OFF THE BEATEN PATH® SERIES

Hawaii

FIFTH EDITION

by Sean Pager
with
Sheryl Groden Pager

Guilford, Connecticut

The prices and rates listed in this guidebook were confirmed at press time. We recommend, however, that you call establishments before traveling to obtain current information.

An additional note: All selections of lodgings and restaurants have been made by the author. No one can pay or be paid to be included in this book.

The detailed route maps provided in this guide should be used in conjunction with a road map. Distances indicated are approximate.

Cover and text design: Laura Augustine
Cover photo: Martin Fox/Index Stock Imagery
Maps on pages 2, 52, 130, 158, 172, and 226 created by Equator Graphics © The Globe Pequot Press.
All other maps by Mary Ballachino.
Illustrations on pages 100, 118, 179, 234 copyright © 1995 by Wren.
All other text illustrations by Daisy DePothod.

ISSN 1535-8313
ISBN 0-7627-1049-7

Manufactured in the United States of America
Fifth Edition/First Printing

To my parents

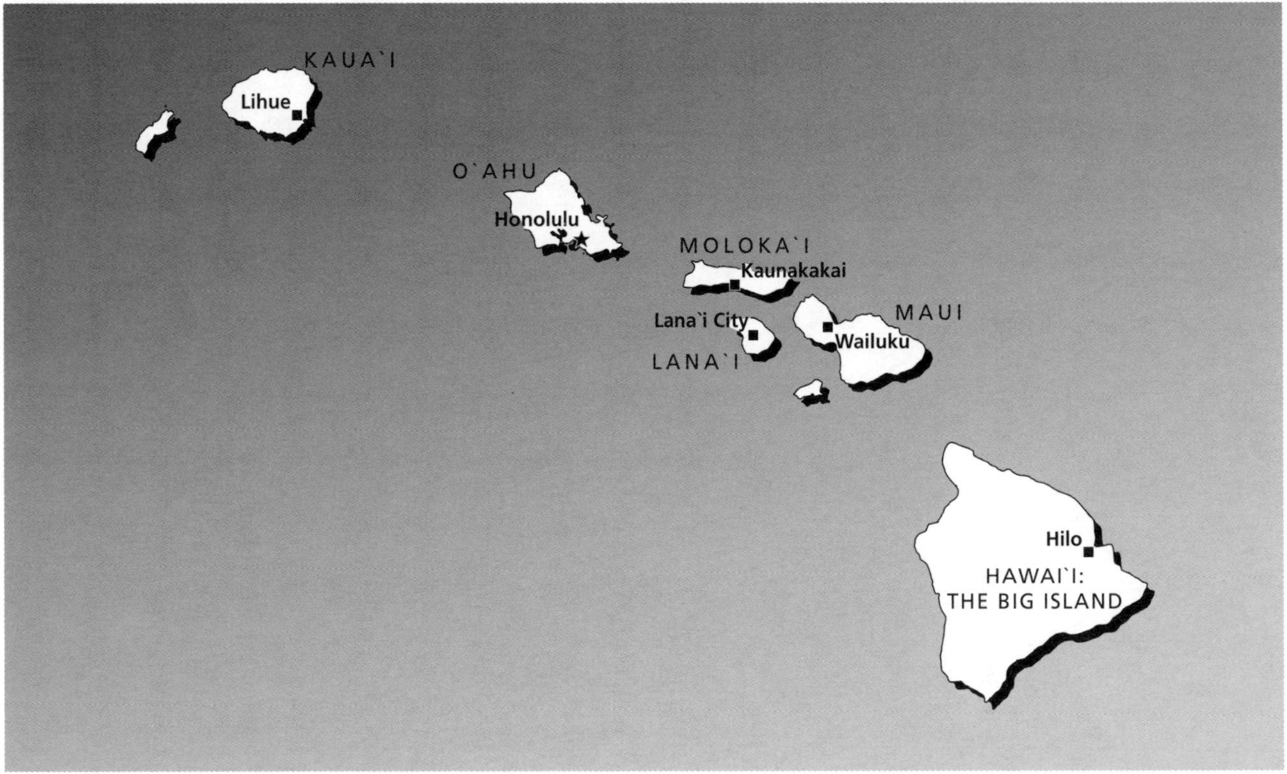

KAUA`I
Lihue
O`AHU
Honolulu
MOLOKA`I
Kaunakakai
Lana`i City
LANA`I
MAUI
Wailuku
Hilo
HAWAI`I:
THE BIG ISLAND

Contents

CONTENTS

List of Maps

LIST OF MAPS

Acknowledgments

As with any project of this scope, many individuals helped bring it to fruition. Special thanks to David Pager for key pinch-hitting on the fifth edition and to Julia King of Aloha Airlines for assisting with travel arrangements. Others, for whose *kokua* I am especially grateful, include the Carolans on Kaua`i; the Shlachters on O`ahu; the Arensdorfs, Jim Grody, and Fern on Maui; Sol Kahoohalahala and John Graham on Lana`i; Jackie Horne, Patti Cook, Punahele Andrade, Kiko Johnston-Kitazawa, and Douglass Bartlett on the Big Island; Torrie Haurez on Moloka`i; Sheila Donnelly Associates; Becker Communications; Marisa Parker at Stryker Weiner Associates; Nathan Kam at McNeil Wilson; Connie Wright; Mary Paterson; Robert Bone; John Mink; Jackie Horne; Matt Cohen; Sheryl the patient; Dave Del Rocco; Sean Shodahl; Devah the Goddess; Martha Yent; and Barbara and David Shideler. Thanks also to many others I met along the way who helped recharge my batteries with the spirit of *aloha.* To all of you, *mahalo a nui loa!*

Introduction

Welcome to Hawaii! These words are heard by almost seven million tourists each year who storm the islands to roast themselves on Waikiki Beach and sip mai tais topped with paper parasols. The tourist industry spends millions to promote the islands' tropical mystique and millions more to manufacture the plastic paradise its visitors demand. Despite this annual onslaught, there remains a Hawaii that few tourists see and many hardly suspect exists. This book will take you there.

Bypass the tourist centers, and you can lose yourself in the midst of untouched natural beauty. You'll travel the back roads that tour buses cannot follow, or take to the hills on foot. Discover beaches empty of human footprints and remote valleys guarding sparkling waterfalls. Experience a Hawaii enriched by its diverse immigrant cultures and native Polynesian roots. You'll learn the legends of prehistoric temples, wander through royal palaces and missionary homes, shop in native craft shops, and sample exotic cuisines. All this awaits you in the Hawaii that lies off the beaten path.

A Setting of Superlatives

I have lived here almost all my life, and I'm still discovering new ways to appreciate Hawaii's charms. These islands encompass some of the most unique terrain on Earth. Between them, they boast the world's best surfing waves, the highest sea cliffs, the rainiest mountain peak, the largest and most active volcanoes, and the clearest night skies. They belong to the longest and most isolated archipelago in the world. More than 90 percent of the plants and animals living here are found nowhere else on the planet.

For all their beauty and wonder, the islands are newcomers as landforms go. They represent the peaks of enormous undersea volcanoes fueled by primeval fires welling up from deep within the earth. Because the ocean floor is shifting northwest over the underlying source of magma, the zone of active volcanism resembles a geological assembly line, with each island forming and then moving over to make way for its successors. The oldest islands, worn away by erosion and sinking under their own weight into the earth's mantle, have all but disappeared, while the youngest island grows larger almost daily as continuing eruptions build new land, much to the delight of tourists lucky enough to witness this volcanic genesis in action.

Long before geology became a science, the ancient Hawaiians understood the natural forces governing their island home. Their legends told of the epic battle between Pele, the fire goddess, and her sister Na Maka o Ka Hai, goddess of the sea. Pele came to Hawaii to escape her older sister's wrath after she had stolen Na Maka's suitor. The sea goddess followed her and flooded the first shallow firepits that Pele had dug. Pele moved from island to island, going southeast down the Hawaiian chain and building newer and taller mountains from the volcanic fires she summoned. Yet, each time, the power of the ocean wore down Pele's island fortresses and drove her onward. Although her current home on the Big Island continues to grow, Pele knows that it too will have to be abandoned in time. Already, new undersea volcanoes farther southeast are rising to form the islands of the future.

Of the 132 volcanic peaks that rise above the highest tide, only the youngest eight were large enough to be settled by the early Hawaiians. Visitors today can explore six of these islands: Kaua`i, O`ahu, Moloka`i, Lana`i, Maui, and Hawai`i ("the Big Island"). Each maintains its own distinct identity. Even within the individual islands, you will marvel at the diversity of habitats. The most obvious contrasts are between windward (northeast) and leeward (southwest) coasts. Crossing a mountain barrier can bring you from rain forest into desert over the distance of a few miles. Weather patterns are also extremely localized. It rarely rains in one place for long, and it's almost always sunny somewhere.

Hawaii's human history is as unique as its natural setting. Polynesian voyagers in double-hulled canoes followed the stars from other Pacific islands across thousands of miles of open ocean to settle these lands more than 1,500 years ago. Although lacking metal, they developed a sophisticated culture governed by inflexible *kapu* (taboos). Elaborate *heiau* (temples) enshrined beautifully crafted *kii akua,* or *tiki* (idols), which accepted divine offerings from a grateful people.

The arrival of the English explorer Capt. James Cook in 1778 brought the archipelago into contact with the modern world. Western weapons enabled a Hawaii chieftain named Kamehameha to forge a unified kingdom, but Western diseases decimated his population. After his death, his son abandoned the old gods and ordered all the *tiki* destroyed in islandwide bonfires. Today only the stone foundations of the *heiau* remain as vestiges of a once flourishing civilization.

Missionaries soon arrived to convert the now-godless people. Newly formed sugar plantations began to import laborers from around the world. Out of this immigrant pool grew a multiethnic society blending

East and West. Now the fiftieth state of the Union, Hawaii is the only U.S. territory formerly a sovereign kingdom. Hawaii also remains one of the few places in the world where no ethnic group can claim a majority.

On the Practical Side

Heading off the beaten path in Hawaii can pose some special challenges. Most of the islands have a single main highway that hugs the coast. The Hawaii Visitors and Convention Bureau (HVCB) has erected roadside marker signs styled in the shape of a Hawaiian warrior to designate the main points of interest. Green mile markers help you keep track of distances, but there are few street signs to guide you along secondary routes. Many places of interest can only be reached by unpaved roads. Because of liability risks, out-of-the-way sites often post discouraging signs while unofficially tolerating access. These artificial deterrents keep tourist hordes away from some of Hawaii's most memorable sights.

As an off-the-beaten-path traveler in Hawaii, you assume certain obligations. These are small islands, with fragile environments. Many of the sites described here rely on their inaccessibility as their only protection against abuse. The state's stewardship has been notoriously lacking. Keep in mind that Hawaii's *heiau* and wilderness remain sacred sites to some, as you'll see by the offerings left (often a simple *ti* leaf wrapped around a rock). Tread lightly wherever you go, and avoid leaving permanent footprints.

Most people come here to bask in Hawaii's natural beauty, and, happily, the best parts are usually free. Natural attractions fall into two main categories: *mauka* (meaning mountain—you pronounce it maow-kah) and *makai* (meaning ocean—you pronounce it mah-kye). You'll hear these two words used frequently in the islands to give directions, as you can almost always use one or the other as a convenient landmark. Going *mauka* (inland) often involves hiking, and Hawaii has some of the world's best trails. Depending on the season, you might be rewarded with guavas, passion fruit, mangos, mountain apples, and other exotic fruits that grow wild in the hills. You needn't worry about poisonous or predatory animals here, but other dangers exist. Volcanic soil and rock can often be treacherously crumbly, undergrowth impossibly thick, and illicit backwoods *pakalolo* (marijuana) patches can put unwary "trespassers" at risk. Stick to posted trails and you'll be fine. Bring mosquito repellant for wet valley hikes and flashlights to explore the occasional cave.

Going *makai* (seaward) eventually means hitting the beach. A simple rule: If a sign says "beach park," you can usually expect facilities (but not necessarily a sandy beach). If it says just "beach," the reverse is usually the case. Keep in mind that all of Hawaii's shoreline up to the highest high-water mark is public property. Public shoreline access, where possible, is required by law. Hawaii has an amazing variety of beaches, but again, the visitor should proceed cautiously. Depending on the season and location, surf and currents can make swimming unsafe. In particular, the northern and western shores of all islands are exposed to dangerous surf in winter. The well-fed reef sharks almost never attack humans in Hawaiian waters, but the occasional jellyfish or Portuguese man-of-war can sting painfully. Razor-sharp coral reefs will cut unprotected feet, and crevices may conceal spiny sea urchins and moray eels. Conditions change rapidly, so never turn your back on the ocean.

You shouldn't overlook Hawaii's cultural offerings, either. In many ways, the Aloha State is still a "foreign" country, and you may as well enjoy its differences. Buy a flower lei to wear. Tune your radio to a Hawaiian music station. Look for ethnic festivities listed in the local newspaper or check out the events calendar at www.gohawaii.com. Sample some exotic foods, and order out a local-style "plate lunch" to eat at a picnic. In addition to the islands' Polynesian heritage, Asian influences are especially strong. You can fill your camera with enough photos of Buddhist temples to fool your friends into thinking you visited the Orient. Most of these temples welcome visitors, but they ask that you remove your shoes before entering. As for shopping, try the gift shops of the attractions listed throughout the guide. Many of them stock unusual items at very reasonable prices.

One of Hawaii's unadvertised charms is its rainbow people, who make up America's true melting pot. Almost everyone speaks English, but you might not feel sure of this when they're laying on the pidgin, a unique local dialect that incorporates foreign words, slang, and a sing-song inflection. Just smile and talk slowly and softly. Hawaiians have always been known for their warm hospitality. Although some locals feel threatened by the tourist industry and resent the ignorant tourists whose money fuels it, if you stay mellow and say *"Howzit"* (hello), you'll still get a lot of *aloha.* The Glossary defines a selection of Hawaiian words used in this guide; many terms are also explained in the text.

For offbeat accommodations, try one of the many bed-and-breakfast outfits (B&Bs). Besides the ones listed in this guide, you can book with several statewide agencies. Those with Internet access can find additional accommodation listings plus other useful visitor information at the following Web sites: www.gohawaii.com; www.planet-hawaii.com; www.alternative-hawaii.com; and www.hshawaii.com. ***All Islands B&B*** (263–2342, 800–542–0344; 463 Iliwahi Loop, Kailua 96734; www.all-islands.com), ***Hawaiian Islands B&B*** (261–7895, 800–258–7895; 1277 Mokolua Drive, Kailua 96734), and ***B&B Honolulu*** (595–7533, 800–288–4666; 3242 Kaohinani Drive, Honolulu 96817; www.hawaiibnb.com) are based on O`ahu. ***B&B Hawaii*** (822–7771, 800–733–1632; P.O. Box 449, Kapa`a 96746; www.bandb-hawaii.com) is based on Kaua`i. ***Hawaii's Best B&Bs*** (885–4550, 800–262–9912; P.O. Box 563, Kamuela 96743; www.bestbnb.com) concentrates on upscale listings. If you want more rugged lodgings, camping is safe and practical on most islands. Contact the ***Department of State Parks*** (587–0300; 1151 Punchbowl Street, Honolulu 96813) to get the scoop on state campgrounds. For ***county campgrounds,*** get in touch with the particular island's department of parks and recreation. Contact Kaua`i's D.P.R. (241–6670) at 4193 Hard Street, Lihue 96766; O`ahu's D.P.R. (523–4525) at 640 South King Street, Honolulu 96813; Maui County's D.P.R. (270–7389) at 1580 Kaahumanu Avenue, Wailuku 96793; and Hawai`i's D.P.R. (961–8311) at 25 Aupuni Street, Hilo 96720. For additional camping options, see chapters on individual islands. Hostel accommodations are also available on most islands; see each chapter listings.

The only regularly scheduled interisland transport is by air. The most extensive flight service is offered by ***Aloha Airlines*** (484–1111, 800–367–5250) and its subsidiary, ***Aloha Island Air*** (484–2222, 800–323–3345), which serves smaller, secondary airports. ***Hawaiian Air*** (838–1555, 800–367–5320) is the principal competitor.

Getting around on the islands themselves will require a rental car, except on O`ahu, where the bus system might be adequate. All the major national firms, as well as local independents, are represented on the larger islands. It is a competitive market, so call around. It also pays to ask your interisland airline for special fly-drive rates.

There are any number of commercial alternatives to driving that will take you off the beaten path—from submarine tours to mountain biking to kayaking. Space does not permit a full listing here, but most advertise in the free, weekly tourist publications available for all islands except Lanai. Specially recommended are the highly informative ***101 Things to Do*** booklets for Kaua`i, O`ahu, Maui and the Big Island; you'll find them at brochure racks throughout those islands; free. Hikers can take advantage of weekend Sierra Club outings on the four major islands. Write the Hawaii chapter office at P.O. Box 2577, Honolulu 96803, or call 538–6616 for a statewide schedule.

As for using the guide itself, you should note that it is written as a narrative, designed to be used on the scene. Attractions are listed geographically in the order you will encounter them, except within individual towns, where accommodations and restaurants are grouped together. Items of special interest appear in boldface italic type. Accommodation prices are based on a double room. Unless noted otherwise, the label B&B implies that continental breakfast is included.

So much for general advice from me. The rest is up to you. Good luck—and get ready for the memories!

Me ke aloha,
Sean Pager

Restaurant prices are given by category based on the cost of an average entree: Inexpensive—less than $10.00; moderate—$10.00 to $15.00; expensive—$16.00 to $25.00; and investment-caliber—more than $25.00.

Note that for all telephone numbers in Hawaii, the ***area code is (808).***

MAP LEGEND

(For all maps except those on pages 2, 52, 130, 158, 172, and 226.)

Streets, highways	———
Unpaved driveable roads	–·–·–·–
Footpaths, trails	- - - - - -
Rivers, streams	~

Kaua`i stands apart from the other islands of Hawaii. The farthest north of the main islands, Kaua`i is the oldest geologically. Six million years have given erosive forces the time to sculpt its mountain slopes with a delicate scalpel. An eternity of waves has wreathed the island in a white lei of sand. Kaua`i is also the wettest Hawaiian island. Its central peak, Mount Waialeale ("overflowing waters"), holds the world's record for annual rainfall. The overflowing waters from such constant precipitation feed Kaua`i's seven full-fledged rivers, where other islands have mere streams. The unrivaled lushness of this "Garden Island" has lured Hollywood here for countless motion pictures.

Kaua`i has always stood apart in human terms as well. The Kaua`i Channel is wider, deeper, and rougher than those between other islands. Scientists think Kaua`i and its nearest neighbor, Niihau, remained fairly isolated in ancient Hawaii. These were the only islands Kamehameha did not conquer. Two invasion fleets failed, one beaten back by storms, the next devastated by sickness. In the end, Kaua`i's King Kaumualii voluntarily acknowledged Kamehameha's sovereignty, but the islands remained a separate kingdom until his death.

Two main highways, Kaumualii (Route 50) and Kuhio (Route 56), reach like arms around the island, with a third main roadway branching off Route 50 to climb the inland heights of Koke`e State Park. Starting from Lihue, the central town, you can drive slightly more than 40 miles in each direction before running into the impassable barrier of the Na Pali Coast. Throughout your stay on Kaua`i, look for the Sunshine Farmers' Markets that rotate through the island towns six days a week. They combine local color with real bargains. Call 241–6390 for the current schedule.

Kaua`i Facts

Nickname: *"Garden Isle"*

Dimensions: *32 x 25 miles*

Highest elevation: *Mt. Kawaikini (5,243 feet)*

Population: *55,983 (1995)*

Principal City: *Lihue*

Flower: *Mokihana*

Color: *Purple*

Kaua`i

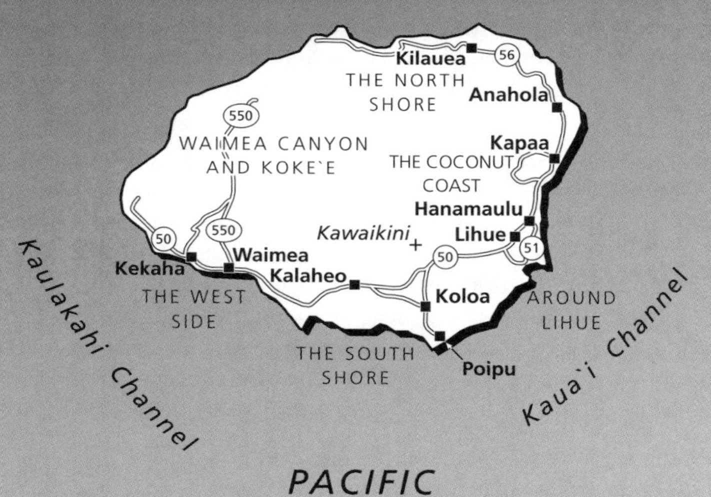

PACIFIC OCEAN

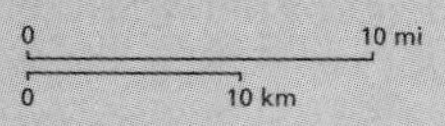

A great way to go off the beaten path on Kaua`i is by paddling a kayak. Even novices can safely navigate the island's rivers to reach secluded waterfalls. Experienced ocean paddlers can explore sections of otherwise inaccessible coastline. Several local firms rent kayaks and supply racks to transport them on your rental car. ***Outfitters Kaua`i*** (742–9667) in Poipu rents mountain bikes and leads a variety of hiking, biking, and kayaking tours. They have a permit for tours in Waimea Canyon and Koke`e, and they also rent camping equipment and supply detailed route maps for suggested activities. ***Kayak Kaua`i*** (826–9844 in Hanalei, 822–9179 in Kapa`a; 800–437–3507) offers similar services on the North Shore and Coconut Coast.

Ecologist Dr. Carl Berg offers custom hiking tours tailored according to interest and ability at very reasonable rates. Call ***Hawaiian Wildlife Tours*** (639–2968). In addition, look in the local paper for listings of the Kaua`i Sierra Club's bimonthly outings. If hiking is out, contact ***Aloha Kaua`i Tours*** (245–6400; 800–452–1113), which has a permit to operate four-wheel-drive tours through the Na Pali Kona Forest Reserve. The air-conditioned vans allow passengers to see the Koke`e area backcountry without the burden of sore feet. Full-day tours include hotel pickup and lunch for $90. They also do shorter excursions elsewhere on the island.

Around Lihue

Located on the southeastern corner of Kaua`i, Lihue serves as the county seat, the main air and sea port, and the midpoint from which highway mileage is numbered. Surrounded by sugar cane and hemmed in on all sides by mountains, Lihue town is relatively new as

Kaua`i Trivia

- *There are more miles of beach per coastline here than any other island.*
- *By law no building here can be taller than a palm tree.*
- *Kaua`i hosts the largest coffee plantation in Hawaii.*
- *Kaua`i's Mount Wai`ale`ale is the wettest spot on earth.*
- *Wailua River is the only navigable river in Hawaii.*
- *Kaua`i is the oldest of the major Hawaiian islands.*
- *Kaua`i's tropical beauty has been filmed in more than sixty Hollywood movies.*

a settlement. The ancient Hawaiians usually bypassed this section of the coast, following instead an inland route behind the mountains. Sugar, centrality, and proximity to O`ahu conspired to put Lihue on the map. Recent tourist developments favoring other coasts have had the opposite effect.

At the junction of the two main highways, turn into Lihue on Rice Street, named for an early manager of Lihue Sugar Plantation. Almost immediately on your left, the ***Kaua`i Museum*** (245–6931) stands behind an imposing classical facade. The well-organized exhibits within cover the story of Kaua`i from many angles. You can see photos of Niihau (as close as most people will ever get), study a model Hawaiian village, rattle a gourd, read excerpts from Captain Cook's log on "discovery" day, and even take a video tour, shot by helicopter, of the island's remote interior. The museum is open Monday–Friday 9:00 A.M. to 4:00 P.M., Saturday 10:00 A.M. to 4:00 P.M. Modest admission.

On the next block the 1913 former historic ***County Building*** reposes in a stately, royal palm–lined park. You can get state camping permits (274–3444) from the State Building behind. Permits for the county's excellent campgrounds (241–6670) are issued at the new cylindrical county building at the top end of Rice Street for $3.00. You can also get them on site for $5.00. But government remains a side interest here. Lihue is still very much a sugar town, and the twin stacks of Lihue Mill belch fumes day and night as a reminder. Haleko Road runs west off Rice Street just inland of the museum, directly behind the mill. On the way down, notice the ***Haleko Shops*** on the right, near the corner. Severely damaged in the 1992 hurricane, these four concrete remnants of the structures and the ornate marble horse trough came from a plantation housing camp for German workers.

Geography of Kaua`i

The oldest and northernmost of the Hawaiian Islands, Kaua`i ranks fourth by size and population. Built from a single massive volcano, the island has been eroded into a series of mountain ridges, valleys, and canyons. Its two central peaks usually remain shrouded in clouds. Of the two, Kawaikini is the highest at 5,243 feet, but Wai`ale`ale, a hundred feet lower, holds the record for the world's highest annual rainfall. The island has 90 miles of coastline (much of it sandy beaches), 16 of which, along the spectacular Na Pali coast, are inaccessible by road.

As a side trip, you can find the ***Church of All Nations*** these devout immigrants built atop "German Hill" on the other side of the mill. (An HVCB marker points up Hoomana Road from Route 50.) This 1885 Lutheran church has an attractive baroque altar inside. But look more closely. The floor is actually bowed like the deck of a ship, with the pulpit the elevated forecastle and the balcony the quarterdeck. The church design symbolizes not only the ship that carried these immigrants to their new home but also the ship of faith that sustained them on their voyage. In the cemetery outside, the German names on the tombstones overlook the cane fields to which they came.

Continuing on Haleko Road past the mill takes you on a winding path through lush jungle. Take the next left onto Nawiliwili Drive, which skirts the cane fields on its way to the harbor. You'll pass a sign on your left marking ***Grove Farm Homestead*** (245–3202). Book well in advance for a tour of this historic estate. Often led by descendants of Kaua`i's plantation families who offer insider "gossip" about the past, the two-hour tours of Grove Farm are offered Monday, Wednesday, and Thursday at 10:00 A.M. and 1:00 P.M. for a modest donation.

The homestead's founder, George Wilcox, was a son of missionaries. He raised tuition for his engineering degree by collecting bird guano to sell as fertilizer. After purchasing the dry land for next to nothing, Wilcox brought irrigation water from the mountains to create a profitable sugar plantation in 1864. A visit to Grove Farm provides a timeless glimpse of the plantation lifestyle he helped pioneer. Designed as a self-contained community, the beautifully maintained grounds still yield harvests of fruits and vegetables. Those who are game can taste raw coffee beans and macadamia nuts.

The Wilcoxes were true pack rats who collected much and threw away nothing. All the furnishings and personal possessions remain as if the inhabitants were due to return momentarily. In the plantation office, where you start your tour, a lone cannonball sits nonchalantly atop the old payroll safe. By the time Grove Farm became a museum, the combination had been forgotten and no record could be found. A safecracker forced the lock and found the combination written inside: "B-A-L-L."

You'll also visit the spartan dwelling of the Moriwake family. Mrs. Moriwake, a picture bride from Japan, lived here with her family through fifty-two years of service as the Wilcoxes' laundress. A print of Mount Fuji on the wall provides a touch of the old country. The main house, built and furnished from beautiful native woods, is where George Wilcox lived with his brother Sam and Sam's family. Among the antique

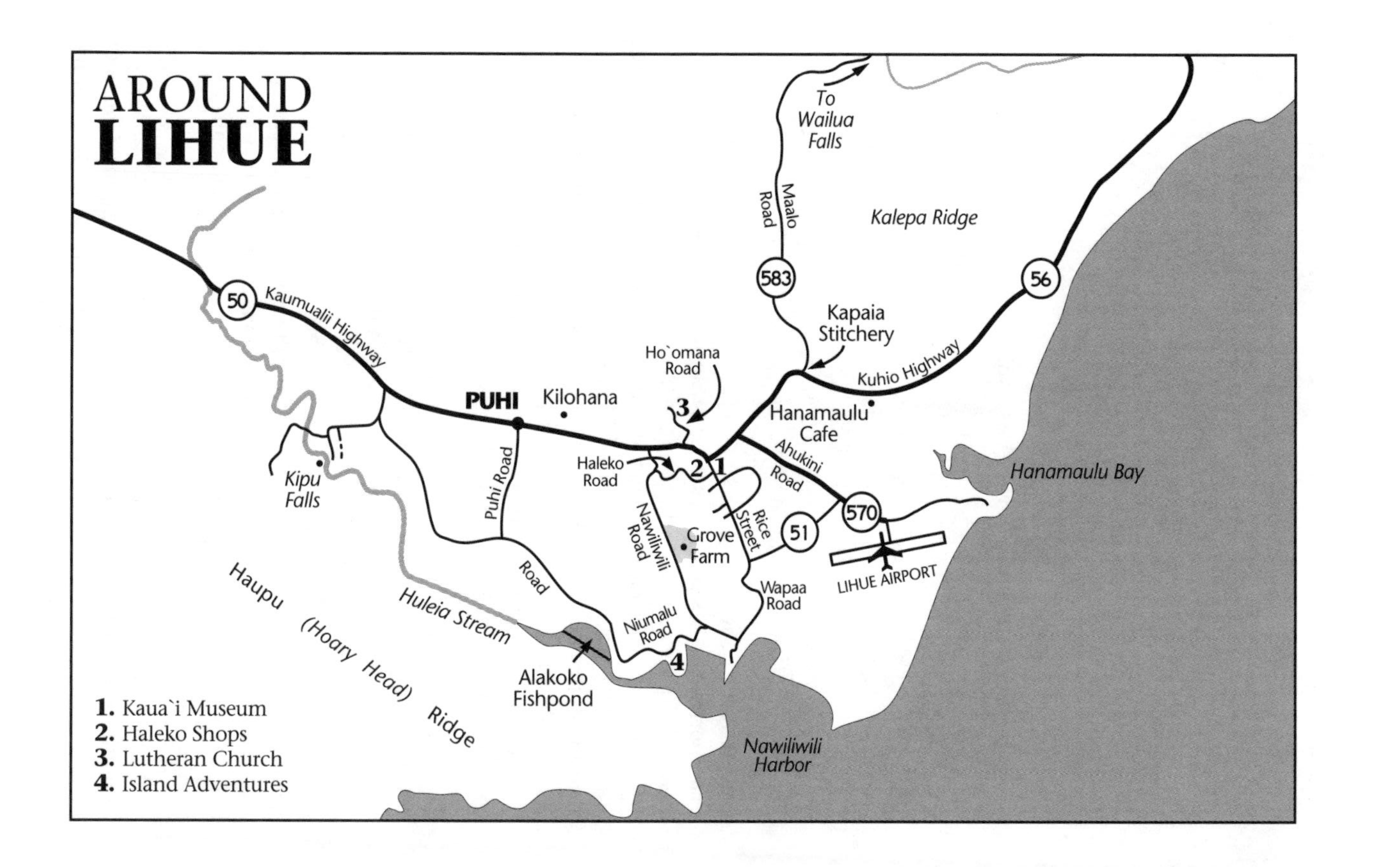
AROUND
LIHUE
To Wailua Falls
Maalo Road
Kalepa Ridge
583
56
50
Kaumualii Highway
Kapaia Stitchery
Kuhio Highway
Ho`omana Road
3
PUHI
Kilohana
Hanamaulu Cafe
Ahukini Road
Haleko Road
2
1
Kipu Falls
Puhi Road
Nawiliwili Road
Grove Farm
Rice Street
51
570
Hanamaulu Bay
LIHUE AIRPORT
Road
Wapaa Road
Haupu (Hoary Head) Ridge
Huleia Stream
Niumalu Road
4
Alakoko Fishpond
Nawiliwili Harbor
1. Kaua`i Museum
2. Haleko Shops
3. Lutheran Church
4. Island Adventures

furniture, you'll find an embroidered settee that Helen Lehman, a long-time house guest, took ten years to complete.

George later built himself a bachelor pad, designed with two bedrooms (winter and summer) draped with mosquito nets, to escape the family bustle. The unadorned rooms are almost bare of furnishings. He would sit in his favorite chair, reading his scientific journals and spitting pieces of cigars into a turtle-shaped spittoon. Although a millionaire, George Wilcox kept his fragments of soap in an old sardine can like the frugal mission son he was.

Nawiliwili Road continues down to its namesake harbor, Kaua`i's main shipping port ever since its completion in 1930. In your mind, try to screen out the heavy dock machinery and industrial warehouses and focus on the lovely setting of the bay, with the Haupu (or Hoary Head) Mountains closing in on its western edge. In the opposite direction, Nawiliwili Beach Park abuts Kalapaki Beach, the site of the Marriott. But you can enjoy the same views at considerably less cost by staying at the ***Garden Island Inn*** (245–7227 or 800–648–0154; 3445 Wilcox Road, www.gardenislandinn.com; info@gardenislandinn.com), across the street from the beach park. The rooms show novel touches such as palm-pattern imprints in the ceiling plaster and original artwork by former "resident artist" George Kosel. Bougainvillea drapes from the balconies, and floral gardens surrounding the inn include carp and turtle ponds. Live-in owners Steve and Susan Layne work hard to make their guests' stay pleasant. With rooms from $75 to $125, the Garden Island Inn could be a real sleeper (no pun intended). If you just want a place to lay your head, try the ***Tip Top Motel*** (245–2333) at 3173 Akahi Street, in Lihue. It's known locally for its bakery/cafe of the same name. Doubles start at $45.

Return to Nawiliwili Drive and turn west onto Niumalu Road 2 blocks above the harbor. Niumalu climbs behind a bulk-sugar warehouse and sidles along the cane fields. Pause at the unmarked turnout ahead for another view of the bay. The road then descends through the rustic Hawaiian village of Niumalu. From the harbor behind Niumalu Park, ***Island Adventures*** (245–9662) leads kayak trips twice a day at 8:00 A.M. and noon up Huleia Stream (which provided the scenery for the opening shots of *Raiders of the Lost Ark*). The two-and-one-half-hour paddle costs $49, snacks included.

At the park, turn right onto Hulemanu Road, which curves uphill again. About 0.5 mile farther, stop at the overlook to view ***Alakoko Fishpond*** tucked below along a bend in Huleia Stream, backdropped by the rugged beauty of the Haupu Mountains. Alakoko is also known as

Menehune Fishpond because of its legendary builders. A supposedly reclusive, pixielike people, the Menehune were said to be expert masons who performed miraculous construction feats overnight for payment in shrimp. Menehune legends are part of the folklore throughout Hawaii, and theories vary as to their origin. The Tahitian word *manahune* means slave. Some say the Menehune were an earlier people who became a hereditary caste of workers. The bird chatter you hear comes from ***Huleia National Wildlife Refuge*** just upstream.

Hulemanu Road continues past the overlook, shadowing the Haupu Mountains as it cuts through green waves of endless cane. All this driving may be making you hot, though. How about a secret waterfall to cool off in? Hulemanu Road goes straight toward ***Kipu Falls,*** our destination, but gets a little bumpy. Instead, turn right on Puhi Road and left at the highway (Route 50). Turn left again on Kipu Road just west of Puhi town. Follow Kipu Road, ignoring the junction on the left with the other end of Hulemanu, and look for a ONE LANE BRIDGE sign. Just beyond the sign, before the bridge, turn onto the dirt road on the left. Park here; the road descends steeply and can be muddy. After a half-mile walk parallel to Kipu stream, a spur trail cuts across to a large pool fed by the falls. A giant Chinese banyan tree growing at the edge of the pool serves as your ladder in and out.

On your way back, you might visit ***Kilohana*** (245–5608), another

Brief History of Kaua`i

Captain James Cook's arrival on the west coast of Kaua`i in 1778 touched off a new era that would transform the Hawaiian islands. A steady stream of Western ships followed in his footsteps, many of them anchoring at the protected Waimea harbor that Cook had described in his journals, making Kaua`i an early center of trade. The separate political status retained by the island in the early days of the Hawaiian kingdom made it the focus of international intrigue, most notably by a German adventurer acting in the service of the Russian czar.

As the site of the Hawaii's first commercial sugar plantation, Kaua`i was also at the forefront of another watershed, the birth of an industry that dominated the islands' socioeconomic landscape for more than a century. Strangely, sugar's successor, tourism, has come later to Kaua`i than some of its neighbors, although the Garden Isle has long been the darling of Hollywood filmmakers. Kaua`i suffered widespread devastation at the hands of two hurricanes, Iwa in 1982 and Iniki in 1992, which has further slowed development on the island.

restored plantation estate on the inland side of the highway. Gaylord Wilcox, the head of Grove Farm, brought renowned architect Mark Potter from O`ahu in 1935 to build his dream house. The name "Kilohana" means "not to be surpassed," and Potter made a strong bid to design and furnish a home worthy of this name. Stop at the carriage house by the Model A Ford to get a map of the thirty-five-acre estate and restored farm area. Or tour the grounds in style in an old-fashioned carriage drawn by Clydesdale horses. Longer "sugar cane" tours are also offered, subject to demand; call 246–9529 to reserve.

The inside of Kilohana is part museum and part boutiques specializing in "Kaua`i-made" wares. Kilohana's courtyard provides a romantic setting for alfresco dining at ***Gaylords*** (245–9593). Continental entrées come with vegetables and fruits from Kilohana's own gardens. Lunch is served Monday–Saturday 11:00 A.M. to 3:00 P.M., Sunday brunch from 9:30 A.M. to 3:00 P.M. Moderate prices. Candlelight dinners are offered nightly from 5:00 to 9:00 P.M. Reservations suggested. Investment-caliber. Kilohana opens daily at 9:30 A.M.

Back in town, dining options consist mostly of mom-and-pop restaurants serving ethnic cuisine in unadorned settings. Two blocks seaward of the County Building, off Rice, a number of eateries cluster around Kress Street. Disguised as a camphouse kitchen with its trademark corrugated orange formica counter, ***Hamura's Saimin,*** 2956 Kress Street (245–3271) ladles out Kaua`i's best bowl of *saimin* (a Hawaiian-Japanese dish based on noodles in broth). Select your own add-ins to slurp with your noodles, find a stool to sit on, but heed the sign on the wall that says PLEASE DON'T PUT GUM UNDER THE COUNTER. Hamura's opens at 11:00 A.M. and stays open late to cater to the postdisco crowd. In the same building, ***Halo Halo Shave Ice*** cranks out a fruity Filipino version of this Hawaiian frozen treat daily until 4:00 P.M.

Around the corner, ***Ma's Family Inc.,*** 4277 Halenani Street (245–3142), serves hearty Hawaiian breakfasts and a famous tripe stew for lunch. Plantation workers stop here for an early morning plate of *kalua* pig (steamed in an underground oven and shredded) with eggs and a free cup of coffee before heading for the cane fields. Note the laundered Calrose rice sacks covering unused tables. Open Monday–Friday 5:00 A.M. to 1:30 P.M., weekends until 11:30 A.M. Other standbys a block away include ***Kun Ja's*** (245–6554), at 4252 Rice Street, for Korean cuisine and ***Kiibo's*** (245–2650), at 2991 Umi Street, for Japanese.

Other Lihue eateries lie along Route 56, north of Rice Street. For those who like seafood, ***Fish Express*** (245–9918), at 3343 Kuhio Highway, across the street from the hospital, offers unbeatable lunch values. Its tiny lunch counter serves gourmet fish specials: choose from among the daily fresh-catch selection prepared in intriguing ways, such as blackened with guava basil sauce or grilled with passion orange tarragon. At a price less than $8.00, you can't eat this well anywhere else on the island. (Fish-haters can sample Hawaiian plates instead.) Hot lunches and dinners are served on weekdays 10:00 A.M. to 7:00 P.M. The deli counter stays open daily until 7:00 P.M. and offers an impressive selection of poke, the local version of seafood salad made from (mostly raw) fish, seaweed, crab, or octopus. For a tongue-tingling taste sensation, try Korean-style kim chi scallops. Also on the highway, at 3125 near McDonalds, ***Oki's Diner*** (245–5899) is as local as they come. It serves old-time favorites like oxtail soup and chicken katsu, as well as dishes named after local politicians. Open 6:00 A.M. to 3:00 A.M.

For beachfront dining and live Hawaiian music, locals favor ***Duke's Canoe Club*** (246–9599), adjacent to the Marriott on Kalapaki Beach. Expensive. If you want a taste of oriental luxury, visit the tea house at ***Hanamaula Cafe*** (245–2511), a yellow building just north and over the hill from Lihue on Route 56 across from a Shell station. The menu at this third-generation Kaua`i establishment includes Chinese dishes, but if you ask for the teahouse, you dine in traditional Japanese fashion, kneeling on futons and tatami mats in front of very low tables. The shoji-partitioned rooms open onto a Japanese garden and koi (carp) pond. Reservations recommended. Open Tuesday–Friday 10:00 A.M. to 1:00 P.M. and Tuesday–Sunday 4:30 to 8:30 P.M.

There are things to see on the way to Hanamaula. One hill closer to Lihue, Route 56 passes through Kapaia, where you can stop to admire the handcrafted fabric creations at ***Kapaia Stitchery*** (245–2281) housed in a red plantation store. You will find everything from traditional kimonos to quilt-making kits—or choose your own fabric and have something custom-made. The price is right and the quality superb. Open Monday–Saturday 9:00 A.M. to 5:00 P.M.

For a scenic jaunt inland, take Maalo Road uphill from the stitchery through 3 miles of sugar cane with steadily improving mountain views. At the end of the road, your reward is a bird's-eye view of mighty ***Wailua Falls,*** featured on the TV show *Fantasy Island.* Those feeling adventurous (and sure of foot) can leave their fellow tourists gawking at the lookout and head 100 yards back up the road. At the far edge of the second guardrail, a steep and very slippery trail leads down to the pool at the base of the falls. Wave to the people above as you backfloat.

The South Shore

Departing west from the Lihue area, the Kaumualii Highway (Route 50) crosses through the Knudsen Gap between Kahili Ridge and the Haupu Range to enter the ***Koloa District,*** birthplace of the Hawaiian sugar industry. The word *koloa* is usually translated as "tall cane," for the region, blessed with ample irrigation and yearlong sunshine, has yielded bumper crops since antiquity.

Turn left on Maluhia Road (Route 520), 5 miles west of Lihue, and head through the ***Tree Tunnel,*** a fragrant double row of overhanging eucalyptus trees planted in 1911. Continue through more exotic foliage, then sugar cane, as you descend upon Koloa Town, now known to tourists as "Old Koloa Town." Maluhia Road ends at a T junction with Koloa Road. On the right-hand side as you enter town, a tiny anonymous park commemorates Hawaii's sugar heritage. Erected in 1985 for the 150th anniversary of commercial sugar production in Hawaii, a small concrete monument symbolizes an opened millstone. Inside, a set of bronze bas-relief carvings portrays the different ethnic groups that figured in sugar's past. Careful readers of the accompanying plaque will notice historical revisionism at work: Someone has taken the haole plantation manager, formerly represented on horseback, out of the scene entirely.

The plaque gives a brief overview of the sugar industry's evolution. The story begins with William Hooper, who arrived from Boston in 1833 at age twenty-four with little expertise in agriculture and no knowledge of Hawaii. Yet somehow he secured enough native cooperation to begin the first large-scale sugar plantation in the islands. The plaque neglects to mention that Hooper and his two partners became embroiled in an international investment scandal and went bankrupt. Despite such rocky beginnings, sugar went on to become Hawaii's dominant industry and the mainstay of its economy for almost a century. Hawaiian plantations today yield more cane per acre and per worker-hour than anywhere else in the world. In spite of this, labor costs and foreign subsidies have put sugar on the decline since World War II. The industry may well die where it began. Kaua`i's plantations are among the last in the state to remain profitable. One quarter of the island's electricity comes from burning leftover bagasse from harvested cane.

Near the monument, a small garden displays different varieties of sugar cane, and behind (partially engulfed by a banyan tree) stand the remains of the third mill built in Koloa.

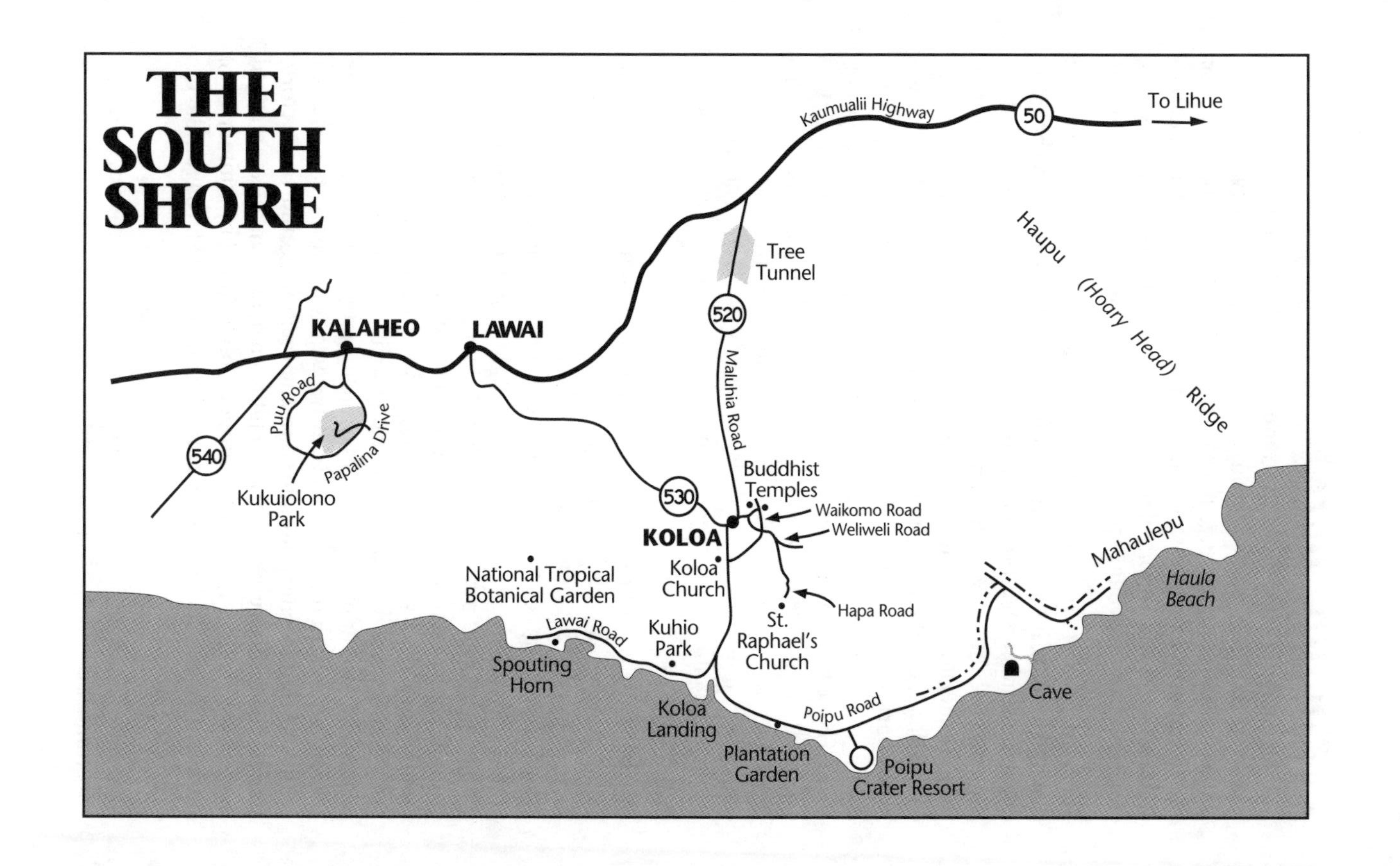

THE SOUTH SHORE
To Lihue
50
Kaumualii Highway
Tree Tunnel
520
Maluhia Road
Haupu (Hoary Head) Ridge
KALAHEO
LAWAI
Puu Road
Papalina Drive
540
Kukuiolono Park
530
Buddhist Temples
Waikomo Road
Weliweli Road
KOLOA
Koloa Church
Hapa Road
St. Raphael's Church
National Tropical Botanical Garden
Lawai Road
Kuhio Park
Spouting Horn
Koloa Landing
Plantation Garden
Poipu Road
Poipu Crater Resort
Mahaulepu
Haula Beach
Cave

Across Koloa Road from the park, the Yamamoto Store is the focus of more town history. On the sidewalk in front of the store stand cartoon-style sculptures by Maui artist Reems Mitchell, depicting a pair of Koloa old-timers, Toshi Freitas, the mechanic and "Chinaman" Lickety Split. Wander into the courtyard behind the store to explore the ***Koloa History Center,*** a collection of exhibits and artifacts portraying aspects of plantation life, from the different immigrant groups housed in camps to the itinerant "drummers" and "shibai" artists who passed through the town hotel.

If you're looking for a bite to eat, ***Koloa Fish Market*** (742–6199), just down the road at 5482 Koloa Road, serves a tasty Hawaiian plate lunch, with rotating multiethnic specialties, plus sushi and an assortment of poke waiting for the choosing behind its small deli counter. Open Monday–Friday 10:00 A.M. to 6:00 P.M., Saturday 10:00 A.M. to 5:00 P.M.

For a tour of Koloa's churches and temples, continue east on Koloa Road to the Big Save market at the corner. Craftsworkers from Japan built the two Buddhist temples here in 1910 to cater to immigrant cane workers. The ***Hongwanji Mission*** has its temple behind the green Y.B.A. (Young Buddhists Association) Hall. Its carved roof and decorative metal inlays form a delicate black-on-white pattern. Around the corner, on Waikomo Road, ***Jodo Mission*** competes with two temples. The smaller original has an elaborate altar inside.

Turning from sutras to rosary beads, follow the signs to ***St. Raphael's Church*** from Koloa onto Weliweli Road (between Maluhia and Waikomo), then right onto Hapa Road to reach Kaua`i's oldest Catholic church. The original Calvinist missionaries strove to exclude Catholicism, convincing their Hawaiian converts that papistry was "just another form of idolatry." Gunboat diplomacy by French warships brought an end to such discrimination.

Several church buildings lie scattered in this peaceful lot, bordered by cane fields, with Koloa's current mill smoking in the distance. The current church dates to 1866, but the graves of Portuguese immigrants in the cemetery are older. In the corner, behind the rectory, stands a beautiful ruinlike shrine built from black lava rocks arranged in steps and levels seemingly at random, highlighted by white marble statuary. The remains of the original 1841 church, rediscovered a century later in an adjacent field, have been shaped into a grotto accented by a giant cross.

Returning on Weliweli Road, turn left on Waikomo Road and notice the rickety plantation homes here, as yet untouched by the tourist traffic a

Jodo Mission

few blocks over. Waikomo Road runs into Poipu Road and ***Koloa Church,*** which dates from 1837. The tall steeple of this New England–style edifice built by missionaries served as a landmark for whaling ships approaching port.

Turn left on Poipu Road and bear left at the Y junction ahead to pass through Poipu Beach, an area thickly populated with plush hotels. A visual oddity among these is the ***Poipu Crater Resort*** (742–2000) off Pe'e Road, the tiny villas of which sprout like acne on the steep walls inside a crater formed by Kaua`i's last volcanic gasp. You might also visit ***Kiahuna Plantation Resort,*** (742–6411), which engulfed the former Moir Garden. Plantation Manager Hector Moir planted this attractive assortment of cacti and succulents suited to Poipu's arid climate back in 1938. In the center of the garden, Moir's plantation home has become ***Piatti's Italian Restaurant*** (742–2216), of San Francisco fame. You can dine either at lana`i tables facing the tiki torchlit gardens or in the elegant, old-fashioned interior. Open nightly 5:30 to 10:00 P.M. Expensive.

Poipu's most notable eatery, however, is the ***Beach House*** (742–1424), at 5022 Lawai Road, on the way to Spouting Horn. The stunning oceanfront location provides the perfect setting for Jean-Marie Josselin's inventive Hawaii Regional Cuisine. Open daily 5:30 to 9:30 P.M. Investment-caliber.

There is little point tarrying in crowded Poipu, though, when the coast is clearer further on in ***Mahaulepu.*** Follow the main cane road extension from Poipu for almost 2 miles until you come to a stop sign at another major cane road. Turn right (following the utility poles) and continue another mile past the quarry. Check in at the guard station to sign a liability release. From here, various turnoffs lead to distinct beaches along the Mahaulepu coast. Mahaulepu means "falling together," referring to the remnants of Kamehameha's abortive 1796 invasion force that staggered ashore here to face a brutal ambush.

Start your exploring at the nearest beach access straight ahead and park at the stone barrier. Walk back toward Poipu until you reach the stream at the end of the beach, and follow the faint trail that runs through cane grass along the far bank. The trail continues a quarter-mile inland and disappears into the mouth of a cave. You have to duck at the entrance, but the rest of the way is OK. Keep a hand above your head just in case, as you grope your way toward the light at the other side. Dense vines hang from the large opening here like a sixties bead curtain. And behind the curtain? A Chinese banyan in a natural courtyard of stone. Come see for yourself! As for the rest of Mahaulepu, you can play Robinson Crusoe, hunting for hidden footprints on a series of deserted beaches alternating with rocky outcrops. Unlike Poipu, this section of the coast actually gained sand during the hurricane. The farthest beach, ***Haula,*** cannot be reached by road; you have to hike 0.5 mile east along low sea cliffs at the foot of the Haupu Mountain Range.

Retrace your steps to the Y junction at the entrance to Poipu Beach, where the right fork, Lawai Road, leads to attractions of its own. Tucked inside the Y is Koloa Landing, a narrow coastal inlet at the mouth of Waikono Stream. Nothing remains of this once-crowded port from whaling's heyday, but accommodation bargains cluster nearby. Book well in advance for any of these. ***Poipu Bed & Breakfast*** (742–1146; 800–808–2330; www.poipu-inn.com) offers cheery lodging in a colorfully restored plantation home with white trellis porches and antique carousel horses in every room. The inn also has a more modern home. Rates run from $125–$165. ***Garden Isle Cottages*** (742–6717; 800–742–6711; www.oceancottages.com) overlook the water (2666 Puuholo Road, Koloa 96756). Nestled in lush gardens, the self-contained units are decorated with the owners' original artwork. Studios begin at $140, two-day minimum. ***Koloa Landing Cottages*** (742–1470) nearby have similar offerings at rates ranging from $85–$140.

For a truly oceanfront setting, continue down the coast to ***Gloria's Spouting Horn B&B*** (742–6995; www.gloriasbedandbreakfast.com; glorbb@gte.net) at 4464 Lawai Road. Here you can curl up in a hammock strung between palm trees in the backyard and bask in the salt spray from the ocean at your feet. Owners Gloria and Bob ("Mr. Gloria") Merkle lost the original Gloria's to Hurricane Iniki. They rebuilt a dream house whose elegant, airy interior belies its fortresslike engineering. The two upstairs rooms have the choicest views, but honeymooners will want to nestle in the "love nest" below, featuring a unique canopy bed fashioned from woven willow boughs. All rooms have four-poster beds with Hawaiian quilts, private baths, and kitchens and cost $250; book well in advance. Full breakfast included. Children under 14 discouraged. Or take to the hills at ***Kahili Mountain Park*** (742–9921) in a secluded meadow above the highway (P.O. Box 298, Koloa 96756). Furnished cabins and more spartan cabinettes rent for $60–$110 and $45, respectively. Fishing and hiking are nearby among these 197 acres of majestic beauty.

The main scenic attraction along Lawai Road is the ***Spouting Horn.*** Hidden behind the tour buses in the parking lot, this surf-driven geyser does its best "thar she blows" imitation through a submerged lava tube. Rumor has it that the spout went much higher before plantation owners dynamited the opening to prevent salt sprays from damaging their crops. On the way to the Spouting Horn, you'll pass another neglected park of historical interest. ***Kuhio Park*** marks the birth site of Kaua`i's favorite son, Prince Jonah Kuhio Kalanianaole, heir to the Hawaiian monarchy and one of Hawaii's first delegates to Congress. The park also includes the remains of an ancient fishpond and a small *heiau.*

At the end of Lawai Road, a 1920s plantation home serves as the visitor center for the ***National Tropical Botanical Garden*** (742–2623). Reserve in advance for one of the three to four tours per day for an experience that even nongreen thumbs will appreciate. Lawai Valley is a sunken oasis of tropical vegetation surrounded by former sugar land. The gardens are roughly segregated into botanical classes and beautifully landscaped around natural streambeds and hillsides. Robert Allerton and his adopted son (some say homosexual lover), John, used their Chicago mercantile fortune to create a tropical Eden here on an estate originally owned by Queen Emma. Emma herself was known as the first Hawaiian monarch to cultivate a garden for aesthetic rather than functional purposes; she began gardening at Lawai in 1870. The Allertons greatly expanded her efforts over five decades in this century and were instrumental in establishing the Tropical Botanical Gardens under congressional charter in 1964. The garden management now oversees the 286-acre property.

On Tuesday through Saturday, walking tours visit the ***Allerton Garden,*** a masterwork of landscape design. The formal geometry of the reflective pools and fountains blends harmoniously with the wildly tropical vegetation, accented by art pieces from around the world. On Monday only, the Lawai Garden tour is offered. Part walking, part riding, it visits endangered sea turtle nests on the beach and takes in the garden's palm collection and native Hawaiian plants, before ending with a stroll through the tropical splendor of the Bamboo Bridge section. Along the way, you gain hands-on exposure to some of the world's most exotic flora and learn their historical, medicinal, and ethnobotanical significance. Taste the five-pointed star fruit, smell a crumpled leaf of allspice, or stroke the "rat fur" of a balsa tree.

Return along Poipu Road until it dead-ends at Koloa Road and turn left onto Route 530, which cuts west through rolling hills carpeted with sugar cane, to rejoin the Kaumualii Highway at Lawai. These upland fields once grew pineapples, but by 1970 all had switched to sugar, a less labor-intensive crop. The old pineapple cannery has been converted to retail space near the junction with Route 50.

Turn left from the end of Route 530 to continue west on Route 50 to the town of Kalaheo. Turn left onto Papalina Drive near the center of town and enjoy the scenic vistas over the Lawai Valley and Poipu Coast on your way to ***Kukuiolono Park.*** This cool hilltop sanctuary includes a nine-hole public golf course and a small pseudo-Japanese garden. Follow the road up to the clubhouse for a panoramic view stretching all the way to Niihau. You can loop back to the highway on Puu Road.

The fields west of Kalaheo have been planted with coffee bushes as a replacement crop for sugar. You can learn more about island coffee (and sample the final product) by stopping at the **visitor center** just ahead on the left. Open daily 9:00 A.M. to 5:00 P.M.

The West Side

About 2 miles west of Kalaheo on Kaumualii Highway, be sure to stop at the ***Hanapepe Valley Overlook*** for a technicolor vision of red canyon walls rising vertically above a tree-carpeted valley floor. Continue on Route 50, which curves around the mouth of the canyon to descend into Hanapepe town. A roadside sign welcomes you to KAUA`I'S BIGGEST LITTLE TOWN, part of an attempt to lure westbound tourists. Fortunately, they have not yet been *too* successful. To see for yourself veer right beneath the bougainvillea-draped cliffs and park on Hanapepe Road.

Hanapepe has its share of history to relate. The valley you admired from above witnessed the bloody suppression of Kaua`i loyalists who revolted against the Kamehameha dynasty in 1824. A hundred years later, sixteen Filipino workers and four police officers were killed here during a plantation strike. But Hanapepe's main attraction springs from its vintage plantation shops still infused with the rhythm of small-town life. Much of *The Thorn Birds* was filmed here.

Begin your walking tour at ***Taro Ko Chips*** (335–5586), a tiny one-room factory that Mr. and Mrs. S. Nagamine have started as a retirement project. The taro they fry in their two woks comes from nearby valley fields that their son now tends. Next, you can explore a series of ***art galleries*** notable not so much for the originality of their work—you can judge that for yourself—as for the accessibility of the tenant-artists, many of whom paint in studios on the premises and are happy to discuss their work. Most stay open Monday–Saturday. ***Kaua`i Fine Arts*** (335–3778) sells a different kind of artwork, though; it specializes in antique maps and prints.

You shouldn't overlook Hanapepe's more traditional vendors, either. Sample the spicy confections at the Crackseed Center or pop inside Yoshiura's General Store, known as the Mikado until World War II. And before you leave, have a swing on the rope bridge over Hanapepe River next to the old church. Continue on the road across the 1911 bridge further downstream. From here, you can turn up Awawa Road into the valley for a scenic digression along the west canyon wall past sugar cane and taro fields. Distinctive for its large forked leaves, the

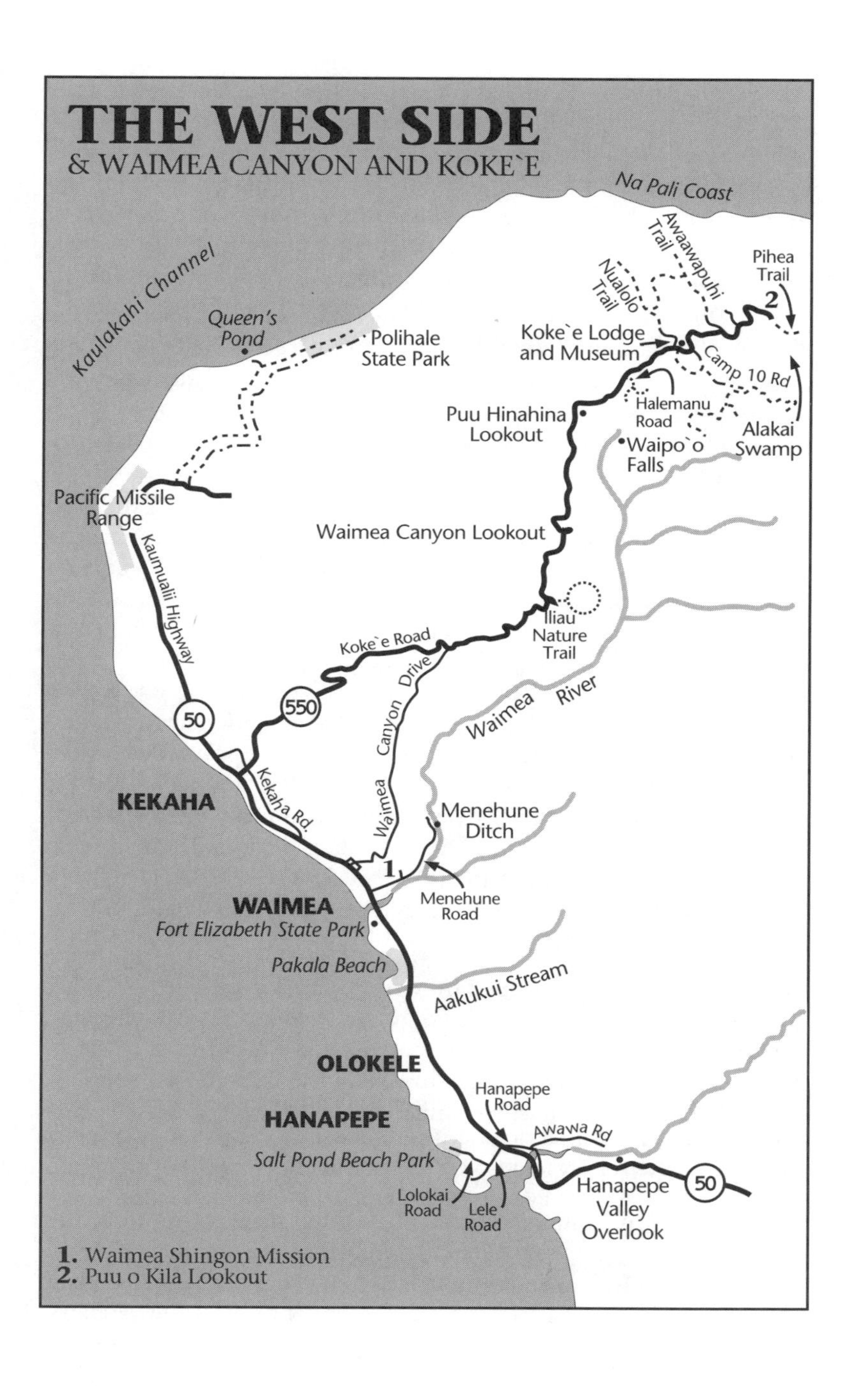

THE WEST SIDE
& WAIMEA CANYON AND KOKE`E
Na Pali Coast
Kaulakahi Channel
Queen's Pond
Polihale State Park
Awaawapuhi Trail
Nualolo Trail
Pihea Trail
2
Koke`e Lodge and Museum
Camp 10 Rd
Halemanu Road
Puu Hinahina Lookout
Waipo`o Falls
Alakai Swamp
Pacific Missile Range
Kaumualii Highway
Waimea Canyon Lookout
Iliau Nature Trail
Koke`e Road
Waimea Canyon Drive
Waimea River
550
50
KEKAHA
Kekaha Rd.
Menehune Ditch
1
Menehune Road
WAIMEA
Fort Elizabeth State Park
Pakala Beach
Aakukui Stream
OLOKELE
Hanapepe Road
HANAPEPE
Awawa Rd
Salt Pond Beach Park
Lolokai Road
Lele Road
Hanapepe Valley Overlook
50
1. Waimea Shingon Mission
2. Puu o Kila Lookout

taro plant served as the Hawaiians' staple crop. They mashed its starchy roots to make poi and cooked the stem and leaves as vegetables. The Hawaiians believed that the taro plant grew from the grave of humankind's elder brother who had died in infancy. Taro was their link to the land and their "staff of life." Back on Hanapepe Road, past Awawa Drive, stop by ***Shimonishi Orchids*** to inspect hundreds of hybrid varieties gilded with dainty colors. Impressionist James Hoyle (335–3582) has moved into a new gallery next door. Hoyle was the first artist to open shop in town. Out on the highway, more galleries await, including "surfboard art."

Naturally, no self-respecting art town could long survive without a decent coffeehouse. ***Hanapepe Cafe*** (335–5011) has the added bonus of being located in Hanapepe Bookstore. In addition to hot java, tasty, albeit somewhat pricey, gourmet Italian-vegetarian meals are served Tuesday–Saturday 9:00 A.M. to 2:00 P.M. and 6:00–9:00 P.M. Expensive. Hanapepe's other notable eatery, the ***Green Garden Restaurant*** (335–5422), sits on the highway. The Hamabata family has built this 1948 landmark into a garden within a garden: Hanging ferns, table orchids, and potted plants decorate the interior, while the spotlit gardens outside splash the huge glass windows with green light. The menu features full dinners of island fare, such as chicken teriyaki and Kiawe-grilled fresh catch in large portions, as well as tempting desserts, such as homemade *lilikoi* (passionfruit) pie, for moderate prices. Open Monday and Wednesday–Sunday 10:30 A.M.–2:00 P.M. and 5:00–9:00 P.M. Plate lunch fans can get their fix at ***Da Imu Hut Cafe.*** Open weekdays 8:00 A.M. to 2:00 P.M., 5:00–8:45 P.M. Lovers of Thai food should backtrack uphill from Hanapepe to ***Toi's Thai Kitchen*** (335–3111) in the Ele`ele Shopping Center open Monday–Saturday 10:30 A.M. to 3:00 P.M., 5:30–9:00 P.M. Moderate.

Near the edge of town, turn left from the highway onto Lele Road, then right onto Lolokai Road to ***Salt Pond Beach Park.*** Besides offering a beautiful protected beach, the park abuts ancient salt ponds used to harvest sea salt. Captain Cook got his salt here, and if you ask someone in the Hui Hana Paakai, which still operates these evaporative basins, you may be able to as well. State health department regulations prevent the "impure" salt from being sold commercially, but the impurities add flavor.

West of Hanapepe, a number of small, working sugar towns are strung along the highway. Looking out onto the horizon, the remote and mysterious islands of Niihau and uninhabited Lehua hover across Kaulakahi Channel. Owned by a missionary-descended ranching family, Niihau is the only private island in the state. The pure-blooded Hawaiians who live here still speak their native tongue and eke out a rustic existence tending the island ranch and gathering honey. Although residents remain free to come and go, uninvited visitors are strictly forbidden. Niihau was the only Hawaiian island "invaded" during the Pearl Harbor attack. A downed Japanese fighter pilot terrorized inhabitants until a large Hawaiian man, disregarding three bullet wounds, literally crushed the pilot with his bare hands.

Past the 18-mile marker in Kaumakani, the ***Niihau Helicopter*** office (335–3500, after hours 338–1234) offers exclusive tours of the "Forbidden Isle," including a forty-five-minute beach landing with swimming and snorkeling if weather permits. The three-and-one-half-hour tours cost $263; reserve in advance. A half-mile farther, turn left onto the main avenue of ***Olokele.*** Shaded by banyan and monkeypod trees, a procession of plantation management homes with old-fashioned lampposts culminates at the sugar refinery. ***Gay & Robinson Sugar Co.,*** headquartered here, is the only plantation still operating on the island and one of the last in the state; it offers tours for those interested in seeing a working plantation up close and personal. The two-hour bus tour follows the cane from field to mill. The main growing season runs from April through October, but the tour operates year-round Monday through Friday, and costs $30. A three-and-one-half-hour tour for $60 also visits Olokele Canyon and includes lunch. Call 335–2824 to reserve a spot. The tour office at Olokele displays various sugar paraphernalia. At 21 miles, ***Pakala*** boasts a famous surfing beach known as Infinities for its endless breaking waves. The unofficial access is via the cattle gate immediately past the bridge over Aakukui Stream. Look out for bulls in the pasture!

From here another 2 miles takes you to Waimea, once the largest settlement on this coast and a historical center of interest. Waimea Bay served as Kaua`i's first major port, beginning with two celebrated British vessels anchored offshore in 1778. A small marker in ***Lucy Wright Park*** marks the spot where Captain Cook first stepped ashore at 3:30 P.M. in January of that year, bringing Hawaii into contact with the modern world. Another modest statue in the center of town commemorates this historic visit by one of the world's greatest explorers and Hawaii's first tourist. Cook's journals became bestsellers back in Europe. His description of Waimea Bay as a safe anchorage on Kaua`i made it the port of call for a steady stream of western vessels crossing the Pacific. Waimea became the island's *de facto* capital as Kaua`i's ruling chiefs gathered here year-round to take advantage of the trading opportunities. Waimea Bay also witnessed the abduction of Kaua`i's King Kaumualii when Kamehameha II invited him on what became a one-way sailing cruise to O`ahu in 1821. Ka`ahumanu, the queen regent, then forced both Kaumualii and his oldest son to marry her. These unorthodox tactics ensured Kaua`i's allegiance to the unified Hawaiian Kingdom.

At the entrance to town, turn left into ***Fort Elizabeth State Park*** to absorb some more history. One of three forts on Kaua`i built by Georg Anton Schaeffer, a German adventurer acting in the service of the Russian czar, Fort Elizabeth dates back to 1815. Schaeffer persuaded King Kaumualii to permit these outposts in defense of Russian trading interests. Other foreign powers objected, and the Kamehameha monarchy protested this bid by Kaumualii to bolster Kaua`i's autonomy. Schaeffer had overstepped himself, and in 1817, having fallen out of favor, he departed the islands for good. Hawaiian troops completed the construction and occupied the fort until 1864, when it was dismantled.

The fort's outer walls are still readily apparent, and a path leads through the main gate to the interior. Climb the steps to the battlements to gain a view of the coast. Inside the fort, various signs along the path label random piles of rubble or empty spaces, according to the architectural feature of the fort believed to have stood there. The most interesting thing at Fort Elizabeth itself is the weeds growing in the lawn out front. No, seriously. Look for the dark green clumps of "sleeping grass" scattered around the parking lot and entrance sign. In reality a relative of the giant koa tree, the "grass" has tiny branches sprouting miniature purple-tinged leaves paired in two symmetric rows. Touching the leaves causes each pair to fold tightly closed as if curled up to sleep.

Cross the bridge over flood-prone Waimea River into town. *Waimea* means "reddish waters." Although Hawaiian legend ascribes the river's color to blood from an unjustly slain maiden, the ruddy water bleeds from a far greater wound—Waimea Canyon. Stop by the public library (on the highway) to pick up a copy of a self-guided walking tour of Waimea's historic buildings.

Highlights include the privately owned ***Gulick-Rowell House,*** begun in stone in 1829 by Rev. Peter Gulick and completed with wooden porches and balconies seventeen years later by Rev. George Rowell. This building is notable for its adaption of New England designs to Hawaiian building materials and climate. Reverend Rowell, "the builder missionary," also completed the current ***Waimea Foreign Church*** in 1859 from sandstone cut nearby. The two buildings stand on Huakai Road one block on either side of Waimea Canyon Drive (Route 550).

Back on the highway, notice the open-wall frame of the old Waimea

Mill. The damage predates Iniki to the earlier Hurricane Iwa in 1982. You'll find a third building by Reverend Rowell opposite the Big Save. After a personal dispute with the established mission, Reverend Rowell built ***Waimea Hawaiian Church*** for his breakaway congregation around 1865. Sunday services are conducted in fluent Hawaiian.

Not included in the walking tour but worth a gander is the ***Menehune Ditch,*** part of an ancient irrigation system diverting Waimea River to surrounding taro fields. Follow the HVCB warrior onto Menehune Road from the highway and drive about 1.3 miles, stopping where the cactus-draped cliffs crowd in on the river. What little remains of the ditch, sandwiched between the road and cliffs, may not impress you, but the significance of this still-functioning watercourse lies in its use of dressed lava stone, which some argue indicates more sophisticated masonry than the Hawaiians were known to have—hence the credit to the Menehunes.

On the way back, you will see taro fields on your right, which the ditch irrigates. A little farther on, follow the sign to ***Waimea Shingon Mission*** at the end of Pule Road, where a sci-fi vision confronts you. Rows of silver, conical-topped cylinders line the temple perimeter, illuminated by red shower-nozzle lights. In the corner, a multiplatform monument supported by these silver cylinders glistens like a wedding cake. Inscribed with oriental characters, each of these bizarre concrete blocks also houses a miniature statuette. These figurines are traditional in Shingon temples. Each represents one of the eighty-eight sins described in Buddhist sutras, and making the tour past all eighty-eight supposedly inoculates one against temptation. But what is unique about this shrine is the unusual shape and appearance of the containers in which the statuettes are housed. They were designed to mimic the appearance of missile shells. Gold-star mothers of Japanese-American soldiers who fought in World War II commissioned these monuments to honor their fallen sons. Ancient Hawaiian burial caves dot the cliffs above.

To explore Waimea's more recent heritage as a sugar town, consider taking the ***Plantation Lifestyles Walking Tour*** (335–2824). The tour visits a real mill camp where Hawaii's multiethnic plantation workers lived with their families as a largely self-contained community. Volunteers, many with first-hand experiences of the camp, tell stories, bringing to life the rich history to which these clapboard homes crowded along dusty lanes bore witness. The hour-long tours are offered a couple times each week. Call to reserve a spot.

Another unique way to experience plantation living is to stay at the ***Waimea Plantation Cottages*** (338–1625 or 800–922–7866). Scattered among clusters of coconut trees in a huge garden lot bordering a silty "black sand" beach on the west end of town, the cottages are renovated homes brought in from sugar camps all along the coast and furnished with understated charm. The resort was started by descendants of Hans Peter Faye, a Norwegian immigrant who rose to become one of the early sugar barons in the area. H.P.'s original home at Mana now serves as its administration building. Rates go from $175–$240 for a one-bedroom. (9400 Kaumualii Highway, #367, www.waimea-plantation.com; waiple@aloha.net.)

If Waimea's sugar heritage lies increasingly in its past, the displays at the ***West Kaua`i Technology and Visitor Center*** (338–1332) chronicle the promise of a hi-tech future. This state-of-the-art multimedia facility, located on the highway at the corner of Waimea Canyon Drive, is part of a campaign to attract technology companies to West Kaua`i. The exhibits describe the activities of some of these companies which rent space at the center. But it has a much broader focus, covering technology used in the region from the days of the ancient Hawaiians to the present-day's solar-powered aircraft tested at the nearby Pacific Missile Range. The center also has a wealth of visitors' information on the island. Open daily 9:00 A.M. to 5:00 P.M.

Back in town, shoppers will enjoy browsing through the inventory of ***Collectibles and Fine Junque*** (338–9855), opposite Waimea Hawaiian Church. You'll find everything from vintage plantation implements to fine china dinnerware. Open Monday–Friday from 11:00 A.M. to 5:00 P.M., Saturday 1:00–5:00 P.M. As for nourishment, Waimea has several options. The hot climate on this side of the island makes it a great place to try shaved ice (a local version of snow cones), and Waimea has some of the best on the island at ***Jojo's*** (338–0056), a colorful roadside shack. Choose from a variety of exotic flavorings, like *li hing mui* (a Chinese tangy salty-sour preserved plum candy), or try *halo halo,* a kind of Filipino tropical smoothie. For more local treats, seek out ***Yumi's*** (338–1731), in the green, barnlike building opposite the library, on the highway (enter the kids' center on the other side). This tiny hole-in-the-wall lives up to its owner's name with fruit turnovers baked fresh each morning. Yumi's also serves a limited menu of local favorites such as *loco moco* (two scoops of rice topped with a hamburger patty, egg, and gravy) and homemade sushi. Open Monday–Saturday 5:30 A.M. to 3:00 P.M.

For dinner, the town favorite is ***Wrangler's Steak House*** (338-1218), decorated in predictable Western style but with a much broader menu than the name suggests. Moderate prices. Open Monday–Friday 11:00

A.M. to 9:00 P.M., and Saturday 5:00–9:00 P.M. The yuppie alternative is **Waimea Brewing Co.** (338–9733), located in the Waimea Plantation Cottages. It claims to be the "World's Western-most Brewpub." Spacious lana`i seating adds to the appeal. A moderately priced menu, including fresh-catch specials, is served daily 11:00 A.M.–9:00 P.M. The quite tasty house brews flow until 11:00 P.M.

If instead of taking Waimea Canyon Drive up to its namesake, you continue west, Route 50 leads next to Kekaha, the largest settlement on the west coast. Kekaha's giant mill sets the tone for this blue-collar community. Just past the mill on Kekaha Road, the former post office building now houses Ray Nitta's ***West Side Woodworks*** (337–1875). Unlike most artisans of his caliber who fashion objets d'art that never get used, Ray's shop is full of beautiful-yet-functional items, from canoe paddles to Zen Buddhist drums. He works mostly in native woods; variable hours.

From Kekaha north stretches an almost endless beach, but the park here has the only facilities before Polihale. Kekaha is also the turnoff for Koke`e Road, an alternate route to Waimea Canyon. Sticking to the coast, Route 50 continues as far as Mana and the Pacific Missile Firing Range at Barking Sands. In dry weather, a portion of the beach here sometimes emits "barking" sounds when you walk on it. Locals, however, say that "the dog stay old already" and has grown silent.

Just as the state highway ends and swings inland to connect with some closed military roads, a single-word sign, POLIHALE, designates the cane road access to ***Polihale State Park.*** The price you pay for admission here is 5 miles along a bumpy dirt road. Your reward is a beautiful desolate beach extending across windswept sand dunes as far as the eye can see.

About 3.5 miles in, the road approaches a large monkeypod tree fronting a scrub-covered hill with another sign indicating Polihale straight ahead. If you turn left at the tree instead, the road leads seaward toward some enormous sand dunes. Park safely so as not to get your wheels stuck, and climb over the dunes to ***Queen's Pond,*** a reef-protected lagoon. This is the only part of Polihale Beach safe for swimming (in moderate surf). After a dip here, continue on to the state park at the end of the road.

As you drive the final miles past the camping area, the mountain ridges edge closer to the shoreline until they loom directly overhead. Beyond Polihale begins the Na Pali Coast, 16 miles of jagged cliffs plunging directly into the ocean. Hanging valleys, hidden sea caves, and ancient ruins lie shrouded in mystery—incomparable and all but impenetrable.

The park itself offers a pleasant setting with beach pavilions and picnic tables surrounded by native beach vegetation. The shrubbery bush covering the dunes here is beach naupaka. Because of its tolerance to salt spray, this is often the closest-growing plant to the ocean. Besides its stubby leaves and small white pods, naupaka is distinguished by its "half flowers" that appear to be missing petals on one side. A related variety, mountain naupaka, shares this trait and is found only atop the highest peaks. According to Hawaiian legend, the two represent parted lovers whose half-formed flowers reflect a single broken heart. Niihau and Lehua float serenely above the horizon, and if you scoop sand near the shoreline, you may find some of the tiny shells from which the famous Niihau necklaces are made.

Polihale means "home of the spirits." At the very edge of the beach, where it tapers off beneath the encroaching cliffline, an ancient *heiau* marks the site from which, according to Hawaiian belief, the souls of fallen warriors would depart the earth to the drumbeat of *kahuna* (priests). A sacred spring still bubbles beneath the sands nearby. Standing amid this desolate setting, the meager trappings of civilization that the park provides seem like alien appendages foreign to and dwarfed by the power of the natural splendor around them. Sunset at Polihale feels like the end of the world.

Waimea Canyon and Koke`e

The drive-by scenery in these adjacent state parks is unmatched in Hawaii. Waimea Canyon serves up eyefuls of choice canyon vistas along the 12-mile cleft in the island's west flank, while higher up Koke`e luxuriates in a cool, nontropical setting with breathtaking overlooks onto the Na Pali Coast. To get to these views, take Waimea Canyon Road, which merges into Koke`e Road near the entrance to the park. Of the two roads, Waimea Canyon offers the most scenic views on the way up from the highway. Stop at the first turnout once you climb above Waimea town for a view of the western coastline. A display board explains the changing land use of this region. As you continue on your way up, note the many dead or toppled trees left in Hurricane Iniki's wake.

Besides checking your gas gauge, it's a good idea to check the weather before embarking on the long haul up the canyon roads. Call the National Guard Station topside at 335–6556, or peer up the valley from Waimea and gauge the cloud cover. Most of the scenery lies at elevations between 3,000 and 4,000 feet. If the whole area appears fogged in, you may prefer to hang out on the beach or tour Waimea town and hope things clear up on top. As a rule, more clouds tend to gather as the day goes on. If the weather looks dicey, head straight to the Na Pali overlooks at the end as they tend to cloud over first. If it does rain while you

Garden Isle Celluloid

*Kaua`i's jagged green mountains and dazzling white beaches would stir any cinematographer's soul. So it's no surprise that the island has become Hollywood's venue of choice whenever a script calls for a tropical setting. Over the years, Kaua`i has doubled for Vietnam's rice paddies (*Uncommon Valor, Flight of the Intruder*), Costa Rican rain forest (*Jurassic Park*), African jungle (*Outbreak*), and even the Australian outback (*The Thorn Birds*). It served as Peter Pan's Never-Never Land* (Hook), South Pacific*'s Bali Hai, television's* Fantasy Island *and the original* Gilligan's Island. *The island has also put in more than a few appearances as itself. Elvis got married at the Coco Palms in 1961's* Blue Hawaii *and returned to croon his way through two other movies set here. More recently, Nicolas Cage and Sarah Jessica Parker's* Honeymoon in Vegas *devolved into a Garden Isle romp. In all Kaua`i has been filmed in more than 60 full-length motion pictures, beginning with 1933's* White Heat. *Stephen Spielberg alone has made four of them, including* Raiders of the Lost Ark.

Almost any oldtimer on the island can tell you stories about how John Wayne came drinking at the local saloon while filming Donovan's Reef. *Or how Frank Sinatra nearly drowned at the beach in Wailua while making* None But the Brave. *With as many as three different movies under production at the same time in recent years and with so many celebrities owning vacation homes on Kaua`i's North Shore, island residents have become almost blasé about their Hollywood connection.*

For visitors to Kaua`i, however, the chance to brush against movie history has proven a great selling point. The official Kaua`i Visitors Bureau Map Guide includes markers of thirty-nine different film locations for visitors to inspect. You can pick one up at the bureau's office at 4334 Rice Street in Lihue, or at many other locations around the island. Local bookstores and giftshops stock copies of The Kaua`i Movie Book, *the definitive guide to moviemaking on the Garden Isle, full of photos and anecdotes about the shoots, as well as its own map of their locations.*

For those wanting help in reaching some of the more out-of-the-way sites (many of which are on private property), Hawaii Movie Tours *(www.hawaiimovietour.com) provides a fully narrated tour service. Their fifteen-passenger vans are equipped with VCRs and surround sound so you can see the actual scenes filmed at each location before you visit. You also learn a wealth of insider gossip about the goings on behind the scenes, and even sing show tunes from* South Pacific. *The five-hour tours run daily, beginning at 9:00 A.M., with lunch and hotel pickup included; they cost $95. Reserve in advance at 822–1192 or (800) 628–8432, as space is limited.*

are up there, don't lose hope. Retreat to ***Koke`e Lodge*** for a cup of hot caffeine and let the trade winds do their work. You may witness some stunning rainbows to reward your patience.

Three designated canyon overlooks along the upper Koke`e Road fill their railings with gawking crowds. The ***Waimea Canyon Lookout,*** first at 11 miles in and 3,120 feet elevation, offers the most dramatic frontal view into the main canyon and its three tributaries. Mark Twain, who toured the Hawaiian Islands in his youth and got in first with most of the quotable quotes, billed this "the Grand Canyon of the Pacific." While nowhere near as large as Arizona's famous hole, Waimea Canyon boasts a lusher climate that adds a vibrant green to the palette of reds, oranges, and browns used to paint its mainland counterpart. Clouds float in and out of the 3,000-foot-deep gorge, redefining the landscape by shape and shadow and sometimes dissolving reality into mist. Helicopters make a less-welcome intrusion to the canyon scenery.

The next stop at ***Puu Ka Pele*** provides picnic tables and a side view of the canyon, while the third turnoff at ***Puu Hinahina*** features yet another angle as well as a separate view toward the coast and out to Niihau. The brightly colored wildfowl you see strutting and pecking in the parking lots are moa, descendants of the original Polynesian chickens brought to Hawaii. Protected by park statute and fed by tourists, their clucking and crowing is heard everywhere. In between these official lookouts, frequent bends in the highway provide space to safely pull over and let you find your own preferred vantage point for absorbing the canyon's grandeur apart from chattering tourists, whirring camcorders, and diesel bus fumes.

An even better option is to take a hike. Everyone, fit or flabby, can and *should* enjoy the ***Iliau Nature Trail,*** a 0.3-mile loop through sporadically labeled native vegetation leading to an impressive canyon overlook and a glimpse of Waialae Waterfall on the far rim. Look for the signposted Kukui trailhead just before the 9-mile point. The stars of the show here are the rare *iliau,* a relative of the silversword plants found on Haleakala and the Big Island that is unique to Kaua`i. These branchless plants topped with spiky leaves wait until the end of their life before erupting in hundreds of yellow blossoms. Branching off from the loop, the longer ***Kukui Trail*** drops 2,000 feet to connect with the extensive trail system and wilderness camps on the canyon floor.

A mile past the third posted canyon lookout, the NASA tracking facilities mark the boundary between Waimea and Koke`e Parks. The first right (Halemanu Road) leads to yet another canyon viewpoint (looking back down the canyon) as well as trails to the Waipo`o Falls and beyond. Unpaved Halemanu Road is often unsuitable for conventional vehicles, but it's less than a mile hike to the lookout just off Halemanu to the right on the ***Cliff Trail.*** Branch left from the trail to the waterfalls for a dip in a refreshing pool surrounded by ginger.

From here on, the main highway moves away from the canyon rim and continues climbing to ***Kanalohulu Meadow,*** the center of Koke`e activity. The god Kanaloa supposedly fashioned this clearing to prevent malevolent forest sprites from preying on passersby. You can get a meal here at the ***Koke`e Lodge*** (335–6061) from 9:00 A.M. to 4:00 P.M. The lodge also rents comfortably equipped housekeeping cabins sleeping three to seven for $35 or $45. Early bookings are essential, especially for weekends (P.O. Box 819, Waimea 96796). ***Camp Sloggett,*** run by the YWCA (245–5959 for YWCA main office), rents space in its lodge and bunkhouse to groups for $20 per person, but you need a minimum of five people on weekdays and more on weekends. Linen not provided; reserve in advance (YWCA, 3094 Elua Street, Lihue 96766). Tent sites are available throughout the park with state permit.

Next to the lodge, the ***Koke`e Museum*** (335–9975), run by the Hui o Laka in honor of Laka, the goddess of the forest, offers hiking information and maps (including a giant 3-D topological map of West Kaua`i with all the trails marked). The two-room museum also crams in a wealth of natural history lore. Well-organized exhibits touch on Hawaiiana, geology, and botany and display stuffed wildlife (including a ferocious boar's head). Be sure to strike the bell stone to hear a working example of these geological curiosities used by the Hawaiians. Open daily 10:00 A.M. to 4:00 P.M. Volunteers also lead guided hikes on Sunday during the summer (call for schedule).

Outdoors enthusiasts will delight in Koke`e's many activities. Hunters (with state permit) track pigs year-round. Frugivores descend upon Koke`e during late June and July for the Menthley plum season. The first Saturday of August kicks off trout season. Anglers can tackle rainbow trout (stocked annually) for the next sixteen days, then on weekends through September. Licenses are available at Koke`e Lodge.

The Camp 10 Road, the second right after the lodge, leads through 2 miles of sylvan splendor to picnic areas around the Sugi Grove. The latter half of the road usually requires four-wheel drive. Cedar, fir, eucalyptus, and even redwood trees line the forest paths here. At dusk, look for Hawaiian bats, the islands' only endemic mammal, fluttering from the treetops.

From Sugi Grove, you can hike to some upper canyon vantage points. But for scenic destinations, most Koke`e trails head for ridgetop views above the Na Pali Coast or make soggy forays through the Alakai Swamp.

You can get a taste of both without departing pavement by continuing on Koke`e Road to the ***Kalalau*** and ***Puu o Kila lookouts.*** Both overlook the lushly carpeted amphitheater of Kalalau Valley 4,000 feet below. Waterfalls spill silently down the razor-slashed walls. Kalalau Beach, the end point of the coastal trail, lies just beyond the left rim of the valley. Uninhabited since the 1920s, the hidden depths of the Kalalau radiate a remote and mysterious power. Here, in a real-life story immortalized by Jack London's pen, Ko`olau the Leper hid with his family to escape exile to Moloka`i. After World War II, Bernard Wheatley, "the Hermit of Kalalau," lived alone in the valley for more than ten years before disappearing.

From Puu o Kila, at the end of Koke`e Road, you can also scan the vast acreage of the ***Alakai Swamp,*** which stretches across the sunken volcanic basin of Kaua`i's original caldera. The remnant of an aborted road project designed to reach Hanalei extends from the lookout along the narrow ridge dividing Kalalau and the Alakai. Free yourself from human static (if not the inescapable buzz of helicopter sorties) by walking a short distance along ***Pihea Track*** and contemplating the changing angles into Kalalau Valley. Follow your nose to the spicy anise aroma of berries from the mokihana trees along this trail. Woven with the equally fragrant leaves of the maile vine, which grows here also, the combination forms Hawaii's most sacred lei.

After 0.5 mile, the "road" narrows; a trail continues to Pihea Overlook, then drops into the murky depths of the Alakai Swamp. The largest wetland area in Hawaii, the Alakai extends to the summit of Waialeale, absorbing the prodigious rainfall this peak attracts. The swamp provides refuge for countless endangered birds shielded from predators in the mire and, at 4,000 feet, out of range of mosquito-borne diseases. Keep your eyes peeled for the brilliant red i`iwi or, if you're lucky, the lime-green nukupu`u. Both have curved beaks; the latter exists today only in the Eastern Alakai. The almost totally endemic vegetation creates a unique environment for hardy souls to explore, but be prepared for rain and mud. Fortunately, a newly built boardwalk bridges the worst patches of muck along the way.

If mud-soaked socks do not appeal, three somewhat drier trails branch off Koke`e Road between the lodge and the Air Guard Station, descending parallel ridges to reach spectacular vantage points overlooking the

Na Pali Coast. Here you can sit, deafened by silence, watching white tropic birds circle in search of nesting sites as mountain goats clamber along impossibly steep ledges. The two overlooks at the end of the ***Awaawapuhi and Nualolo trails*** connect via a third trail. This 10-mile loop makes for one of the most stunning—and demanding—day hikes in Hawaii.

The Coconut Coast

Heading northeast from Lihue beyond Hanamaulu, the Kuhio Highway (Route 56) descends from the edge of the Kalepa Ridge and hugs the coast for the next 10 miles or so. The profusion of coconut trees dotting the golf course on your right makes it immediately obvious how the eastern shore acquired its nickname. Before you fast-forward on to the North Shore, take some time to explore the Wailua River Valley. One of the two most sacred areas in all Hawaii, this lush waterway was the residence of Kaua`i's *alii nui* rulers.

Start your tour on the coast at ***Lydgate Park.*** To get there, turn right onto Leho Road just past the Wailua Golf Course, then right again. The park borders a long, white-sand beach shaded by ironwood trees. Two lava-rock wading pools offer protection against the trade wind–borne swells that buffet the shore. At the far end of the beach road, just below the Aston Kaua`i Resort, scattered clusters of lava rocks mark the remains of ***Hikini o Kala Heiau,*** an ancient sanctuary at the mouth of Wailua River. The *heiau* is one of seven strung along the river valley, culminating in an altar on the summit of Mount Waialeale. Keep in mind that when you look at these *heiau,* you're seeing only the stone foundations and walls. Kamehameha II abandoned the old religion in 1819. On his orders, all the wooden idols and altars in temples throughout the kingdom were burned to the ground. The few that survived are housed in museums. The *heiau* here was part of Hauola Place of Refuge. By reaching this peaceful spot, fugitives of old could gain sanctuary from their persecutors. Notice the small *noni* trees that grow amid the stones here. The pear-sized *noni* fruits bulge like cancerous growths, starting off green and ripening to an unappetizing gray, translucent hue. The fruit has strong medicinal value and is used by some to control hypertension.

The next *heiau* of the Wailua seven lies hidden among the cane fields above the highway, but you can see numbers three and four by crossing Wailua River and turning left from Kuhio Highway onto Kuamo`o Road (Route 580), an ancient roadway once forbidden to commoners. Royalty would beach their canoes and be carried, still seated, along the sacred

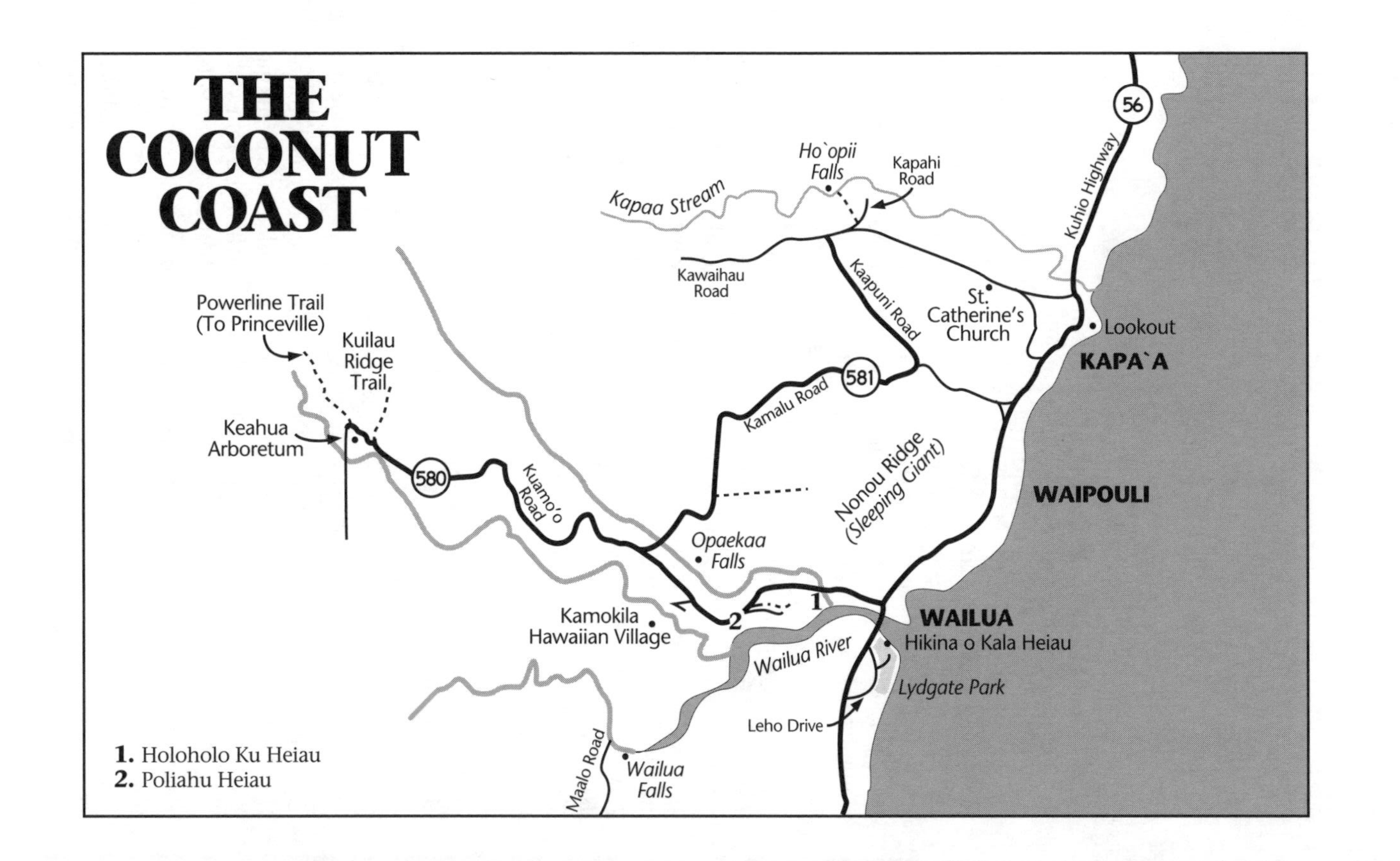
THE COCONUT COAST
Powerline Trail (To Princeville)
Kuilau Ridge Trail
Keahua Arboretum
580
Kuamo'o Road
Kapaa Stream
Ho`opii Falls
Kapahi Road
Kawaihau Road
Kaapuni Road
581
Kamalu Road
St. Catherine's Church
56
Kuhio Highway
Lookout
KAPA`A
WAIPOULI
Nonou Ridge (Sleeping Giant)
Opaekaa Falls
1
2
Kamokila Hawaiian Village
WAILUA
Hikina o Kala Heiau
Wailua River
Lydgate Park
Leho Drive
Maalo Road
Wailua Falls
1. Holoholo Ku Heiau
2. Poliahu Heiau

path to their homes by the lagoon. On your right is the ***Coco Palms Resort,*** the granddaddy of island resorts, built around ancient fish ponds where Queen Kapule, the island's last reigning monarch, once lived. An enormous stand of coconuts encircles the grounds, remnants of an unsuccessful nineteenth-century copra plantation. The hotel itself has a grand old history as a pioneer of Hawaiian resort kitsch from clamshell washbasins to palm-frond chandeliers; it was featured in several Hollywood movies, including Elvis's *Blue Hawaii.* The last of the island's hotels to remain closed after being damaged by Hurricane Iniki in 1992, it is scheduled to re-open the fall of 2001.

Now on to the *heiau.* Only a short distance up the road, in Wailua River State Park, an HVCB warrior points to ***Holoholo Ku Heiau,*** an ancient temple of sacrifice. Some controversy exists as to the authenticity of the ruins. Queen Kapule is believed to have converted the structure into a pigpen. Notice the dense interlocking thickets of *hau* trees planted as a natural barrier around this sacred spot.

A few yards farther, you can visit another set of stones used for birth, not death. ***Pohaku Hoohanau,*** a large stone set against the hillside, marks the site where royal mothers came to give birth in a rustic shelter. Infants born here absorbed the *mana* (spiritual power) of this sacred spot. The umbilical cords were stashed in the adjacent *pohaku piko* following delivery. A special bell stone on the ridge above would be struck on the occasion of a royal birth, sounding the happy news across the valley. A nearby cemetery for Japanese immigrants adds a cross-cultural touch.

Farther on, Kuamo`o Road begins to climb the ridge between Wailua River and Opaekaa Stream. Be sure to stop at the scenic lookout on top to savor the sweeping view of Wailua Valley as you watch riverboats chug slowly upstream. The Wailua River is easily the most navigable river in the state—a Yankee vessel hid here from a Confederate warship during the Civil War. The boats you see today are ferrying tourists to the ***Fern Grotto,*** a natural rock cavity draped with maidenhair ferns. If you can, consider renting a kayak and paddling up on your own (see Introduction). If you do, you can also reach "secret" Ho`olalae Falls by hiking a short distance from the river (ask for directions when you rent your kayak). Interpretive signs at the lookout also identify the adjacent ***Poliahu Heiau.*** The dedication of this temple to Poliahu, the goddess of snow (who lives on the Big Island) is left unexplained.

Your next stop just ahead looks out above ***Opaekaa Falls,*** named for the tiny shrimp that frolic in the pools below. Once a year, while laying eggs, these shrimp dye the water and waterfall red. Walk across to the highway to treat yourself to yet another great view of the main valley. Near the riverbank below, you will see the thatched roofs of ***Kamokila Hawaiian Village*** (823–0559), an authentic re-creation of an ancient Hawaiian community. A guide will walk you around the site, explaining the purpose of each structure. There are also some craft demonstrations. It's very low key, but genuine. Open Monday–Saturday 8:00 A.M.–5:00 P.M. Small admission charge. You can also rent a kayak here, which gives you a put-in site 2 miles up river from everyone else.

Farther up Kuamo`o Road, the Wailua Valley gradually opens into Wailua Homesteads, a vast expanse of green pastures and scattered houses ringed by mountains. The cool, fresh air here brings a welcome respite from the coastal heat. For those wishing to spend the night amid this bucolic beauty, there is no shortage of bed and breakfasts to choose from. Among the most darling is ***Rosewood B&B*** (822–5216; 872 Kamalu Road, www.rosewoodKaua`i.com; rosewood@aloha.net), which rents a charming upstairs room in the main house, an eighty-year-old plantation home, for $85. The real finds, however, are the two private cottages situated on the professionally landscaped one-acre lot. The larger cottage earns its name, Victorian, with white-on-yellow gables and wicker trim. Inside, it's a spacious duplex complete with a skylight and is fully equipped and elegantly furnished. Smaller and more rustic, with its outdoor shower, the Thatched Cottage has guess what kind of roof. The cottages rent for $105 and $125 per day, respectively. For those on a budget, three simply furnished bunkhouse rooms share a bathroom and rent for $40–$50. Rosewood also books vacation rentals elsewhere on the island. Another fashion-magazine contender is ***Inn Paradise*** (822–2542; 6381 Makana Road, mcinch@aloha.net). The three modern, tastefully furnished B&B suites are all in a single unit, which owners Major and Connie Inch originally built for their respective parents. The inn overlooks a 3.5-acre property complete with grazing horses and a rushing stream. Rates run from $70 to $100; two-day minimum stay.

For something more rustic, ***Kakalina's B&B*** (822–2328, 800–662–4330; www.kakalina.com; klinas@aloha.net) offers three studio *hale* on a three-acre working flower farm. The two newer units, Kolu and 'Elua, have the nicest setup and go for $90 and $85, respectively. Those on tighter budgets will have to slum it in Kapaa. ***Kaua`i International Hostel*** (823–6142), opposite the beach park, has dorm beds for $20 and private rooms for $50.

Kuamo`o Road continues to climb deeper into the island interior. At about 5 miles in, a sign warns the road ahead is "unimproved," but it really is not that bad. You pass hillsides carpeted with maidenhair ferns, fragrant patches of yellow ginger, and other exotic flora. At about 6.5 miles from its start, the road crosses Keahua Stream, where you can park and stretch your legs in ***Keahua Arboretum.*** Although most of the plant labels have been lost, nature paths wind along the stream through open meadows and clusters of exotic trees. The Makaleha Mountains, Wailua's rear wall, loom fairly close by, and behind them, the twin peaks of Waialeale and Kawaikiu slash upwards to skewer the clouds.

For those wishing to take in more of the scenery on foot, an excellent network of hiking trail begins near Keahua. The ***Kuilau Ridge Trail,*** one of the most scenic on Kaua`i, has its signposted trailhead on the right of the highway just before you cross Keahua Stream. The 2.1-mile (one-and-one-half-hour) jaunt through diverse vegetation and fruit winds along a steep ridge to reach a shelter–picnic site. Continue on 0.5 mile farther to get the best views. More hardcore is the ***Powerline Trail,*** which starts at the end of the road and leads you on an all-day slog across the mountains to Princeville. On clear days the views are spectacular, but expect thigh-deep mud in patches.

On your way down from Keahua, take the turnoff left onto Route 581 (Kamalu Road), which winds through lush forest and rolling pastures behind Nounou Mountain. About 1.2 miles along, a sign on the right, opposite 1055 Kamulu, indicates the trailhead for the ascent up Nounou, better known as the Sleeping Giant. Hawaiian legend claims the mountain is really the overgrown body of the giant Nounou, whose recumbent form is best viewed from the coast. The trail travels 1.5 miles to Nounou's chin (about an hour's hike) and offers panoramic views from the top.

Route 581 continues for another couple miles of mountain vistas before it swings toward the coast to emerge near the center of Kapa`a. Kapa`a used to be a funky plantation town full of rickety buildings. Unfortunately, the infestation of tourists along this coast has transformed it into an endless sequence of shopping plazas and boutiques. Those of a historical bent will want to seek out the ***Kapaa History Store*** (821–1778), near the first traffic light on the highway. Run by the island historical society, the store displays vintage photographs and other relics and is also the starting point for a guided walking tour of Kapa`a town. The 90-minute tours are offered Tuesday, Thursday, and Saturday at 10:00 A.M. A nearby HCVB warrior along the highway designates the optimum viewing angle to make out the Sleeping Giant's shape, but you can see him from anywhere along the Coconut Coast. (Hint: Nounou's head rests on a pillow above Wailua, and his body stretches north.)

If hunger beckons, you will find the Coconut Coast loaded with restaurants of all stripes strung along the highway. To eat as locals do, visit ***Pono Market*** (822–4581), at the southern edge of Kapa`a, for take-out plate lunch and fresh sashimi and poke. For dinner you might try ***Aloha Diner*** (822–3851), in the Waipouli Complex between Wailua and Kapaa, to sample authentic Hawaiian food. It's a family-run affair, with baseball trophies proudly displayed. Open Monday–Saturday 10:30 A.M. to 3:00 P.M. and Tuesday–Saturday 5:30–9:00 P.M. Also in the same complex is ***KCL Barbeque*** (823–8168), which serves a local/Chinese menu. Both inexpensive.

For more sophisticated fare, ***Caffe Coco*** (822–7990), next to the Wailua Family Restaurant in Wailua, has cultivated the perfect tropical bungalow ambience. A pair of sisters renovated these 1930s Montgomery Ward prefab homes with tin roofs and clapboard walls. One runs the cafe, while the other sells Hawaiian nostalgia kitsch and artsy collectibles next door. Together they planted a wraparound garden full of exotic flowering tropicals and ferns, so dense and lush that you can't even see the buildings from the road. Inside, the cafe displays artwork for sale and is full of idiosyncratic touches. Outside, an assortment of lawn chairs beckon for alfresco dining with live music most evenings. For all the effort put into the decor, the kitchen's no slouch either. The moderately priced menu spotlights local produce and fish, imaginatively prepared with Pacific Rim influences. The only catch is the service, which while well-intentioned, can seem laughably amateurish. Open Tuesday–Sunday 9:00 A.M. to 9:00 P.M.

Those with a yen for Japanese should visit ***Kintaro*** (822–3341), across the street from Caffe Coco, where you can either order *teppan yaki* dishes prepared at your table or sushi and other delicacies from the kitchen. Open Monday–Saturday 5:30–9:30 P.M. Expensive. Thai food lovers locally split their votes between ***The King and I*** (822–1642), in Waipouli Plaza, and ***Mema's*** (823–0899), near Caffe Coco. Both are priced in the moderate range; the latter has the edge on decor, but costs a little more, too.

Finally, for the big splurge of your trip, treat yourself to a meal at ***A Pacific Cafe*** (822–0013) in the Kaua`i Village Center, also in Waipouli. French chef Jean-Marie Josselin's exciting blend of European and Asian cuisines and fresh island produce has put Kaua`i on the culinary map. The menu varies daily according to available ingredients, but fresh fish always features prominently. Taste combinations such as "blackened ahi with papaya salsa" stimulate the imagination, but more important, they actually taste good. Many of the dishes are served on attractive ceramic plates handmade by Josselin's wife, Sophronia. The only quibble here is with the somewhat uninspired decor, but what do you expect when the best restaurant on the island is located in a shopping mall? Open nightly 5:30–9:30 P.M. Investment-caliber prices.

Those craving another waterfall-fed pond to frolic in can take Kawaihau Road off Kuhio Highway (near the north edge of town). On the way, you will pass ***St. Catherine's Church,*** which looks like an aircraft hangar but harbors beautiful murals by prominent local artists portraying Christian scenes in a Hawaiian and Oriental idiom. Continue on for another 2 miles, and then turn right on Kapahi Road, which angles back to end at a dirt road. Follow this dirt road to a narrow trail and keep on the left fork as you zero in on the sound of the falls. Kapa`a Stream funnels over ***Ho`opouli Falls*** into a narrow steep-walled pool formed by an exposed lava tube.

The North Shore

Those striking "Bali Hai" peaks you've admired all the way from Lihue rise from the edge of the Anahola Mountains at the northern limit of the Coconut Coast. North of Kapa`a, Kealia Beach marks the beginning of undeveloped coastline; however, Kuhio Highway turns inland as it climbs over the Anahola Mountains, leaving the beaches ahead hidden from tourist traffic. WARNING: With all North Shore beaches, extreme caution must be exercised while swimming. Dangerous currents form along the coast, and monstrous surf appears during winter.

After crossing the Anahola Mountains, you enter a vast clearing, but surprise, no sugar cane: The climate on the North Shore is too wet. Sugar has given way to niche crops such as the small papaya plantation about 0.5 mile past the 16-mile marker. Turn right here onto Koolau Road to do some exploring. To reach secluded ***Moloa`a Bay,*** take the next right and follow bumpy Moloa`a Road to its end. Park and walk past the cluster of beach homes along the public right-of-way to the beach. Sheltered inside the steep walls of the bay, this beautiful curving strand is bisected by Moloa`a Stream. Windblown debris accumulates at the far end of the beach. You may get lucky and discover a Japanese fishing float, a hollow ball of glass that has floated thousands of miles across the Pacific.

Koolau Road winds uphill past Moloa`a to cross rolling pastureland. For diehards who thought Moloa`a wasn't deserted enough, turn back

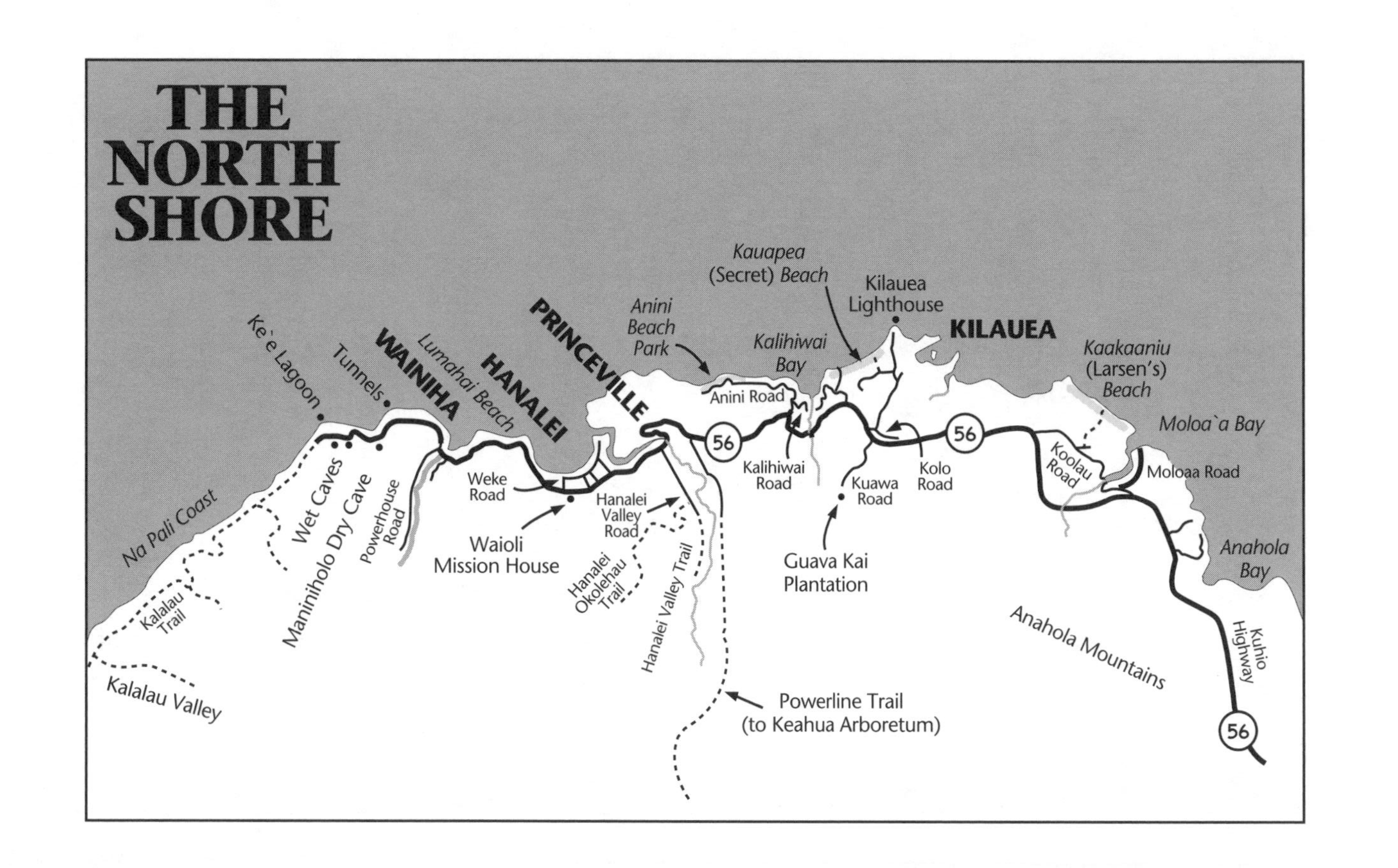
THE NORTH SHORE
Ke`e Lagoon
Tunnels
WAINIHA
Lumahai Beach
HANALEI
PRINCEVILLE
Anini Beach Park
Anini Road
Kauapea (Secret) Beach
Kalihiwai Bay
Kilauea Lighthouse
KILAUEA
Kaakaaniu (Larsen's) Beach
Moloa`a Bay
Moloaa Road
Koolau Road
Anahola Bay
Kuhio Highway
56
Na Pali Coast
Wet Caves
Maniniholo Dry Cave
Powerhouse Road
Weke Road
Waioli Mission House
Hanalei Valley Road
Hanalei Okolehau Trail
Hanalei Valley Trail
Kalihiwai Road
Kuawa Road
Kolo Road
Guava Kai Plantation
Powerline Trail (to Keahua Arboretum)
Anahola Mountains
Kalalau Trail
Kalalau Valley

on the angled cane road on your right just over a mile farther on Koolau Road, then take an immediate left. Follow this second dirt road to the end and hike the remaining 0.5 mile down to ***Kaakaaniu*** or ***Larsen's Beach.*** All this effort guarantees seclusion on a lovely stretch of shoreline that is a traditional harvesting site for *limu,* an edible seaweed. Koolau Road continues past an 1853 cemetery and affords ocean and mountain vistas before it rejoins Kuhio Highway.

At the 23-mile marker you reach the first real settlement on the North Shore at Kilauea. A plantation town that refused to die, Kilauea now thrives on the tourist traffic lured by ***Kilauea Lighthouse.*** Turn right off the highway onto Kolo Road to enter town. You take the first left to reach the lighthouse, but before doing so, have a look at tiny ***Christ Memorial Episcopal Church,*** a charming lava rock edifice set amid a peaceful garden and cemetery. Inside the church are some colorful stained-glass windows imported from England and a hand-carved altar fashioned by a parishioner, Mrs. William Hyde Rice. The present church dates to 1941, but many of the plots in the cemetery hark back to the original Congregational mission church. Farther along Kolo Road, ***Saint Sylvester's Catholic Church*** claims its share of attention for its innovative octagonal design. Inside, painted ceiling panels by Jean Charlot depict the stations of the cross.

At the end of the road, ***Kilauea Point National Wildlife Refuge*** (828–1413) surrounds the old lighthouse standing on Kaua`i's northernmost tip. Stop first at the visitors center to take in some information-packed displays on Pacific wildlife, including a video tour of the remote Leeward Isles northwest of Kaua`i. You can then walk out to the end of the point and enjoy sweeping views along the coast in both directions while looking for the critters you've just read up on. Dolphins, green sea turtles, monk seals, and even humpback whales can all be spotted on occasion, as well as dozens of seabirds whirling overhead.

The old lighthouse is no longer used and is closed to visitors, but a separate set of displays tells the story of its rare "clamshell" lens. Designed by French physicist Augustin Fresnel in 1913, using thousands of fragile interlocking pieces, the four-ton lens beamed its light 20 miles out to sea. Volunteers lead informative and very scenic hikes along the cliffside terrain and native vegetation of adjacent Crater Hill. It is open from 10:00 A.M. to 4:00 P.M. daily. Token admission. On the way to the lighthouse, you'll pass the Kong Lung Center, a historic trading post turned tourist complex. ***Casa di Amici*** (742–1555) serves excellent, albeit very pricey (investment-caliber) dinners nightly 6:00–9:00 P.M.

If you don't know how to spot guavas in the wild, stop by the free visitors center at ***Guava Kai Plantation*** (828–6121). Backtrack on the highway to take Kuawa Road inland just east of the Kolo Road junction. Guavas have such a short shelf life that they aren't even sold in local supermarkets, but the yellow-pink fruit makes tasty juice. Open daily 9:00 A.M. to 5:00 P.M. On the way in, you will pass the ***Native Plant Propagators*** (828–1454). Owner Janet Smith grows only endemic and indigenous plants, those that existed on Kaua`i before humans arrived. You'll find such rarities here as the *ulei* (Hawaiian rose), the only member of the rose family that lacks thorns. Open by appointment.

If you glanced along the western shoreline from Kilauea Point, you probably saw a wide patch of sandy beach. Getting there is another story. ***Kauapea Beach*** once bore the nickname Secret Beach because of its hidden access. The secret is out now, and there is no reason why you should not enjoy its charms. Take Kalihiwai Road, the first right past Kilauea, and then turn right again onto a dirt road. From the end of this road, you have a short (five-minute) hike downhill. Kauapea Beach at the bottom is much bigger than you might expect, but it is partitioned by lava-rock outcrops into cozy subsections. Although calmer in the summer, the beach is not recommended for swimming any time of year due to dangerous currents.

Michelle Hughes rents a pair of one-bedroom cottages on her eleven-acre plot directly above (and with private access to) Kauapea Beach. The newer unit, "Hideaway II," in particular, has a spectacular location atop a knoll, with panoramic views from mountain to ocean. Custom-built and fully equipped, it has all kinds of thoughtful touches and amenities you would never expect in a rental property, from the Japanese ceramic plates in the all-granite kitchen to the double-head shower, which opens onto a private garden and Jacuzzi. It rents for $325, $25 more than Hideaway I. Call 828–2862.

Kalihiwai Road continues on through lush foliage and then curls around the mouth of beautiful ***Kalihiwai Bay*** to descend to yet another pristine North Shore beach. Children swing on a rope over the lagoon formed at the mouth of Kalihiwai Stream. Tidal waves in 1946 and 1957 twice flattened the entire valley. As a result, a broken circuit has left a second Kalihiwai Road joining the highway farther along.

On your way there, park at the scenic overlook near the 24-mile marker and walk onto the highway bridge to savor the tropical vision of Kalihiwai Valley. The waterfall you see upstream can be reached by kayak or jeep trail. The trailhead begins at the next turnout a mile farther at the

FALLING ROCKS sign. Bear left at the meadow. Past the bridge, turn onto the western branch of Kalihiwai Road, choosing the left fork (Anini Road) unless you want to admire Kalihiwai Bay from the other side. Anini Road passes some elegant beach homes (which may explain its good state of repair) on its way to ***Anini Beach Park,*** a huge, grassy expanse with the usual facilities. WARNING: One of the largest fringing reefs in Hawaii protects the coastline here, but dangerous currents still form in the winter, especially through Anini Channel, a gap in the reef where sailboarders romp on windy days. Beyond the beach park on the left, ***Kaua`i Polo Club*** attracts boisterous crowds to its Sunday matches from April to August. Polo, "the sport of kings," was popular among the island's plantation aristocracy. Anini Road hugs the shoreline for another mile, offering coastal views stretching from Kilauea Point to Princeville. A narrow beach lines its length.

Back on the highway, you next pass Princeville Resort. Built onto bluffs overlooking magnificent Hanalei Bay, the ultraluxury ***Princeville Hotel*** (826–9644; 800–826–4400) has perhaps the most scenic location of any in Hawaii. The palatial hotel buildings and grounds take full advantage. Rooms start at $360. If you can't afford to stay here, the unbeatable view may be worth the price of a cup of coffee on the terrace. A small gazebo nearby houses displays on Princeville's royal past.

On the other side of the highway, be sure to stop at the ***Hanalei Valley Overlook*** on the left for one of the classic vistas in Hawaii. The Hanalei River emerges from the mouth of a deep valley and curves gently west through fields of taro toward Hanalei Bay. When it rains in the mountains, tiny waterfalls appear—local lore warns not to visit Hanalei when more than eight cascades are gushing, or you risk being stranded by flash floods. Most of the land before you belongs to the Hanalei National Wildlife Refuge. The Hanalei Valley has been farmed by different people over the years through a cycle of crops. Now, as a protected wildlife refuge, the land has reverted to the taro cultivation of ancient times in a cooperative venture whereby flooded taro fields, regulated by terracing, provide a favorable habitat for endangered wildfowl. Birders can study an illustrated placard to bone up on the different species they might encounter below.

As the highway begins its descent to the valley floor, a wide strip around the first bend allows space to pull over and admire ***Hanalei Bay*** ("crescent bay"), the companion view to the valley overlook. Surfers stop here and check out the breakers through binoculars to decide which part of the bay to paddle out to below. Keen eyes may spot the buffalo that graze in Bill Mowry's farm in front of the bay. Ono's Family Restaurant

Hanalei Rice Mill

Deep within the Hanalei National Wildlife Refuge, unobtrusively located on the banks of the Hanalei River, sits the state's only rice mill. Included on the National Register of Historic Places, the mill was built by a Chinese farmer in the early 1920s. The Haraguchi family purchased the mill in 1924. Rice was harvested here until the 1960s, when it was deemed that taro crops garnered more profit.

The Haraguchi family never intended to restore its historic Hanalei rice mill twice, but hurricanes Iwa and Iniki had other plans. Now the facility has once again been rebuilt and may be open to the public at some point in the future. Call 826–6202 to inquire.

The building and all its original equipment stood in disarray until the early 1980s, when the family formed a nonprofit organization and slowly began moving toward restoration. Their efforts included taking an oral history from family patriarch Kayohei Haraguchi, who died shortly before Iwa demolished the building in 1982. The mill was fully restored and operating as an education center for schoolchildren when Iniki hit in 1992 and again leveled the structure.

The family's homes and farm also were devastated, delaying the mill reconstruction until 1996. Besides rebuilding the mill, workers also labored for months to restore the ancient equipment, which is now fully functional. It's the only such building of its kind in the state.

in Kapa`a serves buffalo meat from this farm.

At the bottom of the hill, you reach the famous single-lane ***Hanalei Bridge,*** a symbolic gateway to the scenic wonders ahead. Mileage numbers are zeroed from this point, and as a practical benefit, weight restrictions prevent tour buses from crossing. One-lane bridges span the 10 miles of highway ahead, enforcing a slower pace of life. Etiquette dictates that you wait until all the traffic from the other side has cleared before crossing and that you wave to acknowledge other motorists' courtesy. Think of it as an excuse to stop and smell the flowers!

To explore the upper valley you saw from the overlook, turn left after the bridge onto Ohiki Road, which heads upriver through the taro fields/wildlife refuge. A turnoff just ahead to the right leads to an old cemetery. A little bit farther on, there's a parking lot where a 0.25-mile nature loop leads to a recently discovered *heiau.* The steep powerline trail behind the cemetery serves as the beginning of the ***Hanalei Okolehao Trail,*** named for the *okolehao* liquor distilled from *ki* plants along this ridge during Prohibition. The 2.25-mile hike takes about two hours and offers great views of Hanalei Bay. Another mile-and-a-half inland, the main road ends at the easier ***Hanalei Valley Trail,*** which heads 2 miles upstream through fruit trees and bamboo forests.

After the bridge, the Kuhio Highway follows the Hanalei River into Hanalei Town. Stop when you spot the soothing green of ***Waioli Huiia Church*** on your left. Come by on Sunday morning, and you will hear the church's famous choir fill the rafters with Hawaiian hymns. The building to the right, ***Waioli Mission Hall,*** built in 1841, housed the original congregation.

The real treat, however, awaits at the end of the long driveway between these two buildings. Park in the lot behind the Mission Hall to visit ***Hanalei Mission House,*** the 1837 residence of the Alexanders, the first missionaries on the North Shore. Restored in 1921 by three Wilcox sisters whose missionary grandparents succeeded the Alexander family here, the mission house is run by the same trust that oversees Grove Farm. Where Grove Farm portrays life during sugar's heyday, this Hanalei museum returns to an even earlier time for a glimpse at the lives of Bedford missionaries in "Owhyhee," as it was referred to back then. Docents lead half-hour tours of the property, revealing the stories behind its contents, while the letters and portraits on display chronicle the early inhabitants. The prefab house and most of the furniture (including a bedwarmer!) were shipped around Cape Horn. The garden in back made this isolated mission self-sufficient in food supplies. Tours are offered Tuesday, Thursday, and Saturday 9:00 A.M. to 3:00 P.M.; donations voluntary; call 245–3202.

From the mission, take any road seaward and then turn right to backtrack along the bay to ***Black Pot Beach Park*** at the mouth of Hanalei River. The park name honors a tradition of seaside festivities held on this spot in decades past. Local fishermen, visiting yacht crews, and anyone else who cared to join in would gather nightly to cook in a communal black pot. "Uncle" Henry Kalani Tai Hook, the unofficial mayor of Hanalei, set records with the enormous outdoor banquets he organized here. An old pier that juts offshore once served to load rice from the valley mill (note the faint rail tracks). Kids play on and around the crumbling pier, and swimming in these estuarine waters is the safest in the bay.

Most of the restaurants in Hanalei cater to tourists so you might want to bring a picnic lunch. Some people are partial to ***Pizza Hanalei*** (826–9494), in the Ching Young Village. What Hanalei lacks in eateries, it makes up for in its bars. ***Tahiti Nui*** (826–6277), on the highway in the center of town, is practically an institution. This South Seas watering hole dates back to thirty-five years ago, when owner Louise Marston

Waioli Mission Hall

arrived as a war bride from Tahiti and fell in love with Hanalei. Polynesian architecture and decor run from floor to ceiling. The glass fishing float lanterns and carved coconut stump barstools are especially nice touches. The restaurant next door is less notable, but the informal luau held Wednesday at 5:00 P.M. is the best commercial version on Kaua`i. Also popular after dark is the ***Hanalei Gourmet*** (826–2524), a deli-bakery-cum-bar housed in the restored 1926 Old Hanalei Schoolhouse across the street.

For those wishing to stay the night, Hanalei has a few options. ***Faye***

Hanalei House and Cottage can be rented from Waimea Plantation Cottages (338–1625). Originally a 1916 retreat belonging to the Faye sugar family, the simple but nicely renovated cottage portion of this three-acre beachfront estate books for $250 a night. Not too far removed from the beach in its name is Carolyn Barnes's ***Bed, Breakfast and Beach*** (826–6111). Her four rooms, all with private baths, start at $75, but the "Bali Hai" suite with wraparound views of Hanalei Bay is worth the extra bucks at $125 (hanaleibay@ad.com). Carolyn is also readying a new place that *is* oceanfront.

Back in town, the ***Historic Bed and Breakfast*** (826–4622; www.historicbnb.com) offers unique lodging in a former Buddhist temple built in 1901, now run by Kelly Sato. Carefully renovated, with original hardwood floors and *shoji* doors, the B&B has three downstairs rooms, two with four-poster bamboo beds and mosquito nets, the third with antique twin beds; all of them share bathrooms and rent for $75-$85. You can also book a variety of rental properties, some owned by absentee celebrities, through ***Hanalei NorthShore Properties,*** P.O. Box 60, Hanalei, 96714 (826–9622; 800–488–3336; www.rentalsonkauai.com).

As Route 56 climbs around the western edge of Hanalei Bay, the road widens at two pullout spaces from which a steep, often muddy trail descends through the forest of *hala* trees to ***Lumahai Beach.*** This lovely strand starred in *South Pacific* as "Nurses' Beach," where Mitzi Gaynor tried to "wash that man right out of my hair." The waters here are very treacherous, so best stick to the sand.

The highway next crosses Lumahai Stream to enter ***Wainiha***—Valley, River, Bay, Beach, General Store. The latter is your last stop for provisions. WARNING: Wainiha quite appropriately means "unfriendly waters." Not only is the beach treacherous, but the river mouth is a nursery for baby sharks—so steer clear. Consider turning inland onto Powerhouse Road to explore wide-mouthed Wainiha Valley, where an early census listed fifty-two residents as Menehunes. You'll pass the standard North Shore offerings of lush vegetation, waterfalls, and ancient taro terraces before ending up 2 miles in at the 1906 hydroelectric power station.

Back on the highway, the YMCA's ***Camp Naue*** (246–9090 for YMCA main office) lies at the 8-mile marker (2080 Hoone Street, Poipu 96756) spread over a choice beachfront lot. Often the site of community functions, the camp also rents dorm bunks for $12 to those who can furnish their own bedding. No reservations accepted, but call ahead to check availability.

As you drive onward, winding through ever denser jungle, the spirit of mystery and romance mounts. After rounding a final curve, the highway crosses a small stream (and quite often vice versa) where, yawning open as if to swallow unwary motorists, ***Maniniholo (Dry) Cave*** appears on the left. Park at Haena Beach Park across the road to explore this cavernous chamber, named for the head fisherman of the Menehunes who lived here. Sinuous vines hang over the rim, and wild taro grows near the entrance. Inside, with the aid of a flashlight, you can follow a passage opening from the back left wall a good distance in before the ceiling becomes uncomfortably low. This ancient lava tube helped form the sea cave through which you entered. Haena Beach Park has facilities, but a nicer stretch of sand lies back around the bend toward Hanalei. Take the beach access road a quarter-mile before Maniniholo Cave to ***Tunnels,*** a popular surfing spot with outstanding snorkeling during calm summer months. Sandlubbers can simply admire the mountain and ocean views.

Kuhio Highway presses on through lush vegetation darkened by the shadow of the mountains overhead. About 0.5 mile past the 9-mile marker, on the mountain side of the road, you will see the entrance to ***Limahuli Gardens*** (826–1053), the North Shore satellite of the National Tropical Botanical Garden in Lawai, which has now opened an environmentally friendly visitors center intended to be functional and visually compatible with its fabulous setting. The structure began as a 10-by-32-foot office trailer, which was transformed into a building resembling a historic, plantation-style home.

The center displays Hawaiian crafts and offers information about the environment and the garden, a seventeen-acre facility that features a large collection of rare and endangered native Hawaiian plants and many tropical species. The plantings here focus on ethnobotany. You can learn about the plants the ancient Hawaiians used in their daily life as you explore this spectacular valley setting. Black lava rock contours the green valley slopes in an age-old system of terraces built for taro. The garden offers stunning views. Guided tours are $15; self-guided, $10. Open Tuesday through Friday, and Sunday, 9:30 A.M. to 4:00 P.M.

Back on the highway, ***Haena State Park*** just ahead was the site of the infamous "Taylor's Camp," a 1960s hippie community started by Liz's brother, Howard, whose free-living style did not include plumbing or waste disposal. State authorities eventually condemned the land. Park at the visitors parking area, cross the street, and take the short but steep trail ahead to the ledge overlooking ***Waikapalae (Wet) Cave.*** To get the full spelunking effect, you should ease your way down to the edge of the water.

Daylight, tinted green by the foliage overhead, filters through the mouth of the cave, and the soundless water inside acquires an eerie blue hue.

A second wet cave, ***Waikanaloa,*** opens onto the highway just ahead. Peering inside, you can see through to a second chamber. The legend of Pele explains how these two caves became wet. It seems the volcano goddess dug her firepits here when she came to Kaua`i in search of a home. Her sister, the ocean, flooded her out of Waikanaloa; Pele tried

Lohiau's House or the Tale of Three Sisters

Countless hikers head into the Na Pali every day without noticing an archaeological site, which the Kalalau trail passes, scarcely 50 feet from the trailhead. Just to the left of the trail, keen eyes will discern the vine-draped lava rock foundation that is reputedly the site of Lohiau's House. Legends recount that Lohiau was a handsome chieftain associated with the hula halau *at the nearby Ka Ulu o Laka temple. When the volcano goddess Pele arrived on Kaua`i, she was fleeing the wrath of her elder sister, a powerful ocean goddess. Hearing the sounds of the drums at Ka Ulu o Laka, Pele drew near to watch the ritual hula. With his graceful dancing, Lohiau won Pele's favor. They vowed to live together as man and wife.*

Unfortunately Pele's older sister, Na Maka o Ka Ha`i, had followed her to the island. When Pele attempted to dig for fire to build a home for her and her beloved, the ocean goddess rushed in with crashing waves to squelch Pele's fire. Pele's flooded firepits remain known as the wet caves of Waikapalae and Waikanaloa. With a heavy heart, Pele had to leave Lohiau in quest of fire elsewhere. As she moved from island to island, Pele longed for her beloved mortal. When at last she settled on the Big Island, her volcanic fires secure in the mighty lava fortress she had built, she sent her younger sister, Hiiaka, to summon her paramour.

Lohiau had since died a lonely death, but Hiiaka was able to recover his spirit, trapped in a flower, and bring him back to life. The two then embarked on an arduous journey down the Hawaiian island chain, battling monsters and overcoming obstacles. Somewhere along the way the two fell in love, although neither dared to speak of it. When at last they came within sight of Halemaumau Crater, Pele's sacred firepit on the Big Island of Hawai`i, the two embraced, as much from relief as repressed longing. Upon seeing them together, Pele's wrath overflowed. Torrents of fire gushed down the slopes causing Lohiau to die a second death engulfed in molten lava. Pele's brothers pitied Lohiau and again brought him back to life. However, Hiiaka had vanished by then. Lohiau wandered aimlessly from island to island until at last he stumbled upon the hula heiau *at Ka Ulu o Laka. A singing contest was in progress, and Lohiau recognized Hiiaka's voice. The two lovers embraced once more and returned to Haena to live happily ever after.*

higher up at Waikapalae, but the ocean followed still. Defeated, Pele took her fires to O`ahu.

As you return to your car with visions of Menehunes and goddesses dancing in your head, keep your eye on the clifftop peaks above the highway. These silent sentinels loom ever closer, choking off the road against the sea, until all at once it ends at Ke`e Beach; beyond lies only the remote Na Pali Coast and the start of the Kalalau Trail. ***Ke`e Beach,*** at the far end of the parking lot, provides ample reward for your perseverance in coming this far. Dominated by the spires of rock overhead and sheltered by a protective reef, this tiny cove offers excellent snorkeling in calm waters and is usually safe for a dip in moderate surf. Long stretches of hidden sandy beach extend around the right side of the lagoon. You can walk there or drive from the parking lot, but the swimming is less protected.

The left side of Ke`e Beach conceals secrets of its own. Follow the short sidewalk strip from the edge of the parking lot toward a narrow trail skirting the edge of the former Allerton estate, just above the rocky border of the lagoon. You get a magnificent glimpse of the endlessly silhouetted *pali* (cliffs) ahead that give this coast its name. Near the end of the point, the trail turns left and climbs steeply through vegetation to emerge in the clearing that was once ***Ka Ulu o Laka Heiau,*** dedicated to Laka, the patron of the hula (dance). The rocky remains of this ancient temple have weathered considerably, but you can still feel the power of the setting, hovering midway between mountain and ocean, encircled by jungle, at the very edge of civilization. The ancient Hawaiians held night rituals on this site, hurling special burning branches from the cliffs nearby in a natural display of fireworks. Hula *halau* still return today to leave offerings and rededicate their arts in this sacred spot.

Across the parking lot from Ke`e Beach begins the ***Kalalau Trail,*** Hawaii's most celebrated wilderness experience. This is no cakewalk. To travel the full 11 miles along the Na Pali coast to Kalalau Beach takes at least two days, and there are numerous spur trails heading inland along the way. State camping permits are required. Along the way, you take in magnificent scenery, lush tropical vegetation, dramatic seascapes, hidden valleys cloaked in mist, and, above all, the magnetic presence of *na pali,* the endless sea cliffs whose sheer edges the trail traverses. Captain Zodiac (826–9371) used to offer dropoff service at Kalalau Beach for you or your pack in one or both directions from May to September. At press time, their permit was in limbo. Call to inquire. A popular day hike goes 2 miles to ***Hanakapiai Beach*** (swimming not recommended) and then an optional 2 miles upstream to ***Hanakapiai Falls*** for a chilling plunge in the pool below.

Those with less time or stamina might consider hiking only 0.5 mile in on the trail until you catch the first full glimpse of the Na Pali coastline spread out before you. You'll know when you're there.

WHERE TO STAY

Garden Island Inn,
3445 Wilcox Road in Lihue;
245–7227, (800) 648–0154.
www.gardenisland.com,
Rates: $75 to $125.

Gloria's B&B,
742–6995,
www.gloriasbedand
breakfast.com, in Poipu,
offers elegant oceanfront lodging. Rooms with four-poster beds and Hawaiian quilts rent for $250.

Waimea Plantation
Cottages; 338–1625,
(800) 922–7866,
9400 Kaumualii Highway.
Charming individual cottage-type accommodations. Rates start at $175.

Rosewood B&B,
822–5216,
www.rosewoodkauai.com,
in Wailua Homesteads,
offers a wide array of lodging, all impeccably maintained on a beautiful country estate.
Rooms: $40–$125.

Inn Paradise,
822–2542,
in Wailua Homesteads,
three-and-one-half-acre estate overflows with country charm. Rooms from $70.

Bed, Breakfast and Beach,
826–6111, in Hanalei,
offers comfortable rooms close to Hanalei Bay from $75.

Historic B&B,
826–4622,
www.historicbnb.com,
in Hanalei, offers lodging in a former Buddhist temple built in 1901.
Rooms with shared bath rent for $75.

For additional accommodations and visitors information,
visit the following Web sites:
www.kauaivisitorsbureau.com; www.hshawaii.com; www.kauai-hawaii.com.

WHERE TO EAT

Gaylord's at Kilohana
near Lihue,
245–9593. Continental entrees come with veggies and fruit grown on property. Revered islandwide for the bountiful Sunday brunch. Expensive-Investment-caliber.

Hamura's Saimin,
2956 Kress Street
245–3271,
Lihue, ladles out Kaua`i's best bowl of saimin. Open from 11:00 A.M. until late in the evening.

The Beach House,
742–1424,
at 5022 Lawai Road,
in Poipu.
Hawaii Regional Cuisine served in a romantic oceanfront setting.

Roy's,
742–5000,
in Poipu Shopping Village at 2360 Kiahuna Plantation Drive. Inventive Hawaii Regional Cuisine. Expensive–Investment-caliber.

Green Garden Restaurant
335–5422,
a landmark in Hanapepe since 1948. Don't miss the homemade passionfruit pie.

Caffe Coco,
822–7990,
on the highway next to the Wailua Family Restaurant in Wailua. Tasty food served in a romantic tropical bungalow ambience. Moderate.

A Pacific Cafe
822–0013,
one of the top venues for Hawaii Regional Cuisine. Located in the Kaua`i Village Center in Waipouli, Kepaa. Investment-caliber.

O`ahu

With 80 percent of the state's population on this island, it's not surprising that O`ahu is commonly (if erroneously) translated as "the gathering place." The fact that the state capitol resides here is almost redundant. On the other hand, officially, O`ahu itself does not exist anymore. The entire island belongs to the City and County of Honolulu, which also includes the uninhabited Leeward Islands that stretch a thousand miles northwest of Kaua`i, making it the largest "city" in the world. This semantic confusion only serves to underline the extent to which Honolulu dominates the islands.

Honolulu Harbor assured O`ahu commercial preeminence, and Pearl Harbor to the west made it a vital strategic asset as well. On the other side of Honolulu Harbor, Waikiki Beach gave O`ahu a jumpstart into tourism far ahead of the other islands. It still bears the brunt of Hawaii's visitors, and some say O`ahu is past its prime. This is grossly unfair. Honolulu has grown into a vibrant, culturally sophisticated city, and O`ahu, although undeniably more built-up than its neighbors, still retains a scenic beauty rivaling the best in Hawaii. What's more, unlike some of the other islands, O`ahu has only one concentrated resort center along a single beach. Much of its shoreline remains public beach park. O`ahu boasts more miles of swimming beaches than any other island, and its surfing beaches on the North Shore are unmatched anywhere.

Measuring 44 by 25 miles in a sort of squashed parallelogram, O`ahu rests on the overlapping slopes of two extinct volcanoes. Their heavily eroded remains extend as parallel mountain ranges running northwest to southeast. Urban Honolulu spreads along the southern shore, walled in by the Ko`olau Mountains, the younger and larger volcanic range.

Downtown Honolulu

The heart of historic Honolulu resides in its downtown area by the harbor. Downtown divides naturally into three sections, reflecting distinct stages in its development. The business district remains at the center, flanked by the enclaves of government and Chinatown. The

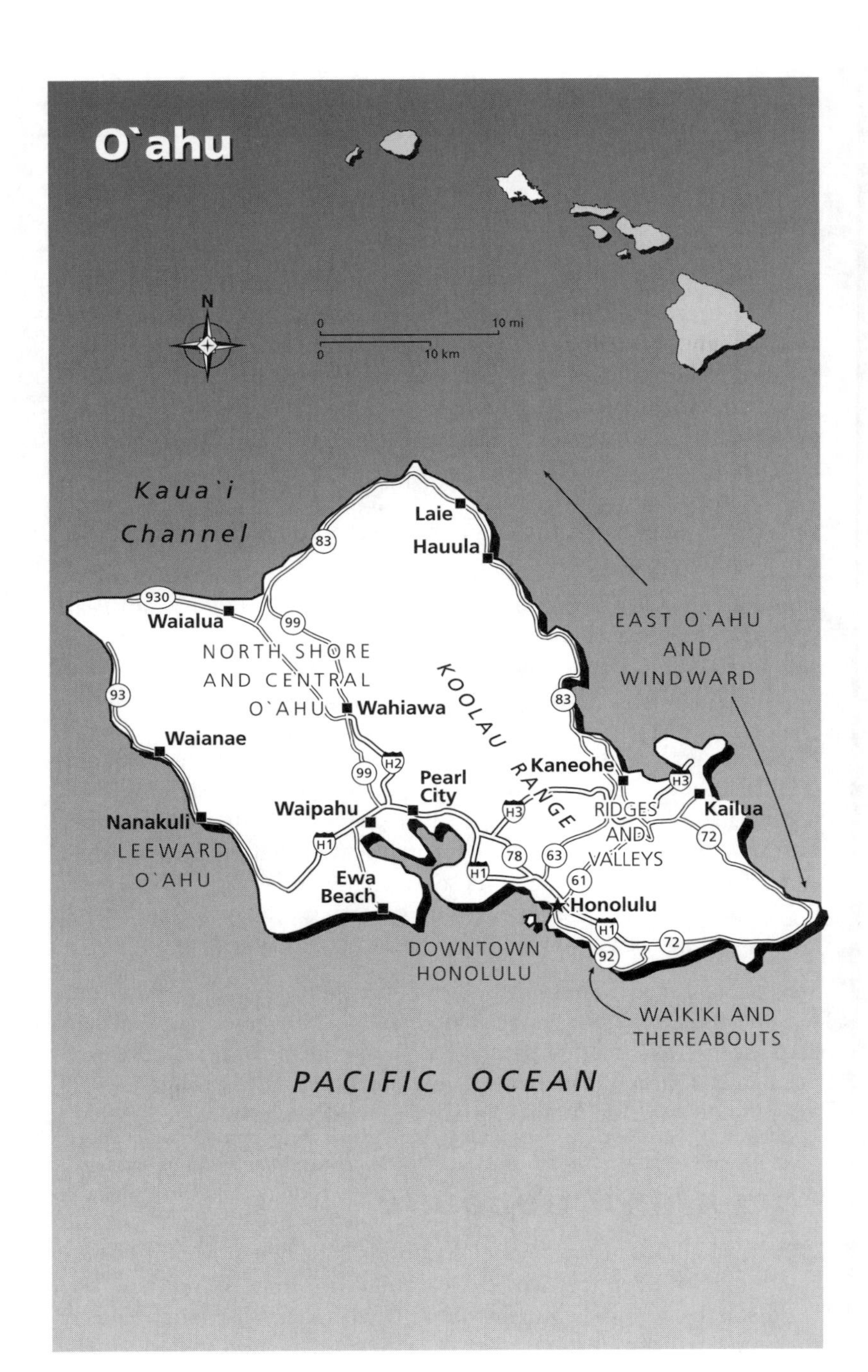
O`ahu
N
0
10 mi
0
10 km
Kaua`i
Channel
Laie
Hauula
83
930
Waialua
99
NORTH SHORE
AND CENTRAL
O`AHU
Wahiawa
KOOLAU RANGE
EAST O`AHU
AND
WINDWARD
93
83
Waianae
H2
99
Kaneohe
H3
Pearl
City
Waipahu
H3
RIDGES
AND
VALLEYS
Kailua
Nanakuli
LEEWARD
O`AHU
H1
Ewa
Beach
78
63
72
H1
61
Honolulu
H1
72
92
DOWNTOWN
HONOLULU
WAIKIKI AND
THEREABOUTS
PACIFIC OCEAN

scarcity of parking makes driving a burden, however. Consider taking TheBus (848–5555; or 296–1818, ext. 8287 for recorded route information). A more expensive option is the ***Waikiki Trolley*** (593–2822), which operates narrated tourist circuits using old-style streetcars.

Begin your tour where the town itself began—at the harbor waterfront. In 1792 William Brown, a British merchant captain, discovered this large protected harbor on O`ahu's southern coast, which he named Fair Haven. Other merchants followed, first China clippers, then whalers. Local inhabitants gathered to barter provisions and sandalwood, and Westerners began to settle as well. A new village arose on the hot, dusty plains inland of the harbor, taking for its name the Hawaiian translation of Fair Haven—Honolulu.

The growing community of *haoles* (foreigners) included all kinds of miscreants who jumped ship and caused trouble. Other menaces came from outside. French warships shelled Honolulu more than once, demanding tolerance of Catholics and lower tariffs on French champagne. A hotheaded British captain briefly took over the entire kingdom in 1843. Still, the harbor commerce brought great wealth to the island kingdom and made for a colorful chapter in Hawaii's maritime history.

The ***Hawaii Maritime Center*** (523–6151) at Honolulu Harbor's Pier 7 explores this ocean heritage, beginning with the ancient Polynesian

Brief History of O`ahu

In 1795 O`ahu bore witness to Kamehameha's final victory, a brutal conquest that made him supreme in the islands. A century later O`ahu also witnessed the overthrow of the monarchy that Kamehameha had established. But of all the landmark events of Hawaiian history, the Japanese attack on O`ahu's Pearl Harbor stands out. December 7, 1941, "the day that shall live in infamy," changed the course of World War II and the postwar order that followed.

In other respects, too, O`ahu occupies center stage in Hawaii. For years the islands remained synonymous with Waikiki in the eyes of the world, and even today Waikiki receives the lion's share of visitors. The military presence at Pearl Harbor and other bases around O`ahu continue to provide an important source of revenue to the state's economy. Likewise, as the state capital and the only major urban population center, Honolulu dominates educational, cultural, and professional life in Hawaii. As the Pacific Rim continues to gain in economic and geopolitical significance, policy makers hope to capitalize on Honolulu's strategic mid-Pacific location.

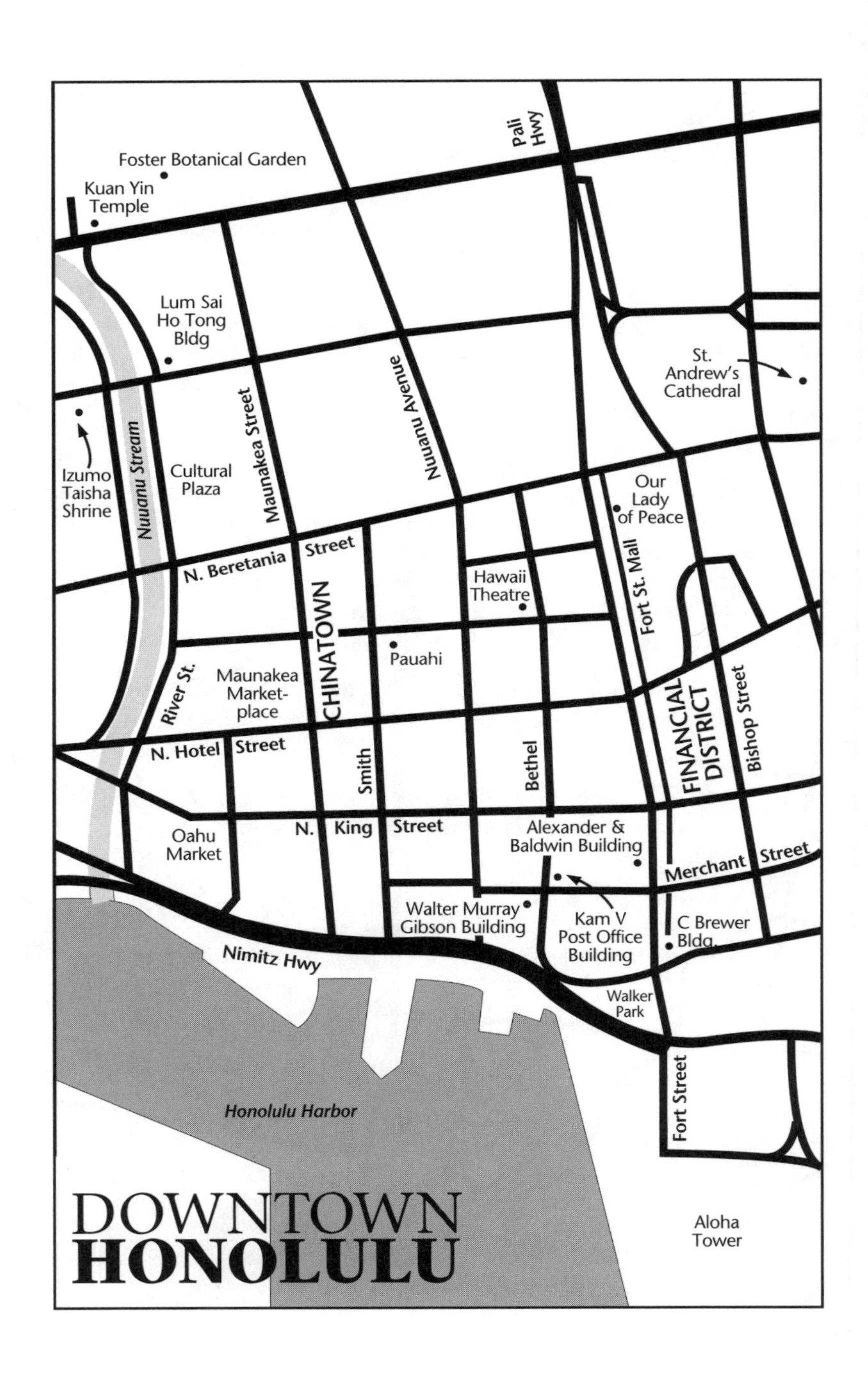
Foster Botanical Garden
Kuan Yin Temple
Pali Hwy
Lum Sai Ho Tong Bldg
St. Andrew's Cathedral
Izumo Taisha Shrine
Nuuanu Stream
Cultural Plaza
Maunakea Street
Nuuanu Avenue
Our Lady of Peace
N. Beretania Street
CHINATOWN
Hawaii Theatre
Fort St. Mall
Pauahi
River St.
Maunakea Market-place
FINANCIAL DISTRICT
Bishop Street
N. Hotel Street
Smith
Bethel
Oahu Market
N. King Street
Alexander & Baldwin Building
Merchant Street
Walter Murray Gibson Building
Kam V Post Office Building
C Brewer Bldg.
Nimitz Hwy
Walker Park
Fort Street
Honolulu Harbor
DOWNTOWN
HONOLULU
Aloha Tower

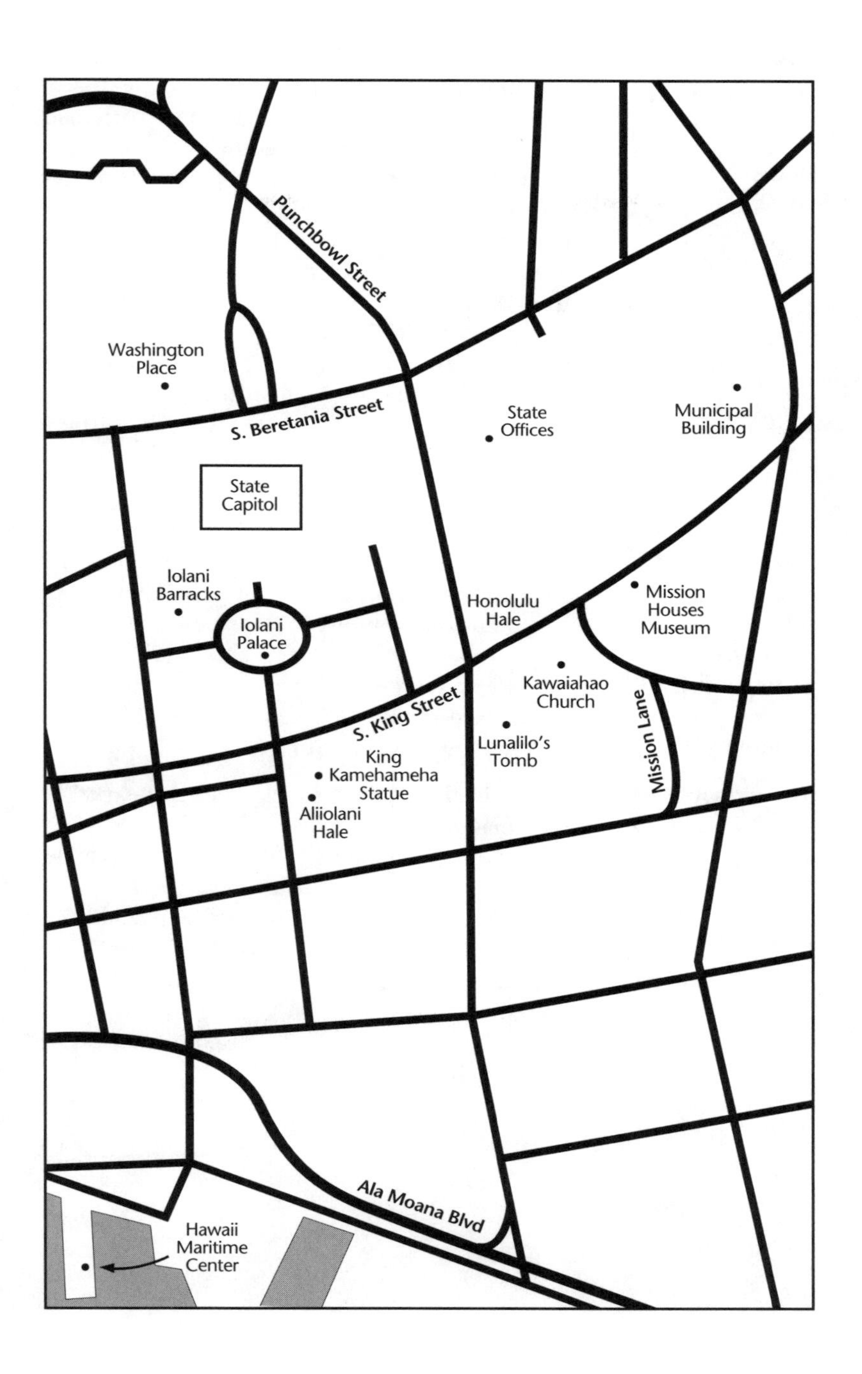
Punchbowl Street
Washington Place
S. Beretania Street
State Offices
Municipal Building
State Capitol
Iolani Barracks
Iolani Palace
Honolulu Hale
Mission Houses Museum
Kawaiahao Church
S. King Street
Mission Lane
Lunalilo's Tomb
King Kamehameha Statue
Aliiolani Hale
Ala Moana Blvd
Hawaii Maritime Center

O`ahu Facts

Nickname: *"The Gathering Place"*

Dimensions: *44 x 25 miles*

Highest elevation: *Mt. Ka`ala (4,020 feet)*

Population: *870,761 (1995)*

Principal City and State Capital: *Honolulu*

Flower: *`Ilima*

Color: *Yellow*

mariners who settled these distant islands and continuing through to the jet age that made tourism king. The center's Kalakaua Boathouse is designed to change the minds of those who think that museum is a four-letter word spelled b-o-r-e. Multimedia exhibits and snazzy decor help bring the subject matter to life. Life-size dioramas of Hawaii's maritime past take you from the cabins of luxury liners to the waterfront tattoo parlors of World War II. Videos of top-rated surfers and sailboarders strutting their stuff accompany displays on these sports. You can also learn how sharks played an important role in Hawaiian culture and admire a 46-foot skeleton of a female humpback whale. Audiocassette tours are offered for a small fee.

Docked outside the boathouse are two important vessels in Hawaiian history. Built in Glasgow in 1878, the *Falls of Clyde* is reputedly the last four-masted sailing clipper afloat. Its worldwide travels included cargo duties in the Hawaiian islands, but it ended up being used as a floating oil depot in Alaska and was slated for grounding in Vancouver, B.C., as a breakwater. Local citizens raised money to save it, and the *Falls* was restored and returned to Honolulu as a museum ship.

The nearby *Hokulea* ("star of gladness") has an even more remarkable story. This replica of the ancient double-hulled Polynesian voyaging canoes was the first to grace Hawaiian waters in more than 700 years. When Western sailors began to arrive in the Pacific, the secrets of ocean seafaring had largely been forgotten in the widely scattered islands of the "Polynesian Triangle." Western egos refused to accept that the Polynesians could have carried out such long-distance exploration centuries

O`ahu Trivia

- *O`ahu is home to world-famous surfing beaches, the state capitol, and a historic naval base.*
- *`Iolani Palace, located in downtown Honolulu is the only royal palace in the United States.*
- *More than 14,000 coral blocks were taken from offshore reefs to build Kawaiaha`o Church in 1836.*
- *Jurisdictionally speaking, Honolulu is the largest "city" in the world.*

before the Vikings. In 1976, the *Hokulea* silenced skeptics by retracing the ancient sea route from Hawaii to Tahiti relying solely on traditional methods of navigation. The Maritime Center is open daily from 8:30 A.M. to 8:00 P.M. The ***Hokulea*** and the ***Falls of Clyde*** close at 5:00 P.M.; $7.50 admission.

To see some maritime history in the making, have a look at Pier 6, adjacent to the center, to see if the *Navatek I* (973–1311) is in port. This 140-foot catamaran uses advanced SWATH technology based on a second sunken hull plus computer-controlled ballast to dramatically improve its stability and reduce the risk of seasickness on the commercial cruise runs it makes. Two-hour cruises cost $45–$120. On the other side of the Maritime Center stands ***Aloha Tower*** (528–5700), built in 1926 as Honolulu's tallest building and recently remodeled as part of a harborfront marketplace. The observation deck is open daily from 9:00 A.M. to 7:30 P.M., and free historic tours of the tower and waterfront are offered at 11:00 A.M. and 1:00 P.M. In former times the tower's four-sided clock face and single-word message greeted passengers arriving on Matson's weekly steamships from the mainland, Hawaii's only link to the outside world before the jet age.

Geography of O`ahu

The third largest island, O`ahu's 112-mile coastline boasts the most swimming beaches of any Hawaiian island, as well as some of the world's most famous surfing breaks. Formed from two overlapping volcanoes, the island's population center, Honolulu, hugs the southern shore. The peaks of the younger and larger Ko`olau range rise over 3,000 feet with nearly vertical cliffs along their windward edges. The older Waianae Mountains harbor the island's summit, Mount Ka`ala, at 4,020 feet.

A mural in the arrival hall recalls the pageantry of "boat day." As island residents gathered, leis in hand, a flotilla of local craft would escort the steamer into dock while the Royal Hawaiian Band played, hula dancers swayed, and boys dived for tossed coins. Olympic gold medalist Duke Kahanamoku set his first swimming record in the water off Pier 8. A century earlier, Honolulu Fort occupied this spot, the focus of several tumultuous events. Today, the only reminder is a solitary cannon on Fort Street. Cross Ala Moana Boulevard to reach ***Walker Park,*** where the cannon mingles with other historical relics from the area's past. Continue across Queen Street to the ***C. Brewer Building.*** Now home to the University of Phoenix, this 1930 beauty huddles at the foot of Fort Street Mall, enclosing its charms in a walled garden. Note the sugarcane motif in the lobby grillwork, recalling the agricultural heritage of C. Brewer, which remains the oldest American company west of the Rockies.

Continue to the end of the block and turn right on Merchant Street, where most of Honolulu's early trading houses set up shop. Just around the corner, look for the ornate facing of the 1905 ***Stangenwald Building,*** Honolulu's first skyscraper. This New York–style brownstone edifice housed a notorious furniture store whose owner had connections with city hall. Word seeped out that madams in the area had to buy their brothel beds here to stay open.

At the next corner, stop to take in the architectural splendor of the ***Alexander & Baldwin Building.*** Originally based on Maui, A&B hired two of Honolulu's leading architects to build this lavish 1929 headquarters as a memorial to its founders. The tile work of the Bishop Street portico depicts Hawaiian fish in a Chinese motif. These and other historic buildings blend seamlessly among the many mirrored glass high-rises nearby. Thanks to downtown's strict zoning laws regulating urban density and greenery, these modern office blocks retain a tropical charm with miniparks, sculpture gardens, and artificial waterfalls. One such park at the corner of King Street and Fort has a noteworthy statue of Robert Wilcox, Hawaii's first congressional delegate. You might also check out Deborah Butterfield's wooden horses on Bishop Street outside the Contemporary Museum gallery in the First Hawaiian building on Bishop Street (the tall one that looks like a giant playing deck with a tilted middle card). Notice that many men working downtown wear reverse-print aloha shirts instead of suits, especially on "Aloha Friday." Welcome to Wall Street in paradise.

Once *haole* business became entrenched in Honolulu, Hawaiian government had to follow, if only to keep an eye on foreign troublemakers. The early Hawaiian monarchs resented the time they were obliged to spend here, preferring the old capitals of Lahaina (Maui) and Kailua (Kona) or even the beach at Waikiki; but finally, by 1850, Kamehameha III yielded to the inevitable and made Honolulu the capital. Government took up its positions to the east of business. Merchant Street appropriately slants into King Street, where most of the historic government buildings cluster. On the way, you may wish to stop at ***Native Books and Beautiful Things*** (599–5511), at 222 Merchant Street, a crafts gallery owned by a consortium of local artisans, working in media from woodcarving to Hawaiian quilts. Open Monday–Friday 8:00 A.M. to 5:00 P.M..

Continue on to King Street, where ***King Kamehameha*** presides in statue form. The heroic image of the king poses with outstretched arm, clad in the traditional yellow feather cloak and helmet of the Hawaiian chieftain. The money for the statue was originally appropriated to commemorate the 100th anniversary of Captain Cook's landing, but most Hawaiians found little to celebrate in that milestone. The committee in charge deemed Kamehameha a better choice to rekindle the people's pride in their own history, leaving Cook's discovery of the islands relegated to a plaque on the pedestal. The statue here is actually a duplicate. The first casting made in Italy was lost at sea, and this one was paid for with the insurance money. (The original was later recovered and is currently displayed on the Big Island, Kamehameha's birthplace.) During Aloha Week and Kamehameha Day, the statue is draped with 18-foot-long leis.

Behind the statue stands ***Aliiolani Hale*** ("house of heavenly kings"). Commissioned in 1869 as a palace for Kamehameha V, the designs were modified for government use. Its attractive Renaissance Revival chambers housed the cabinet and legislature under Kalakaua. Unfortunately, around this time, relations between business interests and the government began to sour, culminating in the 1893 overthrow of the monarchy. Some argue that the paramount interest of sugar plantation owners in protecting their access to U.S. markets made the revolution and subsequent annexation to the union inevitable. (In 1993, President Clinton issued a formal apology for the United States' role in the coup.) Aliiolani is where the fateful events began. *Haole* businessmen occupied the building as the opening move in their bloodless takeover. Once in power, they shifted the executive and legislative organs of government across the street to Iolani Palace and renamed Aliiolani the Judiciary Building. It remains home today to the Hawaii Supreme Court. Step inside to admire the skylit octagonal rotunda. If you arrive Monday through Friday between 9:00 A.M. and 4:00 P.M., you can visit the ***Judiciary History Center*** (539–4999) here. Displays trace the evolution of Hawaiian justice from the days of the *kahuna* (priests) and *kapu* (taboos) through the bumpy transition to Western law under the monarchy.

Facing Aliiolani Hale across the street stands ***Iolani Palace*** (538–1471), the only seat of royalty in America. A palace has stood here ever since Kamehameha III moved his court to Honolulu. Built in so-called American Florentine style, the present two-story palace was occupied by only two monarchs, King Kalakaua and his sister, Queen Liliuokalani, before the 1893 revolution. Then Iolani served as the "Executive Building" under the republican, territorial, and state governments that followed, not to mention its stint as the nerve center for television's *Hawaii Five-0*. With the completion of the new state capitol building next door in 1968, the Friends of Iolani Palace began a $7-million restoration of the palace. They now conduct 45-minute guided tours Tuesday–Saturday 9:00 A.M. to 2:15 P.M., for $15. Book at least a half-hour in advance at the Royal Barracks office (522–0832).

Trivia

Electric lights illuminated Iolani Palace four years before the White House wired up.

Aliiolani Hale

The admission ticket is made up as an invitation to King Kalakaua's ball. You make the magical leap in time after donning protective shoe covers. A guide welcomes you in the name of His Majesty and ushers you through the state rooms of the palace, chatting about royal banquets and distinguished visitors—all in the present tense. Much of the palace's original contents "wandered" during the coup. The kingdom's crown jewels were literally gambled away by a looter ignorant of their true value. The Friends are gradually recovering the original furnishings or commissioning exact replicas. One piece was even found in a local thrift shop! A regal staircase handcrafted entirely from koa wood leads upstairs to the living quarters. The indulgent guides reserve a single original pillar for visitors to stroke. Upstairs, you visit his-and-hers bedrooms in opposite corners of the palace. Kalakaua grew to resent the separate rooms and moved to a private bungalow outside the palace where he could sleep with his queen.

The king's office is dominated by a huge desk cluttered with papers of state written in Hawaiian. Kalakaua was quite the renaissance man: He became the first monarch to sail around the world; he teamed up with bandmaster Henry Berger to compose the islands' anthem, "Hawaii Ponoi"; he mounted a campaign to revive the hula and other aspects of the old culture that the missionaries had suppressed; and he personally recorded many of the legends of his people. The king also took an active interest in the progress of science, and he corresponded with Thomas Edison regularly.

Iolani Palace was one of the most technologically advanced buildings of its age. All the bathrooms had flush toilets. A dumbwaiter outside the dining room connected to the basement kitchen. Electric lights illuminated Iolani four years before the White House wired up. Kalakaua even installed Honolulu's first telephone so that he could call to the royal boathouse. The "Merrie Monarch" had his vices, however, and spending money was one of them. His profligacy helped provoke the overthrow of the monarchy.

The tour culminates in the grand throne room, which spreads across half the ground floor. Decorated in crimson and gold, it has crystal chandeliers hanging from the ceiling and a floral carpet print designed by Kalakaua himself. Bishop Museum has recently returned the original thrones and crowns, which are displayed within, along with a royal *kapu* stick crafted from the tusk of a narwhal. At night, an entire wall of French windows opened onto the garden, admitting perfumed breezes to festive balls that ran into the wee hours of the morning. In less happy times, the wall portraits of past monarchs in this room looked on as

Queen Liliuokalani stood trial for treason after an attempt by her supporters failed to win back her throne. The deposed queen spent nine months confined to the guest room upstairs.

While waiting for your tour to begin, explore the grounds outside. You'll find many exotic trees, such as the banyan "forest" that grew out of two trees planted by Queen Kapiolani. Moving counterclockwise, the next building is the Royal Barracks, a medieval-looking bastion that was moved brick by brick to make way for the new state capitol building. Nearby stands the Royal Bandstand, site of King Kalakaua's coronation, staged nine years into his rule. (His original investiture had been unchivalrously rushed due to rioting by the losing side in the election.) Hawaii's governors today conduct their own inaugural rites at this same pavilion. The Royal Hawaiian Band gives free concerts here every Friday at noon. Farther around the palace is the former Royal Crypt, where Gerrit Judd carried on a literal "underground government" at night during the British occupation of Honolulu.

From the crypt, you will see a small rock platform in the far corner of the palace grounds. This *ahu,* or offering stand, was built from stones hand-carried from each Hawaiian island in 1993 during ceremonies marking the centennial of the overthrow of the Hawaiian monarchy. The structure remains a focus for activists demonstrating for a return of sovereignty to the Hawaiian people. Continuing your circle from the crypt, find your way to the plaque on an upright boulder commemorating Captain Cook. Lying horizontally beneath the monument, an unlabeled stone slab has a far more interesting history. King Kalakaua brought this stone, a *kapu* barrier from the fifteenth-century temple of Liloa on the Big Island, to remind his subjects of the legend of Umi. Born an illegitimate son of the High Chief Liloa, Umi was raised as a commoner. To claim his patrimony, he boldly stepped over this stone to reach a father he had never met. As an illegitimate child, Umi could have been killed instantly for violating the *kapu* of royalty if Liloa had chosen not to acknowledge him. Instead, Umi lived and went on to unify the Big Island.

Turning from the secular to the religious, walk east down King Street from Aliiolani Hale to ***Kawaiahao Church,*** known as Hawaii's Westminister Abbey. Until Iolani Palace, this was Honolulu's largest building. Hiram Bingham, the leader of the early missionaries, drew the plans from memories of his native New England. Almost 14,000 half-ton coral blocks were cut from underwater reefs to build it. Trees from northern O`ahu were floated to Kaneohe and carried over the mountains. Bingham did not remain to witness the church's dedication in 1842; his wife's ill health forced a return to Massachusetts.

From the very beginning, Kawaiahao became an institution of the Hawaiian monarchy. The church provided the setting for royal marriages, funerals, successions, and other courtly ceremonies. Feather *kahilis* (flags) above the velvet pews at the rear of the church signify royal affiliation. Portraits of the entire royal family adorn the walls, with plaques commemorating various historical events. The public is welcome to attend Sunday services, conducted in Hawaiian and English, beginning at 10:30 A.M.

Signposts designate other interesting features around the churchyard. The Gothic-looking crypt near the church entrance figures in a real-life Hawaiian "ghost" story. Its occupant, King Lunalilo, Hawaii's first elected monarch, had died within a year in office. Instead of burial in the Royal Mausoleum, the king's final wish was to be "entombed among my people" in Kawaiahao Cemetery. His successor, King Kalakaua, had lost to Lunalilo in the original election and remained bitter. He refused to order a royal salute from the Punchbowl cannons, saying that if Lunalilo wanted to be buried with the people, he could be buried like a commoner. Instead, eyewitness accounts of the ceremony reported that just as the body was being interred, exactly twenty-one bursts of thunder sounded a supernatural salute to the fallen king.

Surrounded by a wrought-iron fence, the smaller cemetery behind the church belongs to the ***Mission Houses Museum*** (531–0481) across the road. The names on the tombstones reflect the almost incestuous interbreeding between descendants of the various mission companies. Cross Mission Lane to visit the museum's restored mission buildings and learn about the missionaries' lifestyles.

Trivia

Built in 1843, Our Lady of Peace in Honolulu is the oldest Catholic cathedral in the United States.

The first missionaries arrived here in 1820, establishing their headquarters on the outskirts of Honolulu before dispersing to mission stations throughout the islands. In 1821 precut lumber arrived from Boston to erect the Frame House, the oldest Western structure surviving in Hawaii. As many as four mission families lived in this house at one time. Cramped bedrooms with trundle beds reflect the lack of space.

The deep cellar caused suspicion among Hawaiians when it was dug. They thought the missionaries might be hiding weapons. The cellar now houses a diorama of 1820 Honolulu. Note that the ocean came within 300 feet of the Mission Homes before landfills pushed back the shoreline. In 1831 Levi Chamberlain, the mission's secular agent, built a larger building from coral blocks and scrap lumber. Most of the space was taken up by stockpiled supplies waiting to be transferred to the seventeen other mission stations around the islands.

In these crowded conditions, babies were born and Hawaiian orphans taken in. The women were kept busy running the home, teaching school in the parlor, sewing dresses to clothe the congregation, and cooking for the endless succession of Hawaiian visitors that had to be entertained. They had to learn how to prepare native foods in a tropical climate without refrigeration, cooking mostly in a large wall oven. Murky water from the local wells had to be drip-strained through a porous coral stone. Through all of this, Hawaiians crowded at the windows, fascinated by the chance to watch Western women at work. (In Old Hawaii the men did the cooking.)

Meanwhile, the missionary men busied themselves translating the Bible into Hawaiian, writing sermons, and conducting church business. The printing house next door churned out some 30 million pages of Hawaiian-language Bibles and other educational materials by hand. The pages were hung like laundry to dry and then bound with poi. In 1853 almost 75 percent of the Hawaiian population was literate, an achievement exceeded at that time only by New England and Scotland—this from a people who didn't even have a written alphabet half a century earlier.

Heading to Market

For a taste of local color and the chance to pick up some unique souvenirs, visit the Aloha Flea Market (486–1529). Known locally as the "swap meet," the event is held each Wednesday, Saturday, and Sunday in the parking lot of the Aloha Stadium, close to Pearl Harbor. Admission is less than a dollar, and the place is packed with booths selling everything from garage-sale items to exotic foods to custom-designed clothing. You never know when you may stumble upon that rare antique sewing machine, or Japanese glass fishing float lamp that you've always yearned for (even if you didn't know it until now). Or buy some homemade fish jerky to munch on the plane ride back. There are also a variety of food booths where you can sample different island ethnic specialties. The market runs 6:00 A.M. to 3:00 P.M. Come early to catch the best finds and beat the heat.

Another popular market with visitors is the People's Open Market, a farmers' market held Monday through Saturday at different sites rotating around the island. You can talk story with local farmers as you meet the faces behind Hawaii's burgeoning "diversified agriculture" sector and sample exotic fruits and produce. Call 527–5167 for recorded information giving market times and locations.

The missionaries became victims of their own success when in 1863 their governing body in New England withdrew its support, forcing the mission families to seek employment to feed their families. Many left Hawaii, some to continue mission work in the South Pacific. Those who stayed founded the commercial dynasties that came to rule the islands.

The Mission Houses offers guided tours Tuesday–Saturday 9:00 A.M. to 4:00 P.M. for $10.00. All tours are led by docents in period costume. Docents also give walking tours of historic downtown on Thursday at 9:45 A.M. for an additional fee. Reservations are necessary. In addition, the Mission Houses hold monthly classes on crafts such as Hawaiian quilting or *kapa*-making. Call 531–0481 for the schedule. Although separate from the museum, the old mission schoolhouse can be seen nearby on Mission Lane. ***Likeke Hale,*** Hawaii's only surviving adobe building, now serves as a day-care center.

Hovering just outside the downtown area are some other attractions worth mentioning. Two long blocks farther down King Street, the wooded park of ***Thomas Square*** commemorates Admiral Thomas's restoration of Hawaiian sovereignty after British Captain Paulet seized power in 1843. Across Beretania ("Britain") Street on the inland side of the park, the ***Honolulu Academy of Arts*** (532–8701) occupies a rambling Mediterranean villa donated by its founder, Mrs. Charles M. Cooke, in 1927. The thirty galleries surround six garden courts and include a creditable collection of works of European Masters. But the real draw is the academy's top-notch collection of Oriental art, from samurai armor to *T'ang* horses. Guided tours are offered once a day. Academy volunteers serve lunch Tuesday through Saturday from 11:30 A.M. to 2:00 P.M. in the ***Garden Cafe*** for a moderate price. The academy is open Tuesday–Saturday 10:00 A.M. to 4:30 P.M. and Sunday 1:00–5:00 P.M. Admission charge.

On the other side of King Street stands the concert hall of the Blaisdell Center and, farther down to the left, the grand entrance of McKinley High School. Note the Oriental architecture of the ***First Chinese Christian Church*** across the street and the ***Makiki Christian Church*** around the corner, on Pensacola Avenue. The latter has five stories of dreamlike pagoda roofs modeled on Tamon Castle, the first Christian church in Japan.

To stick to a walkable tour, return to Kawaiahao Church and cross King Street to ***Honolulu Hale,*** a.k.a. city hall. Its Spanish Mission architecture became a signature of C. W. Dickey's much-copied Hawaiian Mediterranean style. Take a stroll through the lofty central atrium that often houses art displays. For functional city bureaucracy, such as county camping permits (523–4525), head a block farther to 650 King

Street, the Municipal Building. Or look in the phone book for the nearest satellite city hall. Except for Kualoa, O`ahu county campgrounds carry a security risk. For state camping permits (587–0300), go inland to 1151 Punchbowl Street at the corner of Beretania Street.

Also inland up Punchbowl, the ***State Capitol Building*** stands behind its predecessor, Iolani Palace. The capitol's innovative design draws on elements symbolic of Hawaii: Its two legislative chambers taper vertically like the volcanoes on which the islands rest; its pillars represent palm trees; and the reflecting pools surrounding the capitol symbolize the ocean. You can pick up a brochure covering the capitol district from the governor's office on the fifth floor. Be sure to peek into the legislative chambers. The house has warm earth tones and a chandelier called Sun. The senate has blue shades of sky and sea and a chandelier called Moon. Both chambers feature enormous hanging tapestries by Ruthadell Anderson. Other artwork on the grounds includes *Aquarius,* a mosaic by Tadashi Sato; a statue of Queen Liliuokalani, invariably clutching a fresh flower; and a controversial statue of Father Damien by Marisol Escobar. Damien was a Catholic priest who contracted leprosy while ministering to victims of the disease on the island of Moloka`i. Escobar portrays Damien as a frail old man, deformed but radiating inner peace.

Across Beretania Street, next to the war memorial, stands ***Washington Place,*** the governor's home. John Dominis died at sea soon after building this home for his family. The building's name arose when his widow rented rooms to the United States commissioner. Her son inherited the house and lived there with his wife, Lydia Kapaakea, until she ascended to the throne as Queen Liliuokalani. Later the deposed and widowed queen moved back across the street from Iolani Palace and lived here until she died in 1917. Hawaii's "White House" then became the property of the state.

Walk next door from Washington Place to Episcopalian ***St. Andrew's Cathedral,*** founded by Kamehameha IV and Queen Emma, both ardent Anglophiles. Continue along Beretania to reach the last of Honolulu's Big Three churches. Completed in 1843, ***Our Lady of Peace*** is the oldest Catholic cathedral in the United States. It doesn't look like much from the outside, but the interior has beautiful gilded ceiling panels, statuary, and stained glass. Our Lady stands in front of the top end of Fort Street Mall; ethnic eateries of all stripes line this pedestrian arcade and surrounding alleyways along Bishop Street. Try ***Ba-Le*** (521–4117) for Eurasian sandwiches or green papaya salad;

the name of this Vietnamese chain means Paris. For more substantial Italian fare, follow the downtown lunch crowd to ***Cafe VIII 1/2*** (524–4064) at 1067 Alakeo Street. Open Monday–Friday 11:30 A.M. to 2:00 P.M.

One block past Fort Street you'll find Bethel Street, home to two historic theater venues. The ***Hawaii Theatre*** (528–5535), on the corner of Pauahi, has been renovated to its original 1922 splendor, lavish with murals and gilding. Ask about the "Hawaiian Friday Night" concert series. Tours are offered at 11:00 A.M. on Tuesday for $5.00. Farther down, on the corner of Merchant Street, the ***Kumu Kahua Theatre*** (536–4441) performs in more modest digs in the old Kamehameha V Post Office Building. The theater is known for staging contemporary works dealing with local, Hawaiian themes. While here, take a peek inside the ***Walter Murray Gibson Building*** diagonally opposite. One of the most colorful personalities in Hawaiian history, Gibson came to the islands as a Mormon pioneer on Lana`i. Excommunicated, he entered politics as a Hawaiian populist, rising to power as Kalakaua's "minister for everything" before losing out to the opposing missionary–sugar-growers' faction. This building is the only reminder of his brief, but dazzling, career. Its patterned tile interior looks more like a hotel lobby than the former police station it was.

Moving from the dramatic to the visual arts, the next two streets harbor the galleries of a pair of noteworthy Honolulu artists. ***Pegge Hopper*** (524–1160) has made a name for herself with stylized paintings of giant lounging Polynesian women. Her gallery is located at 1164 Nuuanu Avenue. Open Tuesday–Friday 11:00 A.M. to 3:00 P.M. On the way there, you might stop in at ***Lai Fong*** (537–3497), at 1118 Nuuanu. It's a kind of Chinese department store full of imported fabrics, chinese antiques, and crafts. Lai Fong came to Hawaii as a picture bride and got her start as a seamstress. You can still order tailor-made clothing here.

One block farther, ***Ramsay Gallery*** (537–2787), at 1128 Smith Street, bears another locally prominent name. Ramsay's originals are no longer for sale here, although an extensive collection awaits viewing in the upstairs "museum." It makes something of a statement for historic preservation to realize that many of the subjects of her drawings no longer exist. The rest of the gallery features rotating exhibits from guest artists. The gallery is housed in the historic 1923 Tan Sing building. Basement space is occupied by Ramsay's dermatologist husband (read bankroll). You might poke your head inside to view the Hawaiiana woodblock prints by Dietrich Varez in the stairwell.

Nuuanu Avenue has its own gustatory options as well. Pop inside ***Krung Thai*** (599–4803) at 1028 Nuuanu and choose from a selection of spicy Thai entrees; then carry your goodies out to the back to dine in the garden court. Open Monday–Friday 10:30 A.M. to 2:30 P.M. ***Nayong Filipino*** (531–1846) cooks up earthy Filipino fare at the corner of Hotel Street. The menu features staples such as pork adobo as well as more adventurous choices such as deep-fried pig's feet. Open Monday–Friday 11:00 A.M. to 6:00 P.M. Both inexpensive.

Further up, ***Indigo*** (521–2900), at 1121 Nuuanu, boasts an intriguing Eurasian menu and decor. Moderate prices. Pegge Hopper paintings inside portray the five Chinese elements. It's even nicer in the garden seating out back. The best bets on the menu are the starters. Open Tuesday–Friday 11:30 A.M. to 2:00 P.M., Tuesday–Saturday 6:00–9:30 P.M.

To see a different kind of artistry, pause to smell the flowers at the lei stands on Beretania Street between Smith and Maunakea Streets. The stringers work right in the store, and the variety of colors and textures is staggering. Some have a strong fragrance such as *pikake* (jasmine). Others, such as woven *haku* lei (worn on the head), retain their beauty after drying. Choose one for yourself to enjoy all day. Prices range from about $3.00 into the hundreds.

By now you've reached the border of Chinatown. This part of downtown was developed later than the other two. Sugar plantations began to import Chinese laborers in 1852, but as soon as their contracts expired, the Chinese fled the fields to open shops and small businesses in town. Chinatown soon became a hotbed of gambling, opium dens, and brothels. The Chinatown underground literally ran underground. As developers remodel the buildings here they keep finding tunnels. Old-timers even whisper of secret trapdoors used to shanghai unwary sailors. A Honolulu detective named Chan Apana prowled this turf. Most people know his fictionalized name, Charlie Chan.

This crowded enclave of wooden shops and homes burned to the ground twice. The second blaze in 1900 started when the Board of Health torched homes contaminated with the bubonic plague and the fire spread. The Chinese suspected a *haole* conspiracy to drive them out. During World War II the rebuilt district became a G.I. vice center. Chinatown today thrives as a magnet for immigrants from the entire Orient. Its mysteries unfold like layers of a fortune cookie.

The Chinese Chamber of Commerce (533–3181) and Hawaii Heritage Center (521–2749) each offer weekly walking tours of Chinatown on

Tuesday and Friday morning, respectively. But it can be just as much fun to poke around on your own.

Walk down Maunakea to the corner of Hotel Street. This is the center of Chinatown, where the lion dancers prance during the Chinese New Year. Hotel Street is also Honolulu's principal red-light strip, flush with peep shows and porn shops on adjacent blocks. With its ornate pagoda roof, ***Wo Fat,*** Hawaii's oldest Chinese restaurant, keeps a benevolent watch over the comings and goings at the corner from its second-story perch. Still more eating possibilities lurk within the multiethnic food court of ***Maunakea Marketplace*** on the opposite corner. A statue of Confucius presides over the courtyard. Farther up Maunakea Street on the corner of Pauahi, ***A Little Bit of Saigon*** (528–3663) serves decent Vietnamese cuisine. Roll your own spring rolls with moistened rice paper. The same family runs the equally popular ***Duc's Bistro*** (531–6325), an elegant French-Vietnamese restaurant a few doors down. ***Won Kee*** (524–6877) and ***Legend*** (532–1868), seafood restaurants in the Chinatown Cultural Plaza each have their following. For the best dim sum in Chinatown, hit ***Mei Sum*** (531–3268), at 65 North Pauahi Street (at the corner of Smith) to devour these Hong Kong–style delicacies by the cartload.

A potpourri of vintage Chinatown shops line the rest of Maunakea Street. The buildings here mostly date from the two decades following the 1900 fire. Pretend you're Marco Polo as you peek inside darkened noodle factories amid clouds of flour. Inhale the wafts of incense that escape from hidden shrines. You'll also find acupuncture clinics, martial arts studios, Asian groceries and importers, watch repair shops, and tattoo parlors. Much of the action is out in the streets themselves. People of all ages scurry about on their dubious missions. You'll hear bantering in a dozen Asian dialects.

Stop inside ***Shung Chong Yuein,*** a cheery Chinese bakery at 1027 Maunakea, to munch on almond cookies or *manapua,* a local version of dim sum. Across the street, you can balance your yin and yang with an herbal prescription from ***Fook Sau Tong.*** The rows of shelved jars and wooden drawers bearing mysterious labels in Chinese characters emit intriguing smells.

Lower Maunakea has a string of antiques shops and art galleries. ***Aloha Antique Collectibles*** (536–6187) is a dragon's lair of hoarded treasure, including Niihau shells, samurai swords, Tibetan bronze, vintage aloha shirts, and much more. The trick is to find anything. ***Bushido*** (941–7239), toward Waikiki at 1684 Kaeakava, is less claustrophobic. It specializes in Japanese weaponry.

Continuing your exploring on King Street, heading away from the capitol, you'll pass the open-air ***O`ahu Market,*** where vendors display food products such as pig snouts, quail eggs, and lotus roots. You can sample all sorts of exotic fruits you may not have seen before. Open daily until 2:30 P.M. The last block before Nuuanu Stream has mostly Vietnamese shops and restaurants. If you don't want a full meal, just sit by the window at ***Ha Bien*** (531–1185), at the corner of River Street, and sip a flavorful "mix drink" composed of pomegranate juice, coconut milk, and translucent seaweed.

Farther up River Street, across Beretania, stands a statue of Chinese nationalist leader Sun Yat-sen, who got his education here in Honolulu. The Filipino community has placed a statue of its own hero, Jose Rizal, across the bridge. Listen to the click-clack of mah-jongg played by old men at the pavilion tables.

Inside the cultural center, you can buy Chinese-language magazines, including *Playboy,* from ***Dragongate Bookstore*** (just don't try to claim you bought it for the articles). A smattering of English-language works on Chinese folklore are also on sale. The Asian Mall and upstairs Sun Yat-sen Hall display vintage photos, including some "class portraits" of Sun and his Chinese émigré cohorts plotting their revolution in Honolulu.

The **Lum Sai Ho Tong** has its headquarters at the corner of River and Kukui Streets. The many tongs in Chinatown served as cultural societies for immigrant clans. If the gate to the stairway is unlocked, you can visit the elaborate Taoist shrine on the second floor. Across the river, the ***Izumo Taisha Shrine*** houses the *kami,* Okuninushi-No-Mikoto, a universal god of love and happiness. The shrine property was seized during World War II and only returned by court order in 1962. Shinto services usually are held on the tenth day of each month, and members also visit at significant milestones in their lives, such as reaching the ages of three, five, seven, sixty-one, and eighty-eight.

Continue up River Street across Vineyard Boulevard to visit a temple for yet another Eastern religion, Buddhism. The ***Kuan Yin Temple*** (533–6361) has Western-style walls joined to a traditional Chinese ceramic tile roof. Inside, enormous statues stand behind the altars, the largest of which represents the bodhisattva, Kuan Yin, goddess of mercy. Wei Tor (faith) and Kuan Tai (truth) guard her flanks. You can burn a stick of incense to add to the fumes already present. Some worshipers even burn money. Temple priests and priestesses rattle joss sticks to tell fortunes. Open to visitors daily 8:30 A.M. to 2:00 P.M.

Trivia

Foster Botanical Garden, on O`ahu, was built in 1855 and is Hawaii's oldest garden.

After all this urban exploration, you can seek refuge in the shady confines of nearby ***Foster Botanical Garden*** (522–7065), Hawaii's oldest botanical garden. William Hillebrand, physician to the royal court, started the gardens in 1855 with specimens he gathered during his travels in India. Many of the tallest trees date to these first plantings, such as the massive kapok tree that rises 161 feet high and has a trunk more than 20 feet wide. You may recognize kapok floss, which comes from the tree's seed pods, as the filler in life preservers. Other names you've heard but may never have seen in the wood, including allspice, chocolate, cinnamon, nutmeg, vanilla, and chicle, grow in the economic section—extra points if you recognized the last one as the main ingredient of chewing gum.

The park also has some truly bizarre specimens named for fruit resembling cannonballs, sausages, and "dead rats" (the baobab). Some of the rarest plants, such as a Hawaiian *loulu* palm taken from upper Nuuanu Valley, are believed to be extinct in the wild. The Friends of Honolulu Botanical Garden offer free tours on weekdays at 1:00 P.M. They also organize weekend educational programs in all four of Honolulu's botanical gardens as well as leading hikes islandwide. Call 537–1708 to inquire. Foster Botanical Garden is open daily from 9:00 A.M. to 4:00 P.M. Admission is $5.00.

If you need a waterfall in your garden to meditate properly, little-known ***Liliuokalani Gardens*** lies close at hand. Take Nuuanu Street across the freeway and turn left on School Street. The second right, a small side street, leads to the banks of Nuuanu Stream. Queen Liliuokalani used to picnic here, and so can you. Most of the plants here are native species.

Ridges and Valleys

Above the city, the ridges of the Koolau Mountains reach like fingers toward the sea, with a series of valleys spaced in between. As Honolulu grew, the city pushed inland from the harbor first into Nuuanu ("cool height") Valley. Hawaiians preferred the mild climate and lush beauty, and the many churches and consulates here seem to echo this view today. As you enter the valley, Asian temples predominate along upper Nuuanu Avenue. Most of these also function as cultural centers. Ironically, some of the only civilian casualties of the Pearl Harbor attack happened when a stray artillery shell exploded in one such Japanese-language school.

1. Thomas Square
2. Academy of Arts
3. Foster Botanical Garden
4. Queen Emma's Summer Palace
5. National Memorial Cemetery of the Pacific
6. Hawaii Nature Center
7. Contemporary Museum
8. Puu Ualakaa State Park
9. Lyon Arboretum
10. Waioli Tea Room
11. Manoa Valley Inn
12. Manoa (AYH) Hostel
13. Dae Won Sa Temple
14. Ala Moana Beach Park
15. Royal Hawaiian Hotel
16. Army Museum
17. Sheraton Moana Surfrider
18. Waikiki Aquarium
19. Hale Aloha Hostel
20. Damien Museum
21. Diamond Head lookouts and beach
22. Bailey's Antique & Thrift

See also Downtown Honolulu map detail on pages 54–55

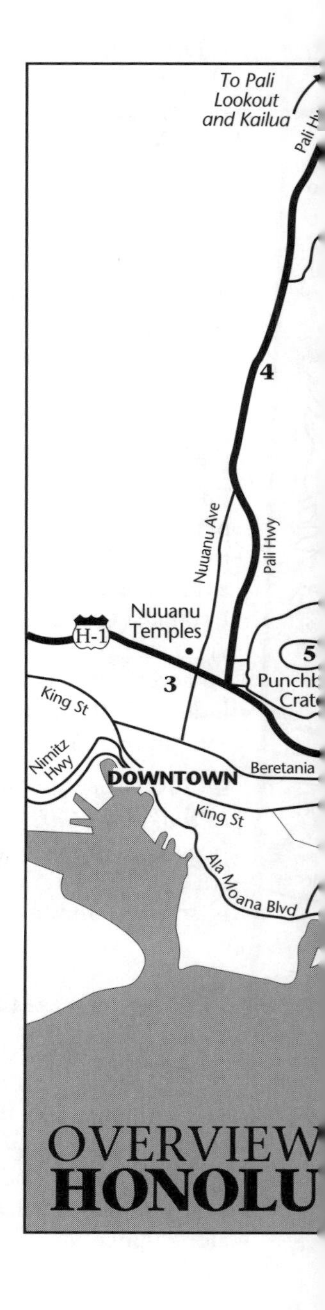

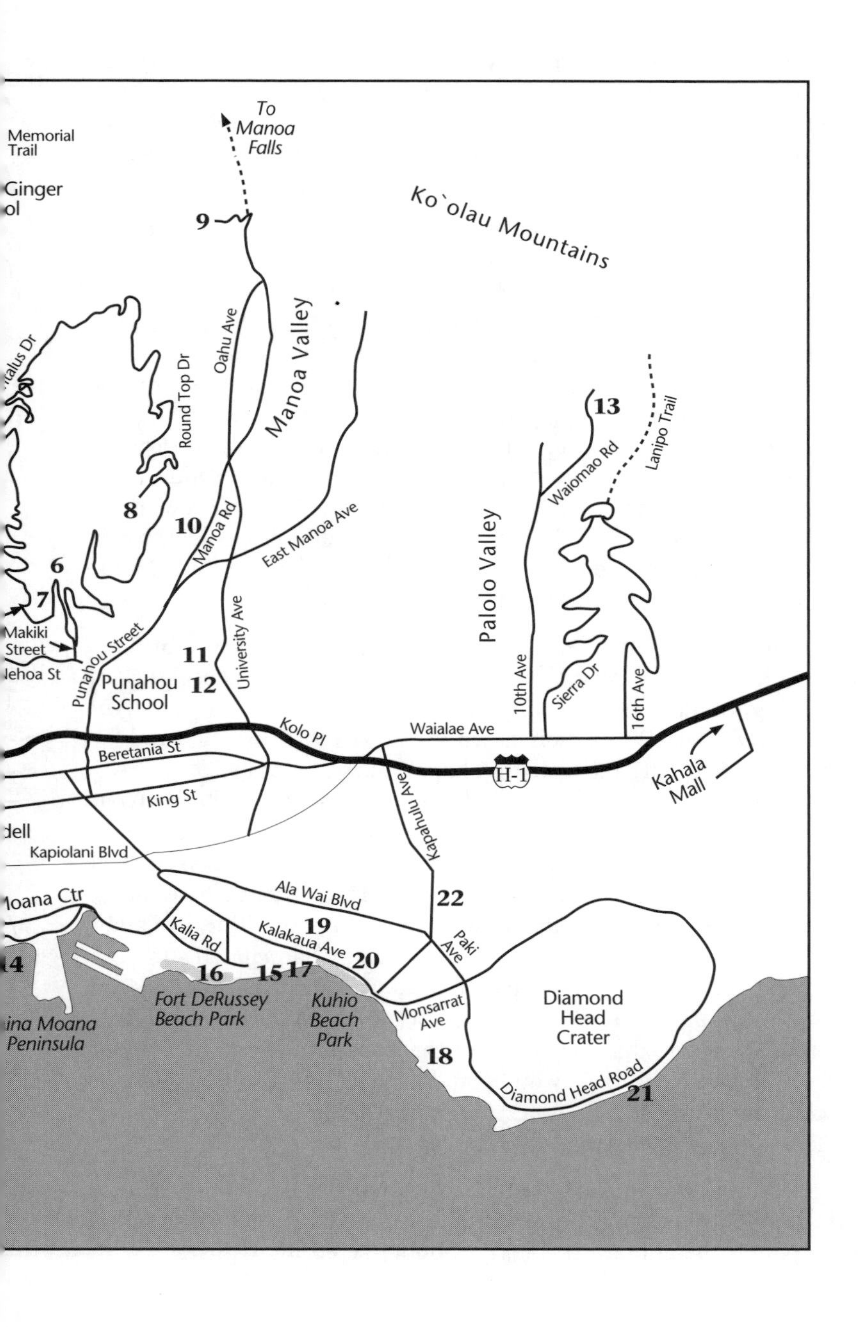

To Manoa Falls
Memorial Trail
Ginger
ol
Ko`olau Mountains
Manoa Valley
Oahu Ave
Round Top Dr
Manoa Rd
East Manoa Ave
University Ave
Palolo Valley
Waiomao Rd
Lanipo Trail
10th Ave
Sierra Dr
16th Ave
Makiki Street
Punahou Street
Punahou School
Kolo Pl
Waialae Ave
Beretania St
King St
H-1
Kahala Mall
Kapahulu Ave
Kapiolani Blvd
Ala Wai Blvd
Kalia Rd
Kalakaua Ave
Paki Ave
Monsarrat Ave
Diamond Head Crater
Diamond Head Road
Fort DeRussey Beach Park
Kuhio Beach Park
Peninsula
9
8
10
6
7
11
12
13
22
19
20
16
15
17
18
21

First up as you cross the freeway on Nuuanu Avenue is the ***Chinese Buddhist Society*** building on your left. The large meeting hall has a lovely altar in back. A couple doors farther along is the ***Soto Mission.*** The stylized geometry of this Japanese Zen Buddhist temple reflects the Soto sect's homage to Buddhism's Indian origins.

The ***Myohoji Temple*** comes next on the right, two blocks farther at 2003 Nuuanu. It's set back from the street along the banks of Nuuanu Stream, sheltered beneath high-rise condos. As you continue on Nuuanu up a short hill, take a peek left down Judd Street at the traffic light to see what seems to be another Oriental temple. In fact, you're looking at St. Luke's Episcopal Church. Just ahead, turn right on Craigside Drive to visit ***Honolulu Memorial Park.*** Sloping down the gulley of Nuuanu Stream, this Japanese cemetery enjoys a picturesque setting highlighted by detailed replicas of two famous buildings in Japan. The Sanju Pagoda is an enlarged model of the one in Nara's Minami Hokke-ji Temple. A winding garden path leads to a replica of the Kyoto Kinkaku-ji ("golden pavilion"). Note the phoenix on the roof, a symbol of immortality. Both buildings serve as columbariums for cremated remains.

Just uphill on the left side, the Ten Ri Kyo faith (an offshoot of Buddhism) maintains a small shrine within a charming Japanese garden. On the right-hand side, turn through wrought-iron gates into the ***Royal Mausoleum*** (587–2590). Completed in 1865 as the burial ground for Hawaii's royalty, the mausoleum chapel takes the shape of a Greek cross. Remains from earlier royal graves were transferred here, except for those of Kamehameha I, whose burial place remains a secret as was the old Hawaiian custom. The chapel did not hold all the caskets, and they were moved into underground crypts. Three trusted *haole* advisors also occupy places of honor here. John Young helped train Kamehameha I's army; Robert Wylie served as Kamehameha III's foreign minister; and Charles Bishop founded Bishop Estate, which remains the state's largest landowner. William Maioho, the curator, is a descendant of the chiefly line that has guarded the Kamehameha family bones since antiquity. He is usually on hand during the week to show visitors around, but it may be a good idea to call first. The Mausoleum is open Monday–Friday, 8:00 A.M. to 4:30 P.M.

Turn left on Kawananako Place to see the final temple of the strip, ***Hsu Yun Temple.*** This one is Chinese Buddhist and has bolder colors than its Japanese neighbors. Inside, its double-sided altar glistens with gold-trimmed grillwork, and incense perfumes the air. You can follow the life of the Buddha through illustrated serial posters around the room. Two other buildings behind the temple house cremation urns stacked in crowded rows of bleachers. Full-time monks live next door, praying for Earthly peace.

From the end of Nuuanu Avenue, take the overpass to get onto the Pali Highway heading toward Kailua. About a mile along, turn right after the first traffic light to ***Queen Emma's Summer Palace*** (595–3167). Emma's uncle, John Young II, erected the house, which arrived prefab from Boston in 1847, and called it Hanaiakamalama ("adopted child of moonlight"). Emma inherited the property and spent a lot of time here with her husband, King Kamehameha IV. Feather *kahilis,* emblematic of royalty, stand in every room. Woven *lauhala* (pandanus) mats cover the floors, except for Western carpets in the Edinburgh Room, an extension built in anticipation of a visit from the Duke of Edinburgh. The building lacks the imposing appearance of Iolani Palace, but a visit here provides a much more personal experience. Docents guide you around the palace, and almost every item of furnishing has a story.

A rare feather cape that Kamehameha I won in battle displays the yellow feathers of the now-extinct *`o`o `a`a* bird. A tiger-claw necklace from an Indian maharaja and a lithograph of Napoleon III number among the many gifts from monarchs around the world. Notice the tiny red jacket that belonged to Prince Albert. Like many little boys, the royal heir wanted to be a fireman when he grew up, so the Honolulu firefighters made him a miniature uniform.

Despite these tokens of happy times, a sense of tragedy pervades the house. Prince Albert, the only child ever born to Hawaiian royalty after Kamehamaha I, took sick and died at the age of four in 1862. A silver christening cup and holy water sent by Britain's Queen Victoria, who had agreed to be the child's godmother, arrived only hours after his death. Albert's father, the king, blamed himself for his son's death and shut himself in the Summer Palace for almost fifteen months of mourning before dying of what the community called "a broken heart."

Faced with a double bereavement and a house full of painful memories, Emma took to traveling and social work. She auctioned off much of the home's furniture to help fund the Queen's Hospital, which she and her husband had founded. Later the house itself was scheduled to be torn down and the grounds converted into a ballpark, but the Daughters of Hawaii intervened. They restored the palace, recovered much of the original contents, and now operate it as a museum. The palace welcomes visitors daily 9:00 A.M. to 4:00 P.M. for a small admission fee.

A trio of Oriental temples flanks the Summer Palace. The most interesting of the three, the Shinto shrine of ***Daijingu,*** sits behind the palace on

Paiwa Road. Stone lions guard the entrance, and offerings of hundred-pound rice bags and three-gallon jugs of soy sauce rest before the altar.

About 0.5 mile from the Summer Palace, turn right onto Nuuanu Pali Drive for a scenic detour. The road winds through 2 miles of lush rain forest and bamboo thickets. Halfway along, following a sharp bend in the road, look for a turnoff into a small forest clearing. (You'll recognize it by the litter.) The ***Judd Memorial Trail*** begins here, an easy 1.3-mile loop that leads to a grove of Norfolk pines named for an early forest ranger. Locals come here to mud-slide down the hill slopes on plastic bags, large pieces of cardboard, or *ti* leaves (the Old Hawaiian way); you can wash off in Jackass Ginger, a naturally formed pool reached by taking the right fork of the trail immediately across Nuuanu Stream. Nuuanu Pali Drive continues past a grassy embankment, where kids fish for crayfish in the stream pools, before rejoining the Pali Highway.

As you continue through rain forest on the highway, glance up at the steep walls of the valley above you. Waterfall paths scar the green cliff faces; if it has been raining, the walls sparkle with rivulets. A mile farther, take the turnoff to the ***Pali Lookout*** for a magnificent view of O`ahu's windward coast. From this clifftop perch you see at once the dramatic contrast between the two sides of the Koolau Range. The gentle ridges and valleys that slope upward from the "town" side terminate here in an unbroken wall of *pali* (cliffs). Rising vertically as high as 3,000 feet, these Koolau cliffs tower above the bowl-shaped coastal plains below. Their wind-eroded face is cloaked in greenery, moistened by a misty crown of rainclouds that the trade winds deposit on their peaks. At just under 1,200 feet, the Nuuanu Pali represents a low point in the chain; jagged spires on either side of the pass rise a thousand feet above. Winds funneling through the pass often reach gale force, so hold onto your hat and tether small children securely (just kidding).

The view below encompasses the sweep of Kaneohe Bay, the largest in the state. Below the lookout, the Pali Highway emerges from tunnels to descend to Kailua, the next bay off to the right. Part of the original Pali Highway follows an ancient Hawaiian pathway from the lookout itself. You can walk along this abandoned road to enjoy the view in solitude.

Kamehameha's conquest of the islands reached its terrifying conclusion in 1795 at this very spot. His army had routed a combined opposition of O`ahu and Maui chieftains and driven them up Nuuanu Valley. Many of the defeated warriors leaped over the cliffs to avoid capture. More than 800 skulls have been found at the bottom.

The windward coast is described in a later section; for now, let's stay in town. To the right of Nuuanu Valley, the green volcanic form of Punchbowl Crater rising above downtown Honolulu makes a striking landmark, whose English name makes obvious visual sense. Hardened ash ejected during violent steam explosions formed this tuff cone in less than a day. *Puu o Waina,* its original Hawaiian name, translates to "hill of sacrifice," an ironically appropriate epithet for the ***National Memorial Cemetery of the Pacific*** (532–3720) inside. Ernie Pyle, the famous World War II correspondent who covered one battle too many, and Ellison Onizuka, a Hawaiian-born astronaut who died in the *Challenger* crash, lie entombed here along with countless others. You enter from the mountain side. Volunteers from the American Legion offer walking tours of the cemetery on weekdays. The $15 fee includes transport from Waikiki. Call 946–6383 to make advance reservations. Open daily 8:00 A.M. to 6:30 P.M.

The various ridges above Honolulu have dense housing tracts whose twinkling lights at night reflect the star-filled sky. Most have scenic drives leading up, the oldest and nicest of which is the Tantalus/Roundtop loop, inland and east of Punchbowl. Take Punahou Street off King past the cactus-covered walls of missionary-founded Punahou School. Turn left onto Nehoa Street at the light and then right 2 blocks up Makiki Street, which takes you to the start of the loop. Bear left onto Makiki Heights Drive. Just ahead at the hairpin bend, outdoors enthusiasts can stop in at the ***Hawaii Nature Center*** (955–0100) to get maps and advice on the network of trails that crisscross the ridges. Two of the trails begin right behind the center. Open daily 8:00 A.M. to 4:30 P.M. The center also conducts hikes and interpretive activities around the island on weekends for a small fee. Call to reserve a spot.

For more civilized pleasures, continue up the road to the ***Contemporary Museum*** (526–0232). The museum occupies the elegant 1925 designer home of the three-acre Spalding Estate. Creative remodeling allows the museum to display its rotating art exhibits in unique multilevel galleries. A specially built pavilion houses the one permanent exhibit, a colorfully robust environmental installation by David Hockney that re-creates the atmosphere of his opera designs for Ravel's *L'Enfant et les Sortileges.* Outside, Japanese-inspired gardens slope into a ravine below. The museum also has a pleasant outdoor cafe serving moderately priced lunches 11:30 A.M. to 2:30 P.M. Open Tuesday–Saturday 10:00 A.M. to 4:00 P.M., Sunday noon–4:00 P.M.

Makiki Heights Drive runs into Tantalus Drive, which takes you to the top of the loop. The road passes more elegant homes (one of which was the residence-in-exile for Ferdinand and Imelda Marcos) spaced between amazing rain-forest growths of bamboo, ferns, and philodendron creepers. Roll down your window to inhale the smell of ginger and *pikake* (jasmine) flowers. With every bend in the road, you get treated to another breathtaking view of Honolulu. Tantalus Drive climbs to 2,000 feet and then loops back as Roundtop Drive on the other side of the ridge, providing new viewing angles to contemplate. Halfway down, take the turnoff to ***Puu Ualakaa State Park*** and walk out onto the lookout platform at the lower parking lot. Be sure to bring your wide-angle camera lens because all of Honolulu spreads out below your feet.

Next up comes Manoa ("vast") Valley, an enormous clearing famous for its "Manoa mist," whereby the sun shines through a veil of mist-like rain and forms intense rainbows. This time take Punahou Street to its end and bear left on Manoa Road.

Follow this tree-lined drive just under a mile into the valley, and on your left you'll see the entrance to the ***Waioli Tea Room*** (988–5800), at 2950 Manoa Road. Owned by the Salvation Army, the restaurant here dates back to the 1920s. Photos from the tearoom's past hang alongside portraits of Hawaiian royalty. Grab a table in the open air *lana`i* and enjoy light cafe fare while admiring the lushly tropical garden. Another attraction on the property is the ***Robert Louis Stevenson Grass Shack,*** brought here from Waikiki, in which the author penned some of his famous works. Open daily from 8:00 A.M. to 4:00 P.M.

Lyon Arboretum (988–0456). Harold Lyon was a sugar botanist in the 1920s. He belonged to an elite team of roving naturalists who traveled the world, paddling upriver through Malaysian jungle or scaling South American peaks, in a never-ending search for specimens of interest or value to the Hawaiian sugar industry. He introduced several thousand new plant species to the islands, many of which you can see today growing in a seminatural state in the 194-acre grounds of the arboretum.

A Hawaiian garden displays the trees and plants used in ancient times. They are grouped according to usage: Foods include mountain apples and breadfruit; clothing came from *wauke* bark (a mulberry); musical instruments could be a gourd or bamboo rattle; building materials ranged from vines to trees; medicines came from almost anything. You can see how limited the original flora of the islands was, but the Hawaiians found ingenious uses for almost everything. Open Monday–Saturday 9:00 A.M. to 3:00 P.M. Donation. The arboretum also offers regular tours as well as other interpretive activities and classes. Call for schedule.

Just ahead, the road ends at the trailhead to ***Manoa Falls.*** Although often muddy, this popular trail offers a delightful stroll through rainforest jungle, some of which was planted by the arboretum. Look for mountain apples and guava along the way, and expect mosquitoes. The veil-like ribbon of the 100-foot waterfall spills into a shallow pool less than a mile up the canyon. It takes about forty-five minutes going up. Just before you reach the falls, the Aihualama Trail branches off to the left to connect with the Tantalus trail system. The first part of the trail offers a good view across Manoa Valley.

At the mouth of Manoa Valley on the east side is O`ahu's most intimate luxury accommodation, the ***Manoa Valley Inn*** (947–6019; 800–634–5115), at 2001 Vancouver Drive, off University Avenue. This three-story mansion bristles with gables and buttressed eaves. Built in 1919 by businessman John Guild and now on the National Register of Historic Buildings, the home was refurbished by Crazy Shirts owner Rick Ralston with nostalgic touches, from patterned wallpaper to brass fixtures. Many of the antique furnishings come from Ralston's personal collection. All the necessary ingredients for gentle living are supplied in this self-styled country inn: croquet and billiards, a veranda facing a shady yard, wine, daily newspapers, and fresh-cut flowers. Rooms range from $99 to $190, Continental breakfast included. A block seaward of the inn at 2323A Seaview Avenue, you can obtain far more modest lodging at Hosteling International's ***Manoa Hostel*** (946–0591).

Waialae Avenue, the continuation of King Street, leads past other ridges and valleys of interest. Palolo Valley hides a startling sight in its rear canyon, the ***Dae Won Sa temple.*** Take Tenth Avenue deep into the valley and bear right on Waiomao Street. You'll see the gaudy colors of the temple's pagoda rooftops before you get there. Hawaii's first Korean Buddhist temple is a massive complex. Fierce larger-than-life statues of "Buddha's guards" secure the entrance to the three temple buildings. The oldest one, on the right, displays the most authentic architecture. Inside, bleacher rows of golden miniature Buddhas surround a central altarpiece. The entire building swims with colors and textures that make the mind boggle. Flower children will appreciate ***Kawamoto Orchid Nursery*** (732–5808) just around the bend at 2630 Waiomao Road.

The next ridge is Maunalani Heights. Take Wilhemina Rise to Maunalani Circle to reach the trailhead for ***Lanipo.*** This is the best of the many ridge hikes leading up to a Koolau *pali* overlook. You pass through a variety of vegetation, including seasonal strawberry guavas, and are afforded great views into the surrounding valleys; the thin ribbon of civilization along the coast recedes with every mile into virgin forest. Three miles along you reach a staggering panorama of the windward coast, 2,500 feet below. The hike is strenuous and takes at least three hours going up. Make sure

Manoa Valley Inn

it's clear up top before setting out, or your only view will be of your hands groping 2 feet in front of you in the mist.

Waikiki and Thereabouts

Waikiki (see map on pages 72–73) is like a concrete castle guarded by a less-than-shimmering moat. It's a giant tourist mill, cut off from reality and quarantined lest it contaminate the rest of Honolulu. Yet, Waikiki has its own perverse charm in spite of its monumental tackiness and congestion. Long before the first tourists arrived, Hawaii's royalty luxuriated on the golden crescent of Waikiki Beach and surfed its endlessly rolling breakers, with the regal profile of Diamond Head Crater rising in the distance. As the birthplace of Hawaiian tourism, Waikiki has an added nostalgia lacking in other island resorts. While today's clamorous crowds may detract from the beach's beauty and the high-rise hotels block each other's views, Waikiki still remains a world-class resort destination. You may not like it, but you owe yourself a look.

In days gone by, most of Waikiki inland of the beach was a wetland with fifty-one acres of fish ponds surrounded by taro and rice paddies. The word *waikiki* means "spouting waters." Beachgoers increasingly complained about the swarming mosquitos bred in "the swamp," and in 1922 the Ala Wai Canal drained the land, allowing Hawaii's first destination resort to be born. Emerging from the primordial slime, greedy developers soon raised a bumper crop of architectural hideousness. The main thoroughfares are Kalakaua Avenue, heading toward Diamond Head past the beach hotels, and Ala Wai Boulevard, running toward Ala Moana along the canal, where outrigger canoe teams practice.

When local people go to the beach in town, they usually head for Ala Moana Beach Park, just west of Waikiki. ***Aina Moana*** (Magic Island), an artificial peninsula at the Waikiki end of the park, offers great views and protected swimming. Crossing the bridge over the Ala Wai Canal and harbor, Ala Moana Boulevard enters Waikiki itself. To hit the beach, make a right on Kalia Road after the road curves past the Hilton Hawaiian Village and stop at ***Fort Derussey Beach Park,*** one of the two public areas bordering Waikiki Beach. Southern Californians at heart can find pickup games of two-person beach volleyball here. Actor Tom Selleck used to play almost every Sunday while filming the TV series *Magnum P.I.* The ***U.S. Army Museum*** next to the park bristles with weaponry of varying ages and has some realistic Vietnam-style dioramas for Rambo types wanting to experience jungle combat. Open Tuesday–Sunday 10:00 A.M. to 4:30 P.M. Free.

Saratoga Road leads from the museum back inland to Kalakaua Avenue. On Wednesday and Friday between 10:00 A.M. and noon, you can visit the ***Urasenke Foundation*** (923–3059), at 245 Saratoga Road to watch a ritual performance of the *cha-no-yu,* the ancient Japanese tea ceremony. Around the bend on Kalakaua sprawls the massive ***Royal Hawaiian Shopping Center*** (922–0588), which offers free lessons in hula and Hawaiian crafts on weekday mornings. If you shop here, visit the ***Little Hawaiian Craft Shop*** (926–2662) on the third floor of building B. Unlike the other Waikiki souvenir shops that have plastic, made-in-the-Philippines inventories, this one has the real stuff, from Niihau shell leis to handmade feather work. The shop thrived for years in Pearl Ridge Shopping Center before moving to Waikiki, so you know they don't sell only to tourists. Prices aren't low, but the selection can't be beat. Another place to drop an eye is the ***Ukulele House*** (923–8587) in building A. You'll find everything you need to learn to strum these "jumping fleas" of the islands. Both shops open daily 9:30 A.M. to 11:00 P.M.

Threaded between the A and B buildings of the shopping center, Royal Hawaiian Avenue ushers the faithful to the vintage hotel of the same name. It's worth making the pilgrimage to the ***Royal Hawaiian Hotel*** (923–7311, 800–325–3589; 2259 Kalakaua Avenue, Honolulu 96815) to bask in the lingering romance of Old Waikiki. Built in 1927 as the glamor destination Matson needed to attract passengers on its luxury liners, the "Pink Palace" welcomed an endless stream of Hollywood stars. Its Valentino-era Moorish architecture and quiet, grassy courtyard remain an island of grace amid an ocean of vulgarity. Rooms in the historic wing feature four-poster beds, floral wallpaper, and Queen Anne furnishings. Rates begin at $310. Farther down Kalakaua, the ***Sheraton Moana Surfrider*** (922–3111; 800–325–3535) claims its own share of nostalgia. Step through the elaborate Colonial porte cochere that fronts the lobby to travel back in time. Built in 1901, the Moana was Waikiki's first hotel. Live music plays throughout the day in the rear banyan tree court, where Robert Louis Stevenson once composed and the Prince of Wales caroused. The historical room above the lobby chronicles this glamorous past with photos and memorabilia, and the hotel offers free historical tours on weekdays at 11:00 A.M. and 5:00 P.M. The guest rooms have been refurbished with period touches, such as Hawaiian quilts on the beds and old-fashioned fixtures for the plumbing. Rates begin at $265.

Beyond the Moana the shoreline reverts to public park with lots of waterfall thingies burbling out of nowhere; there are several features of interest (not counting the ones in swimsuits on the beach). Right next to the Police Substation, four large boulders lounge incognito in the sand. A plaque explains how these ***kahuna stones*** came to contain the healing powers of four powerful *kahunas* ("one who knows the secrets") visiting from Tahiti in the thirteenth century. Not far from the stones stands a bronzed statue of Duke Kahanumoku, a Waikiki "beach boy" who was an Olympic swimming gold medalist in 1912 and 1920 and became an international surfing hero and unofficial ambassador for the islands. Local surfers bemoan the fact that the statue has its back to the ocean, something an experienced waterman like the Duke would never have done while living. Modern-day ***beach boys*** ply their trade from a concession stand nearby. For $5.00 you can help paddle an outrigger canoe out to sea and ride the waves in. For $25 you can get an hour's surfing lesson with individual instruction. The waves here offer long, gentle rides, making Waikiki the best place on the island to learn to surf. If you rent a board on your own, you'll want to get one with a leash so that the board stays with you.

Continue down the street to watch old-timers face off on the checkered tables of the Kuhio chess pavilions. Across the street, look for the blue V-shaped roof of St. Augustine Church. Take a moment to pop inside the ***Damien Museum*** (923–2690) in back to see memorabilia of the "Martyr of Moloka`i." Open Monday–Friday 9:00 A.M. to 2:00 P.M. Free.

The main hotel strip ends at Kapahulu Avenue opposite the entrance to the Honolulu Zoo. The city is constructing an elaborate and controversial burial mound nearby, "Na Iwi Kupuna Waikiki," which translates roughly as "the bones of our ancestors in Waikiki," and will house just that (said bones having been unearthed during recent work on a water main). Look for a schedule of nearby bandstand events and read some park history at the corner kiosk. You can shop for sidewalk art along the fence on Monsarrat Avenue on weekends. The zoo itself is fairly standard, but visitors (especially prospective snorkelers) definitely should visit the ***Waikiki Aquarium*** (923–9741) farther along Kalakaua Avenue. It isn't a big facility, but the exhibits illustrate the colorful diversity of marine life surrounding these islands. You can see some of the world's first chambered nautiluses hatched in captivity, watch Hawaiian monk seals perform, and even handle marine life in the "Edge of the Reef" exhibit. Ask about reef walks and other aquarium excursions. Open daily 9:00 A.M. to 5:00 P.M. Admission $7.00.

Next to the aquarium, note the elaborate facade of the oceanside ***War Memorial Natatorium.*** An enclosed, salt-water bathing pool built in honor of Word War I vets, the natatorium has been the subject of a decade-long debate: What do you do with an aging war monument no one wants to use anymore? The city recently restored the facade, but the state health department still can't bring itself to sign off on reopening the pool due to sanitation concerns about water circulation.

Kapiolani Park sprawls along the opposite side of the street. A staging ground for community activities on weekends, it is also a top-rated kite-flying venue. You can request a free demo/lesson from ***Kite Fantasy*** (735–9059) by appointment. Across the street is the ***New Otani Kaimana Beach Hotel*** (923–1555; 800–356–8264; 2863 Kalakaua Avenue, Honolulu 96815). This small "boutique" hotel enjoys a less frenetic, off-Waikiki location on Sans-Souci Beach, another Robert Louis Stevenson hangout. Rooms start at $135. The hotel's ***Hau Tree Lana`i*** restaurant sits right on the beach. For lodging in Waikiki proper, hostelers can hole up in Hosteling International's ***Hale Aloha*** (926–8313; 2417 Prince Edward Street). For a B&B alternative, artist Joanne Trotter rents two suites with private baths in her gracious estate on the slopes of Diamond Head, overlooking Waikiki. The rooms rent for $115 and are full of original artwork and heritage koa furnishings, including a 100-year-old bed that belonged to Princess Ruth. Call ***Diamond Head B&B*** (923–3360).

Kalakaua Avenue ends near the foot of ***Diamond Head Crater.*** The largest of the tuff cones on the island, Diamond Head received its English name when British sailors caught the glint of what they thought were diamonds reflecting from its slopes. King Kamehameha I promptly slapped a *kapu* (taboo) on the entire mountain, only to discover the "gems" were calcite crystals. You can enter the crater interior via a military tunnel through the inland walls. To do so, turn left onto Paki Avenue, then right at the traffic lights onto Monsarrat. A paved road less than a mile long leads through the tunnel. The military installations inside share space with a state park that the public can visit from 6:00 A.M. to 6:00 P.M. From the parking lot a well-graded trail ascends the 760-foot summit, emerging through the inside of a World War II bunker. The panoramic view from the top extends over half the island. The hike up takes about a half-hour. Bring water and a flashlight.

If you'd rather sun by the shore than hike in the hills, turn right from the end of Kalakaua onto Diamond Head Road, which skirts the seaward edge of the crater around the southern tip of the island. The road climbs high onto the slopes past Diamond Head Lighthouse. Just ahead, a paved pathway leads down the steep cliffside to ***Diamond Head Beach,*** a secluded gem. A fringing reef extends close to shore, making swimming difficult at this spot. Surfers and sailboarders who come here launch through a reef channel a few hundred yards to the left. Keep walking that way toward Black Point, and you'll find some nicer swimming holes and maybe a stretch of sand to call your own.

You can also watch the action from up top at the two lookout points a little farther along. During summer, the surf off Diamond Head reaches as high as 8 feet, providing exciting conditions for expert wave riders.

The first lookout offers a view east of distant Koko Head and Koko Crater and has a plaque commemorating Amelia Earhart's solo flight across the Pacific.

If instead of continuing on Kalakaua past the zoo, you turn left up Kapahulu Avenue, you'll come to some interesting antiques stores. Step inside ***Bailey's Antiques & Aloha Shirts*** (734–7628), at 517 Kapahulu, and you enter a three-ring bazaar. The eclectic inventory creates a carnival atmosphere rich in color and texture. Most of the items fit the category of Hawaiiana kitsch and collectibles, such as the dancing hula-girl lamps popular in the 1950s. Bailey's specializes in classic aloha shirts, including original 1940s "silkies" whose wild floral patterns became a symbol of the islands. Some of the shirts have celebrity connections and fetch upwards of $1,000. You can also find contemporary reproductions for about $50 and used shirts for under $20. Owner David Bailey scours thrift shops in California to find these forgotten treasures and has been known to buy the shirt off a stranger's back. Open daily 10:00 A.M. to 6:00 P.M.

Other antiques shops space themselves along Kapahulu, with the biggest cluster at the far end near the freeway. Most of the five antiques shops in back of the ***Kilohana Square*** shopping complex, at 1016 Kapahulu, mostly specialize in decorative art and furniture from the Orient. On the way down, you might also stop in at Aunty Mary Lou's ***Na Lima Mili Huli No`eau*** (732–0865), at 726 Kapahulu, a craftshop devoted to featherworking. (The name means "skilled hands touch the feathers.") Students take lessons here and then sell their completed projects by consignment. Open Monday–Friday 9:00 A.M. to 9:00 P.M., Saturday 9:00 A.M. to 5:00 P.M.

Kapahulu also has a variety of good restaurants. At the high end of the spectrum, ***Sam Choy's Diamond Head*** (732–8645), at 449 Kapahulu, caters to a local crowd, serving gourmet versions of island food in giant portions. Open Monday–Thursday 5:30–9:00 P.M., Friday–Sunday 5:00–9:30 P.M. Investment-caliber prices. ***Hee Hing*** (735–5544), downstairs, has decent Chinese fare. ***Irifune*** (737–1141), at 563 Kapahulu, serves slightly offbeat, garlicky Japanese dishes in a funky venue for inexpensive prices. Open Tuesday–Saturday 11:30 A.M. to 1:30 P.M. and 5:30 P.M. to 9:30 P.M.

A couple blocks farther, ***Ono Hawaiian Food*** (737–2275), at 726 Kapahulu, has the real product. The lines outside the door are both a deterrent and a recommendation. Open Monday–Saturday 11:00 A.M. to 7:30 P.M. Inexpensive. And to experience trendy, "revolving sushi service," try ***Genki Sushi*** (735–8889), at 900 Kapahula. A conveyer belt trundles

Trivia

Oahu boasts more miles of swimming beaches than any other island.

rotating menu samples around the restaurant; after you make selections, your order is prepared fresh. Open daily 11:00 A.M. to 3:00 P.M., 5:00–9:00 P.M., and until 10:00 P.M. on Friday–Saturday. Inexpensive.

The Kapahulu area used to be heavily settled by Honolulu's Portuguese community. Near the inland end of Kapahulu, ***Leonard's Bakery*** (737–5591) keeps tradition alive with fresh-baked Portuguese *pao doce* (sweetbread) and hot *malasadas* (doughy, holeless donuts). Stop by for a gustatory treat.

Just Up the Freeway

Believe it or not, although stuck in the middle of the Pacific Ocean, Hawaii has its own "interstate" highways. The main route through town is the H–1 Freeway. Take any on-ramp and head west to see some more of Honolulu. If you really want to scratch the soul of Hawaii, visit the ***Bishop Museum*** (847–3511), a repository of Hawaiiana from A to Z. Princess Bernice Pauahi, the last heir of the Kamehameha dynasty, left her immense landholdings to educate Hawaiian students at nearby Kamehameha Schools. Her private possessions, however, were left to benefit all of us as the beginnings of the museum established by her American banker husband, Charles Bishop. Today, a century later, the museum's exhibits have swollen to include 76,000 Hawaiian artifacts alone, not to mention 13.5 million insect specimens. Bishop Museum has become the world's leading research institution on Pacific cultures. To reach it, take the Houghtailing Street turnoff from the H–1 Freeway and take the second left.

Budget plenty of time for your visit, as there's lots to see. The bulk of the exhibits fill the massive Hawaiian Hall inside the castlelike main building. The three levels focus on different periods, beginning with precontact Hawaii and continuing through the turbulent changes of the nineteenth century to today's multiethnic society. From the ceiling hangs the 50-foot skeleton of a sperm whale. You'll find most of the old Hawaii exhibits on the ground floor. Here you can meet the gods: those fiercely scowling akua (idols) that survived the 1819 abolition of the old religion. In the entrance room, look for Kukailimoku, the personal war god of Kamehameha I. The great conqueror carried this flaming orange-feathered apparition into battle, and its wide staring eyes were witness to the years of carnage. You might also see Kamehameha's full-length yellow feather cloak. Specially trained "bird men" had a full-time job trapping the more than 100,000 *mamo* birds needed to gather the plumage for the cloak. Each bird yielded only a few yellow feathers plucked from among the black. Upstairs you will find relics of missionaries and mariners, costumes of kings, and immigrant heirlooms all jumbled together much like the history of Hawaii. Hall tours are offered twice daily on weekdays.

You can compare the Hawaiian exhibits with the displays from other Polynesian islands in the hall next door. Adjacent rooms house artifacts from the related Micronesian and Melanesian peoples. If you're not clear which islands fit where, just consult the color-coded maps.

Open Monday–Saturday, the Planetarium introduces you to the world of stars. Thrice daily shows highlight topics of astronomical interest. Try to catch the live hula performances weekdays at 11:00 A.M. and 2:00 P.M. You can also watch demonstrations of Hawaiian crafts such as featherwork, quilting, or lei making. Cultural enthusiasts might also consider taking the museum's Ho`ike`ike tour—a full day program which includes a guided tour and lessons in Hawaiian lei-making and hula. Reservations required. Bishop Museum is open daily 9:00 A.M. to 5:00 P.M.; $14.95 admission.

Past the museum, the freeway splits temporarily, with H–1 bending seaward to the airport. Continue straight on what's now Route 78 for another mile. Take the Puuloa Road/Tripler Hospital turnoff and make a quick right into ***Moanalua Gardens*** (833–1944). Prince Lot, who later became Kamehameha V, kept a summer home here, where he encouraged a partial revival of the hula art forms. The annual Prince Lot Festival commemorates his efforts with a weekend of Hawaiian dance beginning the third Saturday of July. The prince's elaborate cottage still stands beside koi and taro ponds. The garden is open during daylight hours; free.

You can soak up additional historic scenery by hiking the nearby ***Kamananui Valley Trail,*** which passes petroglyphs and other historic sites deep into the valley. Kamehameha I (Lot's grandfather) capped his conquest of O`ahu by sacrificing rival chief Kalanikupule on an altar here. Stop by the Moanalua Gardens Foundation (839–5334), just behind the gardens at 1352 Pineapple Place, to purchase an interpretive trail guide keyed to numbered posts along the way ($5.00). Open Monday–Friday 8:30 A.M. to 4:00 P.M.

The best signs to follow to the Pearl Harbor and *Arizona* Memorial are along H–1. If you're already on Route 78, follow signs to the Aiea exit, about 4 miles farther, and turn left over the bridge. This section of

JUST UP THE FREEWAY

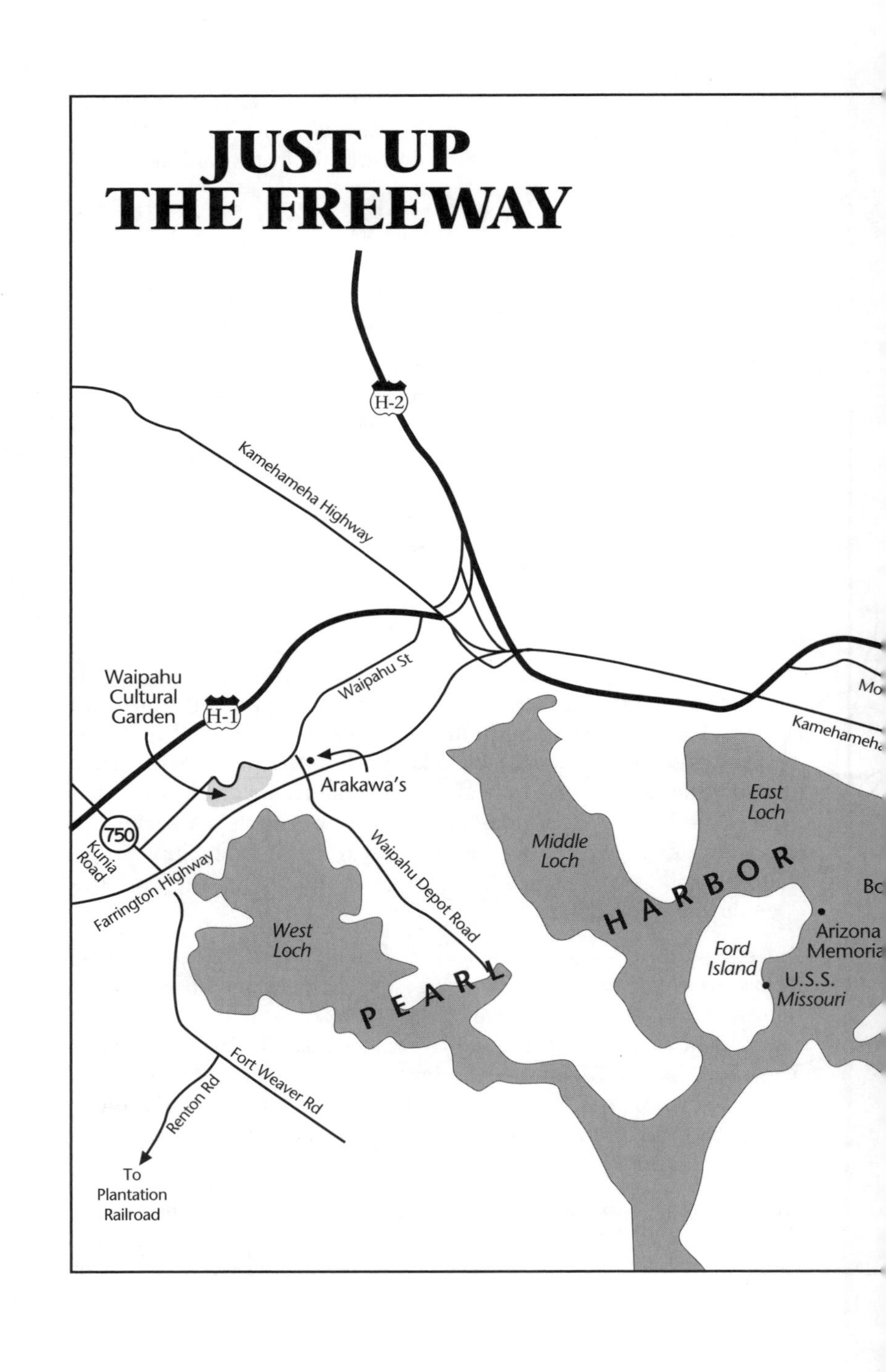

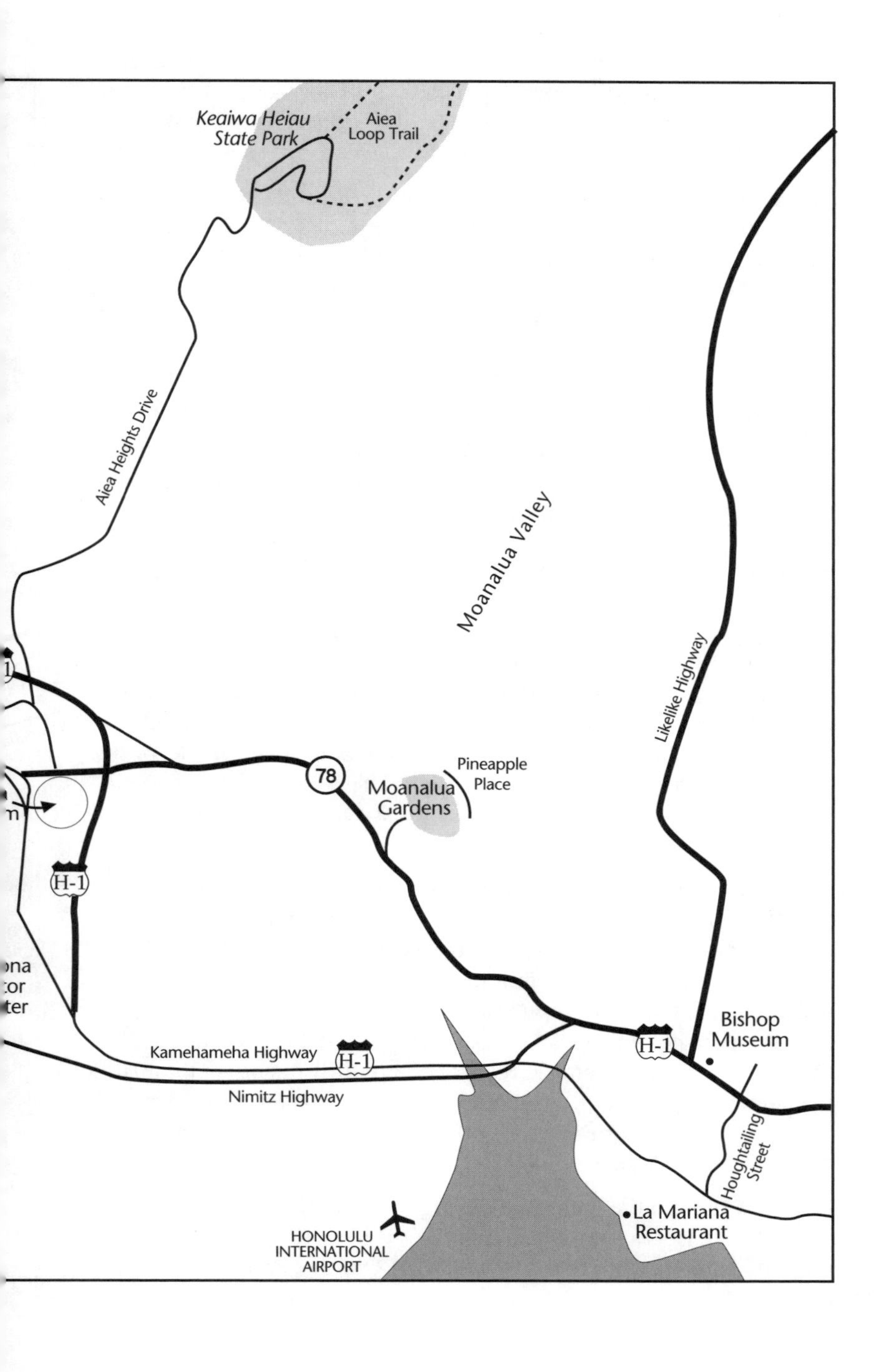

Keaiwa Heiau
State Park
Aiea
Loop Trail
Aiea Heights Drive
Moanalua Valley
Likelike Highway
78
Pineapple
Place
Moanalua
Gardens
H-1
Bishop
Museum
Kamehameha Highway
H-1
Nimitz Highway
Houghtailing
Street
HONOLULU
INTERNATIONAL
AIRPORT
La Mariana
Restaurant

Kamehameha Highway runs past the stadium along the East Loch of Pearl Harbor. The cauliflowerlike lochs of this enormous inland lagoon were cut by river valleys during a time of lower sea levels. Oyster beds thrived in the shallow flats, hence the name Pearl.

The American military acquired base rights to Pearl Harbor during King Kalakaua's reign in exchange for tariff-free access to U.S. markets for Hawaiian sugar, but they didn't get around to dredging the harbor opening until 1902. Hawaiians were perturbed when the U.S. Navy chose to dig its dry dock on the very island where the shark goddess, Kaahupahau, supposedly lived. Their dire warnings came true when, four years into construction, a structural collapse wiped out all the work that had been done so far. A giant shark skeleton was found amid the rubble.

The Japanese attack on December 7, 1941, brought Pearl Harbor before the eyes of the world and catapulted the United States into World War II. Contrary to popular belief, the attack did not come entirely without warning. A Japanese minisub had been found and disabled near the mouth of the harbor hours earlier. Experimental radar stations even tracked the incoming attack squadrons (until their commander told them to turn off their screens). More intriguing yet, American intelligence forces had recently cracked the Japanese code and by monitoring cable transmissions were alerted to the likelihood that Japan was planning a military strike. Some have suggested that top American officials secretly planned to absorb the damage so as to commit the United States to entering the war against Hitler. These "conspiracy theorists" claim that the fortuitous absence of the carrier fleet at the time of the attack was more than a stroke of luck.

You can grapple with your own interpretation as you come face to face with the monuments left from that day's violence. Take the turnoff from Kamehameha Highway to the **Arizona *Memorial*** (422–0561). The white concave hull of the monument sits like a shroud across the sunken hull of the battleship *Arizona*. More than a thousand sailors and marines perished in this single battleship's destruction—almost half the total deaths in the attack. Most of the victims remain entombed in the ship, which sank within minutes of the explosion in the forward-deck powder magazine. Half a century later the *Arizona* continues to bleed, oozing gallons of oil every week.

Free boat trips to the memorial depart from the National Park Service visitors center on a first-come, first-served basis. Browse the open-air museum exhibits while you wait your turn. One display tells the story of Hawaii's Americans of Japanese descent. At a time when mainland cities were incarcerating their Japanese populations, Hawaii's Japanese-Americans refused to allow their patriotism to be doubted. Their patient resolve won them the chance to prove themselves in combat in Italy, where they became one of the most decorated battalions in U.S. military history. Equally compelling is the story of Admiral Yamamoto, a Harvard-educated military genius who masterminded the Pearl Harbor strike despite a personal opposition to the war. The museum is open daily 7:30 A.M. to 5:00 P.M.; tours run from 8:00 A.M. to 3:00 P.M.

During busy months the wait for the tour can last for hours or even sell out entirely. Come early to reserve a space, and then amble over to nearby ***Bowfin Park*** (423–1341). You can take in the exhibits of the Pacific Submarine Museum and then enter an actual World War II submarine, the USS *Bowfin,* moored nearby. Open daily 8:00 A.M. to 5:00 P.M.; admission $8.00. On Wednesdays and weekends, check out the massive "swap meet" flea market at nearby Aloha Stadium from 6:00 A.M. to 3:00 P.M.

At Bowfin Park you can also purchase tickets for Pearl Harbor's newest visitor attraction, the ***USS Missouri*** (423–2263). One of the most formidable battleships ever built, the *Missouri* saw duty in three wars from World War II to the Persian Gulf. It earned its spot in the history books, however, not for its role in the fighting, but rather as the place where World War II ended with Japan signing instruments of surrender on its aft deck. Anchored only a thousand yards from another World War II battleship, the sunken USS *Arizona,* the two form perfect bookends to America's involvement in the war, from defeat to victory.

Much of the ship is still undergoing restoration, but you can hit the highlights, including the main bridge, armory, wardroom, the panoramic views from the "flying bridge," the retrofitted Tomahawk missile launchers, and, of course, the "surrender deck." Exhibits recount the details of daily life aboard ship, and war stories abound, including a heart-stopping moment when a Japanese kamikaze pilot slammed his fighter plane into the starboard side of the ship. Part of the experience is merely appreciating the size of this floating behemoth. Launched in 1944, the *Missouri* was the last battleship the U.S. Navy ever built and one of the largest. Its entire 887-foot-long hull is encased in steel armor plating more than a foot thick. Its massive 16-inch guns, each weighing 116 tons and measuring 65 feet in length, are capable of launching a shell as heavy as a Volkswagen Beetle more than 20 miles—with accuracy. Just designing the *Missouri* took 175 *tons* of blueprint paper. Built in three years, the ship required more than three million man-days to complete. The USS *Missouri* is open daily 9:00 A.M. to 5:00 P.M. Tickets must be purchased by 4:00 P.M. and cost $20 for a guided visit or $14 for self-guided.

Going straight from the same Aiea freeway exit puts you on Moanalua Road (moving parallel to and inland of Kamehameha Highway, past the stadium). Turn right at the mall just ahead and take Aiea Heights Drive up the hill to ***Keaiwa Heiau State Park.*** You get some good views of Pearl Harbor and Central O`ahu on the way up. The *heiau* sits at the park entrance, one of the few healing temples of ancient Hawaii that remain. Here the *kahuna lapaau* (medicine men) mixed herbs and prayers to cure a variety of ailments. Many of the medicinal plants they used still grow around the *heiau* grounds, including *noni* fruit for blood pressure; *kukui* nuts for a laxative; *hau* flowers for childbirth; and *ti* leaves for warding off evil spirits. The rest of the park consists of groves of ironwoods and eucalyptus and cool fresh air. At the top of the road, the ***Aiea Loop Trail*** offers an easy 4.5-mile hike through a variety of forest cover and occasional views. You can see the wreckage of a C-47 cargo plane about 3 miles along on your right. The round-trip trek takes about three hours.

Eating Off the Beaten Path in Honolulu

Honolulu's restaurants are every bit as international as its populace. The variety of restaurants here is probably unequaled in a city of its size. Cross-pollination between these diverse culinary traditions has led to some unusual hybrids. Amid the creative energies unleashed by such culinary fusion, a new school of Hawaii Regional Cuisine (HRC) has emerged. Its leading proponents are scattered among the islands, but common threads link the restaurants. Following the trend of New American regional cuisine, the menus revolve around island-grown produce and fresh seafood, much of which is typically served crusted in, say, a coating of macadamia nuts, then seared, blackened, or wok-charred, and sauced with Pacific Rim flavorings that enhance classic French reductions. Presentations dazzle with vertiginously layered towers erected in the center of the oversized plate and with a multicolored wasabe/sesame/miso/ginger-something drizzled around the edges. Decor is deliberately understated, often with an open kitchen as the centerpiece, and the service is casual, albeit attentive.

Many of today's top HRC performers got their start in hotel restaurants on the neighbor islands. But almost all of them have opened restaurants in Honolulu of late, and the competition has gotten fierce. The current pack of eponymous eateries includes ***Roy's*** (396–7697), ***Chef Mavro's*** (944–4714), ***Padovani's*** (946–3456), ***Onjin's Cafe*** (589–1666), and ***Sam Choy's Diamond Head*** (732–8645). All of these have investment-caliber prices (Onjin's is a tad cheaper). The top dog in town, by most counts, remains ***Alan Wong's*** (949–2526), at 1857 S. King Street. His ever-changing menu harmoniously combines an innovative use of ingredients with classical cooking techniques. The Chinese pork-hash crusted *opakapaka* (pink snapper) is but one example of improbable combinations that you have to taste to believe. Investment-caliber prices. Open nightly 5:00–10:00 P.M. Other standouts include Russel Siu's ***3660 On the Rise*** (737–1177), at 3660 Waialae Avenue, in Kaimuki, which is slightly less expensive than the rest; open Tuesday–Sunday 5:30–9:30 P.M.; and Hiroshi's Fukui's ***L'Uraku*** (955–0552), at 1341 Kapiolani Boulevard, near Ala Moana, whose Japanese-accented menu mirrors the ultra-minimalist decor. Investment-caliber prices. Local people favor Sam Choy's other restaurant, ***Breakfast, Lunch and Crab*** (545–7979), at 580 North Nimitz Highway, just north of downtown, which serves less pretentious dishes in hearty portions. The centerpiece of this cavernous brewpub is an old fishing sampan with tables in the cabin. Expensive.

If Hawaii Regional Cuisine represents the future of Hawaii's restaurants, ***La Mariana Restaurant*** (848–2800), located in the sailing club of the same name, retains something of its past. To get here, take Sand Island Access Road from Nimitz Highway north of downtown and look for the sailing masts on the right after the first traffic light. Having survived at least one tidal wave and several lease foreclosures, this rustic beach shack has been around ever since Keehi Lagoon was opened as a "poor man's yacht club." The Polynesian kitsch decor harks back to the classic South Seas restaurants of the 1920s and '30s—and with good reason: Owner Annette Nahinu bought much of it from her more illustrious, but less long-lived, predecessors such as Trader Vic's and Don the Beachcomber. To mention the lighting alone, a circus sideshow of multicolored bulbs illuminates your choice of lamps made from shells, bamboo, puffer fish, and Japanese fishing floats. Thronelike rattan chairs encircle wooden tables; carved tikis serve as pillars; and, of course, the ubiquitous fishing nets drape both ceiling and walls. No fewer than two trees grow within the restaurant, while a row of coconut palms frames the harbor views. The moderately priced menu consists of local American fare, highlighted by daily fresh fish specials. Open daily 11:00 A.M. to 3:00 P.M. and 5:00–9:00 P.M., bar service daily until midnight with live music and dancing on weekends. Something of the same atmosphere (minus the kitsch) can be found at the ***Willows*** (952–9200) at 817 Hausman Street, near the university. They serve an expensive Hawaiian buffet, Monday–Friday 11:00 A.M. to 2:00 P.M. and nightly 5:30–9:30 P.M.

For ordinary good food, try these ethnic restaurants the average tourist might not find.

The ***Indian Bazaar*** (949–4840) at 2320 South King Street, between McCully and Isenberg Streets, dwells in a minimall opposite Kozo's Sushi. You get three tongue-tingling tastes of Madras curry for one low price from a mostly vegetarian, cafeteria-style selection. There are a few tables, but it's nice to take your food to Stadium Park across the street. ***Kozo's Sushi*** (973–5666) itself is a good place to try for inexpensive, "fast food" sushi; there are many branches city-wide. Open Monday–Saturday 11:00 A.M. to 9:00 P.M. and Sunday 11:00 A.M. to 7:00 P.M. Around the corner of the park at 909 Isenberg, ***Maple Garden*** (941–6641) specializes in Northern Chinese dishes for moderate prices. A multicolored herd of Chinese horses gallop madly across the restaurant walls, painted by local artist John Young. It's open daily 11:00 A.M. to 2:00 P.M. and 5:30–10:00 P.M.

To get your just desserts, head for the homemade ice cream and pastries at ***Bubbies'*** (949–8984), opposite Varsity Theater, a block inland on University Avenue from King Street.

Continuing east on King Street leads to Waialae Avenue, where ***Beau Soleil*** (732–0967) welcomes patrons with its cheerful Mediterranean decor and gourmet menu. There is a daily choice of two entrees plus salad and dessert for a moderate price. Open daily 7:00 A.M. to 2:00 P.M., and Tuesday–Saturday 5:30–9:30 P.M.; B.Y.O.B.

Finally, Thai food fans should continue up the hill to ***Champa Thai*** (732–0054), at 3452 Waialae Avenue, in Kaimuki. Open Monday–Friday 11:00 A.M. to 2:00 P.M., and 5:00–9:30 P.M. nightly.

A Night on the Town

Waikiki is the entertainment capital of Hawaii. It has plenty of nightclubs for owls on the prowl, and almost all the big hotels book prominent local entertainers to perform at dinner shows. For free outdoor entertainment, pick an evening with clear skies and stroll along Waikiki Beach. At night the beach is empty. Instead of human static, you hear the gentle lap of waves against the shore. Stars twinkle in the velvet night, and the phosphorescent glow of breaking surf blends with the lights of cruise ships offshore. As you walk, you hear the sounds of the many hotel shows staged on oceanfront lanais and can linger to watch part of the acts.

If you feel like stopping in for a drink, a good candidate is ***Duke's Canoe Club*** (922–2268) in the Outrigger Waikiki. Top-notch local entertainers perform contemporary island music most nights from 4:00 to 6:00 P.M. and on weekends also from 10:00 P.M. to midnight. In between, the "aunties" serenade individual tables. Another good venue for Hawaiian (not in Waikiki) music is ***Chai's Island Bistro*** (585–0011) in the Aloha Tower Marketplace downtown.

For zany local comedy, much of it disguised in pidgin idioms, don't miss ***Frank de Lima's*** version of nondiscriminatory humor—he puts down every ethnic group equally. Frank's current roost is the ***Captain's Table*** at the Hawaiian Beach Hotel (922–2511), with performances Friday and Saturday at 8:30 P.M. If your night on the town stirs an appetite, the ***Wailana Coffee Shop*** (955–3736), at 1860 Ala Moana Avenue, serves good-value grub amid pseudo-Hawaiian decor. Open twenty-four hours. Night action outside Waikiki centers around two zones of interest: Collegiate crowds gather at a cluster of bars near the intersection of King and University. Young professionals favor downtown's ***Restaurant Row,*** at the ocean end of Punchbowl Street and the harborside ***Aloha Tower Marketplace.***

Honolulu has plenty to do besides nightlife. A constant succession of cultural festivals celebrate Hawaii's diverse ethnic heritage. During the summer, almost every weekend, Japanese temples schedule *bon* dances to honor ancestral spirits, and the public is always welcome to join in. Local hula *hulau* also hold fundraisers at sites around the island—a great way to catch authentic Hawaiian culture. Look at the Friday newspaper or *Honolulu Weekly* to see what's on. A number of groups schedule ***hiking trips*** on weekends. Besides the Foster Botanical Garden, and Hawaii Nature Center hikes, the Sierra Club (538–6616), and Hawaiian Trail and Mountain Club (P.O. Box 2238, Honolulu, 96804) lead hikes on most weekends.

Michael Walther's ***Oahu Nature Tours*** (924–2473; 800–861–6018) offers a daily schedule of interpretive outings; he charges $37 for a half-day trip.

Those of a crafty bent might consider taking a Hawaiiana class. Besides the Royal Hawaiian Shopping Center (see Waikiki section), other places offering instruction in Hawaiian crafts and hula include the ***Waikiki***

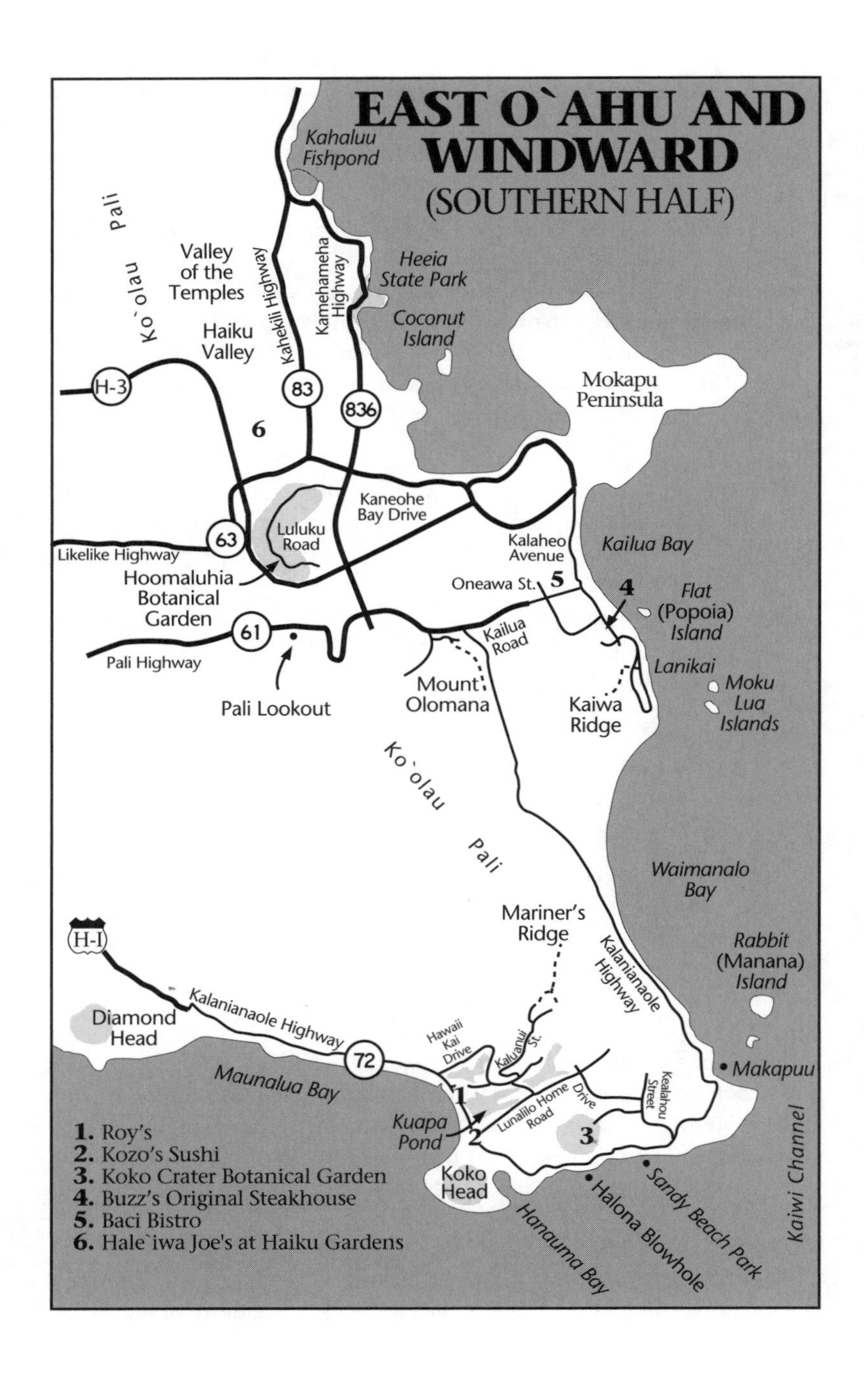
EAST O`AHU AND WINDWARD
(SOUTHERN HALF)
Kahaluu Fishpond
Ko`olau Pali
Valley of the Temples
Haiku Valley
Kahekili Highway
Kamehameha Highway
Heeia State Park
Coconut Island
Mokapu Peninsula
H-3
83
836
6
Kaneohe Bay Drive
Luluku Road
63
Likelike Highway
Hoomaluhia Botanical Garden
Kalaheo Avenue
Kailua Bay
Oneawa St.
5
4
Flat (Popoia) Island
61
Pali Highway
Kailua Road
Lanikai
Mount Olomana
Kaiwa Ridge
Moku Lua Islands
Pali Lookout
Ko`olau Pali
Waimanalo Bay
Mariner's Ridge
Kalanianaole Highway
Rabbit (Manana) Island
H-I
Diamond Head
Kalanianaole Highway
Hawaii Kai Drive
Kaluanui St.
72
Makapuu
Maunalua Bay
Kealahou Street
Lunalilo Home Road
Drive
Kuapa Pond
1
2
3
Kaiwi Channel
Koko Head
Sandy Beach Park
Halona Blowhole
Hanauma Bay
1. Roy's
2. Kozo's Sushi
3. Koko Crater Botanical Garden
4. Buzz's Original Steakhouse
5. Baci Bistro
6. Hale`iwa Joe's at Haiku Gardens

Community Center (923–1802) and the ***Lyon Arboretum*** (988–0456). ***Temari Center*** (735–1860) specializes in Asian and Pacific artforms, often bringing in guest artists from Japan and elsewhere. Sign up in advance because these classes do fill up quickly.

Anyone with a taste for the macabre should check into the excellent ghost tours offered by ***Honolulu TimeWalks*** (943–0371). Master storyteller Glenn Grant has filled several volumes with the ghost tales he has collected over the years. He leads a walking tour of spooky Old Honolulu on Wednesday nights for $10. TimeWalks also offers a bus tour of haunted locales around the island on Fridays and Saturdays for $30. Call for current schedule as other tours may be added, and, again, book well in advance. Those with an interest in World War II history will appreciate the unique tour offered by ***Home of the Brave*** (396–8112). Guides dressed in World War II air corps pilot uniforms lead a half-day excursion to military bases and other sites associated with wartime history, bringing them to life via recordings of actual news bulletins, music, and speeches which aired during the war. The tours run weekdays, beginning 6:20 A.M and returning by 1:30 P.M.; the cost is $69. More conventional walking tours covering island history and archaeology can be arranged through the ***Hawaii Geographic Society*** (538–3952). They charge $24 for groups of four or less. ***Kapiolani Community College*** offers its own "stories of Honolulu" walking tours. Call 734–9234 for information.

East O`ahu and Windward

All right, enough big-city stuff. You came here to see natural beauty, and O`ahu's got plenty—outside Honolulu. To do the main "circle island" tour, driving up the windward coast and back through the center in a single day, is impractical, though. If you're based in Honolulu, take advantage of the scenic trans-Ko`olau highways—the Pali, Likelike, and H–3—to break the trip into smaller loops.

Start the southern circuit on Kalanianaole Avenue at the east end of H–1, "heading Koko Head" (which is how locals say "go east" when you're east of Diamond Head). Four miles along the highway you reach Hawaii Kai, a large suburb built around a converted fish pond. ***Mariner's Ridge*** is one of the few built-up hillsides here. If you take Kaluanui Street off Hawaii Kai Drive all the way to the top, there's an excellent one-and-a-half-hour hike to a Ko`olau *pali* overlook. It's similar to Lanipo but not as long or hard, and the view is almost as good.

Surprisingly, out here in the s'burbs you'll find one of the best restaurants on the island. ***Roy's*** (396–7697) showcases the inventive talents of chef Roy Yamaguchi. Combining Oriental instincts with classical training, Roy has helped pioneer the new Hawaii Regional Cuisine, with dishes such as Opaka paka with macadamia-nut lobster sauce. His restaurant occupies space in the Hawaii Kai Corporate Plaza, overlooking Maunalua Bay across the highway; turn off at Keahole Street. Open nightly 5:30–10:00 P.M. Live music on weekends; for a quieter meal, ask for a table outside. Investment-caliber prices.

Another good dinner bet nearby is ***Portlock's Restaurant*** (394–5550), at 377 Keahole behind Long's Drugs in Kuapa Kai Shopping Center (not on Portlock). They serve an eclectic menu in a cheerful Latin American space overlooking the marina (former fish pond). Open Tuesday–Sunday 5:30–9:30 P.M.

After Koko Marina, the divided highway ends. Continue up the hill between Koko Head and Koko Crater, two large tuff cones formed during O`ahu's most recent eruption. (Not to worry, it happened about 100,000 years ago.) At the top of the hill, turn right into ***Hanauma Bay Beach Park*** (395–2211). Peering over the rim into this unique indentation on Koko Head's east flank from the parking lot, you won't need a Ph.D. in geology to recognize that the bay was once a volcanic crater. Part of a chain of craters along the east coast, Hanauma's seaward wall has yielded to the assault of the ocean. Faced with this violent intrusion by her sister into her last-ditch refuge, it's easy to see why Pele moved on. She left us to enjoy a unique, sheltered bay with large coral deposits and a white sand beach.

As a state underwater park off-limits to fishing, Hanauma has blossomed into a natural aquarium with fish of every shape, stripe, and color. You'll see giant rainbow parrotfish, banded convict tangs, exotic Moorish idols, and maybe even reed-thin trumpetfish. The different schools glitter like so many points of light. The bay has become popular with tourists, but such exquisite beauty is worth sharing. You walk or ride a trolley down the steep path to the beach. A concession rents snorkeling equipment at the pavilion below, and if you want to make yourself really popular with the fish, buy some food packets. Note: Due to overcrowding, the park is closed on Tuesday and exercises capacity controls on parking.

Before you leave Hanauma, take a walk around the left side of the bay past some interesting tidepools. Keep a watch for waves that sometimes sweep over the ledge. After you round the far rim, it's only a few more yards to the ***Toilet Bowl,*** a unique rock formation. Incoming waves are channeled into an exposed lava tube; as they ebb and flow, they "flush" a small pool at the end in a vigorous imitation of your household porcelain pot. The rocks around the edge are slippery, but inside it's safe and loads of fun. If you want to explore some more, you can hike along the spine of the crater by taking the blocked-off road that splits off near the entrance from the highway.

Past Hanauma Bay the highway swoops around another sunken crater (used as a firing range), then clings to the striated slopes of ***Koko Crater,*** which overlooks the deep blue of the Kaiwi Channel. This is the sort of drive you see featured in sports-car commercials. You wind in and out of the volcano's ridges and grooves while, beneath the highway, the ocean crashes against the coast in a fury of foam and spray. Across the channel, Moloka`i darkens the horizon. If conditions are clear, you can make out Maui and Lana`i as well.

Less than a mile along the road, look for a small stone monument on your right, a hundred yards *before* the ***Halona Blowhole*** parking lot where the tour buses disgorge their loads. Pull over here instead and walk up the steps to this fishing shrine built by the Honolulu Japanese Casting Club. Carved into the upright rock, O Jisan, a guardian spirit, keeps a watchful eye on anglers casting from the wave-swept lava shelf below. The view from the monument extends along the coast in both directions. Below to your left, the tiny picturesque cove you see earned a cameo in the "kiss in the sand" scene in *From Here to Eternity.* Beware of currents beyond the rim if you swim here. Just around the cove, the Halona Blowhole sprays a fine mist through a hole in the lava shelf, driven by incoming waves that fill a sea cave underneath.

Past the blowhole, the highway straightens as it descends to the flat coastline of ***Sandy Beach.*** The bodysurfing here is famous, but for experts only. Because of the steep slope of the beach, waves crash with spine-snapping force directly onto the shore, and the undertow from the backwash is fierce. Red flags mean stick to the sand. In the summer, when trade-wind swells build up, the surfing circuit migrates here for bodyboarding contests. Youngsters favor "Sandy's" year-round as the hangout of choice for sand, sun, and scoping. The windswept field next to the beach is popular for stunt kites.

Just ahead you might turn up Kealahou Street and take another left to visit the ***botanical gardens*** inside steep-walled Koko Crater. Known as Kohelepelepe ("the fringed vagina") to the ancient Hawaiians, the crater's resemblance to that portion of the female anatomy is explained by legend. It seems that the swinish pig-god Kamapuaa had been in

Makapuu Point

amorous pursuit of Pele. To distract him, Kapo, Pele's sister, threw her magically detachable vagina to O`ahu; its imprint remains on this spot. Notice that, as with Diamond Head, the higher southwestern walls reflect the direction of the trade winds when the crater formed. The garden inside mostly features xerophytic plants appropriate to the dry climate. Open daily 9:00 A.M. to 4:00 P.M.

After Kealahou Street, Kalanianaole Highway turns inland and climbs through a funnel-shaped valley between the edge of the Ko`olau Mountains and Makapuu Point. On your right, halfway up, look for a turnoff to a paved road with a locked gate. You can park here and hike 1.4 miles to the road's end at the scenic ***Makapuu Lighthouse*** at the eastern tip of the island. It's a great place to watch whales in winter.

You get a lesser version of the same view from the lookout farther ahead on the highway. Take a deep breath as you approach the top. More than half the windward coast unfolds before you, bordered by the bluest of ocean. From this side-on perspective, it's easy to trace the boundaries of the original 5,000-foot volcano that formed this half of the island. Instead of ending at the vertical wall of the windward cliffs, picture the Ko'olau ridges continuing to rise to a summit peak hovering somewhere above the present coastline and then descending roughly symmetrically on the other side. The line of islands dotting the coast offshore formed as rift eruptions along the outer flank of this now-vanished mountain.

Anchored in the blue waters closest to the lookout, Rabbit and Turtle islands are the southernmost members of this chain of offshore islands. The larger of the two, Rabbit Island got its name from a rabbit farm that once flourished on its scrub-covered slopes. Appropriately, the island's shape resembles the profile of a giant rabbit's head swimming offshore. Walk a little ways onto Makapuu Head for a better view along the coast. Notice the many rounded boulders here, garlanded by tiny orange blossoms of *ilima* scrub. These are river stones. The hanging valley you just drove up was gouged by an ancient river that drained the slopes of the mountain that was.

The highway descends from the lookout to picturesque ***Makapuu Beach.*** The waves here outdo even Sandy's and funnel into the cliff-ringed bay year-round. Surfers of all kinds come here, but inexperienced swimmers should stay out of the water. Look up to the sky to see the black *iwalani* ("bird of heaven") frigates that circle effortlessly above, watching for fish. These winged pirates often steal the catch from other birds. Trade winds running into the wall of the Ko`olau cliffs create a constant updraft that hang gliders also can enjoy. Launching from the clifftop, these daring flyers have set endurance records at this spot.

Across the road from the beach park, Sea Life Park (259–7933) operates a popular Sea World–type attraction. Open daily 9:30 A.M. to 5:00 P.M.

A couple miles farther on Kalanianaole Highway, you reach ***Waimanalo Beach,*** a magnificent strand that stretches more than 3 miles around the gentle curve of Waimanalo Bay. The city and state beach parks here are

The Case of the Missing (Half) Island

One of the most striking features of O`ahu is its Ko`olau Mountain pali, *a wall of sheer cliffs that extend along half the island from Waimanalo to Waikane. Rising more than 3,000 feet at their highest point, the* pali *dominate the landscape of the southern windward coast. Their characteristic fluted indentations add an element of delicate beauty to the drama of their near-vertical slope.*

This sheer cliff face stands in marked contrast to the gently sloping ridges of the Ko`olau Mountains' leeward slopes, which reach like so many fingers toward the coastal settlements of Honolulu with deep valleys etched in between. Trails leading up these ridges to a pali *overlook offer some of the island's most dramatic vistas. But what accounts for this very different topography on either side of the same mountain mass? Originally, the Ko`olau—along with most of the island—formed as a single volcano with roughly symmetrical edges. The summit of this ancestral volcano, which once reached perhaps 5,000 feet in elevation, was centered above the windward coast, roughly where Kailua and Kaneohe are today. Somehow, a huge chunk of this island mass disappeared along its southern windward edge, leaving only the leeward slopes whose abrupt end at the* pali *bears witness to a now-vanished mountain.*

As to that much, the geological evidence is clear. The chain of islands dotting the windward coast offshore mark the outer edges of where the Ko`olau Volcano once stood. Geologists tried to account for this disappearing mountain by relying on the normal forces of erosion—the constant tradewinds that

(continued on the following page)

lined with ironwood trees and both are popular with weekend picnickers. Waimanalo Beach does get waves, but an offshore reef provides some protection. Its shallow waters offer an ideal learning ground for bodysurfing and boogie boarding.

As you move north, the Ko`olau cliffs grow taller and more lush as they recede from the shoreline. The interior plains area of Waimanalo is mostly farms run by Hawaiian homesteaders. Signs advertising accommodations here are for horses. Turn up any country road and you'll see pig farms, equestrian stables, and fruit and vegetable gardens galore.

Farther on, ***Honolulu Polo Club*** takes to the field on the inland side of the road every Sunday at 2:00 P.M. from May to October. Listen for the thunder of hooves. As the highway continues, it skirts the green peaks of ***Mount Olomana*** ("forked mountain"). Rising 1,643 feet from flat surroundings, this daggerlike spire often splits the clouds.

On the other side of Olomana, Kalanianaole Highway runs into Kailua *weather the windward side—the ocean waves that tear against the coast. The problem was that O`ahu is simply not old enough (geologically speaking) for these slow-moving forces to have carved away that much rock in such a short time. It was a mystery.*

A decade ago, however, an unmanned navy submarine made a remarkable discovery. Operating in very deep waters many miles off the coast of O`ahu, the sub was searching for the "black box" flight recorder from a downed airplane. The sub's sonar revealed a strange accumulation of debris—giant boulders, rubble, etc.—piled along the ocean floor. Subsequent investigation revealed that this debris had the same geologic composition as the Ko`olau Mountains. The stuff down there had come from up above.

Scientists calculated that for so many tons of rock to have traveled so far and so deep offshore, it had to have been moving very, very fast to have built up enough momentum. This discovery led to a new explanation for the formation of the pali. *Geologists now believe that somehow half of the island all at once took a cataclysmic plunge into the sea.*

It turns out the Ko`olau* pali *are not the only example of such massive island-wide landslides. The sea cliffs along the north shore of Kaua`i and Moloka`i also appear to have formed in similarly abrupt fashion. The impact of so much rock crashing into the ocean all at once gave rise to some amazing splash waves. Scientists have traced a massive prehistoric tsunami that flooded the island of Kaho`olawe up to the 500-foot level to one such monster landslide along the Big Island's Kona coast.

For young islands, Hawaii's geologic history has been anything but dull.

Road opposite Castle Hospital. A right turn takes you past ***Kawainui Marsh,*** a waterfowl sanctuary, into Kailua Town. Continue through the town until you dead-end into Kalaheo Road, which runs along the coast. Turn right to get to ***Kailua Beach Park.*** Curving around from Mokapu Peninsula, Kailua Bay shelters its turquoise waters behind an outlying reef, where turtles are common. Flat (Popoia) Island floats offshore, but it's a long swim out. Sun worshipers delight in the fine white sand of Kailua Beach, and the onshore winds and calm seas make ideal learning conditions for windsurfing. But when the wind kicks up, the same onshore breezes turn the beach into a desert sandblast and whip the bay into a frothy mass of whitened chop. That's when Robby Naish, Kailua resident and eight-time world-champion windsurfer, rigs up. You can rent equipment or arrange lessons at ***Naish Hawaii*** (262–6068), the Naish family shop on Hamakua Drive (the first cross street as you enter town on Kailua Road). The windward coast is also ideal for kayaking, as both Kailua and Kaneohe Bay have numerous islands and sandbars to paddle to. The view from the water looking back at the Ko`olau Mountains is unsurpassed. You can rent equipment from ***Twogood Kayak*** (262–5656) at 345 Hahani Street. The more adventurous can go tandem paragliding with an instructor for $150, or kite surfing with an instructor for $15 an hour. These services are offered by ***Gravity Sports*** (261–7873) at 767B Kailua Road.

If you continue east from Kailua Beach around the tip of Puu Halo Ridge, you enter Lanikai, a secluded residential area ringed by mountains and blessed with azure waters that beckon toward a distant pair of island peaks, the Moku Luas. Park and walk up any beach access path. If you come here at night during summer, you might see glow-in-the-dark plankton wash ashore, miniature phosphorescent specks that sparkle in the sand.

You can scale Kaiwi Ridge behind Lanikai for breathtaking coastal vistas. Turn up Kaelepulu Drive and pass the turnoff to the country club. The trail begins just before the entrance to the Bluestone Estates, starting from a driveway off to the left and running outside the wire fence of the estates. After the first hundred feet you get on top of the ridge, and the views get better and better. You'll pass some military bunkers higher up. The ultimate panorama arrives with the second bunker about a half-mile along.

If you linger to catch the sunset, you might end your day with a steak dinner or fresh grilled fish at ***Buzz's Original Steakhouse*** (261–4661). Resembling an oversized treehouse, with a *hau* tree growing through the roof, Buzz's sits directly across the street from Kailua Beach Park. Ask for the table where Bill and Hillary dined. Open daily 11:00 A.M. to 3:30 P.M. and 5:00–10:00 P.M.

Other Kailua eateries cluster in town, near the main commercial intersection between Kailua Road and Oneawa Street. One block seaward at 30 Aulike Street, ***Baci Bistro*** (262–7555) serves fresh-made pasta and other Italian staples in an inviting, covered lana`i. Open Monday–Friday 11:30 A.M. to 2:00 P.M., nightly 5:30 to 10:00 P.M. On the other side of Oneawa, ***Casablanca*** (262–8196), at 19 Hoolai, belies its name with a cheerful blue exterior. Inside you'll find exotic Moroccan cuisine served Monday–Saturday 6:00–9:30 P.M. If you're in town before 6:00 P.M., be sure to stop at ***Agnes Portuguese Shop*** (262–5367), at 46 Hoolai, to sample ethnic specialties including bean soup, sweetbread, and hot *malasadas* (a kind of donut). The *malasadas* are made fresh to order—yum! Closed Monday.

To spend the night in Kailua, you can't beat the value offered by ***Kailua Beachside Cottages*** (262–4128; pats@aloha.net; www.10kvacationrentals.com/pats). Several units abut Kailua Beach Park (three have ocean views). The rentals range in price from $65 to $500 for an oceanfront unit right on the water. Three-night minimum. Over in Kaneohe ***Alii Bluffs B&B*** (235–1124; 800–235–1151; www.hawaiiscene.com/aliibluffs; donm@lava.net) offers two rooms for $60–$70 in a home full of Old World antiques and original oil paintings, overlooking the bay. Otherwise, ***Hawaiian Islands Bed & Breakfast*** (261–7895; 800–258–7895; www.lanikaibb.com) has the local B&B market pretty much cornered with almost a hundred listings in the area. Rooms with private baths start at $45.

Backtrack on Kailua Road past Castle Hospital. A mass of green mountains surrounds the road. Mount Olomana juts out on the left, with the Oneawa Hills to the right. Straight ahead, the corrugated cliffline of the Ko`olau *pali* march forward with Puu Konahuanui, the highest peak at 3,150 feet. To the right, the deeply notched V of Nuuanu Pass stands out.

To call it a day, continue straight on the Pali Highway and return through the pass into town. Those undeterred by Olomana's jagged profile can attempt the ascent from this side. The climb takes about one-and-a-half hours. The view is fabulous. To reach the start of the ***Olomana Trail*** from the highway, take the first left after the hospital, then turn left again immediately and bear right after the bridge. Otherwise, to continue circling the island, turn right onto Kamehameha Highway, a mile farther. This road cuts behind the Oneawa Hills to reach Kailua's next-door neighbor, Kaneohe.

Two miles along, past the elementary school and just before the Windward Mall, turn left at Luluku Road for a restful visit to ***Hoomaluhia*** ("peaceful place") ***Botanical Garden*** (233–7323). The road climbs into the lush Ko`olau foothills through banana farms at the edge of the park. Encompassing 450 acres of former farmland, the county's newest botanical park remains more of a forest reserve than a landscaped garden. The towering curtain of *pali* overhead creates a magnificent natural setting, while the thirty-two-acre artificially created lake provides the flood protection buffer that led to the park's creation.

Stop at the visitor center a mile from the park entrance to pick up information on the park's offerings and take in some exhibits on Hawaiian ethnobotany. From here you can drive the 2 miles of winding road past endlessly varied vegetation, with views of Kaneohe Bay and the hypnotic presence of the *pali* above. For those willing to walk, a number of trails meander through the gardens. Various sections have been planted with specimens from Africa, India, tropical America, Polynesia, and

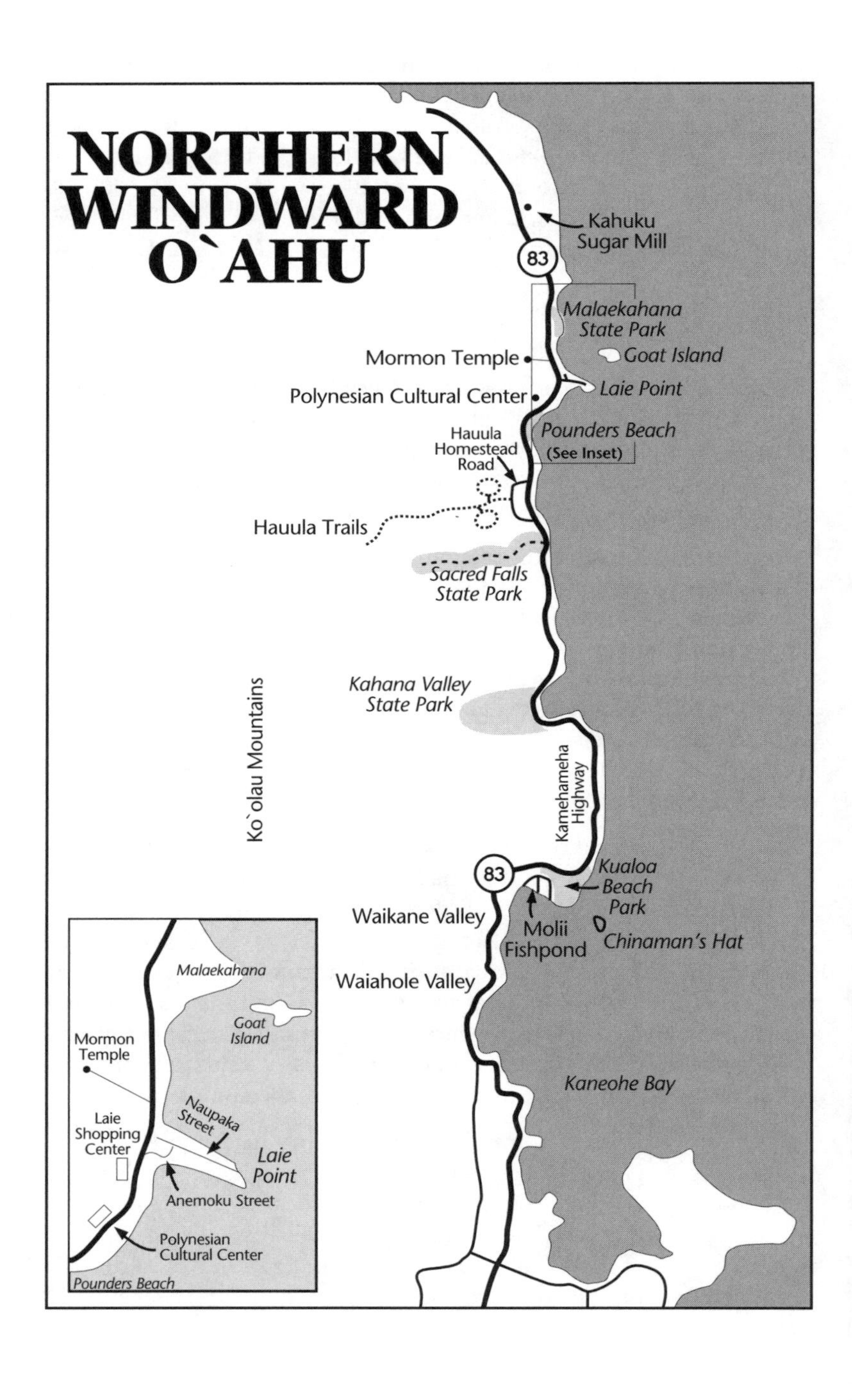
NORTHERN WINDWARD O`AHU
Kahuku Sugar Mill
83
Malaekahana State Park
Mormon Temple
Goat Island
Laie Point
Polynesian Cultural Center
Pounders Beach
(See Inset)
Hauula Homestead Road
Hauula Trails
Sacred Falls State Park
Kahana Valley State Park
Ko`olau Mountains
Kamehameha Highway
83
Kualoa Beach Park
Waikane Valley
Molii Fishpond
Chinaman's Hat
Waiahole Valley
Kaneohe Bay
Malaekahana
Goat Island
Mormon Temple
Naupaka Street
Laie Shopping Center
Laie Point
Anemoku Street
Polynesian Cultural Center
Pounders Beach

Hawaii. Ask the staff at the visitor center for free self-guiding pamphlets. The garden schedules a variety of walking tours, usually on weekends, as well as evening moonwalks. Camping allowed by advance permit Friday–Sunday. Open daily 9:00 A.M. to 4:00 P.M.

After relaxing in Hoomaluhia, those continuing onward have to make a difficult choice. Two different routes will take you north. If you like ocean views, stick with Kamehameha Highway. You'll wind through residential gardens past stunning ocean vistas. You can stop at ***Heeia State Park*** (247–3156) at the beginning of the coastal stretch to learn some of the history of the area. Friends of Heeia staff the visitor center Monday–Friday 8:00 A.M. to 4:30 P.M. The park itself juts onto Kealohi Point in the middle of Kaneohe Bay, the largest in the state. Coconut Island, the biggest of many offshore islands in view, appeared on television as *Gilligan's Island.* To the right of the point, you can see Heeia Fishpond, one of several ancient ponds along Kaneohe Bay.

If you prefer the majesty of mountains, turn left at the main intersection at the end of the mall. From here, Likelike Highway tunnels back to Honolulu. To stay on the windward side, take the next right onto Kahekili Highway to continue north in the shadow of the Ko`olau *pali.* A left turn on Haiku Road, at the fourth traffic light, leads you to Haiku Gardens, where ***Hale`iwa Joe's*** (247–6671) serves pleasant, open-air dinners for moderate prices. Farther along you'll pass the ***Valley of the Temples,*** an interdenominational mortuary park and the late Ferdinand Marcos's temporary resting place. The Byodo-In Temple at the back is particularly picturesque. Token admission charge. The eyesore you see in the misty depths of Haiku Valley is H–3, a newly opened and highly controversial trans-Ko`olau route.

The two highways reunite at Kahaluu Fishpond. To visit the secluded ***Gallery & Gardens*** (239–8146), at a nearby mountain retreat, take the second left onto Wailehua Road, and then bear right on Lama`ula Road and head up the hill. The experience is akin to a multicourse banquet of the senses. More than fifteen years of botanical plantings enhance the already beautiful natural setting, with exotic flowers to smell and seasonal fruits to taste. Ask to try "magic fruit" (sepotia berry), which turns sour tastes to sweet. Bird songs from the aviary and wind chimes provide soothing melodies. The architecturally intriguing, Japanese-style gallery blends well with the beautiful artwork it contains. Open Saturday, Sunday, and Monday 10:00 A.M. to 5:00 P.M., or by appointment.

Around the next ridge are Waiahole and Waikane valleys, havens for rural Hawaiians, with backyard taro and sweet potato patches. The demise of

O`ahu's sugar industry has freed up irrigation water for these traditional crops that used to be diverted to the leeward side of the island. At the corner of the Waiahole Valley Road, the rickety wooden 1904 ***Waiahole Taro Factory*** is back in business. They make poi on Thursday night and sell it fresh with Hawaiian plate lunches on Friday from 10:00 A.M. to 2:00 P.M. Note the traditional poi pounder mounted near the factory sign.

The highway leaves the valleys to slope along hills where cattle graze. As you begin to curve around the northern edge of Kaneohe Bay beneath the imposing Kanehoalani Ridge, look through the forest on the right-hand side to catch glimpses of ***Molii Fishpond,*** the only pond on the island in continuous operation since ancient times. Its harvest includes mullet, *moi,* and tilapia.

At the far rim of the bay, pause for a scenic break at ***Kualoa Beach Park.*** *Wiliwili* trees, flaming red in late winter, line the entry road. A narrow sandy beach with adequate swimming borders the long grassy park. The views back around the bay and inland along the Ko`olau wall are breathtaking. Note the turtle shape of Kaneohe peninsula—the other side of the bay—now well in the distance. Gates are locked at night here for secure camping.

Kualoa has a long history as one of the most sacred spots on the island. O`ahu chieftains brought their children here to learn the necessary arts with which to rule. Passing canoes had to lower their sails out of respect. Offshore, Chinaman's Hat bears a close resemblance to the headgear of Chinese immigrants. Hawaiians call the island Mokolii, meaning "little dragon," because their legend says the island is really the tail of a dragon that the goddess Hiiaka slew during her trip back from Kaua`i. People do wade out to the island at low tide, but you need footwear to walk on the sharp coral and you may have to swim some of the way. It's about 500 yards out.

Continue along the highway past the smokestack of an 1864 sugar mill. As you round the tip of Kanehoalani Ridge, brace yourself, because in the miles ahead your eyes will struggle with divided loyalties. On the ocean side, a series of picturesque bays beckons. In the sun's golden light, these shallow lagoons shimmer like liquid jewels of turquoise, sapphire, and emerald. On the mountain side, you peer into virgin green valleys bordered by steep cliffs. You'll want a third eye to negotiate the bends in the road! A string of hamlets spaces out the scenery. You can stop at any of the beach parks along the way for a dip. During the week, your only company may be a few fishermen casting bamboo poles or throw-nets from the reef.

About 3 miles along, the road curves around the deep indentation of Kahana Bay. Pass some overgrown fish ponds and turn left into ***Kahana Valley State Park.*** Extending inland the length of the valley, this is the only publicly owned *ahupuaa* in the state. *Ahupua`a* were the old wedge-shaped land sections that ran from the top of the mountains down to the sea, making each community self-contained in the raw materials needed for everyday life. Kahana Valley still contains about thirty-one families whom the state has incorporated into a "living history" program to teach schoolchildren about the valley's heritage. You can turn up the road to the park orientation office and chat with the staff, if anyone is in. If not, obtain a trail map for a valley hike from a rack outside, or take a swim in the stream mouth or ocean. The many tall trees with red-tinged leaves around here are known as false *kamani,* or tropical almonds.

Past Kahana Bay in Kaaawa, look for the 1921 federal flatbed truck parked in front of ***Ahi's Restaurant*** (293–5650), a funky green bamboo cantina. The menu at this longtime family-owned eatery is standard local American, with tasty shrimp specials. Grab a table out back to enjoy the mountain views. Open Monday–Saturday 11:00 A.M. to 9:00 P.M.

Four miles farther, ***Sacred Falls State Park*** offers one of the most popular hiking trails on the island. It's a fairly easy 2.2-mile hike into a narrow canyon. You have to cross the stream a few times to reach the 87-foot falls at the top. In summer, look for mountain apples, Hawaii's only native fruit. They look like small, wax apples but taste more like pears. The pig-god Kamapua`a supposedly haunts this valley. You might do as locals do and wrap a *ti* leaf around a rock as a peace offering. Flash floods and falling rocks do happen, so it doesn't hurt to have the gods on your side. You can swim in the pool under the falls and picnic on the rocks. Just don't bring a ham sandwich! Apparently someone did, because seven people were killed by a rockslide in 1999; at press time the park remained closed indefinitely. Call 587–0300 to inquire. As you leave the park, smile at the "Old Hawaiian Church" nearby.

About a mile up the road, next to the 21-mile marker, you'll see the ruins of Lanakila Church next to its replacement. If you turn up Hauula Homestead Road and then continue a few hundred yards straight ahead on the unpaved Maakua Road, you'll reach the heads of three less-traveled trails. You can choose from a scenic 2.5-mile loop up the ridges on either side of the valley on the Hauula and Papali trails, or hike and rock-hop 3 miles upstream to a small waterfall pool at the back of ***Maakua Gulch.*** From there, ropes lead to a series of larger pools and falls.

Past the 20-mile point, ***Pounders Beach*** has a lovely setting and bodysurfing waves that live up to its name. Next comes the overwhelmingly Mormon town of Laie. You'll see the thatched roofs of the ***Polynesian Cultural Center*** (293–3333) run by the church on your left. Authentically re-created villages from the major Polynesian islands are "populated" by Polynesian students attending the nearby Hawaii campus of Brigham Young University. It's fairly educational but definitely geared to tourists. Admission is $27. Open Monday–Saturday 12:30–6:00 P.M. If you visit the center, consider returning at 7:30 P.M. for the Polynesian revue, which has a cast of more than 100 performers. Admission to the Center and dinner show is $49.

Past the cultural center, opposite Laie Shopping Center, turn right onto Anemoku Street and then right again on Naupaka Street to the tip of ***Laie Point.*** A magnificent view awaits at the end of this narrow peninsula. You can see the green mass of the Ko`olau Mountains stretching as far back as Kaneohe. Waves crash against the many islets offshore, one of which has a natural *puka* (hole) gouged through its middle. Anglers cast their lines into the teal-colored sea. As you continue north on the highway, gaze back along the stately drive that leads to the ***Mormon Temple,*** the self-styled "Taj Mahal of the Pacific."

Malaekahana State Park, a mile farther, enjoys a truly idyllic location. Deep deposits of white sand are piled along this mile-wide bay. The steep hills backing the beach offer shade from beautifully diverse forest. If you wade a few hundred yards through the shallow waters, you'll reach ***Goat Island,*** a seabird sanctuary. You can explore the island perimeter with views along the coast, but don't disturb the nesting sites in the center.

The Kahuku section of the beach, accessed by a separate entrance, has some rustic cabins available for rent maintained by friends of Malaekahana; they rent for $60 on weekdays, slightly more on weekends. Call 293–1736 for information.

Beyond Malaekahana you enter Kahuku, a former plantation town largely settled by Samoans. The ***Kahuku Sugar Mill,*** which closed in 1971, still stands in the center of town. You can ogle its innards in a free self-guided tour. The flywheels, crushers, clarifiers, and myriad connecting pipes are all color-coded in bright paint. When operational, the mill could churn through fifty tons of fresh cane an hour, burning the leftover bagasse for power. Gift shops and restaurants crowd the machinery in the factory center, taking the edge off the heavy industrial atmosphere.

You'll also notice some roadside shrimp stands, which, until recently, sold shrimp from local aquafarms. A disease wiped out those ponds' stock, but cultivation may resume in the future. Just ahead, the Tanaka Plantation Store complex is home to ***The Only Show in Town*** (293–1295)—for antiques, that is. The tiny store is crammed with antique bottles, vintage campaign buttons, classic aloha shirts, and much more. Open daily 11:00 A.M. to 5:30 P.M. The highway continues around the northern tip of the island, but it runs inland and you hardly notice the bend. Windmills on the ridge above the highway make up an experimental energy project.

North Shore and Central O`ahu

As you begin to curve south away from the windward coast, the hills get closer to the shoreline and cattle graze in pasture. Suddenly, on your left, the surfing murals on the side of the Sunset Beach Store tell you that you've arrived at the North Shore—two words that excite the fantasies of surfers around the world. Forget about all of that Beach Boy-esque Californiana that Hollywood spawned in the 1950s. Surfing was born in the Hawaiian Islands, and the North Shore of O`ahu remains the supreme venue for the sport. Winter surf hits the north and west shores of all the islands, but Nature and her handmaiden, Geology, have conspired to make O`ahu stand supreme. All along this coast, incoming ocean swells, having traveled thousands of miles from storms off Alaska, reach the beaches and rise to form the most perfect tubes, the biggest breakers, and the ultimate surfing challenge in the world.

Winter surf typically lasts from November to April, during which time the professional surfing circuit descends in force. If your visit should overlap with a major competition, the spectacle is worth taking in. The hype and hoopla of big-time surfing—with its corporate sponsors, rock music, and bikini beach contests—electrify these normally sedate beaches. Competitors are judged on the size of the waves they catch, the length of their ride, and the "radicalness" of their maneuvers.

Most of the contests are held at Sunset Beach, which stretches for more than 2 miles of wide, steeply sloping sand. The different surfing breaks all along have names like Gas Chambers, Velzyland, and Banzai Pipeline. WARNING: At any place along the North Shore, when it's pumping, the waves can snap surfboards and spines. The backwash and undercurrent of these breakers can hold you underwater for up to five minutes. Needless to say, you shouldn't even walk near the shoreline. Even when the surf is down, currents pose a danger all winter.

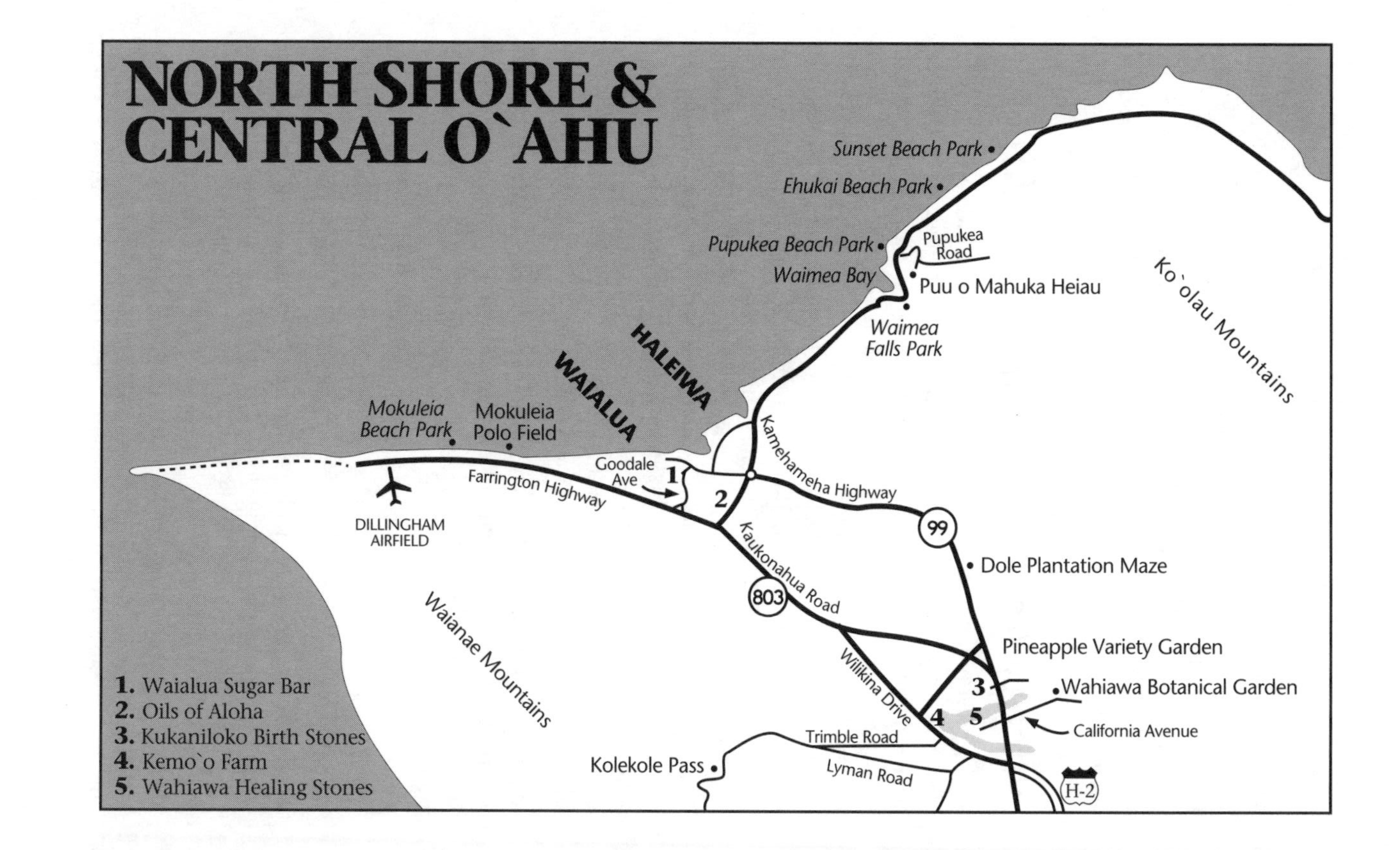
NORTH SHORE & CENTRAL O`AHU
Sunset Beach Park
Ehukai Beach Park
Pupukea Beach Park
Pupukea Road
Waimea Bay
Puu o Mahuka Heiau
Waimea Falls Park
Ko`olau Mountains
HALEIWA
WAIALUA
Mokuleia Beach Park
Mokuleia Polo Field
Goodale Ave
Kamehameha Highway
Farrington Highway
DILLINGHAM AIRFIELD
99
Dole Plantation Maze
Kaukonahua Road
803
Waianae Mountains
Pineapple Variety Garden
Wahiawa Botanical Garden
Wilikina Drive
California Avenue
Trimble Road
Kolekole Pass
Lyman Road
H-2
1. Waialua Sugar Bar
2. Oils of Aloha
3. Kukaniloko Birth Stones
4. Kemo`o Farm
5. Wahiawa Healing Stones

The ***Banzai Pipeline*** has a special notoriety as the home of the "world's most dangerous wave." As big swells rise from the deep into the sudden shallow of a coral shelf, their acceleration causes the top part of the wave to curl over into a tunnel of breaking fury that combs over waters only inches deep and filled with razor-sharp coral. On days when the surf swells above 15 feet, you will find but a handful of diehards willing to brave the "tube ride" off Banzai reef. To watch them cut and slash their way in, stop at Ehukai Beach Park, the second beach park along Kamehameha Highway, opposite the elementary school. The Pipeline breaks just to the left of the park.

By the way, you should know that Hawaiian wave heights are measured from behind. Because the water in front of a rising wave drops an equal amount, the waves will appear twice as high from the beach. It's quite a show.

In total contrast, during the summer, Sunset Beach, like all of the North Shore, transforms into a glassy lake. The expanses of white sand broaden as the beach reclaims sand carved away by the winter surf. At the end of the day, the placid waters reflect the unforgettable sunsets that are its namesake.

Beyond Sunset Beach the coastline turns rocky. Few people surf here, but ***Pupukea Beach Park*** has its own attraction. The waters offshore are a marine conservation zone. During calm summer months, Shark's Cove, at the north end of the park, offers especially breathtaking underwater terrain, flush with fish, seaweed, coral, and lava cave formations. Don't worry: "shark's" is a misnomer.

To the left of the cove is the site of a former rock quarry. An ancient coral reef has been excavated, leaving a horseshoe-shaped outer wall enclosing a shallow lagoon. During winter, huge waves flood the walls; as the water level inside rises, a swift current draining out to the cove can sweep the unwary off their feet. The sound and spray can be mesmerizing, but stay out of the water at these times.

Turn left up Pupukea Road at the Foodland supermarket, just past the quarry. Climb a half-mile uphill and take the turnoff on the right for ***Puu o Mahuka Heiau.*** Several speed bumps later, you reach O`ahu's largest ancient temple. The low, terraced walls slope in sections down a grassy field overlooking the angled coastline. In 1793 three British sailors from one of Captain George Vancouver's ships ended up as sacrifices here. Walk to the far side of the *heiau* to peer down into lush Waimea Valley and Waimea Bay. On the other side of the valley, cane fields cover the ridge plateaus.

Across the highway from "three tables" reef at the southern edge of Pupukea Beach Park, ***Backpackers Vacation Inn & Hostel*** (638–7838; backpackers@aloha.net; backpackers-hawaii.com) was started by Mike Foo, a local-boy-turned-surfing-legend. When Mike left to paddle his surfboard around the world, his sister Sharlyn took over operations and has expanded them considerably. In addition to a hostel bunk, you can rent private rooms, cottages, and apartments in the area—some are actually beachfront. For a unique experience, ask to stay in "plantation village," a lane of tiny clapboard homes formerly used by immigrant cane workers. The colorfully painted cottages offer a range of lodging options, from dorm beds for $17 to private units with kitchens from $45 to $55. Oceanfront studio apartments rent for $80–$100. South of Pupukea, ***Saints Peter & Paul Mission*** has a tall tower and an unusual origin. The church building was erected as a rock-crushing plant during the construction of the highway and only later was converted to a mill of a more spiritual nature. After passing the mission, the highway curves around the mouth of world-famous ***Waimea Bay.*** The island's highest rideable surf breaks on the bay's outer bowl, with monster combers that sometimes tower more than 30 feet. Expert bodysurfers tackle an equally daunting shorebreak. In the summer, calm returns as crystalline waters mirror the beauty of Waimea's picture-postcard setting. Then you can join locals in diving off "the rock" on the left side of the bay.

Inland from the bay, ***Waimea Valley Adventure Park*** (638–8511) spreads across the entire valley. If you want to get an idea what Puu o Mahuka might have looked like in ancient times, you can inspect the restored ***Hale o Lono Heiau*** near the parking lot free of charge. While nowhere as big as its neighbor up on the ridge, the structure includes a reconstructed oracle tower, offering stand, and drum house that are considerably more photogenic. If you pay admission to the park, you can explore other archaeological sites, including a reconstructed Hawaiian village. You can also try your hand at Hawaiian crafts and games, watch and learn hula, and explore the gardens whose thirty-six sections include more than six thousand species of plant life from the world over, including the only known specimen of *Kokia cookei,* a flowering tree of the hibiscus family. Narrated tram tours are included in the admission price, but it's nicest just to roam around on your own. At the back of the valley, cliff divers plunge 60 feet from the top of Waimea Falls in acrobatic displays, and visitors are welcome to swim in the natural pool below at other times. Open daily 10:00 A.M. to 5:30 P.M. Admission $24.

Past Waimea Bay, Kamehameha Highway continues through dairy

pastures past hidden surfing beaches. Ahead in the distance Haleiwa sits at the crook in the angle formed by the coastline. The highway turns inland as Kaukonahua Road. Haleiwa took its name from an early mission outpost here. It grew into a popular seaside resort when the Haleiwa Hotel opened at the end of the railroad line in 1899. Things quieted down after the war, but hippies and surfers brought the town back to life in the 1960s, and artists have made up the most recent wave of invaders. Many of the original plantation shops remain along the highway, nestled in between modern plazas full of boutiques. The town's commercial district stretches almost a mile.

If you didn't get to see surfing on the beaches, you might stop first before the bridge at ***Surf and Sea*** (637–9887), the biggest of the many surf shops in town. Continuous surfing videos inside offer a vicarious substitute. All the top brands of boards and designer beachwear are here, blazing with neon color. You can buy or rent all types of watersport equipment, as well as intriguing accessories like Dr. Zogg's Sex Wax (for your surfboard).

For more conventional surfing exhibits, continue into town to the ***North Shore Surfing Museum*** (637–8888) in the North Shore Marketplace. A variety of displays and memorabilia recount the story of how "Hawaii's gift to the world" became an international craze and icon of free-spirited youth. Open daily 9:00 A.M. to 7:00 P.M. To get there, cross the arching concrete bridge over the Anahulu River. The attractive ***Liliuokalani Church,*** on your left at the second cross street, was founded in 1832 and rebuilt in 1961. Queen Liliuokalani attended services here during her frequent vacations in Haleiwa. In 1892 she presented the church with an elaborate seven-dial clock that Queen Victoria had given her. Instead of numerals, the hour hand points to the twelve letters in Liliuokalani's name. You can still see it ticking today.

Across the street, ***Matsumoto's*** perpetuates another longtime Haleiwa tradition. This forty-year-old plantation store cranks out the most famous shave ice on the island, packed into paper cones. Choose from a range of tropical fruit–flavored cane syrups to sweeten your ice or ask for a "rainbow" of any three. Local connoisseurs eat theirs with sweet *azuki* beans or ice cream on the bottom.

For a more substantive repast, visit ***Cafe Haleiwa*** (637–5516) near the south edge of town, owned by Duncan Campbell, a noted surfboard designer. The surfing posters on the wall reflect the clientele who come by for an early morning feed before hitting the waves. The food's great, but the catch is that they close daily at 2:00 P.M. Farther down, ***Kua Aina***

Sandwich (637–6067) reputedly serves the island's best, including a hefty grilled mahimahi sandwich and great burgers. Open daily 11:00 A.M. to 8:00 P.M. Or, if it's a caffeine fix you crave, visit ***Coffee Gallery*** (637–5355) in the North Shore Marketplace. Order from an impressive collection of coffees grown on four different Hawaiian islands, and sip your java in a *très* funky painted/mosaic lana`i. If you want a sunset dinner to remember, double back to ***Jameson's by the Sea*** (637–4336) across from the harbor. The menu features fresh seafood among other items. But the real feast is the view from the second-floor tables as the sun drops behind Kaena Point, bathing the water and harbor sailboats in a rosy glow. Dinner is served nightly 5:00–9:00 P.M. Expensive.

Having catered to base needs like food and surfing, it's time for the finer things in life, namely art. Haleiwa has no shortage of galleries in which to browse. In the center of town ***Wyland's Gallery*** (637–7498) has the biggest name, though the artist's most famous works don't fit in his gallery. Robert Wyland paints giant murals of humpback whales around the world to promote marine conservation (and himself). Inside, you'll find works in various media by a range of artists revolving around a basic ocean theme. For women's clothing check out ***Oogenesis Boutique*** (637–4580), which features the work of Inge Himmelmann, a German fashion designer who's been working in Haleiwa since the hippie days.

After disporting yourself in Haleiwa, continue straight on Kaukonahua Road, past the rotary, following the sign to Mokuleia. About a half-mile farther, on your right, you'll pass the ***Oils of Aloha*** (637–5620) set up in a former movie house. The company is most notable for producing a unique line of cosmetics made from kukui nuts. The *kukui,* a relative of the castor bean, is Hawaii's state tree, whose versatile nuts had many uses in ancient times. The word *kukui* literally means "light"; the oil-rich nuts are known in English as candlenuts and were used as just that. The meat from the *kukui* nut also served as a potent laxative, and the shells were polished for jewelry. *Kukui* oil has useful skin care properties, and the nut company concentrates on this angle. A *kukui* tree grows right outside the nut company building, which unfortunately is not open to visitors.

Continue on Kaukonahua Road until it runs into Farrington Highway. Turn right, and then, a half-mile along, exit right from the rotary onto Goodale Avenue to enter Waialua. Waialua is Haleiwa's less glamorous twin across the bay. While Haleiwa has always been a resort and recreation center, Waialua has schlepped along as a working sugar town. Now that sugar has ended, its fortunes are uncertain, although a portion of former sugar land has been replanted with coffee. Because it's off the highway, few people come here. You'll see some vintage clapboard homes and the red-dirt-stained remains of the former mill.

Goodale Avenue intersects Kealohanui Street near the mill on the left. Turn right instead to imbibe the unique atmosphere of the ***Sugar Bar*** (637–2220). At first glance the neoclassical architecture and the inscription BANK OF HAWAII may mislead you. But people here prefer to drink with their money rather than bank it, so Peter Birnbaum, a German restaurateur, converted this abandoned building into a saloon. A sign near the entrance says NO LIFEGUARD ON DUTY, and it's that kind of place. Things get pretty rowdy here, especially on Sunday when the bikers roll in. But folks coexist peacefully enough. They have to—this is the only decent bar for miles. The tables outside face the cane fields. (One of them has toilet seats instead of chairs.) Open daily from 11:00 A.M.

Return to Farrington Highway and continue west through the cane fields. ***Mokuleia Beach Park*** arrives a few miles farther along, but the wide sandy beach stretches for miles on either side, and unmarked turnoffs from the highway allow you to find secluded spots. Swimming can be hazardous, especially during winter surf. If you think beaches are too down-to-earth, continue on to Dillingham Airfield where ***glider rides*** (677–3404) take off daily from 10:00 A.M. to 5:00 P.M. You pay $100 for a twenty-minute ride for one, $120 for two.

Mokuleia has a couple of attractive accommodation options for those who want to spend more time on the North Shore. The ***Hawaii Polo Inn's*** (949–0061, 800–669–7719; www.hawaiipolo.com, info@hawaiipolo.com.) beach cottage sits on a five-acre beachfront estate near the polo grounds. Decorated with polo club memorabilia from its years as a guesthouse for visiting polo players from the world over, the fully-equipped one bedroom cottage rents for $110 ($15 surcharge December–February). More spartan quarters can be had at ***Camp Mokuleia*** (637–6241), which offers bed-and-breakfast lodge rooms on a beachfront lot for $65–$75 per couple. ***Camp Erdman*** (637–4615; www.camperdman.net) has cabins for $80–$160. Both allow tent camping for a nominal fee.

The road ends at the start of ***Kaena Point Nature Preserve,*** a unique coastal habitat of endangered wildlife and plants. Kaena Point lies 2 miles farther, but the walk from the Waianae side is more scenic. Backtrack on Farrington Highway and continue on as the highway begins to climb onto the Leilehua Plateau between O`ahu's two mountain ranges. At a certain elevation you emerge from some trees, and *voilà*, something's changed. Instead of tall cane grass walling you in, you find

Sugar Bar

that your gaze stretches unobstructed across miles of spiky pineapple rows. James Dole introduced Hawaii's first commercial pineapples in nearby Wahiawa. Unlike sugar cane, the plants are not native, but thanks to Dole, they soon became an international symbol of the islands. You can still see heavily garbed workers stooped over the fields, planting and harvesting by hand.

Four miles along the highway, take the right fork 2 more miles to Del Monte's ***Pineapple Variety Garden*** to see all the unique forms these thorny bromeliads take. ***Dole Plantation*** (621–8408) has its own touristy visitors center, 1 mile angling back on Kamehameha Highway (Route 99), which includes the "world's largest maze" planted from hibiscus and other tropical flower bushes. Open daily 9:00 A.M. to 6:00 P.M. Small admission charge for maze.

If not, continue on 0.5 mile past the garden in the same direction, turn right at the traffic light onto an unpaved plantation road. A few hundred yards into the pineapple fields, you'll reach a tight ring of eucalyptus and palm trees encircling a cluster of largish boulders. Hawaiians called this curious oasis ***Kukaniloko,*** and women of royal descent came here to give birth so that their children would be born with the necessary *mana* to rule as kings and queens. If you look to the Waianae Mountains in the

Stone Age Magic

The ancient Hawaiians practiced a religion that was basically animist. They believed that everything in nature had a spiritual dimension that people needed to respect. Canoe builders would say a prayer before cutting down the giant koa *trees. Fishermen would leave offerings at fishing shrines to thank the ocean gods for its bounty. So it was with* pohaku, *the Hawaiian word for stone or rock.*

Even today in this modern age, stories still abound of farmers who clear giant boulders from their fields only to return the next morning and find the stones back in their original position. Hawaiians explain this by saying that the pohaku *"did not want to be moved." Certain* pohaku *were inhabited by powerful spirits whose influence men and women could elict through ritual offerings. For example, barren women would seek out fertility stones known to exist on each island, of which Moloka`i's phallic rock is the most famous example today. Travelers crossing over dangerous terrain would leave offerings at guardian stones, such as the giant boulder at Kolekole Pass. The sacred birth stones at Wahiawa's Kukaniloko provide yet another well-known example.*

Wahiawa is home to another set of somewhat more abscure pohaku, *the so-called Wahiawa Healing Stones, which have their own curious history. Although the stones have an ancient lineage, the origins of their healing powers remain shrouded in mystery. The stones came to the public's attention in the 1920s after some well-publicized miracles and, for a time, attracted mass pilgrimages, which continued until the outbreak of World War II.*

Although largely forgotten since then, the stones continue to attract visitors from diverse religious backgrounds. Housed in a makeshift cinderblock shrine of sorts, the stones had a statue of the Virgin Mary placed beside them for many years. More recently, the stones have been adopted by a group of local Hindus, who perceive one of the stones to be a Shiva lingam and another to bear the likeness of the elephant god Ganesh. The Hindu community has built a newer marble structure around the stones and visit on the morning of the third Sunday of each month to conduct pooja, *a ritual ceremony.*

If you would like to visit the stones, too, you can find them in Wahiawa town on California Avenue, 0.5 mile west of Kamehameha Highway (the opposite direction from the botanical garden), at the corner of Kaalalo Place just past the elementary school.

distance, you can trace a profile of the *wahine hapai* (pregnant woman) to the right of the V-shaped Kolekole Pass. Kamehameha I wanted to send his sacred wife, Keopuolani, to O`ahu to bear his first child at these birth stones, but she took sick and couldn't leave the Big Island. Some say Liholiho's early death at age twenty-six sprang from this inauspicious birth.

Continue on the same road, and you'll cross Lake Wilson, an artificial reservoir used for sugar irrigation, on your way into Wahiawa town. Wahiawa grew up as a plantation town, but its lifeblood today rests in the mammoth Schofield Army Barracks nearby as the countless fast-food and chain restaurants attest.

For a quiet picnic spot, turn left up California Avenue, the second cross street, and go about 0.5 mile to the ***Wahiawa Botanical Garden.*** Sugar planters began the twenty-seven-acre garden as an experimental forest growth in the 1920s. The mature trees now rise majestically from the slopes of a sunken ravine, leavened with ferns, palms, and other tropical plants. Open daily 9:00 A.M. to 4:00 P.M. Free.

South of town you can loop back around the lake to Schofield Barracks. Across the highway from the base, stop at ***Kemo`o Farm*** (621–8481) for a touch of local nostalgia. The farm got its start in 1916 with the valuable swill contract from Schofield and gradually expanded to include a market and a popular lakeside restaurant. The restaurant has changed ownership, but in the adjacent saloon you can see a shot taken of thirsty hordes awaiting Kemoo Farm's first shipment of beer after Prohibition. The bar today is better prepared; it stocks 130 kinds of lagers and ale.

To crown your Central O`ahu visit in spectacular fashion, enter the barracks and ask the guard to direct you to ***Kolekole Pass.*** (Lyman or Trimble Road will put you on the main road up.) You can see the deep notch in the mountains as you drive up. About 5 miles from the entry gate, you reach a parking area at the top. On your right, a tall white cross stands on a nearby hill facing back toward central O`ahu. A short hike in the opposite direction brings you to a spectacular overlook onto the Lualualei Valley on the Waianae Coast. It's less panoramic than the Nuuanu Pali, but at 1,720 feet the clifftop perch is just as exhilarating, and you may well have it all to yourself. Watch your footing, though; no handrails here!

On the way to the overlook, you pass ***Kolekole Stone,*** a massive boulder along the trail. An eroded basin on the top of the stone drained by curious troughlike ridges has given rise to some latter-day legends about gruesome human sacrifices. Actually, Hawaiian executioners dispatched their victims without bloodshed; a mangled corpse was not a fitting offering to place before the gods. An older, perhaps more comforting, tradition holds that the stone is inhabited by a guardian spirit that keeps watch over travelers crossing this lonely mountain pass. Kolekole Road continues over and down to the other side of the pass, but only military types can drive it.

Departing from the outskirts of Wahiawa and Schofield, the H–2 Freeway whisks you back to Honolulu. As you leave the central plateau, you see mountains on both sides, pineapple fields, steep gulches, and then suddenly the blue lochs of Pearl Harbor stretched out below.

Leeward O`ahu

Having done Honolulu and the "circle island" drive(s), it's time to "head Ewa," which is the local version of "go west" toward the Ewa District. Honolulu itself is moving this way. Having spread all the way east to Hawaii Kai, Honolulu has shifted course to ooze into the "Second City" of Leeward O`ahu (see map on page 112). Few tourists make it out here. Few rainclouds come this way, either. That's what "leeward" means (sheltered from the wind). All this land was originally scrubland, too arid even to support cattle. But underground, where the folds of the island's two volcanoes had overlapped, millions of gallons of fresh water waited to be tapped. In 1877 a canny Scotsman named James Campbell bought 40,000 acres of the "worthless" land and successfully dug a series of artesian springs that made him an instant millionaire. The sugar cane that once covered these lands is being replaced by diversified agriculture, although the biggest new crop is housing projects.

To the west of the modern Pearl City metropolis, the town of Waipahu grew up a separate plantation community. To explore, take the Waipahu exit from H–1 and get onto Farrington Highway. About 1.5 miles along, turn up Waipahu Depot Road toward the sugar mill.

At the mill turn left onto Waipahu Road, and just ahead on your left is ***Hawaii's Plantation Village*** (677–0110) surrounded by taro fields. You enter the park through a "time tunnel" to get to an authentically recreated nineteenth-century plantation camp inside. You can then wander through life-size dwellings representative of the many different ethnic groups that worked Hawaii's plantations.

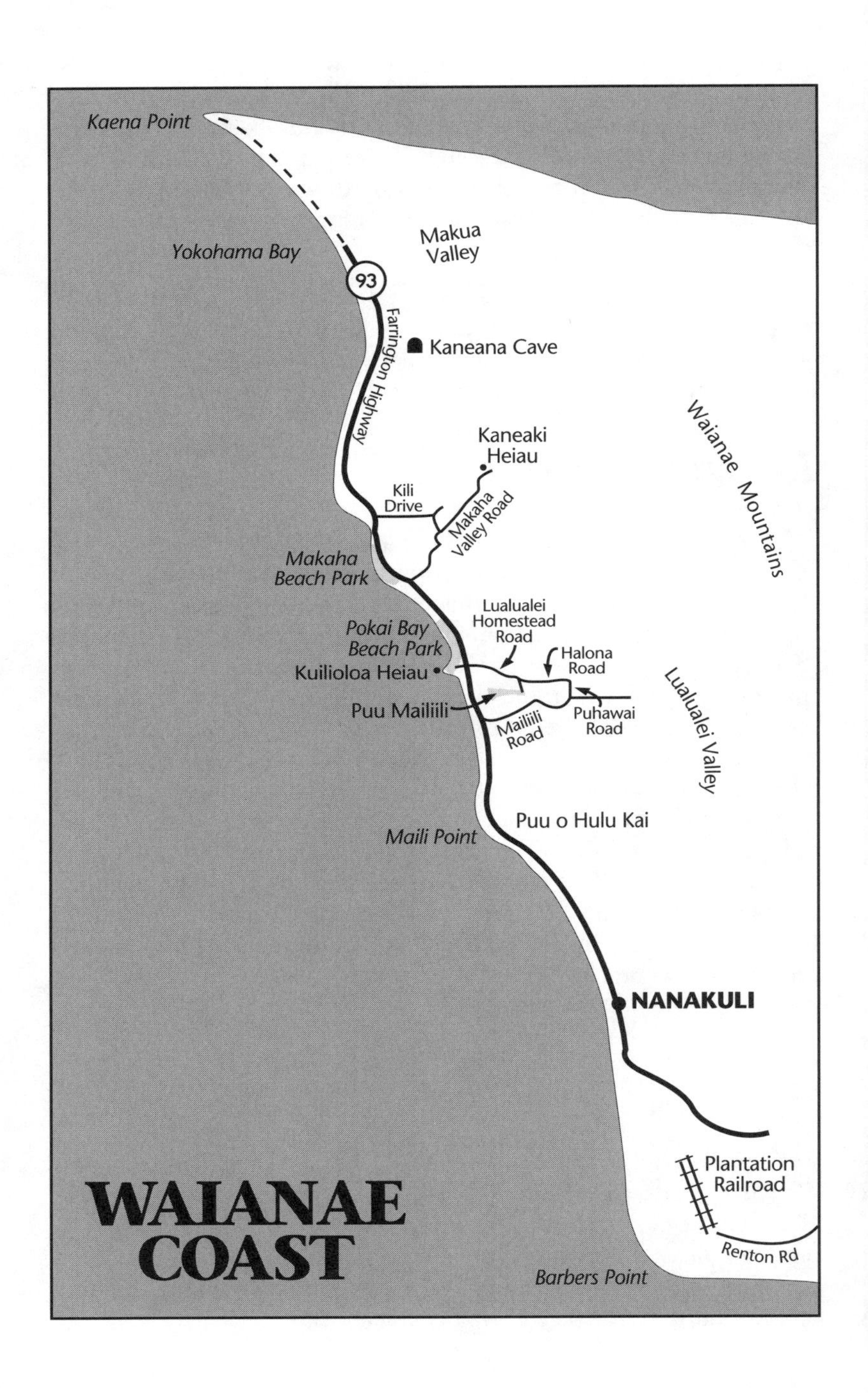
Kaena Point
Makua Valley
Yokohama Bay
93
Farrington Highway
Kaneana Cave
Waianae Mountains
Kaneaki Heiau
Kili Drive
Makaha Valley Road
Makaha Beach Park
Lualualei Homestead Road
Pokai Bay Beach Park
Halona Road
Kuilioloa Heiau
Lualualei Valley
Puu Mailiili
Mailiili Road
Puhawai Road
Puu o Hulu Kai
Maili Point
NANAKULI
Plantation Railroad
WAIANAE COAST
Renton Rd
Barbers Point

The garden organizers have acquired many unique items, such as an antique *tofu-ya,* used to grind bean curd in Kahuku, and the Inari Shinto Shrine, rescued from destruction in Moiliili. Some of the displays offer hands-on learning; others provide fascinating vignettes. Learn the folklore that guided immigrant women facing childbirth in a foreign land. Master a few phrases of "pidgin," the linguistic potpourri by which the different immigrant groups communicated. Inspect Filipino fish traps and Chinese herbal medicines. These are the ethnic threads that contribute to Hawaii's rich social tapestry today. Open Monday–Friday 9:00 A.M. to 4:30 P.M. and Saturday 10:00 A.M. to 4:30 P.M. Tours are offered on the hour until 3:00 P.M.; $7.00 admission.

Continue on Waipahu Street to Kunia Road (Route 750). A right turn here will get you back on H–1. If it's a Sunday, you may want to turn left for a historic train ride. Take Fort Weaver Road 2.5 miles, then turn right on Renton and drive until it ends at Ewa station of the ***Hawaiian Railway Society*** (681–5461). An old navy diesel locomotive hauls passenger cars on a ninety-minute round-trip every Sunday at 12:30 and 2:30 P.M. Along the way you'll hear the story of O`ahu's railway and plantation history. Adult admission is $8.00. Reserve ahead of time to travel in style on the "parlor car" for $15.

As you drive along the southern slopes of the Waianae Mountains, you gaze over a vast sunken plain that starts with Ewa cane fields and housing subdivisions and extends across Pearl Harbor all the way to Diamond Head. All this land rests on an enormous coral shelf formed at a time of higher sea levels. H–1 peters out as it rounds the bend of the mountains. Continue northwest on Farrington Highway to sidle up the shoreline of the Waianae (or leeward) Coast.

Sheltered behind O`ahu's tallest mountains, this dry coastal stretch provides refuge to Hawaiians clinging to a traditional rural lifestyle. Many are homestead farmers who received land grants through the Hawaiian Homelands Act. Almost everyone keeps a few pigs or chickens in their backyard, and subsistence fishing remains an important source of food. Extended families still gather for weekends on the beach.

Most tourists are put off by the region's lingering bad reputation. On the whole, you'll find the people here more overflowing with aloha spirit than anywhere else on O`ahu. Unfortunately, some residents (justifiably) feel that this open-hearted, giving nature has left them dispossessed of their land, and now they want to keep what's left to themselves. Visitors used to be a target for some of that resentment. The Waianae Coast has scenery rivaling the most beautiful in Hawaii, with miles of coral beach backed by rugged mountains that open into rural valleys. It would be a shame to miss. If you exercise common sense with valuables, maintain a low-key profile, and stay away from groups of drinking locals, you should have no problems here. WARNING: As with the North Shore, beaches along this coast are exposed to winter surf; swimming is often unsafe.

Farrington Highway meets the coast at the Kahe Point Power Plant. Ignore this monstrosity and instead gaze ahead to the majestic sweep of the Waianae Coast spread before you. The rocky headland of Maili Point dominates the arcing shoreline, with taller mountains silhouetted beyond. The beach park on your left bears the unofficial name Tracks because of the railroad tracks from former sugar trains that parallel the highway. Continue north past other beach parks through the town of Nanakuli, where you can peer into the remote depths of Nanakuli Valley. Near the north edge of town, you pass the ***Samoan Assembly of God,*** only one of the many picturesque churches along the way.

Beyond Nanakuli, Farrington Highway skirts the Puu o Hulu Kai, the headland at Maili Point, to reach the town of Maili. Here you get a frontal view into the staggering expanse of ***Lualualei Valley,*** the ancestral firepit of the Waianae Range. Two tall, red antennae near the mouth of the valley and a whole farm of smaller structures behind it make up the Navcom Radio Transmitting Facility for which the navy has sequestered most of the valley floor. Puu Mailiili, another headland, walls in Maili's northern limits. Consider turning onto Mailiili Road at the edge of town to circle inland around the hill past some homestead plots. You'll see dairy farms, vegetable plots, and more stunning valley scenery. Two miles in, turn left on Puhawai Road and left again on Halona. This will take you past some curious Quonset hut homes and back onto Lualualei Homestead Road to rejoin the coast.

Cross Farrington Road and continue straight onto Kaneilio Point at the southern tip of ***Pokai Bay Beach Park.*** Walk out on the peninsula through a coconut grove to ***Kuilioloa Heiau*** at the end. Built on three neatly terraced platforms, the *heiau* enjoys sweeping views along the coast. Pokai Beach, the beautiful sandy strip curving north behind the breakwater, offers the only winter-safe swimming on the Waianae Coast. It serves as a popular canoe-launching site. Inland, the rear wall of Waianae Valley rises to Mount Kaala, the 4,020-foot pinnacle of O`ahu.

As far as restaurant selection goes, the Waianae Coast features drive-ins galore, a handful of Chinese chop sueys, and not much else. This would be a good place to acquire a taste for a plate lunch, which dominates the menus here. Try the ***L&L Drive In*** (696–7989) near the entrance to the beach park for a wide selection of multiethnic entrees served with the standard two scoops of rice and macaroni salad. Open daily 6:00 A.M. to 11:00 P.M.

A worthwhile stop at the Waianae mall is ***Na Hana Lima*** (696–5462), an artisans' cooperative owned by Waianae Coast residents whose "working hands" (the store name) excel at a variety of traditional Hawaiian crafts. Open Monday–Saturday 9:00 A.M. to 5:00 P.M.

Continue north to Makaha, the next town and valley on Farrington Highway. The name Makaha means "savage," referring to a clan of highway robbers who long terrorized passersby. The savage predator today is resort development. At the rear of this steeply grooved valley lies ***Kaneaki Heiau,*** which has been reconstructed in a similar fashion to the one at Waimea Valley. To get there, take Makaha Valley Road inland, zigzagging left past the Sheraton Resort, then right on a road through the housing estate. Entry is permitted only Tuesday–Sunday 10:00 A.M. to 2:00 P.M.

Loop back along the north side of the Makaha valley on Kii Drive to ***Makaha Beach Park*** on the coast, where pro surfing began. Spectators flock to this wide crescent of steeply sloping sand every year for the Buffalo Big Board Surfing Classic in March. Competitors ride vintage "tankers"—long boards up to 12 feet long and weighing more than eighty pounds—as did the surfers of old.

Two miles farther, look for ***Kaneana Cave*** on the right side of the highway. The cave opening faces north, so you have to look behind you as you drive. Carved by wave action during a time of raised sea levels, the narrow, high ceiling of the cave slants 450 feet into the mountain flank. The cave's legendary denizen was a shark-man named Nanaue who used his dual nature to prey on unsuspecting victims in the area.

Just ahead the mountains recede, opening into the amphitheatral bowl of ***Makua Valley.*** This seemingly pristine valley harbors a deadly secret. The military has long used the area as an artillery range, and unexploded shells litter the valley floor. Across the highway, Makua Beach continues the pearly white lining of the Waianae coast. Farther up the road, the beach at ***Yokohama Bay*** marks the end of the highway. You can sift for tiny puka shells in the sand.

From here a rugged jeep trail continues 2 miles to Kaena Point. The Waianae coast curves majestically into view, stretching back as far as Kepuhi Point. On the way, you pass more caves. Look also for *ilima,* a native ground cover that thrives along the roadside. The tiny, pale-orange blossoms of the plant are O`ahu's official flower. Threaded by the hundreds, they form an unusual crepe-paper lei. Pregnant women used to chew the buds to stimulate their muscles during childbirth. Waves breaking near the point sometimes reach 40 feet during winter, a height unequaled anywhere else in Hawaii. During calmer summer months, the tidepools can be fun to explore.

Kaena Point itself is a narrow, sand-dune peninsula protruding from the tapered ridge of the Waianae Mountain Range. This westernmost promontory was another legendary "jumping off" place for the souls of O`ahu's fallen warriors. A coast guard observation tower stands at the far end of the point. If you climb the swaying ladder to the top, you can get an exquisite view of this desolate, windswept peninsula. Incoming waves, angling from both sides of the point, sweep across a string of rocks offshore. On a clear evening, this is also a great spot to watch for the elusive "green flash" that occurs when the sun sets over a cloudless ocean horizon. Shield your gaze until the instant when the last puddle of molten sun oozes out of view. Instead of orange sun, a brilliant spot of green light will shine for the briefest moment.

WHERE TO STAY

Manoa Valley Inn,
947–6019
at 2001 Vancouver Drive, off University Avenue. This three-story mansion exudes a wonderful historic air. Rates start at $99.

Royal Hawaiian Hotel,
2259 Kalakaua Avenue,
923–7311
(800) 343–9136. Although not exactly "off the beaten path," this pink palace is a landmark in Waikiki and the historical grandeur it possesses offers a unique type of luxury. Rooms start at $310.

Sheraton Moana Surfrider,
922–3111 or
(800) 325–3535,
in Waikiki,
is expensive and ultra-luxurious but definitely a place you'll remember. Built in 1901, it was restored to perfection and the Old World charm remains intact. Rooms from $265.

Kailua Beachside Cottage,
262–4128,
offers quiet retreats on the scenic windward side. Rates start at $65.

Hawaiian Islands Bed and Breakfast,
261–7895 or
(800) 258–7895,
has a humongous variety of rentals with more than one hundred listings in Kailua alone.

Backpackers Vacation Inn & Hostel,
638–7838,
on the North Shore near Waimea Bay,
offers great rooms close to all the surfing hot spots. Rates start at $45 for doubles.

Hawaii Polo Inn,
949–0061 or
(800) 669–7719,
a secluded cottage near Mokulei Beach on the North Shore; rents for $110 ($125 December–February).

WHERE TO EAT

Hau Tree Lana`i,
923–1555,
beachfront with unsurpassed views. It's situated at the far east end of Waikiki. Moderate prices.

Ono Hawaiian Food,
737–2275,
at 726 Kapahulu Avenue. *The* place on O`ahu to go for an authentic Hawaiian meal.

Alan Wong's Restaurant,
949–2526,
at 1857 South King Street, offers state-of-the-art Hawaii Regional Cuisine. Investment-caliber prices.

Maple Garden,
941–6641,
specializes in Northern Chinese dishes for moderate prices. It's at 909 Isenberg Street, near the corner of King Street.

Sam Choy's Breakfast, Lunch and Crab,
545–7979,
at 580 North Nimitz Highway, a cavernous brewpub with hearty fare in hefty portions. Expensive.

Buzz's Steakhouse,
261–4661,
across the street from Kailua Beach Park, surf 'n' turf menu makes a nice end to a day on the beach.

Roy's,
396–7697,
inventive East-West cooking in a raucous Hawaii Kai eatery. Expensive–investment-caliber.

Jameson's by the Sea,
637–4336,
brings sunset serenity to your North Shore sojurn. Expensive.

Located midway between the bustle of Honolulu and Lahaina, the island of Moloka`i clings to a seclusion that has long been its birthright. With a legacy of ancient sorcery and the stigma of its leper colony, Moloka`i's image as the "Lonely Island" was until recently reinforced by a declining population. Moloka`i likes to bill itself as the most Hawaiian of the visitable islands; almost half its inhabitants share native Hawaiian ancestry. From a visitor's viewpoint, Moloka`i also remains one of the least "spoiled" islands. It contains only one resort and a handful of smaller hotels. There are no traffic lights or shopping malls on the island. Instead, Moloka`i offers a laid-back atmosphere, a lingering glimpse of "Old Hawaii," and a low-key tourist industry conducted with a genuine warmth that has given Moloka`i its new nickname, the "Friendly Isle."

Moloka`i stretches 37 miles from end to end but no more than 10 miles in width. Three main highways partition its interior, making exploration fairly simple. The road east, Route 45, is named for Kamehameha V. Running to the west, Route 46 goes by the name of Maunaloa Highway. Branching north from the Maunaloa Highway, Route 47 provides the only access to the island's north shore. Moloka`i hides much of its scenery within a remote interior, inaccessible by road and often private property to boot. Most visitors will be content to spend a day or so exploring the roadside attractions in each direction. ***Budget*** (567–6877; 800–527–0700) and ***Dollar*** (567–6156; 800–800–4000) rent cars at the airport; reserve early for weekends. For a less-corporate alternative, ***Island Kine Auto Rental*** (553–5242; e-mail: fishin@aloha.net) has a mixed fleet of quality used cars, which they rent out of Kaunakakai town. Free airport pickup and personalized advice included. Island Kine also rents a limited number of four-wheel-drive vehicles.

Moloka`i Facts

Nickname:
"The Friendly Isle"

Dimensions: *38 x 10 miles*

Highest elevation:
Kamakou (4,970 feet)

Population: *6,745 (1995)*

Principal city:
Kaunakakai

Flower: *White Kukui blossom*

Color: *Green*

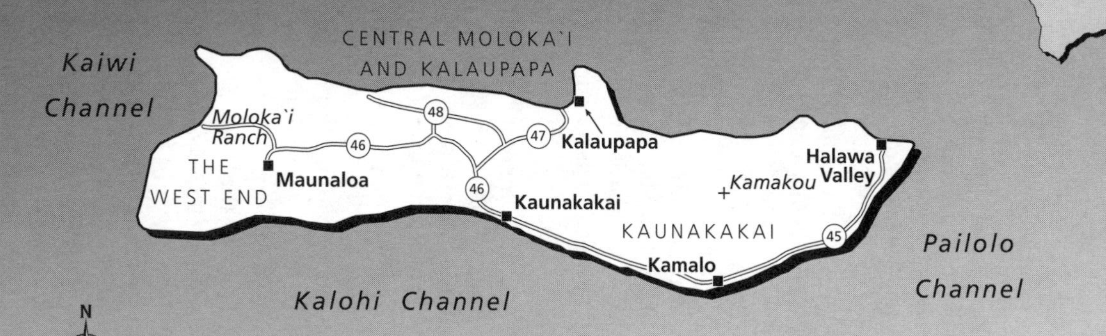
Moloka`i
PACIFIC OCEAN
CENTRAL MOLOKA`I
AND KALAUPAPA
Kaiwi
Channel
Moloka`i
Ranch
THE
WEST END
Maunaloa
48
46
47
Kalaupapa
Kaunakakai
KAUNAKAKAI
Kamakou
Halawa
Valley
45
Kamalo
Pailolo
Channel
Kalohi Channel

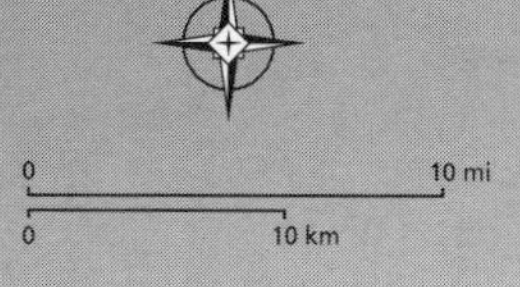
N
0
10 mi
0
10 km

For those who want to see more, two local residents offer their expertise and access to the action traveler. Alex Puaa's ***Moloka`i Off-Road Tours*** (553–3369) will take you four-wheeling. Walter Naki's ***Ma`a Hawaii*** (558–8184) has a number of guiding services, including hiking. His specialty is snorkeling, though: He will guide you through Moloka`i's reef environment, roust an octopus for you to play with, and, if you wish, spear fish for your dinner.

While planning your stay, contact the ***Moloka`i Visitor Association*** (553–3876, 800–800–6367, or interisland 800–553–0404), a publicity organization for the entire island.

Kaunakakai & Things East

Begin your sightseeing on Moloka`i by heading into town. Located midway along the island's south shore just off Route 45, the single-block business district of Kaunakakai comes as close to urban clutter as Moloka`i gets. The aging wooden storefronts have been described as Western, but the palm trees give the game away. Walking the strip along Ala Malama, the main drag, will put the rest of the island in perspective and get you in the right frame of mind.

Geography of Moloka`i

Fifth largest of the Hawaiian Islands, Moloka`i's elongated shape represents the union of two volcanoes with a third. Reaching a summit of 4,970 feet at Kamakou, the mountains of eastern Moloka`i are much taller and greener than arid western Moloka`i, whose highest point barely tops 1,000 feet. The cliffs along Moloka`i's largely inaccessible northern coast, from Kalaupapa east, soar to more than 3,000 feet in elevation, rising directly above the ocean. They are held to be the tallest sea cliffs in the world.

You will find most of the island's nonhotel restaurants here. All offer down-home local cooking at budget prices. Dining atmosphere not included. ***Big Daddy's*** (553–5841) offers a selection of authentic Filipino dishes, such as chicken papaya and pork adobo, as well as traditional Hawaiian *lau-lau.* For dessert ask for *halo halo* ("mix mix"). You will get a colorful parfait of shaved ice, fruit, gelatin, and sweetened milk that you then "mix mix." Open daily 10:30 A.M. to 4:00 P.M.

Kanemitsu Bakery (553–5855) produces a repertoire of island-flavored breads famous throughout the state, from onion-cheese to guava and mango. They bake every day but Tuesday. Nearby, ***Outposts Natural Foods*** (553–3377) offers a tropical juice bar from 10:00 A.M. to 3:00 P.M., closed on Saturday; both serve full meals as well. ***Oviedo's Lunch Counter*** (533–5014), another tasty Filipino kitchen hidden in dingy quarters, waits at the end of the strip; open daily,

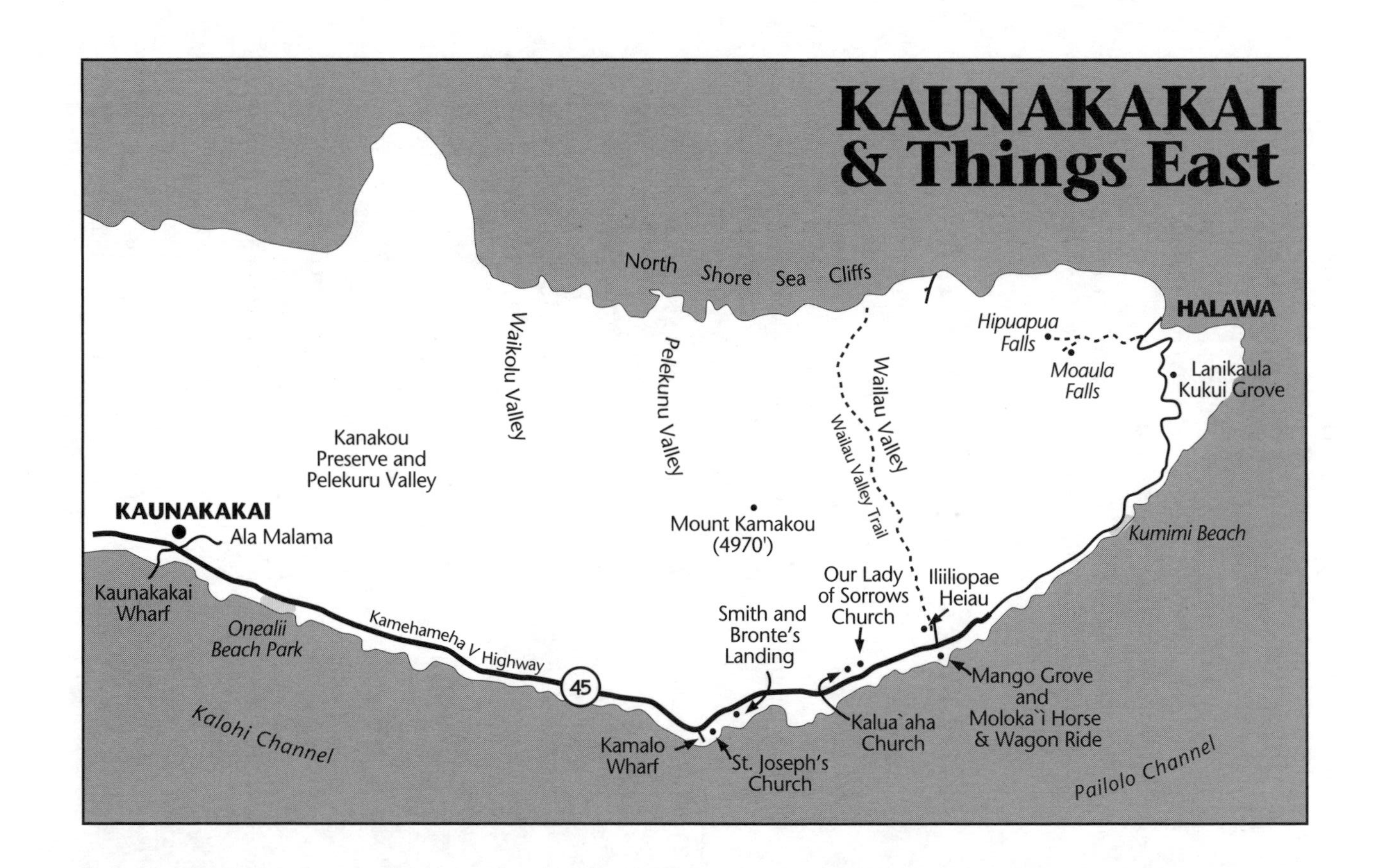
KAUNAKAKAI
& Things East
North Shore Sea Cliffs
HALAWA
Hipuapua Falls
Moaula Falls
Lanikaula Kukui Grove
Waikolu Valley
Pelekunu Valley
Wailau Valley
Wailau Valley Trail
Kanakou Preserve and Pelekuru Valley
KAUNAKAKAI
Ala Malama
Mount Kamakou (4970')
Kumimi Beach
Our Lady of Sorrows Church
Iliiliopae Heiau
Smith and Bronte's Landing
Kaunakakai Wharf
Onealii Beach Park
Kamehameha V Highway
45
Mango Grove and Moloka`i Horse & Wagon Ride
Kalua`aha Church
Kamalo Wharf
St. Joseph's Church
Kalohi Channel
Pailolo Channel

10:00 A.M. to 6:00 P.M. Meanwhile, across the highway on Wharf Road, ***Moloka`i Pizza Cafe*** (553–3288) fills another vital niche in the island repertoire; they also serve pasta, fish and chicken. At the end of Ala Malama, across from the baseball diamond, stands the Mitchell Pauoli Center (553–3204), where you can get camping permits to tent in county parks. The state issues its camping permits next to the post office in Ho`olehua town (near the airport).

It is worth driving to the end of ***Kaunakakai Wharf,*** where barges unload supplies from Oahu but no longer head out laden with pineapples. The wharf extends almost a half-mile offshore due to the shallow mud flats along this coast. As you savor the view of Moloka`i's southern shoreline and its three neighbors across the Kalohi Channel, you'll see why Mark Twain called Hawaii "the loveliest fleet of islands anchored in any ocean." From left to right are Maui, Kaho`olawe, and Lana`i. You may also see O`ahu rising in the distance above West Moloka`i. At the base of the wharf, the stone foundation behind the canoe club was the site of King Kamehameha V's summer retreat.

Moloka`i Trivia

- *The water reservoir in Kualapu`u holds 1.4 billion gallons and is the largest rubber-lined reservoir in the world.*
- *The highest sea cliffs in the world rise above Moloka`i's north shore.*
- *At one time, Moloka`i led the world in honey production, before disease damaged the hives.*

A number of fishing boats dock here (some available for charter), and anglers cast their lures right from the wharf. Thanks to ***Moloka`i Ice House*** (553–3054), a fisherman's cooperative at the wharf's end, you too can share in their catch. A deli counter inside showcases a variety of fresh-catch and seafood delicacies, including several different kinds of poke (island-style salads made with raw fish and seaweed). Open Monday–Saturday 10:00 A.M. to 6:00 P.M., Sunday 9:00 A.M. to 3:00 P.M.

About 1.5 miles east of Kaunakakai, the Polynesian rooftops of the ***Hotel Moloka`i*** (553–5347, 800–272–5275) appear on a cluster of low-rise bungalows facing the ocean. The simple, but recently refurbished rooms here start at $80, with rates rising to $135 for ocean views or kitchenettes. The real charmer of the property is the hotel restaurant (553–5347). Decorated in the nostalgic style of Old Hawaii, the dining area spreads across a large oceanfront lana`i with carved-*tiki* pillars, rattan paneling, and lava rock sidewalls. Plop yourself down in an oversized patio chair and gaze out through the palm trees to views across the Pailolo Channel. At night, *tiki* torches flicker in the ocean breeze as locals gather to hear live music from island performers. Menu choices here embrace an eclectic mix of steak, pastas, and seafood, with lunchtime sandwich choices. Preparations are simple, but tasty, and prices moderate. Open daily from 11:00 A.M. to 9:00 P.M., with breakfasts served weekends from 7:00–10:30 A.M.

Four miles east of town is ***Onealii Beach Park.*** The beach here is still muddy and flat, but it's a nice spot with coconut trees and the remains of a fish pond. These shallow, protected waters were ideal for such ponds, and more than sixty of them ring the coastline, some dating back as early as the thirteenth century. The Hawaiians were the only Polynesian people to practice aquaculture, building saltwater enclosures as big as football fields from coral and lava rock, with intricate sluice gates. Some of the ponds have been restored, and aquaculture is again becoming an industry on the island, restoring Moloka`i's reputation as the "land of the fat fish." Another thing being restored on the island is its population of native geese. If you call in advance, a visit to nearby ***Nene O Moloka`i*** (553–5992) will put you face to feather with Hawaii's state bird. This captive propagation site also has a collection of native plants and displays on migratory birds, but the stars of the show are the nene, "the most endangered goose in the world." Open weekday mornings at 9:00 A.M. by appointment; call one week in advance.

For an aerial view, take the next left up to ***Kawela Plantation,*** a new hillside housing division. As you climb, vistas extend along the south shore, revealing the outlines of several more fishponds fronting the deep cobalt blue of the channel seas.

Brief History of Moloka`i

While ancient Moloka`i's reputation for sorcery protected the island from marauders, the people of Moloka`i were skilled in other arts as well. As the legendary birthplace of the hula, both men and women excelled at this traditional dance form. Aquaculture was also practiced here to a greater extent than on other islands. Fishponds all along the south shore of the island ensured a reliable source of sustenance.

Modern history has been less kind to the island. The establishment of a leprosy settlement at Kalaupapa in 1864 made the island a byword for the horrors of that disease. The close of the pineapple plantations on the island in recent decades has left a legacy of economic hardship. Today almost 20 percent of the island's population remain unemployed, the highest rate in the state. Moloka`i residents remain stoic about their island's future. Having seen the social and economic dislocation caused by development on the neighboring islands, many prefer to keep Moloka`i the way it is.

The road ahead is rich in Hawaiian history in other ways as well. Kamehameha I landed on this coast near Kawela with an invasion force of canoes that was said to stretch over 4 miles. Slingshot stones from the fierce battle still litter the scrub-covered foothills. The conqueror's prize was a child bride. Keopuolani, one of Maui's highest-born chieftesses, had fled during Kamehameha's invasion of that island. By capturing and later marrying her, Kamehameha assured his heirs of the *mana* necessary to rule.

As you drive farther east, the mountains inland grow taller and the vegetation becomes more lush. Just after the 10-mile marker, where the highway makes a sharp veer to the left, take a dirt road turnoff to the right and drive out to the abandoned wharf at Kamalo. Absorb the views of the coast and the islands offshore, then gaze up at the mountains behind you. ***Mount Kamakou,*** the highest peak directly above, forms the pinnacle of the island at 4,970 feet.

Around the bend from ***Kamalo Wharf,*** on the ocean side, stands ***St. Joseph's Church.*** Built by Father Damien, the celebrated priest of Kalaupapa, in 1876, it is the second oldest church on the island. An often lei-draped statue of Damien greets visitors in front of the chapel. The door is rarely locked, so be sure to take a peek inside.

Continuing east on Kamehameha V Highway, you will pass (in addition to many more fish ponds) a wooden sign on the right indicating the site of ***Smith and Bronte's Landing.*** In 1927, these pioneering aviators abruptly ended the first civilian flight from the United States mainland to Honolulu when they ran out of fuel here after twenty-five hours in the air. Both survived the crash. A few miles farther on, a large wooden cross on the left marks the barnlike ruins of ***Kalua`aha Church.*** This first outpost of Christianity on Moloka`i was built by the original missionary congregation in 1844. The mission's location here reflects the original population center around the lusher east and north coasts. Two hundred yards farther, Damien's second church, ***Our Lady of Sorrows,*** built in 1874, stands in much better repair.

Moloka`i's eastern shore remains the population center for island B&Bs and vacation rentals. Most of these keep fairly full, so book early. One of the nicest is ***Kamalo Plantation*** (558–8236). Glenn and Akiko Foster also rent a B&B suite in their home for $75, plus a private studio cottage for $85. Their landscaped gardens include fruit orchards as well as a former *heiau* and a Hawaiian pony named Koko. In addition, the Fosters have recently acquired an oceanfront two-bedroom cottage farther east at the 20-mile-mark, which they plan to rent for $120. Other

Our Lady of Sorrows

rental options on the east end include ***Honomuni House*** (558–8383), ***Dunbar Beachfront Cottages*** (558–8153, 800–673–0520; molokai-beachfront-cottages.com), and ***Swenson Vacation Rentals*** (553–3648). The latter two have several properties, some oceanfront. Finally, ***Pu`u o Hoku Ranch*** (558–8109) rents a two-bedroom cottage, about 25 miles out, surrounded by acres of open ranch land and forest, with great hillside views. The simply furnished, but fully equipped rental is a steal at $85.

Past the 15-mile marker, the highway passes a giant mango grove. Reputedly the world's largest, the patch features thirty-two different varieties of these prolific fruit trees spread over forty-nine acres. It was planted in the 1930s by Hawaiian Sugar as an experimental venture. To meet the new owners, follow the roadside sign up a driveway to the ***Moloka`i Horse & Wagon Ride*** (558–8380). When he has enough business to do the wagon rides, Junior Rawlings leads his horse-drawn wagon down a bumpy path through the grove and then across the highway to Ili`iliopae Heiau. Afterward, guests return to an oceanside Hawaiian feast where they learn Hawaiian crafts and a basic hula. The enterprise is so refreshingly low-key and amateurish that even those who normally shun group tours might not mind this one. Tours depart daily at 10:00 A.M., numbers permitting. On "off" days, Rawlings offers a longer horseback tour and omits the lunch segment. The cost is $50 for either format. Reservations preferred.

If you don't take the wagon ride, you should still make a point of visiting ***Ili`iliopae Heiau*** on your own. The entrance is a few hundred yards past the wagon-ride sign on the other side of the highway and through the gate immediately after the bridge. Don your safari camouflage (and mosquito repellent) and strike out on the jeep trail into the jungle. At the end of the road, cross the streambed. Hidden in the vegetation on the far side, Ili`iliopae makes a dramatic and mysterious appearance.

The *heiau* is much bigger than it appears, extending almost 300 feet across the valley. It was once even larger, but, according to legend, a flood washed away half the structure. The story goes that a father whose sons had been sacrificed by an evil *kahuna* as temple offerings had petitioned the shark god for vengeance. The flood waters carried the evil priest and his attendants out into the ocean where a gathering of sharks waited. What you see today is just the foundation of a once elaborately designed complex. Imagine that the vegetation fronting the *heiau* was cleared all the way down to the shoreline so that the temple could be clearly seen by canoes crossing the channel from Maui. You can see that Ili`iliopae was once a formidable structure indeed.

The *heiau* is also the starting point for the ***Wailau Valley Trail,*** an all-day hike over the mountains to that remote North Shore valley. Legend—backed by geology—holds that the lava rock used in this *heiau* originated in Wailau Valley and was carried overland along this trail by a human chain. Anybody in reasonable shape should consider hiking a short way up this steeply climbing trail (look for the red trail ribbons at the *heiau* "viewing platform"). Even going a few hundred feet up the ridge slope earns you a breathtaking view of the full *heiau* as well as of the fishponds along the coast. Those who go farther will find that the trail becomes quite overgrown and muddy as it continues. It takes a half day of slogging up the ridge to reach the top for a view of the even steeper valley on the other side—assuming the almost permanent clouds don't rain out your visibility. If they do, you can console yourself by exploring the moss-covered "enchanted forest" that this constant precipitation supports.

Continuing on the highway, you'll pass the ***Neighborhood Store 'n Counter*** (558–8498), your last chance to stop for supplies or take-out lunch. Open 8:00 A.M. to 6:00 P.M. every day but Wednesday. As you drive onward, look for the ubiquitous *hala* (pandanus) trees, whose knotted fruit are often called tourist pineapples. The fruits are not as edible as the pineapples they resemble, but the tuft-tipped "nuts" made serviceable paintbrushes, and the *lauhala,* the long fibrous leaves, were woven into mats. The trees along this shoreline are said to derive from an ancestral tree whose stiltlike roots upset the fire goddess Pele's canoe. The enraged goddess tore the tree to bits, sending splinters flying in every direction. They took root in the fertile soil. Of course, almost every rock in Hawaii has its story to tell, but here on Moloka`i, more people remember.

As you continue east, the highway narrows to a single lane, and the scenery grows more and more dramatic as the road curves around one spectacular cove after another. The tiny beaches nestled along the coast, beginning at the 20-mile marker, are all superb for snorkeling or fishing, but they can get rough, especially in winter. ***Kumimi Beach,*** at 21 miles, has facilities. From here you get a first glimpse of Moku Honii, an offshore island used for bombing practice in World War II. The West Maui Mountains loom across ***Pailolo Channel*** as if it were a mere puddle. The highway then makes an abrupt turn inland winding around—and through—some interesting rock formations before climbing to the lush pastures of ***Puu o Hoku Ranch*** (558–8109). In addition to its bread-and-butter cattle business, the ranch has diversified into niche crops, such as *`awa,* a Polynesian stimulant used in traditional rituals and now a popular ingredient for alternative medicines. The ranch headquarters on the oceanside of the highway (just before the 25-mile point) sells samples of *`awa* health drinks.

On top of the hill, just seaward of the ranch headquarters, the sacred ***Lanikaula Kukui Grove*** grows on the spot where a powerful sixteenth-century *kahuna* ("one who knows the secrets") lies buried. Lanikaula's influence pervaded Hawaii and made Moloka`i, an island dedicated to spiritual pursuits, off-limits to warfare. Lanikaula died betrayed by a visiting *kahuna* from Lana`i. His sons planted these light-green *kukui* (candlenut) trees to conceal their father's final resting place. Moloka`i's isolation continued in the seventeenth century, belligerently enforced by the *Kalaipahoa,* whose magic poisonwood led other islands to give Moloka`i a wide berth. As these legends testify, Moloka`i's "Lonely Island" reputation long predated leprosy. You can feel some of that loneliness today as you approach the North Shore. Once populous, it is now largely deserted due to lack of road access.

Somehow, after leaving the main ranch, the highway manages to lurch around even wilder turns, and the vistas across lush canyons leading to the ocean become ever more stunning. You fight desperately to keep your eyes on the road, knowing that any driver coming around the blind turns ahead will be equally seduced by the magnificent views. Your patience will be rewarded, for just as the scenery reaches its climax, a wide turn allows space to pull over and absorb your first lingering view into ***Halawa Valley.*** A pair of waterfalls topple over cliffs at the back of the steep-walled valley. Halawa Stream descends from there through a thousand shades of green to emerge at an estuary at the mouth of a horseshoe-shaped bay complete with black sand beach. As soon as you can tear yourself away from the lookout, maneuver the last hairpin turns to the valley floor where you can enjoy Halawa up close.

One of the oldest settled valleys in Hawaii, ***Halawa*** continued to support a thriving community that supplied most of the island's taro long after the more remote North Shore valleys had been deserted. Then tragedy struck, beginning with a 1946 tidal wave that devastated the valley. Today only a handful of diehards remain in this Shangri-la. Some have begun to farm taro again. Unfortunately, other valley residents are now claiming that the main hiking trail to the waterfalls passes through their private property and are demanding that visitors pay to take a guided tour. In fact, the trail follows a century-old public roadway and such demands appear extortionate. To avoid this, travelers can obtain a permit at the Puu O Hoku Ranch office (above).

To visit the falls, park near the pavilion and walk back up the dirt road into the valley past the photogenic green Halawa Church. The trail begins at the end of the road and almost immediately crosses Halawa Stream before heading up the slope of the valley. Follow the orange trail markers and enjoy the tropical fruits along the trail as it climbs a series of lava rock terraces built for taro farming. An hour or two of hiking leads to ***Moaula Falls,*** the lower of the two falls visible from the lookout.

Trivia

The first Hawaiian fossils were discovered on Moloka`i, lodged in sandstone at the Mo`omomi Dunes.

Hawaiians used to drop a *ti* leaf in the pool below before swimming to see if the mo`o lizard for whom the falls are named was prowling underwater. The superstitious or cautious of mind can continue up the streambed to the larger ***Hipuapua Falls*** and bathe in its pool *sans* mo`o.

There are showers back at the park pavilion to wash off any mud collected on your descent, and the bay itself stays sufficiently sheltered to permit swimming in all but the roughest weather. Camping at the pavilion is not permitted, but Puu o Hoku Ranch tolerates tenters on its land by the south shore of the bay. Beyond Halawa, inaccessible by land, begins the spectacular Moloka`i North Shore, where a 1,750-foot waterfall (the state's highest) topples from the slopes of the world's highest sea cliffs. The stormy weather and winter surf that pummels this rugged coastline are such that even boat traffic to the North Shore is largely restricted to the summer months.

Central Moloka`i and Kalaupapa

One-and-a-half miles west of Kaunakakai, the hundreds of coconut trees swaying in the ocean breezes make up ***Kapuaiwa Grove,*** a royal coconut grove planted for Kamehameha V (whose nickname was Kapuaiwa, "mysterious taboo") on the site of seven sacred ponds. It was once much larger, but adjacent construction, an encroaching coastline, and basic neglect have all taken their toll. Still, the grove—one of the few such sites remaining—merits a visit. Just beware of falling coconuts.

Strung like a cordon against temptation, eight different congregations of Moloka`i worshippers gather on Sunday at ***Church Row*** across the street. Any denomination with Hawaiian members can build here. Some of the services are still conducted in Hawaiian, and visitors are welcome. Locals boast that the only traffic jams on the island occur here on Sunday morning.

After Kapuaiwa, the highway climbs inland past a plumeria flower farm. Just shy of the 4-mile mark (0.5 mile before the junction between Routes 46 and 47 and immediately preceding the white concrete bridge), an unmarked forest preserve road on the right leads the intrepid explorer 10 miles through the island's lush interior to the ***Waikolu Lookout.*** The road quickly becomes unpaved and in all but the driest weather will require a four-wheel-drive vehicle to get to the end. Ignore the many turnoffs to smaller hunting trails.

About 9 miles in you pass a famous ***sandalwood pit,*** dug in the shape of a ship's hold to measure an exact cargo of the fragrant wood for export to China. Run as an exclusive monopoly of Kamehameha I, the going rate was to exchange a full cargo of sandalwood in return for the brig that carried it. The king amassed a fair-sized fleet in this fashion. You aren't likely to see any sandalwood near the pit today, or anywhere else in Hawaii, either. After Kamehameha's death, greedy chieftains inherited the franchise and led long forays into the mountains, eventually harvesting Hawaii's sandalwood to virtual extinction. Some credit the tree's demise to commoners who, tired of being forced on these expeditions away from their fields and fishing, deliberately pulled out saplings by the roots.

A mile farther, the road ends at a picture-perfect view of ***Waikolu*** ("three waters") ***Valley,*** one of the three major valleys of Moloka`i's virtually inaccessible North Shore. Stretched out 3,000 feet below, furrowed by waterfalls and carpeted in lush vegetation, this valley supplies much of the island's water. Try to arrive in the morning before the clouds move in. Beyond Waikolu lies the entrance to the ***Kamakou Preserve,*** a fragile parcel of native rain forest managed by the Nature Conservancy of Hawaii. You can hike along a boardwalk trail through Pepeopae Bog to an overlook into Pelekunu Valley, yet another inaccessible North Shore valley. The stunted, rain-drenched native vegetation in this summit "cloud forest" makes the trip one of Moloka`i's most unique experiences. The only problem is getting here. Be sure to call the ***Nature Conservancy*** (553–5236) office in Kualapuu before entering the preserve because the area is subject to violent weather changes. If possible, contact them months in advance to reserve a spot on either of their all-day excursions into the preserves at Kamakou and Mo`omomi. These are staged monthly and are offered for the cost of a donation.

To get to ***Kualapuu,*** take the turnoff north on Route 47 and head uphill 2 miles until the intersection with Farrington Highway (Route 48). The plantation village of Kualapuu stretches to the left, behind the now-derelict pineapple factory on the corner. On the right, across the road from the factory, is the former headquarters building for Del Monte Pineapple, now home to a new island crop, coffee. You can sample a cup of the house brew at the rather generically named ***Coffees of Hawaii*** (567–9241; 800–709–2326) espresso bar. The product is Moloka`i-made from seed to cup. Open Monday–Friday 8:00 A.M. to 3:00 P.M.; and Saturday and Sunday 9:00 A.M. to 3:00 P.M. Java junkies can also take a wagon tour of the fields and processing plant, which is offered weekdays at 10:00 A.M. and 1:00 P.M. for $14. Kualapuu's claim to fame rests in its reservoir ("the world's largest rubber-lined body of water"),

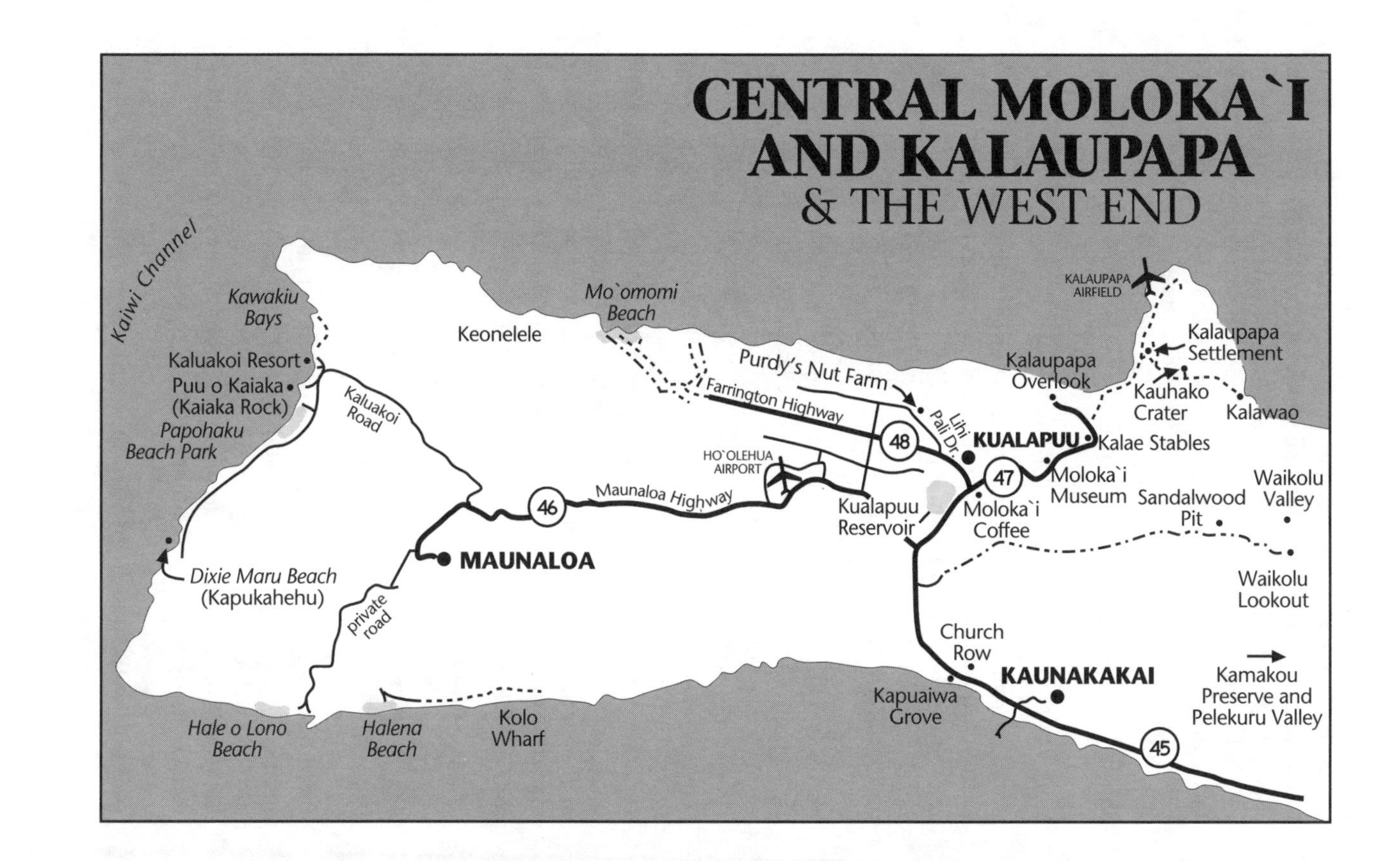
CENTRAL MOLOKA`I
AND KALAUPAPA
& THE WEST END
Kaiwi Channel
Kawakiu Bays
Kaluakoi Resort
Puu o Kaiaka (Kaiaka Rock)
Papohaku Beach Park
Kaluakoi Road
Dixie Maru Beach (Kapukahehu)
private road
Hale o Lono Beach
Halena Beach
Kolo Wharf
Keonelele
Mo`omomi Beach
MAUNALOA
46
Maunaloa Highway
HO`OLEHUA AIRPORT
Farrington Highway
Purdy's Nut Farm
48
Lihi Pali Dr.
KUALAPUU
47
Kualapuu Reservoir
Moloka`i Coffee
Moloka`i Museum
Kalae Stables
Kalaupapa Overlook
KALAUPAPA AIRFIELD
Kalaupapa Settlement
Kauhako Crater
Kalawao
Sandalwood Pit
Waikolu Valley
Waikolu Lookout
Church Row
Kapuaiwa Grove
KAUNAKAKAI
45
Kamakou Preserve and Pelekuru Valley

which houses irrigation water piped from the rain-drenched North Shore via a 5-mile tunnel bored through the mountains. You can dine here in the renovated ***Kamuela's Cookhouse*** (567–9655). The country Hawaiian decor complements the tasty, local American specialties served here at moderate prices. Open Tuesday–Friday 6:30 A.M. to 2:30 P.M., 5:30 to 8:30 P.M., Saturday and Sunday 8:00 A.M. to 2:00 P.M.

Head west on Farrington Highway and enter Ho`olehua, a larger community engaged in diversified agriculture. In 1921, after Congress passed the Hawaiian Homelands Act, the homestead program began here on Moloka`i. At first Hawaiian farmers struggled on the tiny lots they received. Most ended up leasing their land to the pineapple companies. Since pineapple's demise in 1982 and with today's better capital and water allocation, the homestead program is at last reaping some successes.

After passing the island's high school, turn right up Lihi Pali Drive and look for the sign outside ***Purdy's Nut Farm*** (567–6601). Visit this single-acre orchard on Hawaiian homestead land Monday through Friday, 9:30 A.M. to 3:30 P.M. Saturday, 10:00 A.M. to 2:00 P.M. and one of the Purdys will tell you everything you want to know about macadamia nut farming and provide hands-on demonstrations. You can also try or buy their home-roasted nuts, which taste much better than the commercially packaged version.

Speaking of nuts, while in Ho`olehua, you might also take advantage of the unique "post-a-nut" service offered by the local post office. Postmaster Margaret Keahi-Leary keeps a supply of coconuts on hand that await your inscription with a felt marker pen to mail as mementos to friends and family back home. All you have to pay is postage (around $3.00 for a 2-pound nut). Margaret stocks her basket with unhusked brown nuts. Green coconuts contain water and are thus much heavier. Both are edible if you strip off the outer husk and crack the inner nut. The post office is located at the corner of Farrington Highway and Puu Pele`ula. Open Monday–Friday 8:00–11:30 A.M., 12:30–4:30 P.M.

Farrington Highway turns to dirt a couple miles outside town, but the road is usually in good condition. If you're game, follow it as far west as you can go to beautiful ***Mo`omomi Beach.*** It's popular with locals for unofficial camping. Turnoffs along the way lead to other nice locales; the whole coastline is studded with tiny strands of deserted beaches hidden between rocky outcrops. The land west of Mo`omomi, Keonelele, "the flying sands," belongs to the Nature Conservancy and consists of windswept sand dunes covered with native vegetation. Entrance by road requires permission, but you can follow a coastal trail on foot from Mo`omomi to take in the rugged isolation of the terrain. The first Hawaiian fossils were found lodged in sandstone here, and the cliffside sea caves harbor ancient burial sites.

Return to Kualapuu and continue north on Route 47. As the road begins a winding ascent, the landscape becomes pastoral and the air cool and fresh. About 2 miles up the road, a wooden signpost announces the ***Moloka`i Museum & Cultural Center*** (567–6436) on the left. One of the first in the islands and the oldest left standing, the ***Meyer Sugar Mill,*** the museum's principal attraction, has been restored to working order. Rudolf Meyer left his native Hamburg to seek his fortune in the California gold rush. His ship detoured in the Pacific, however, and he ended up taking a surveying position on Moloka`i during the Hawaiian Kingdom's land reform of 1848. Meyer married a Hawaiian chieftess and stayed on as an overseer, managing what has now become Moloka`i Ranch, while wearing many different hats as a government official. His venture into sugar, beginning in 1878, was never entirely successful.

Almost all the original machinery of the mill—a mule-driven crusher, copper clarifiers, redwood evaporating pans—survives in working condition. The mill's exhibits provide a fascinating glimpse into nineteenth-century industry in Hawaii. The adjacent cultural center focuses on Hawaiian crafts, including *lauhala* weaving, woodcarving, lei stringing, and quilting. While on the premises, take the time to inspect the Meyer family cemetery nearby and unwind in its shade and solitude. Visible on the hill above the parking area is the original Meyer family home. It has a reputation for being haunted and is closed to the public. Meyer Sugar Mill receives visitors Monday through Saturday 10:00 A.M. to 2:00 P.M. Admission charges are nominal.

Farther uphill through green fields of grazing bovines, you reach ***Kalae Stables,*** home base for the "world-famous Moloka`i mule ride" to ***Kalaupapa*** (flat leaf) ***Peninsula.*** The descent to Kalaupapa begins at the UNAUTHORIZED PERSONS KEEP OUT sign just ahead, where the highway turns left. The trail drops 1,600 feet over a mere 3 miles and has twenty-six switchbacks. Manuel Farinha, a Portuguese immigrant, carved the trail while hanging from ropes over the cliff; but it's named for Jack London, who descended it in 1907 and wrote of his experience. (There's a lesson here.) The views along the trail are predictably stunning, but you need to make special arrangements to enter Kalaupapa settlement (keep reading for details).

Continue by car into Palaau State Park around the corner. The road ends at the official ***Kalaupapa Overlook,*** where you can take in the unearthly view of the leaflike peninsula jutting out into the Pacific from beneath the impossibly steep cliffs of Moloka`i's North Shore. From the same parking lot you can take a short hike through ironwood pines to ***Phallic Rock,*** which, when seen, needs no explanation. Barren women spent the night in this forest in order to conceive, and offerings are placed on the rock to this day. Camping in Palaau (at a safe distance from phallic effects) is allowed by state permit. Call 984–8109 (Maui office).

A visit to ***Kalaupapa National Historic Park*** will almost certainly provide the highlight of any Moloka`i experience. It is essential if one is to comprehend the emotional scars of this one-time "Lonely Island." Leprosy (Hansen's disease) was first observed in Hawaii in 1835 and soon grew to epidemic proportions. The biblical stigma (and physical repulsiveness) of the disease moved missionary doctors to push for drastic quarantine measures. (Never mind that leprosy is now known to be one of the *least* contagious diseases and that Hawaiians were already dying in droves from almost every other Western illness.) The physical isolation of Makanalua ("the given grave") Peninsula made it a natural place to exile leprosy patients, a process that began in 1866. Honolulu's finest turned a blind eye to the appalling conditions on the peninsula, while many victims took to the hills to escape banishment.

Flows from ***Kauhako Crater*** created the 2-mile peninsula as a geological afterthought, long after the rest of Moloka`i had taken shape. As a

Priapic Geology

Precontact Hawaiians believed various stones were inhabited by spirits and held magical powers. Among the more famous of these stones is Moloka`i's Phallic Rock, located in Palaau State Park. The legend is that the male fertility god Nanahoa lived nearby and was caught staring at a beautiful young girl who was admiring her own reflection in a pool. Nanahoa's wife, Kawahuna, saw her husband leering, and in a storm of jealousy attacked the young girl by yanking on her hair. Nanahoa became outraged in turn and struck his wife, who rolled over a nearby cliff and turned to stone. Nanahoa also turned to stone, appropriately enough, some might say, in the shape of a penis, and according to legend, he still sits today in full erect form. Barren women make the pilgrimage to this rock, where it's said if they spend the night and pray for fertility, they could be blessed with a child.

There was once a female stone (the wife) that stood next to the male. As the legend suggests, this stone has since fallen down the hillside.

natural viewing platform from which to marvel at Moloka`i's stunning northern coastline, the beauty of the peninsula provides a serene counterpoint to the saga of its troubled past. A visit to Kalaupapa, however, does not wallow in the misery caused by man's inhumanity to man as much as it celebrates the redemptive qualities of human compassion and altruism. You will learn of the *kokuas* (helpers) who volunteered to follow their loved ones into exile and who lived out their lives among the diseased. You will pay homage to the courage of Father Damien, a Catholic priest who came here alone to minister to the afflicted and helped transform their lawless purgatory into a life of newfound dignity.

Damien eventually contracted leprosy and died among those he had come to serve. His work did not lack controversy. The Protestant establishment resented his interloping presence and went to great lengths to discredit him. Conflicts with his own bishop had for a long time jeopardized Damien's nomination for sainthood; in 1996, he was beatified by the pope—a preliminary step to eventual canonization. During Damien's lifetime, his plight attracted headlines around the world, and soon others came to labor alongside him. The original settlement at rainy Kalawao was moved to more hospitable Kalaupapa, a fishing village on the other side of the peninsula. Bit by bit, the suffering of leprosy patients abated, and the advent of sulfone drugs in the 1940s offered a permanent cure to the progress of the disease. Despite this, the isolation laws governing the settlement were not rescinded until 1969. Children under sixteen remain barred from entry even today.

Trivia

Meyer Sugar Mill on Moloka`i was built in 1878; it is the oldest mill still standing in Hawaii.

The classic way to get to Kalaupapa has always been to take the ***Moloka`i Mule Ride*** (567–6088 or 800–567–7550; www.muleride.com) out of Kalae Stables. Bumper stickers on Oahu advertise "I'd rather be riding a mule on Moloka`i." The ride and tour cost $150, which includes lunch. The other options are flying and hiking, with direct flights from Ho`olehua ("topside") or Honolulu available. Kalaupapa tours are offered Monday–Saturday. Nonmule riders should book directly with ***Damien Tours*** (567–6171; best times to call are 7:00–8:00 A.M. or 7:00–9:00 P.M.), which runs the three-hour ground tours of Kalaupapa in a rickety old school bus. All-day tours can also be arranged. If you hike in, your ground tour is only $30. Air packages vary greatly as a number of small charter airlines compete. ***Moloka`i Air Shuttle*** (545–4988 in Honolulu; 567–6847 in Moloka`i) had the best rate as of this writing ($70 roundtrip). Ask Damien Tours or your travel agent for advice on current service. If

View from Kalawao, Kalaupapa Peninsula

you're lucky, you'll get owner Richard Marks' personal attention on your tour. Marks, the sheriff of Kalawao County (distinct from the rest of Moloka`i, which is part of Maui), is an extraordinary man. A self-taught authority on leprosy and its history and a former patient himself, he has had audiences with the Pope and Mother Teresa. The depth of his personal involvement with Kalaupapa past and present makes the whole experience come alive.

Trivia

The highest sea cliffs in the world are on Moloka`i.

All the tours cover the basic fixtures and monuments of Kalaupapa settlement, where more than forty of the original patients still reside. You then cross the peninsula to the earlier settlement at Kalawao. Here you visit ***St. Philomena Church,*** which Damien built. Note the square holes he cut in the wooden floor so ailing worshipers could spit without feeling self-conscious. Nearby you stop for a picnic lunch at a stunningly beautiful site overlooking the mouth of Waikolu Valley and Mokapu Island. (Those who hike or fly in should bring their own food.) If time permits, ask to take a short hike to the rim of ***Kauhako Crater*** (400 feet) for an awesome view of the entire peninsula. A "bottomless" lake, the habitat for at least one species of shrimp found nowhere else in the world, fills the crater floor.

The West End

Moloka`i's coastline lacks good swimming beaches. The south coast consists of shallow mud flats, and the North Shore is mostly inaccessible. The tiny beaches and coves on the east coast have their charm, but they are peppered with rocks. It is along the west coast (see map on page 142) that Moloka`i has stationed its major white-sand creations. Not coincidentally, it's also the site of the island's only real tourist resort.

The Maunaloa Highway (Route 46) heads west past Ho`olehua Airport, where it climbs the gentle slopes of its namesake, the 1,381-foot volcano that formed this half of the island (not to be confused with the vastly bigger Mauna Loa on the Big Island). The slopes of the mountain yielded an ultra-hard basalt prized for making adzes and other tools. The name of the resort in this region, Kalauko`i, translates to "the adze pit." The other outstanding feature of West Moloka`i is its red volcanic soil that blows in the constant tradewinds and sooner or later daubs everything (tree trunks, houses, cars) with its ruddy palette.

To hit the beaches on the other side of the mountain, take the signposted turnoff on the right to ***Kaluakoi Resort*** (552–2555). The road down traverses extremely dry scrub land whose rolling hills are covered with thorny *kiawe* (mesquite) trees. *Kiawe* briquettes make great barbecue, as any native of the American Southwest will testify. What's more, the pollen from the tree's flowers makes great honey. Moloka`i at one time led the world in honey production, before disease struck the hives. Island honey is still sold in stores and makes a popular gift item.

Kaluakoi Resort, the hotel and two condominiums, and the scattering of surrounding private estates were only part of an ambitious development plan for the West End, whose unrealized boundaries are indicated by the miles of paved roads leading nowhere. Residents of Moloka`i remain skeptical of these plans, and limited water allocation (largely controlled by the Hawaiian Home Lands Commission) has proved an effective obstacle to further development. For now, the focus of West End development has shifted to Maunaloa. As resorts go, Kaluakoi is not a bad place, especially to wander around at night and gaze at Honolulu's lights across Kaiwi Channel. Strangely enough, Kepuhi Beach fronting the hotel is rocky and often unsuitable for swimming. Note: At press time, the resort had recently changed ownership and has been closed "temporarily," with its future uncertain.

Land of Powerful Prayer

*Ancient Hawaiian name chants record that Moloka`i was known in olden times as* Moloka`i pule o'o, *"land of powerful prayer." Legends of sorcery on the island abound. Some of this magic was benevolent. The island's most powerful* kahuna, *Lanikaula, became famous throughout Hawaii for his wisdom and learning. Chiefs from all of the islands would travel to his home on the island's east end to seek his counsel. During Lanikaula's lifetime Moloka`i became a spiritual haven, off-limits to warfare. Unfortunately, Lanikaula was betrayed by a visiting fellow* kahuna *from Lana`i named Kawelo, who stole a stool sample from the sage and used it to work a magic death-by-constipation on his erstwhile colleague.*

The west side of the island became equally famous for a more ferocious style of magic. Discovered in a dream by the chief Kaneiakama, a miraculous stand of trees suddenly appeared on the slopes of Maunaloa, into which the Kalaipahoa, *or "poisonwood gods," entered. Birds flying over the trees would drop dead out of the sky, and chips sent flying from an axe blow would poison woodcutters sent to harvest the timber of these magical trees. Under the guidance of Kaneiakama, the Moloka`i priests finally learned how to harness the power of the* Kalaipahoa *through ritual offerings. From the wood of the trees, they carved fearsome* ki`i *(god images) whose magic rendered the island immune to attack from its neighbors. Traveling war canoes gave the western coastline of Moloka`i a wide berth. Also at Maunaloa lived Kapo, an early master of the hula and legendary relative of the volcano goddess, Pele. Embittered at her younger sister Laka for her greater fame as a hula dancer, Kapo is reputed to have turned to* ana`ana *(black magic) in her old age.*

If you walk a few hundred yards north across the golf course, past the tenth hole, you'll reach ***Pohaku Mauliuli,*** a patchy sand beach sheltered beneath the eroded face of blackened cinder cone. Known as Make ("dead") Horse to locals after an unfortunate equine fell from the cliffs, the beach's deep waters offer exciting terrain for experienced snorkelers. Almost a mile farther north, tucked inside tiny coves along the rocky shoreline, the determined beachgoer can enjoy the island's finest strands at ***Kawakiuniu and Kawakiuiki*** ("big and little Kawakiu") ***Bays.*** To get there, you must choose between hiking along the coast or bumping along the jeep road that splits from the road to the Paniolo Hale condos, passing the fourteenth-hole restroom. Stay on the left fork to follow the coastline. The two coves are sheltered from the elements, but in winter the waters may be too rough for swimming.

Immediately south of Kepuhi Beach and Kaluakoi Resort, ***Puu o Kaiaka,*** or Kaiaka Rock, a massive basalt outcrop, juts into the ocean. Of spiritual significance to the ancient Hawaiians, Puu o Kaiaka was the site of a *heiau* that was demolished by army bulldozers in the 1960s. If you scramble up the short jeep trail leading from Kaiaka Road to the top, you will, in addition to having breathtaking views of the western coastline, come upon some curious concrete block structures that resemble a modernistic rendition of the *heiau* the army destroyed. In fact, the blocks are the forgotten remains of a cable-car winch erected by Libby Pineapple Company to lower their fruit to ships anchored offshore. The pineapple offerings ceased flowing from this sacred spot when Kolo Wharf was built.

On the other side of Kaiaka Rock, the vast windswept sands of Papohaku Beach extend for 2 miles of white powder, accessible through several turnoffs from Kaluakoi Road. Sand from the beach was for years illegally mined to replenish Waikiki's own diminishing strands. ***Papohaku Beach Park*** offers attractive facilities maintained by Kaluakoi Resort. (WARNING: Offshore currents make the waters unsafe at times, and the wind can generate a fierce sandblast.) Every May, a festival at the beach park commemorates the legendary birth of the hula on Moloka`i. Turnoffs farther along Kaluakoi Road lead to additional beaches, most of them unblemished by human footprints. ***Kapukahehu,*** the last beach before the paved road ends, is known to locals as ***Dixie Maru*** after a Japanese fishing boat that shipwrecked offshore. The beach's tiny cove may be more sheltered than those before it.

To escape the coastal heat, follow the Maunaloa Highway for another 2 miles past the turnoff into Maunaloa Town, a tiny former plantation community nestled among cool pine trees. After Dole Pineapple pulled out of the island in 1975, Maunaloa became a virtual ghost town that nobody visited. Jonathan Socher's ***Big Wind Kite Factory*** (552–2364) almost single-handedly put Maunaloa back on the map. Jonathan's elaborate designs translate the artistic visions of his wife, Daphne, into airborne motion. The tiny front-room shop comes alive with colorful kite fantasies, from dancing hula girls to pineapple windsocks. Tour the factory in back where the Sochers happily demonstrate the finer points of kite making. Big Wind also imports high-performance stunt kites, for which Jonathan gives free lessons. In an adjacent room, the Sochers operate ***Plantation Gallery*** to showcase the craftwork of local artists as well as carefully chosen imports from Bali, where the Sochers vacation. Open Monday–Saturday 8:30 A.M. to 5:00 P.M. and Sunday 10:00 A.M. to 2:00 P.M.

In recent years Maunaloa has witnessed a number of great changes. ***Molokai Ranch*** (552–2791; centralized reservations: 877– 726–4656), which owns most of the land on this half of the island, has carefully nurtured its plans for controlled development in a number of complementary ventures. To start with, the ranch literally rebuilt the town of Maunaloa, replacing its worn-out plantation homes with updated models. Moloka`i's first movie theater (a cineplex no less) and fast-food franchise (KFC) have opened here. A few of the original homes were relocated and will form the basis for a museum and cultural center across from the visitors center. Larger show homes invite inspection by

The Birth of Hula

As the home of the fearsome Kalaipahoa, *or "poisonwood gods," Maunaloa was once feared throughout the islands. Yet, its other legacy as the legendary birthplace of the hula gives Moloka`i a more enduring claim to fame. The graceful movements of this traditional dance have long been synonymous with the romantic image of the Hawaiian islands around the world. Although the story of the hula's creation varies greatly among sources, many accounts credit an early hula school established at Ka'ana as the progenitor of the art form. The demand for hula soon exceeded the limited capacity of the school. Accordingly, Laka, a* kumu hula *(dance teacher), left Ka`ana to travel to the other islands, spreading the art of hula throughout Hawaii. Today, Laka is revered as a goddess and patroness of the dance. Every year, Moloka`i celebrates* Ka Hula Piko *(the birth of hula) through offerings at Ka'ana and an islandwide hula festival held at Papohaku Beach Park. The annual celebration takes place on the third Saturday of May. If you plan to attend, book your Moloka`i stay early as the island fills up.*

Big Wind Kite Factory

prospective buyers. A new, upscale restaurant, ***The Village Grill*** (552–0012), occupies the building of the one-time plantation infirmary. Decorated in Western style, with optional lanai seating, the grill serves a fairly basic surf 'n' turf menu, with a few local ethnic specials at lunchtime. Dinner prices run in the expensive range. Open Monday–Friday 11:30 A.M. to 1:30 P.M. and nightly from 6:00 to 9:00 P.M.

The Ranch has also launched some less conventional tourist ventures, transforming portions of its surrounding property into a kind of eco-tourist resort. Offering an ersatz "camping" experience combined with a smorgasbord of daily activities, the Ranch caters to well-heeled travelers who want to experience the great outdoors without roughing it. Overnight guests lodge in "tentalows," a kind of hybrid tent/bungalow with fabric walls built over wooden platforms. The solar-powered tentalows come equipped with comfortable beds, self-composting toilets, and outdoor showers. The Ranch has built three different campsites, each the staging ground for various activities. The Paniolo camp has a central location that enjoys cool, hilltop views. Kolo offers the most privacy, with rounded yurts pitched along a craggy, desolate bluff overlooking the ocean. These are currently reserved for group lodging. Kaupoa boasts the nicest beach, but its tentalows are somewhat crowded together. The campsites serve three meals daily, although only breakfast is included in the daily rate. The food is actually quite good and may include fresh shrimp from the ranch's own aquaculture farm. Evening entertainment is provided and the whole operation is conducted in refreshingly low-key Moloka`i style. Rates range from $205–$255, per person, per night, exclusive of activities.

Moloka`i Night Life

Folks in Honolulu will tell you nothing happens on the island of Moloka`i after dark. But like most places, the truth is you just have to know where to go. In Kaunakakai, the hot place to be (literally) is the alley in back of Kanemitsu Bakery where locals gather for fresh-baked bread, hot out of the oven starting around 10:15 P.M. every night but Monday. Here's how it works. You enter the alley to the right of the bakery storefront and head for the light at the end. Most nights you'll find a line already formed there. If not, knock on the door under the light. You have to knock hard to be heard. Eventually, footsteps will approach and the door will open about 8 inches wide, no more. A voice will ask you what kind of bread you want. You counter by asking what do they have. You may have a choice of toppings, either butter with cinnamon sugar or cream cheese with guava jelly. Once your order is placed, the door slams shut again and the footsteps disappear. You wait in the alley, inhaling the aroma of fresh-baked bread, impatient with anticipation. Eventually, the door cracks open once more and a hand extends your order to you. You pay and wait for change, clutching the piping hot bread. The loaves are cut lengthwise down the middle with the toppings slathered inside. You may just have to take a bite right there. Stroll back down the alley to the street and chew the rest under the streetlight.

Daily activities include kayaking, mountain biking, canoeing, and a ropes course. Urban cowboys can ride herd (literally) by signing up for the ranch's ***Cattle Trail Drive*** or hone their skills in rodeo games. Especially recommended is the ***Onaohilo Cultural Hike,*** a fascinating foray into the history and culture of old Hawaii. The 90-minute hike visits an archaeological site and interprets its significance. Guides weave a mixture of storytelling with excerpts from traditional Moloka`i *mele* (chants). Ranch activities are open to visitors staying elsewhere. Call 552–2791 or sign up at the "outfitters center" in Maunaloa. Overnight guests pay from $20–$80 per activity, with day guests paying slightly more.

Much of the Ranch land around the campsites and elsewhere remains fenced-in cattle pasture. The Ranch has preserved public access to Hale O Lono Harbor on the island's southwestern coast. To get there from Maunaloa, turn onto the paved road just above the outfitters center. The road turns to dirt before passing the rodeo arena. Farther along, take the right fork and follow the bumpy road 2 miles down to the harbor. There is a small swimming beach nearby. In October competitors launch from Hale O Lono for the annual Moloka`i-to-O`ahu canoe races, a 40-mile paddle through monstrous swells and fierce channel currents. The ranch allows camping at both Hale O Lono and Kawakiu Bay. The Ranch has also built more traditional quarters in Maunaloa town. The 22-room ***Molokai Ranch Lodge*** cultivates the rustic charm of a gentleman rancher's manor and overlooks sweeping hillside views. Rooms start at $305, with meals equally exorbitant.

WHERE TO STAY

Dunbar Beachfront Cottages
558–8153 or
800–673–0520,
molokai-beachfront-cottages.com. The name says it all, $125, three-night minimum.

Hotel Moloka`i,
553–5347 or
800–272–5275,
has rooms by the sea from $75.

Kamalo Plantation B&B,
558–8236,
a lush oasis on the island's east end; rooms start at $75, with private cottages for $85 and $120.

Puu o Hoku Ranch,
558–8109,
offers secluded cottage on the far eastern tip of Moloka`i for $85.

Moloka`i Ranch,
(877) 726–4656,
offers upscale "camping" with a smorgasboard of action adventures to choose from. Rates start at $205.

Paniolo Hale Resort Condominiums
552–2731 or
800–367–2984, paniolo-haleresort.com/condos. Hawaiian ranch-style two-story units located on Kaluakoi Resort. $95

WHERE TO EAT

Hotel Moloka`i,
553–5347. Charming oceanfront dining in a nostalgic Old Hawaii setting. Moderate prices.

Kanemitsu's Bakery,
553–5855,
Kaunakakai. An impressive selection of breads that are coveted statewide.

Kamuela's Cookhouse,
567–9655.
A renovated plantation eatery. Good,casual fare. Inexpensive.

Moloka`i Pizza Cafe,
553–3288,
in Kaunakakai. A menu full of variety, casual fare. Inexpensive.

Ohia Lodge,
552–2555. West-end dining with good views and a great salad bar. Located at the Kaluakoi Hotel and Golf Club. Expensive.

Village Grill,
552–0012. Plantation tavern in Maunaloa serves steak and seafood menu. Expensive.

For additional accommodation options and other visitor information, visit:
www.molokaihawaii.com
www.visitmolokai.com

Lana`i

For a small island, Lana`i has seen a lot of changes. In a legendary past, Hawaiians shunned the island, believing it to be inhabited by a nasty breed of *akua* (spirits). Kaululaau, the mischievous son of a Maui chieftain, was banished here for chopping down his father's breadfruit trees. He defeated the *akua* and opened Lana`i to human habitation. Mormon settlers came here beginning in 1853, hoping to build a "City of Joseph" as a model of earthly peace. The mission folded when the settlers discovered that their leader, Walter Gibson, had secretly registered title to the land in his own name. The Mormon Church promptly excommunicated him and relocated to Laie on Oah`u. Undeterred, Gibson brought in new settlers and converted the entire island into an open cattle

Brief History of Lana`i

Lana`i's history is full of larger-than life figures whose arrival left it forever transformed. Dreamers and schemers such as its legendary pioneer, Kaululaau, whose mischievous ways led to his banishment there, also found salvation on Lana`i. A more recent visionary, Walter Murray Gibson, came to the island as a Mormon leader and later used it as the springboard for his spectacular, if short-lived, political career as a populist demagogue. George Munro, another pioneer, brought his own vision of reforestation to restore the island's ecological balance.

Pineapple King James Dole combined innovative methods of mass production with mass marketing to make the pineapple synonymous with Hawaii the world over. But in Hawaii, he made pineapple synonymous with Lana`i, transforming the island's population and economy in the process. Lana`i became the world's largest pineapple plantation, although it was not the first place in Hawaii that pineapple (not a native fruit) was grown.

Ironically, Lana`i claims distinction for another "first" regarding a different crop: sugar. The Polynesians grew sugar cane, but never produced refined sugar. In 1802, a Chinese man on Lana`i is believed to have been the first to have done so. Sugar would go on to transform Hawaii, becoming the dominant crop in the islands, but not on Lana`i.

Lana`i

Kalohi Channel

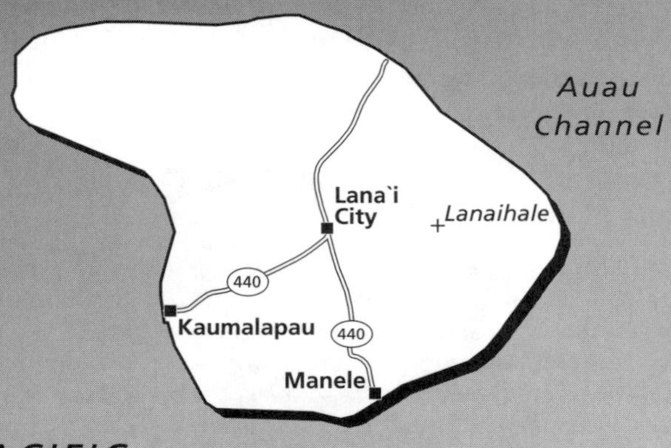

PACIFIC
OCEAN

Kealaikahiki
Channel

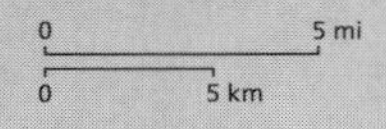

range, which he managed until King Kalakaua appointed him prime minister.

Unrestricted grazing turned the already dry landscape into a barren wasteland. The arrival of New Zealand naturalist George Munro, who was called in to manage the ranch, helped reverse some of the damage. Munro literally replanted a forest with introduced flora, including the Norfolk Island pines that have become a local trademark. While Munro worked to undo the excesses of ranching, Jim Dole introduced a different type of pine as ranching's replacement, purchasing the entire island in 1922 to begin the world's largest pineapple plantation. Castle & Cooke, the current owner, has phased out pineapple production in recent years, shifting workers from agriculture to hotel work in two newly opened resorts. The erstwhile "Pineapple Island" is now being promoted to well-heeled vacationers as "Hawaii's Private Island."

Lana`i Facts

Nickname:
"Pineapple Isle"

Dimensions: *18 x 12 miles*

Highest elevation:
Lana`ihale (3,370 feet)

Population: *9,734 (1995)*

Principal city: *Lana`i City*

Flower: *Kauna`oa*

Color: *Orange*

These changes mean less than they might sound. The substitution of tourists for pineapples might seem like a backward step, but less than one-fifth of the island ever grew pineapples to begin with. Shaped roughly like a kidney, Lana`i measures 18 miles long by 12 miles across. Adventurous travelers will have no difficulty losing themselves amid untamed wilderness and hidden locales. As you explore, you cannot help but stumble upon a variety of wildlife. Axis deer and mouflon sheep mingle with countless game fowl that flourish here in the absence of the mongoose found on other islands. You probably will want to rent a jeep to get around. Be prepared for unchivalrous bumps and thick red clouds of dust. Be warned that landmarks might change as fields are abandoned, and with them the access roads cleared through the bush. Get good directions and advice on weather and road conditions before setting out anywhere away from pavement. The only game in town for car rentals is Dollar Rent-A-Car (800–800–4000), and the prices reflect it.

Lana`i City

Though a small island, Lana`i has always thought big. Its tiny town has been optimistically named Lana`i City and is situated in the center of the island with plenty of room to grow. An elevation of 1,650 feet keeps cool breezes blowing through Lana`i City even during summer. Most of the houses here date from the town's origins in 1922. Their brightly colored iron roofs punctuate the green of the ubiquitous Norfolk Island pines. Almost all Lana`i's inhabitants live here in town, the majority of them of Filipino extraction. More by tradition than function, the plantation horn still sounds every evening, although thankfully the 4:30 A.M. wake-up calls have ceased. Sunday cockfights, although illegal, remain a fixture of island social life.

Geography of Lana`i

Sixth largest of the Hawaiian Islands, Lana`i is the smallest island open to visitors. Formed from a single central volcano, it has 47 miles of coastline, two resort hotels, few roads, and only a handful of swimming beaches. The island summit at Lana`ihale reaches 3,370 feet and the widest point of the island spans 18 miles.

Dole Park, a grassy square shaded by rows of Norfolk Island pines, occupies the town center. Lana`i's few commercial buildings mostly cluster around the park. Visit the ***Lana`i Art Program*** (565–7503) to view the work of local artists and take classes to create your own. Stop by **Pele's Other Garden** (565–9628) to munch healthy deli food. Open Monday–Saturday 11:00 A.M. to 7:00 P.M. The ***Blue Ginger Café*** (565–6363) serves inexpensive local-style meals daily from 6:00 to 9:00 P.M. It doubles as a bakery. ***Tanigawa's*** (565–6537) operates a lunch counter every day but Wednesday from 6:30 A.M. until 1:00 P.M. ***Henry Clay's Rotisserie*** in the ***Hotel Lana`i*** (565–7211; 800–795–7211) serves moderately priced dinners featuring spit-roasted meats as well as some Cajun specialties and pizza. Open nightly 5:30–9:00 P.M. Built in 1925 as a clubhouse for Dole executives, the hotel's eleven rooms rent for $95–$140, less than half the rates charged by its upmarket sisters, the ***Manele Bay*** and ***Koele Lodge*** resorts. Call 565–3800 or (800) 321–4666 for centralized reservations for the upscale resorts. ***Dreams Come True*** (565–6961; 800–566–6961) offers B&B rooms with private baths in a restored plantation house for $99.

You might contact statewide B&B agencies for alternatives (see the Introduction). Camping at Hulopoe Bay is private, scenic, and peaceful and even offers solar-heated showers. The bay is a Marine Life Conservation area, so while there's no three-prong fishing allowed, you can snorkel to your heart's content. Permits are issued for a seven-night maximum stay and the fee is $5.00 per person per night and a one-time $5.00 registration fee. For more information, contact the ***Lana`i Company*** at P.O. Box 310, Lana`i City 96763; 565–3978.

Branching Out

From Lana`i City, paved roads cut across an inland plateau and drop sharply to the coast on each of Lana`i's three sides; hunting tracks climb the slopes of the central mountain and, together with the former pineapple field roads, partition the island's interior. Begin by heading west on Kaumalapau Highway, the only road truly deserving the designation of highway. As the main access road to the airport and harbor, it is wide, well graded, and smoothly paved and thus, as you might expect, has little of interest lying along it. Drive down to the harbor anyway. The transition from the flat tableland to the steep slope down the coast offers some vistas over the craggy gulches, sheer cliffs, and rocky sea stacks that characterize Lana`i's western shore. The very industrial-looking harbor squats beneath the rocky cliffline from which it was blasted. It may no longer buzz with its previous pineapple-related activity, but it and the airport are still Lana`i's main gateway to the outside world.

Lana`i Trivia

- *Luahiwa Petroglyphs are considered among the best-preserved in all the islands.*
- *There are no traffic lights on Lana`i.*
- *Lana`i is the former home of the world's largest pineapple plantation.*

A side trip from Kaumalapau to Kaunolu, on the other hand, demonstrates the reverse trade-off and offers a fascinating destination—an ancient village that was Kamehameha I's favorite fishing retreat—at the price of a hellishly difficult access. Definitely get current directions for this one: As empty pineapple fields are converted to pastures, new fences might arise. For one possible route, turn left at the stop sign onto Kaupili Road, just past the airport turnoff as you are coming down the highway. The road deteriorates to gravel and then dirt as it winds through some curves and then follows a fenced border along the former pineapple fields. You soon will see the island of Kahoolawe ahead on the horizon. As you drive, scan the southwestern tip of the island, on your right, for a tiny lighthouse; this is your destination. You should find the road down to Kaunolu 2.1 miles from the highway, where the fencing ends at a runoff ditch. The 3-mile descent is incredibly steep and rocky. Do not attempt this unless you are experienced at handling a four-wheel-drive vehicle.

A bruising half-hour ride along the left side of a gully down brings you to ***Kaunolu Bay,*** whose archaeological treasures constitute a National Historic Landmark. The stone foundations of more than a hundred Hawaiian homes cling to the slopes above this tiny cove. Tufts of *pili*

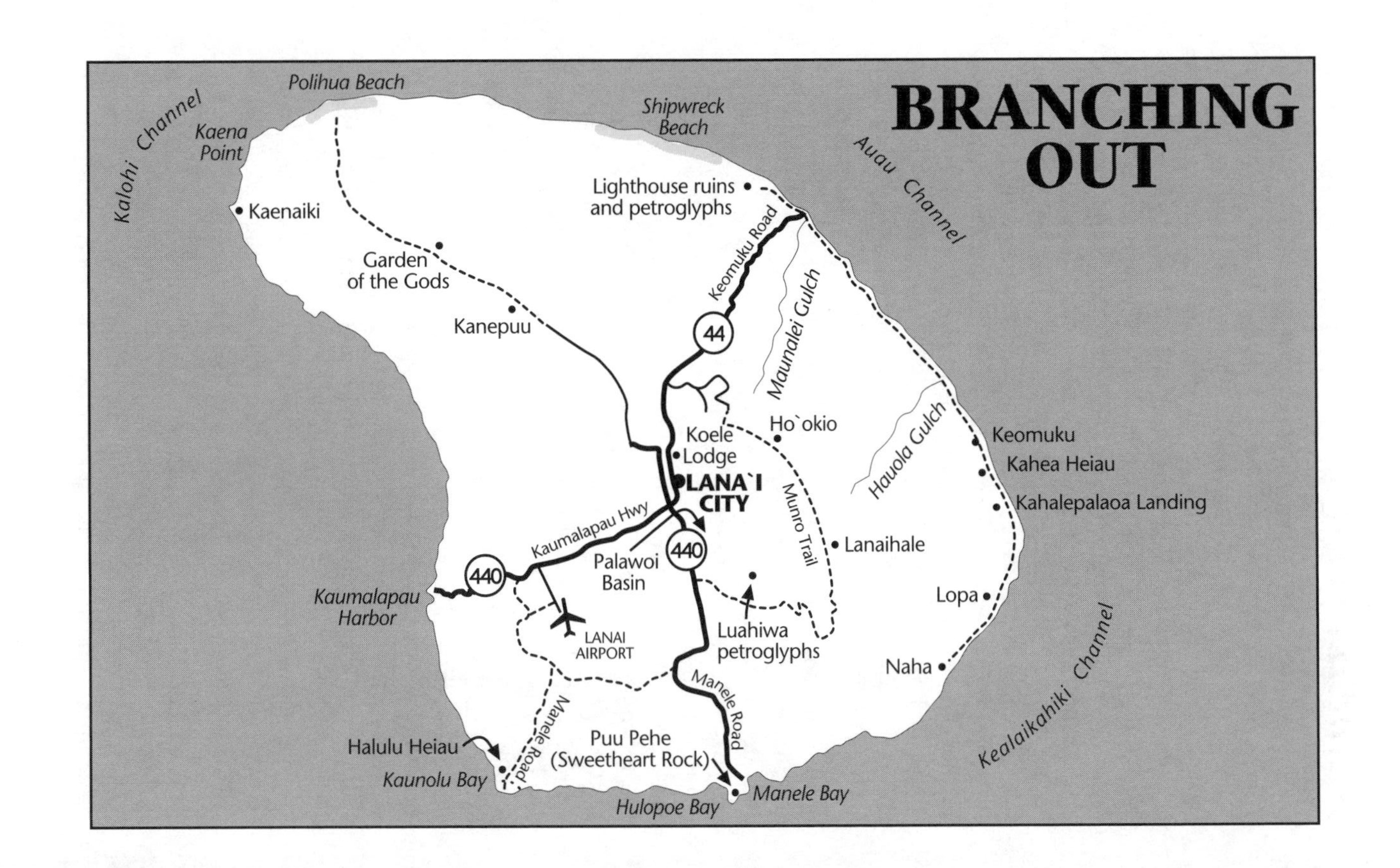
BRANCHING OUT
Polihua Beach
Kalohi Channel
Kaena Point
Kaenaiki
Garden of the Gods
Kanepuu
Shipwreck Beach
Lighthouse ruins and petroglyphs
Auau Channel
Keomuku Road
44
Maunalei Gulch
Hauola Gulch
Ho`okio
Koele Lodge
LANA`I CITY
Munro Trail
Keomuku
Kahea Heiau
Kahalepalaoa Landing
Lanaihale
Kaumalapau Hwy
440
Palawoi Basin
Kaumalapau Harbor
LANAI AIRPORT
Luahiwa petroglyphs
Lopa
Naha
Kealaikahiki Channel
Manele Road
Puu Pehe (Sweetheart Rock)
Halulu Heiau
Kaunolu Bay
Hulopoe Bay
Manele Bay

grass used for thatching grow wild in the rocky terrain. If you wet the wisplike seeds of the *pili,* they will rotate—a unique self-planting mechanism adapted to intermittent rainfall. Just to the right of the *kiawe* tree at the end of the trail, on a bluff overlooking the dry streambed of the gully, you can find the terraced foundation believed to be the site of King Kamehameha's house. Facing Kamehameha's house, on the bluffs across the gully on the right side of the bay, stands ***Halulu Heiau;*** and on the far side of this bluff, a small gap in the rocky rim marks the entrance to ***Kahekili's Leap,*** named for Kamehameha's

Kahekili's Leap

greatest rival, the High Chief of Maui, who excelled at cliff diving. Try to picture the fertile setting this former streambed once supported that attracted Kamehameha here.

Climb down the slope to the base of the bay, then walk up the streambed. On your left you will pass a narrow rock wall enclosure that formed part of a shelter for repairing canoes. Above on your right, you can now clearly see the terracing of Kamehameha's house site. Climb up the opposite wall of the gully to reach the *heiau.* Kamehameha rebuilt the temple after he conquered Lana`i, making it one of the last monuments to the old gods. Its carefully fitted rock walls stand in excellent repair. (Please take care that they remain so.) Walk over to Kahekili's Leap for a dramatic view of ***Pali Kaholo,*** Lana`i's tallest sea cliff, which rises 1,000 feet above deep-blue ocean. At the base of the cliff, the pounding surf echoes inside a large sea cave like rolling thunder. Kamehameha's warriors used to dive from the ledge you are standing on to prove their loyalty and courage. The mere imagining of the 62-foot plunge into the Pacific—with a 15-foot rock outcrop to clear at the base—should be enough to give most visitors a jolt of vertigo.

Your next excursion takes you south on Manele Road, descending from Lana`i City through the historic Palawai Basin. Once the caldera of the volcano that formed Lana`i, the basin became the site of the short-lived Mormon settlement and later cradled Dole's first pineapple fields. The foothills east of the Palawai hold some of the best-preserved ***petroglyphs*** in the state. To probe their secrets, look for the large water tower on the hillside above the basin. On the right of the water tower is a wide gulch, and to the right of the gulch grows a stand of trees where the petroglyphs lurk. To get there, turn left on Hoike Road, a former pineapple road marked by a yield sign (facing south). Turn left at the second irrigation ditch and follow the water pipe to the third power pole where a NO TRESPASSING sign marks the beginning of the trail up to the petroglyphs. The petroglyph-laden rocks are located at the far lower edge of the trees amid a clump of exotic-looking sisal plants with spiky leaves and tall central stalks. A jeep trail leads up the hill to the first carved boulder. Proving that on Lana`i nothing comes easily, the better-preserved, more intricate carvings lie on rocks farther up the slope. Patterned images of canoes, warriors, and animals abound. One shows a man on horseback, dating its origin to after the arrival of Western ships, but no one today can explain why these carvings were made or what they signify. Please be respectful of their fragile condition.

Continue along Manele Road as it rises out of Palawai Basin and then descends steeply to the coast. You will see Kaho`olawe again across

Kealaikahiki ("the way to Tahiti") Channel and maybe the twin towers of the Big Island beyond. Two beautiful bays await you at the end of the road. Both are marine-life conservation zones offering excellent snorkeling. ***Manele Bay*** arrives first on your left, its former black sand beach now converted to a small-boat harbor. Guarded by fortresslike cliffs, the cove offers views of Maui's Mount Haleakala rising above the clouds on the horizon. ***Expeditions*** (661–3756) offers ferry service to and from Lahaina Harbor on Maui five times daily. The fee is $25 one-way.

An extension of Manele Road curves west to ***Hulopoe Bay*** around the point. Hulopoe Beach, often called Manele as well, dazzles visitors with its wide crescent of snowy white sand edging a lovely bay. The shorebreak can be rough in summer, suitable for bodysurfing. A pod of spinner dolphins frequents the waters offshore. (Federal law prohibits harassment of this endangered species.) Unfortunately, this idyllic location has not gone unnoticed. Day-trippers from Maui now come daily, and the 250-room Manele Hotel perches on the bluffs above the bay. Note the murals showing Kaululaau's legendary deeds at the hotel's entrance. You might also ask about the hotel's weekly coastal hikes along the historic Fisherman's Trail. The ninety-minute guided hikes cost $15 for nonguests. Call 565–7700, ext. 2088.

For seclusion, walk around the left side of the bay, past some enormous tidepools, to the cove at ***Puu Pehe.*** Also known as ***Sweetheart Rock,*** it was named for a legendary beauty who drowned in a nearby sea cave, where her jealous husband had confined her, and was buried on this giant sea stack. You can sun yourself on the hidden beach below, although the water is too rocky for good swimming. Walk to the far edge of the bluffs facing Sweetheart Rock for a sweeping view of Lana`i's southern coast, with the mountains of Maui and Kahoolawe, and sometimes even the Big Island, visible across the sea.

Keomuku Road, Lana`i's third paved road, departs north past the Koele Lodge Hotel. ***Kalokahi o Ka Malamalama,*** the tiny church next to the lodge, survives from the ranch days. You can attend Sunday services in Hawaiian here. The road then climbs past guava trees and curves right toward Lana`i's eastern shore. Just beyond the bend, a small paved road on the right leads to the old Koele cemetery and the start of Lana`i's famous ***Munro Trail.*** This 9-mile-long jeep path showcases much of the exotic vegetation that Munro introduced to reestablish a viable watershed in the island's upcountry. The trail climbs the summit of 3,370-foot ***Lana`ihale*** ("house of Lana`i"), which resembles a second-story addition to the island. Rising steeply above the surrounding tableland, the Hale, as locals call it, presents panoramic views of Lana`i and up to five other islands in the chain. Look for guavas and thimbleberries along the trail. Do not attempt the ascent if it has been raining or looks like it will start.

From the cemetery, bear left to avoid the golf course and look for a small sign marking the Munro Trail's entrance into the forest proper. If you are traveling on foot, it might be easier to take the newly created ***Koloiki Ridge Trail*** that begins behind Koele Lodge and joins the Munro Trail halfway along. Ask the concierge for a self-guiding pamphlet. (Guided, interpretive hikes are also available.) After descending through forest for the first few miles, the trail then climbs to reach a telephone relay station overlooking the steep walls of Maunalei ("mountain lei") Gulch, named for the wreathlike clouds so often draped around the mountain here. In 1778, Kalaniopuu's invasion force from the Big Island laid siege to Lana`i's last defenders in this valley. The trail continues along the ridgeline above the upper valley to overlook a lower middle ridge, Ho`okio, where keen eyes can still discern the ***Ho`okio Notches,*** carved by the stalwart Lana`i warriors to fortify their stronghold. Kalaniopuu eventually starved them out, then proceeded to massacre and pillage the entire island.

At 4.7 miles, just before the summit, a side trail heads left through eucalyptus trees for a view of ***Hauola Gulch,*** a 2,000-foot gash in the mountain's side, the deepest on the island. From the windswept, rain-soaked summit, you get the island's best views, provided the Hale breaks free from its cloud cover. The trail then descends steeply down the drier backside of the mountain to link up with Hoike Road, the main jeep access from Palawai Basin.

Keomuku Road continues northeast and begins another bumpy, winding descent to the coast. The stacks of rocks you see along the highway here and elsewhere are not ancient Hawaiian monuments but rather a form of graffiti. While Hawaiians did use such cairns as trail markers, these were built by latter-day visitors to "ward off the ghosts." Game abounds in this area, and if you're not careful, you could violate hunting regulations by running over a few wild turkeys with your car.

The paved road ends at the bottom of the hill. An unpaved extension on the left, fairly easy going, leads north to ***Shipwreck*** or ***Kaiolohia Beach.*** Situated equally between the islands of Maui and Moloka`i offshore, this long, desolate beach gets battered by fierce trade winds and ocean swells funneling through the Pailolo Channel. Littered with debris that drifts across its protective outer reef, the beach has witnessed countless shipwrecks and intentional groundings since the days when flotillas of whalers laid anchor in the famous Lahaina waters off Maui. Although swimming is less than ideal, beachcombers will have a field day. As you drive farther, notice the dwellings of "Federation Camp" built from driftwood and salvaged wreckage. Filipino fishermen built these as weekend shelters during the 1930s. At the end of the drivable road, a path leads to the site of a former lighthouse. Offshore, an abandoned World War II Liberty Ship lists just beyond the reef, stubbornly holding out against the punishing waves.

Heading in the other direction from the end of paved Keomuku Road requires a jeep to reach Keomuku itself and points beyond. To navigate the 12-odd miles to Naha on the southeastern coast takes at least an hour. Four miles along you reach the ghost town of ***Keomuku,*** headquarters of the hapless Maunalei Sugar Company. Gibson's daughter started this short-lived venture at the turn of the century. The plantation was visited by the plague in its first year and was forced to fold after the second year, when the sweet well water mysteriously turned brackish.

Ka Lanakila o Ka Malamalama, a picturesque wooden church nestled in a coconut grove, remains the only intact building in Keomuku. Behind the church, three large whaleboats rot on what used to be shoreline in 1935. Soil runoff has added the new land. Less than a mile farther south, you'll pass ***Kahea Heiau,*** whose stones were pilfered to line the plantation railbed. Hawaiians believe such desecration led to Maunalei Sugar's demise.

Beyond the *heiau* lies the old sugar dock, ***Kahalepalaoa Landing.*** Queen Ka`ahumanu came from Maui near the end of her life to preach to Lana`i's people on this spot and convert them to Christian ways. Today, Maui day-trippers follow in her footsteps to indulge in more hedonistic pursuits at Club Lana`i. The road turns inland from here, with the coast hidden behind a forest of *kiawe* trees, and emerges a few miles farther along at Lopa, where the beach is somewhat more sheltered than the windswept coast farther north. Traveling an additional 2 miles brings you to ***Naha*** and the end of your jeep trail. Another abandoned fishing village, Naha had one of the island's few fishponds, and its walls can still be traced offshore. According to legend, after outwitting all the *akua* on the island, Kaululaau built a huge bonfire here to signal his victory to the people of Maui. Beyond Naha, an ancient pasved trail built by the Hawaiians leads over the mountains to Palawai; for now, however, you will do better to backtrack on Keomuku Road.

The last compass direction accessible from Lana`i City by road is to the northwest. Your route follows what Lana`i maps euphemistically label Kanepuu Highway. In reality, it's a dirt-road extension of Fraser Avenue from town. Follow this road as it curves to the left, then take the first right. After passing through former pineapple fields for the first few miles, you reach the lowland forest of ***Kanepuu.*** Munro recognized the value of this pristine habitat of native plants and trees and planted a surrounding rectangle of eucalyptus trees and sisal plants as a windbreak. Today, the Nature Conservancy continues to preserve this bastion of native vegetation that includes rare Lana`i sandalwood and Hawaiian gardenia. Interpretive signposts line a short nature walk.

The edge of the forest brings an abrupt transition to a now-barren landscape, weakened first by overgrazing and then stripped entirely of vegetation by the punishing winds that sweep across the north coast. At about 7 miles in, you come to a series of bizarre rock formations covering a rugged landscape of peaks and canyons. Welcome to the ***Garden of the Gods.*** The beauty of this bleak terrain lies in the burning mineral colors of its soil and eroded rock. The changing hues at sunset become dramatic. Not far from here is where legend says the treacherous *kahuna* Kawelo engineered the death-by-constipation of Moloka`i's sage, Lanikaula, by burning his rival's stool in a magic fire. As you listen to the wind howl across the rocks, it is easy to imagine that a few of the *akua* have lingered to haunt this desolate spot.

Trivia

The temperature of the sand in which turtle eggs incubate determines the sex of the hatchlings.

Beyond the Garden of the Gods, the road deteriorates as it drops steeply to the coast. WARNING: Do NOT continue if it has been raining here or looks likely to start. If you do go all the way, you will reach beautiful ***Polihua*** ("bosom of eggs") ***Beach,*** a former haven for green sea turtles coming to deposit their eggs. Lana`i chants tell of Pele's love for turtle meat. Perhaps the goddess has been especially hungry, as the species is now endangered; nest sites should not be disturbed. Offshore currents make swimming risky, but it is a quiet spot to look for whales passing through Kalohi Channel and to watch the clouds blow across Moloka`i. Kaena Point to the west served as a penal colony for women between 1837 and 1850; thieves and adulteresses were forced ashore here to fend for themselves. In fact, the concept of adultery did not exist in Old Hawaii. Missionaries had to make do with translating the seventh commandment as "Thou shalt not sleep mischievously."

Apparently, the exile system was no more successful than the commandment. Male convicts from Kaho`olawe swam ashore to Maui and stole canoes that they promptly used to liberate the women on Lana`i.

Farther around the point, at Kaena Iki, lies Lana`i's largest *heiau.* This ancient temple is difficult to find and hard to reach, but as you survey this lonely corner of the island, just knowing it exists adds a touch of mystery.

Where to Stay

Dreams Come True,
565–6961 or
(800) 566–6961,
has B&B rooms for $99.

Hotel Lana`i,
565–7211, or
(800) 795–7211,
hotellanai.com,
is a quaint eleven-room structure that's been accommodating guests since 1925. Recently renovated. Rooms from $95.

Lodge at Koele,
565–7300 or
(800) 321–4666,
www.lodgeatkoele.com,
is an upscale resort that exudes the aura of an Old English hunting lodge. Rooms from $400.

Manele Bay Hotel,
565–7700 or
(800) 321–4666,
www.manelebayhotel.com,
also an upscale resort with a Mediterranean feel, sits, on bluffs overlooking Lana`i's best beach. Rooms from $375.

Where to Eat

Blue Ginger Cafe and Bakery,
565–6363,
offers inexpensive local-style meals in Lana`i City.

Henry Clay's Rotisserie,
565–7211,
serves American/Cajun cuisine nightly.

Manele Bay Hotel and Lodge at Koele provide a variety of upscale dining options.

Pele's Other Garden,
565–9628,
in Lana`i City,
serves healthy deli food.

Tanigawa's,
565–6537,
in central Lana`i,
operates a simple lunch counter every day but Wednesday.

While today's college athletes boast "We're Number One," Maui's warriors of old had an equivalent slogan in Hawaiian: *"Maui no ka oi"* ("Maui is the best"). Sailboarders agree. They come from around the world to frolic at the beaches of the island's windy central isthmus. Humpback whales also make Maui their winter destination of choice. Although they visit all the Hawaiian islands, the biggest groups gather in sight of Maui's coastline. The island has much to recommend to other visitors as well. Within an area not much bigger than O`ahu, Maui boasts a 10,000-foot volcano, a historic whaling town, a rain forest laced with countless waterfalls, and miles of beach colored with white, red, and black sands.

Maui Facts

Nickname:
"The Valley Isle"

Dimensions: *48 x 26 miles*

Highest elevation:
Haleakala (10,023 feet)

Population: *105,429 (1995)*

Largest city: *Kahului*

County Seat: *Wailuku*

Flower: *Lokelani (a rose)*

Color: *Pink*

The island of Maui takes its name from a demigod, "Maui of a Thousand Tricks," whose exploits form legends across Polynesia. Maui's magic fishhook pulled up the first islands from the Pacific floor so that man could have a place to live. Maui pushed up the sky so that man could stand erect. Maui stole fire to warm man's hearth. It was on the island of Maui that the demigod performed his most celebrated feat: slowing the passage of the sun. Some say that the shape of the island resembles the trickster's body. The West Maui Mountains are the demigod's head, with Haleakala's girth a limbless torso to the east. A narrow isthmus forms the neck between these mighty mountains, fetching Maui its nickname of the Valley Isle.

The Isthmus and Points South

Maui's population centers on the northern tip of the isthmus, the nape of Maui's neck. Modern Kahului has the main airport and harbor. In the foothills to the west, its older brother, Wailuku, retains prominence as the seat of Maui County and has the historical flavor

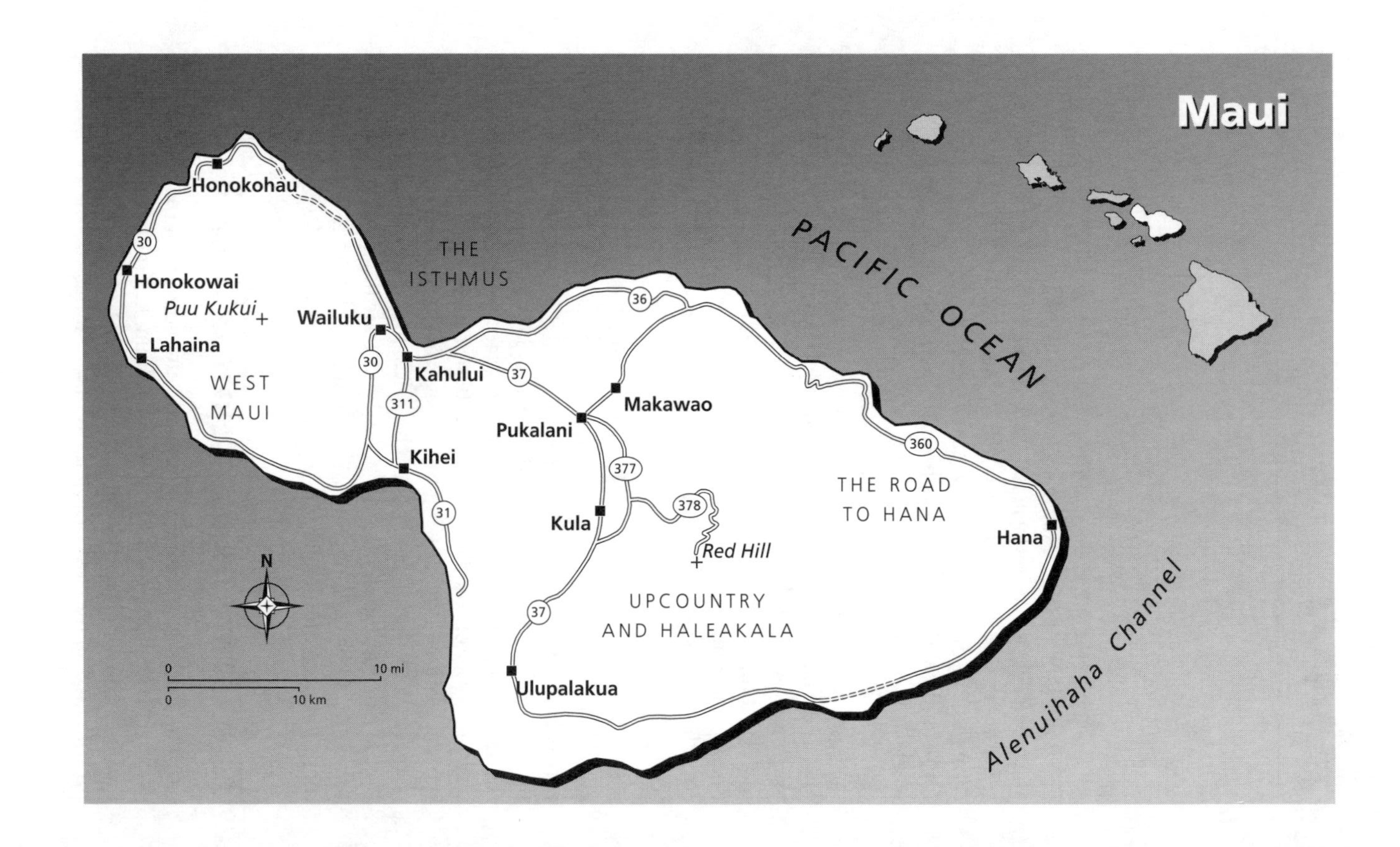
Maui
PACIFIC OCEAN
Alenuihaha Channel
Honokohau
Honokowai
Puu Kukui
Lahaina
Wailuku
WEST MAUI
THE ISTHMUS
Kahului
Kihei
Pukalani
Makawao
Kula
Red Hill
Ulupalakua
Hana
THE ROAD TO HANA
UPCOUNTRY AND HALEAKALA
30
311
31
37
36
377
378
360
N
0
10 mi
0
10 km

Kahului lacks. As Ka`ahumanu Avenue (Route 32) heads west from Kahului, it slopes uphill to become Main Street in Wailuku. At the top of Main Street, begin your tour at the ***Bailey House Museum*** (244–3326). This restored mission station portrays both the lifestyle of the early missionaries and the Hawaiian culture that preceded them. The Wailuku mission began in 1833 under Reverend Green, who established a young women's seminary on the property. The main goal was to instruct them in "employments suited to their sex," primarily to produce suitable companions for the graduates of the boys' school over the mountains in Lahaina.

In 1837, Reverend and Mrs. Green were joined and eventually replaced by the Baileys, who converted the adobe building to coral stone in 1841. Young women in the seminary donated their hair as the binding agent for the plaster. Edward Bailey was a multitalented man who later left the mission to manage Wailuku Sugar Company. An accomplished artist, he gifted posterity with oil paintings of nineteenth-century Maui, many of which adorn the museum.

Brief History of Maui

As the second largest island in Hawaii, Maui chieftains long rivaled those of the Big Island in the bid for preeminence. In the mid-eighteenth century, a Maui warrior by the name of Kahekili embarked on a bold mission of conquest, uniting O`ahu, Moloka`i, and Lana`i under his rule. Had his conquests continued, we might today know the archipelago as "the Maui islands" instead of Hawaii. Instead, Kahekili was eclipsed by a younger warrior from the Big Island, named Kamehameha, who eventually succeeded in unifying the entire island chain under his rule.

Maui's most enduring legacy in the newly unified kingdom of Hawaii was wrought by two women. Keopuolani, a Maui princess of the highest rank, became Kamehameha's "sacred" wife. Her royal lineage (superior to his own) ensured that his heirs would have the mana *to rule and became the foundation for the Kamehameha dynasty. But Kamehameha's favorite wife, Ka`ahumanu, played an even greater role in Hawaiian history. Also Maui born, Ka`ahumanu's willful nature led to a stormy relationship with Kamehameha during their marriage. After his death, Ka`ahumanu served as regent, sharing power with Liholiho, Kamehameha's heir. To consolidate her position, Ka`ahumanu maneuvered Liholiho into overthrowing the* kapu *(taboo) system that repressed women; she later encouraged the advent of Christian missionaries. Ka`ahumanu also succeeded where even Kamehameha I had failed in "conquering" the northernmost island, Kaua`i. She accomplished this by the novel strategem of abducting and then simultaneously marrying both Kaua`i's former King, Kamuali`i, and his eldest son.*

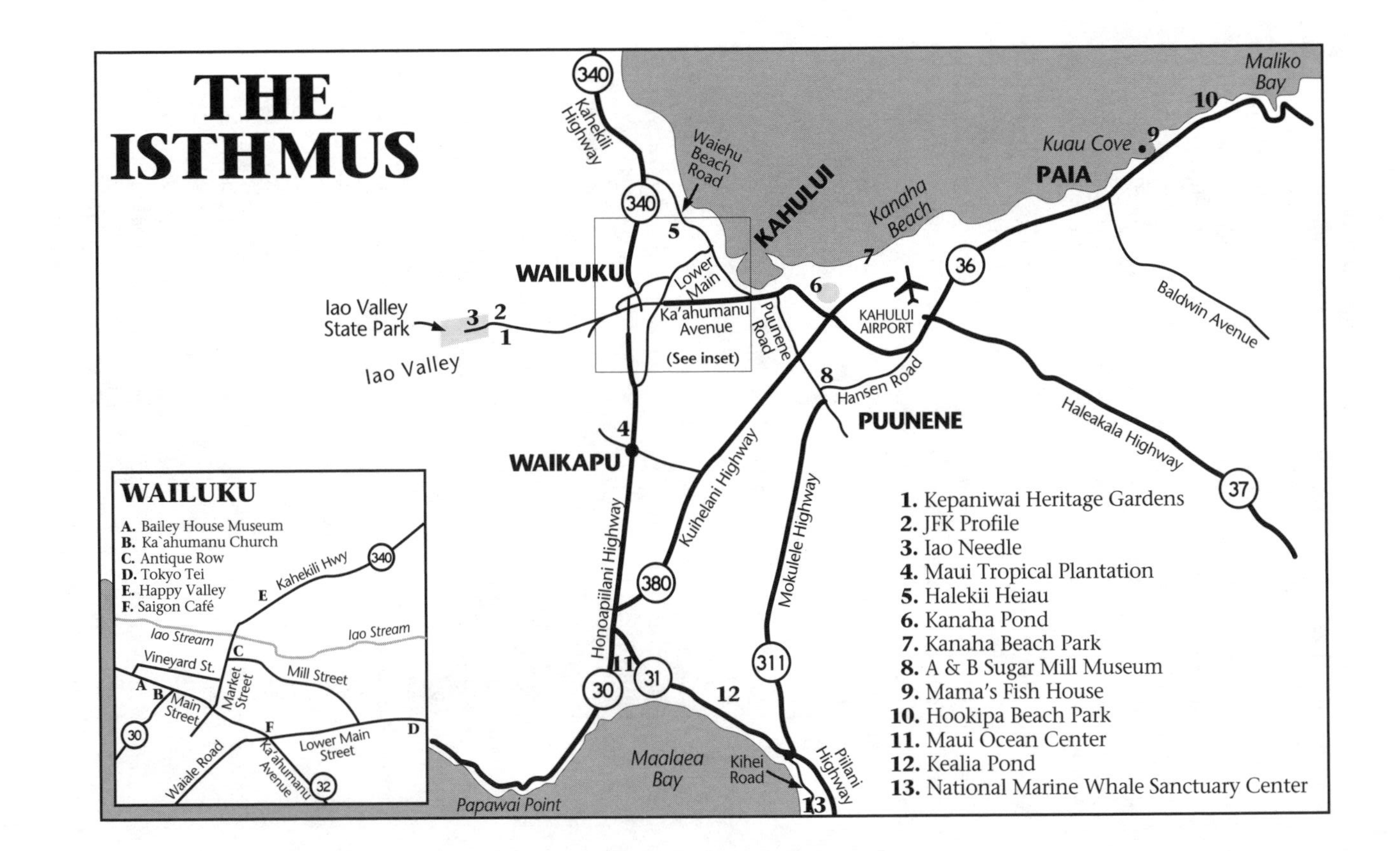
THE ISTHMUS
Maliko Bay
10
Kuau Cove
9
PAIA
Kahekili Highway
340
Waiehu Beach Road
KAHULUI
Kanaha Beach
7
5
WAILUKU
Lower Main
6
36
Iao Valley State Park
3
2
1
Ka'ahumanu Avenue
(See inset)
Puunene Road
KAHULUI AIRPORT
Baldwin Avenue
Iao Valley
8
Hansen Road
PUUNENE
Haleakala Highway
4
WAIKAPU
Kuihelani Highway
Mokulele Highway
37
380
Honoapiilani Highway
311
11
31
30
12
Maalaea Bay
Kihei Road
Piilani Highway
Papawai Point
13
1. Kepaniwai Heritage Gardens
2. JFK Profile
3. Iao Needle
4. Maui Tropical Plantation
5. Halekii Heiau
6. Kanaha Pond
7. Kanaha Beach Park
8. A & B Sugar Mill Museum
9. Mama's Fish House
10. Hookipa Beach Park
11. Maui Ocean Center
12. Kealia Pond
13. National Marine Whale Sanctuary Center
WAILUKU
A. Bailey House Museum
B. Ka`ahumanu Church
C. Antique Row
D. Tokyo Tei
E. Happy Valley
F. Saigon Café
Kahekili Hwy
E
Iao Stream
Iao Stream
C
Vineyard St.
Mill Street
A
B
Main Street
Market Street
F
Lower Main Street
D
Waiale Road
Ka'ahumanu Avenue
32

The upstairs rooms of the Bailey home feature missionary-period furnishings, including some beautifully patterned Hawaiian quilts in the bedroom. Hand-operated spinning wheels and looms fill the parlor room, sewing having been one of the principal employments taught at the seminary. The rooms below are devoted to Hawaiiana. Jewelry junkies will marvel at the variety of materials Hawaiians used for necklaces. Instead of perishable flower leis, the well-dressed Hawaiian could wear a strand of shells, *kukui* nuts, feathers, teeth, or even human hair. The museum also offers examples of rare Hawaiian *kapa,* some of the most beautiful bark cloth produced in Polynesia, sadly a lost art form. Another room displays the enormous *ipu,* or Hawaiian gourds, decorated to be used as containers, musical instruments, or lamps. Open Monday through Saturday 10:00 A.M. to 4:00 P.M.; modest admission charge. Before you leave, ask about the self-guided ***walking tour*** to explore other historic buildings in Wailuku.

Geography of Maui

Maui is the second largest of the Hawaiian Islands. Built from the overlapping flows of two volcanoes that meet along a narrow isthmus, this natural wind tunnel makes the "Valley Isle" a mecca for windsurfers. Of the two landmasses the western Maui mountains are older and more heavily eroded. Their summit at Puu Kukui reaches 5,788 feet. Haleakala, the volcano that forms eastern Maui, rises gently to a 10,023-foot summit and harbors an enormous erosive crater within.

Walk a block downhill to High Street where ***Ka`ahumanu Church*** sits in Honolii Park. Its weighty steeple points heavenward in classic New England style, while the white walls and green roof invert the colors of the cloud-draped West Maui Mountains behind. Named for Queen Ka`ahumanu, an early convert to Christianity, the present structure dates to 1876, but its predecessors go back to the earliest missionaries. Wailuku's government buildings huddle under shady trees nearby. The State Building at 54 South High Street issues state camping permits, dispenses hiking guides, and books cabins; call well in advance for the latter (984–8109). Open Monday–Friday, 8:00 A.M. to 3:30 P.M. Camping in the county's Kanaha Beach Park is not recommended.

So much for religion and power. Now for shopping. Stroll north on Market Street, 2 blocks below High Street to explore ***Antique Row,*** a strip of antiques stores and galleries with catchy names like Memory Lane and Sheila's Junktique. You never know what treasures you might discover as you sift through Asian and Pacific artifacts, genuine antiques, and various arts and craftwork. For classic aloha-wear, check out ***Sig Zane's*** at 53 Market Street.

Wailuku's unpretentious eateries mostly follow Hawaii's ethnic contours. Somehow it ended up with two Thai restaurants, though. Folks differ on which has the best food, but ***Saeng's*** (244–1567), at 2119 Vineyard Street, has the edge on decor with a pleasant garden lana`i in back. Open weekdays 11:00 A.M. to 2:30 P.M. and nightly 5:00–9:30 P.M. Moderate. If you're here for lunch, you could also try a *pain fourré* sandwich from nearby ***Maui Bake Shop & Deli*** (242–0064).

Locals all over Maui rave about the Vietnamese cuisine at the ***Saigon Cafe*** (243–9560) at 1792 Main Street. (The steak dishes on the menu are holdovers from the cafe's former incarnation as Naokee Steak House.) Be warned: The sign for the cafe is not visible from Main Street itself. You'll find it near the bridge where Ka`ahumanu Avenue crosses over Lower Main, at the corner of Kaniela and Main Streets. Open 10:00 A.M. to 9:30 P.M. daily.

Back in Wailuku, heading north (downhill) on Market across the Iao Stream bridge leads you into Happy Valley for more dining options. You won't find the "action" this former red-light district once attracted, though all eleven of Maui's hostess bars hover nearby. But the restaurants and shops here are even less tainted by tourist dollars than Wailuku. Visit ***Aki's Hawaiian Food and Bar*** (244–8122) for *ono kaukau* (good eats) at budget prices. Open Monday–Saturday 11:00 A.M. to 9:00 P.M. and Sunday 5:00–9:00 P.M. Or check out the deli case at ***Takamiya's Market.*** Prepared foods range from *poke* (raw fish and seaweed salad) to *bento* (Japanese box lunches).

Just before the bridge, Mill Street leads east off Market Street into

Maui Trivia

- *More humpback whales congregate in the warm waters offshore from Maui than near any other island.*
- *Haleakala is the world's largest dormant volcano.*
- *Built in 1801, the Brick Palace in Lahaina is Hawaii's first western building.*
- *Pi`ilani heiau, Hawaii's largest, was built in A.D. 1400 near Hana.*
- *Mosquitoes first arrived in the islands in 1872, as unknown passengers in Lahaina, Maui, aboard the* Wellington, *a merchant ship.*
- *A drop in sea level during the Ice Age joined Maui with neighboring islands Moloka`i, Lana`i, and Kaho`olawe, forming a single landmass.*

Wailuku's industrial sector along Lower Main Street. ***Tokyo Tei*** (242–9630), 1063 Lower Main Street, ensconced in an ugly two-story office complex, has served tasty Japanese fare since 1935. Open Monday–Saturday 11:00 A.M. to 1:30 P.M. and 5:00–8:30 P.M., Sunday 5:00–8:00 P.M.

For late-night dining you have to go to Kahului. Visit ***Koho's*** (877–5588) in Kahului's Ka`ahumanu Shopping Center for local diner fare. Open Sunday and Monday, 7:00 A.M. to 10:00 P.M.; Tuesday through Thursday, 7:00 A.M. to 11:00 P.M.; Friday and Saturday 7:00 A.M. to midnight. Worth a visit any time of day, ***Mañana Garage*** (873–0220), at Ka'ahumanu and Lono Avenue, across the road from Chevron, serves hip Latin fare prepared with an island flair in a sleek, industrial setting. Open Monday–Saturday 11:00 A.M. to 2:30 P.M., 5:00–9:30 P.M., with late-night menu until 11:00 P.M.

Wailuku sleeps as cheaply as it eats, with a number of flophouses catering to transients and workers. The influx of windsurfers to Maui's North Shore has led some to upgrade. The best of the bunch are the ***Banana Bungalow*** (244–5090), at 310 North Market Street, and the ***Northshore Inn*** (371–4131), at 2080 Vineyard Street. Both offer doubles for $40 and dorm beds for $16.

Wailuku does offer one luxury accommodation option in ***The Old Wailuku Inn at Ulupono*** (244–5897; 800–305–4899; www.maui-inn.com; 2199 Kaho`okele Street, 96793). Built in 1924 by a wealthy island banker as a wedding gift for his daughter-in-law, the inn has been lovingly restored to evoke the nostalgic grandeur of that earlier era. Woven *lauhala* mats rest on hardwood floors while full-size Hawaiian quilts drape over the beds. A variety of Hawaiian heirlooms and antique furniture from the Orient enhance the period look. The inn also pays tribute to Hawaii's "Poet Laureate," Don Blanding, and contains several features inspired by his poems. Views from the breakfast room encompass Haleakala, while the front porch faces Iao Valley. The seven rooms range in price from $120–$180 and include a full breakfast; two nights minimum.

To visit a far older shrine than Ka`ahumanu Church, continue down the hill on Lower Main and turn left onto Waiehu Beach Road. Cross Iao Stream and turn left at Kuhio Place, then left again up Hea Place to ***Halekii Heiau.*** Built atop a massive sand dune overlooking Kahului Bay, the temple was partially reconstructed in 1958, but the carved wooden images (*kii*) that presumably stood here no longer exist to deter invaders.

While in Wailuku, every Maui visitor must undertake the pilgrimage into ***Iao Valley,*** by far the largest, steepest, and deepest cleft in the West Maui Mountains. The head of the valley opens onto the ancient crater that formed this half of the island. Its rear wall rises 5,788 feet to ***Puu Kukui,*** the highest peak on West Maui. Because of this western mountain screen, darkness comes early to the valley. Mornings can be memorable as the sunlight descends the ridgetops probing through the mist. Equally dramatic are late afternoons, when the clouds that crowd into the narrow valley opening reflect ethereal bolts of sunlight that backlight the stage.

To get there, take Main Street west past the Bailey House and bear left onto Iao Valley Road. Drive into the steep-walled canyon entrance and watch the scenery unfold. The valley gradually widens as its walls grow taller, serrated by narrow side canyons and hanging valleys. Waterfalls concealed in these dark crevasses often spray mist that the sun's probing rays transmute into rainbows.

Kepaniwai, a clearing halfway up the valley, literally means "damming of the waters." The name has its gruesome origins in a battle in which Kamehameha's Western cannons massacred Maui defenders in a carnage that left Iao Stream literally dammed by piles of corpses. Today, ***Kepaniwai Heritage Gardens*** on the bank of Iao Stream celebrate Hawaii's diverse ethnic heritage. As you roam the grounds, try to puzzle out the different motifs, from a Japanese sculpture of cane workers to a traditional Filipino bamboo house. Local kids of all ethnic groups come here to splash in the stream and fish for tadpoles in the ponds. Free. The ***Hawaii Nature Center*** (244–6500) next door showcases a different facet of Hawaii's diversity, with hands-on, interactive exhibits focused on Iao Valley's ecology. The center offers hikes and other interpretive activities. Open daily from 10:00 A.M. to 4:00 P.M. Admission $6.00.

The road continues deeper into the valley through a winding gorge. Pause to squint at the ***JFK Profile,*** a natural rock formation noticed only after President Kennedy's death. Ahead is ***Iao Valley State Park.*** Various paved paths crisscross the valley floor, and hiking trails lead up the different tributary branches of Iao Stream as well as up a central ridge to the tableland above the upper valley floor. Wherever you roam in the park, your eyes are drawn toward ***Iao Needle,*** a basalt spire jutting 1,320 feet above the valley floor. A narrow ridge actually connects the Needle to the valley wall, but its freestanding illusion is maintained until you walk behind it.

South of Wailuku, the Honoapiilani Highway (Route 30) continues out of High Street to reach the small pineapple plantation town of Waikapu, home of ***Maui Tropical Plantation*** (244–7643). This 112-acre "work-

Iao Needle

ing farm" showcases Hawaii's agricultural history and diversity. It's worth visiting but would seem less of a tourist trap if the gift shop did not sit firmly athwart the entrance. If you skip the narrated ride, admission is free. Open daily 9:00 A.M. to 5:00 P.M.

Don't let the sedate pineapple fields around Waikapu fool you; the rest of the isthmus "raises cane." Surrounded by tall, waving cane fields, the tiny town of Puunene sits southeast of Kahului at the intersection of Puunene Avenue (Route 350) and Hansen Road. Puunene centers around its sugar mill, a monster of hissing pipes and ducts and throbbing machinery. As with all mills in Hawaii, visitors are barred for safety reasons. But at Puunene, the curious can learn the sugar story—and even see a working

Humpback Heaven

Like many species, humpbacks head south for the winter as Arctic ice packs encroach on their summer feeding grounds off Alaska. Fashionable humpbacks gather in Hawaii; roughly 3,000 whales, more than two-thirds of the north Pacific population, winter in island waters. The whales begin arriving in November, reaching peak numbers by February, and stick around until about May. They do not eat while in Hawaiian waters, as their preferred food, krill (a tiny shrimp), is not found in tropical oceans. Instead, the humpbacks live off stores of blubber accumulated over the summer and devote their time to other pursuits.

Topping their list of vacation activities is reproduction. Whales breed and then give birth a year later in the warm, sheltered waters offshore from all the major Hawaiian islands, with the largest numbers gathering around Maui. Female humpbacks calve every two to three years, with a ten- to twelve-month gestation period. Their newborns measure 12 to 14 feet and weigh two tons. Drinking fifty to one hundred gallons of milk, these will grow as much as one hundred pounds per day, reaching up to 50 feet long and forty tons by maturity.

Humpbacks communicate through unusually complex whale songs, haunting rhythmic melodies that extend from the subsonic range to high-pitched whistles and can travel over hundreds of miles of open ocean. Only male humpback whales sing complete songs; the tunes they use vary by region in the Pacific and evolve over time.

Humpbacks are also known for their playful acrobatics, often leaping from the water or splashing with their flukes and fins. The purpose of this behavior is not well understood, yet it makes for fascinating whale watching. Any number of whale-watching tours operate during the season from Lahaina or Malaia harbors. Those prone to seasickness might consider going with Seabird Cruise's Navatek (873–3475; 888–8481–6787), which uses boats equipped with SWATH technology, a system whereby a submerged second hull and a computer-controlled ballast provide added stability. At press time, the boat was being refurbished, but is expected to resume operation in Spring, 2002.

For more information on humpbacks, contact the National Marine Sanctuary in Kihei (see page 182).

scale model of a mill—by visiting the ***Alexander & Baldwin Sugar Mill Museum*** (871–8058) right across the street.

Housed in a turn-of-the-twentieth-century plantation superintendent's residence, the museum brings to life the people and events that created Hawaii's once dominant industry. Begin by mastering Arithmetic Lesson number 1: Constant Sunshine Plus a Ton of Water Equals a Pound of Sugar. Maui's isthmus gets plenty of sunshine, but the water comes from irrigation. In 1878, Samuel Alexander and Henry Baldwin, children of Lahaina missionaries, began the Hamakua Ditch, a 50-mile engineering miracle that tunneled and bridged its way across Haleakala's rainy windward gulches to tap millions of gallons of water. You can see remnants of it on the drive to Hana. In addition to its inherent difficulties, the project became a race against time. If they didn't finish in a year, the water rights and all their work would go to their rival, Claus Spreckels, who held financial strings on King Kalakaua. They made it—barely.

With the increase in irrigated lands under production, a labor shortage arose. Different immigrant groups were brought in to work the fields and were housed in separate camps with names like "Ah Fong" for the Chinese and "Codfish" for the Portuguese. Such segregation helped new arrivals adjust to the culture shock of relocation and also prevented a united labor front from forming. Photo murals illustrate the different pastimes these plantation workers indulged in: sumo wrestling for the Japanese, cockfights for the Filipinos, with baseball serving as the one "melting pot" sport. The museum is open Monday–Saturday (also open Sunday February through March and July through August) from 9:30 A.M. to 4:30 P.M.; $5.00 admission.

South of Waikapu, Route 30 leads to Ma`alaea Bay on the isthmus's southern shore. The ***Maui Ocean Center*** (270–7000) here presents a fascinating introduction to Hawaii's underwater environment. Grasp a squishy sea cucumber in the "touch pool." Test your knowledge of cetacean trivia by playing the "Humpback Dating Game." Stroll through a glass tunnel that leads into a 750,000-gallon "open-ocean" tank with sharks and other colorful fish swimming overhead. Naturalist talks/feedings are scheduled at different tanks throughout the day. Open daily 9:00 A.M. to 5:00 P.M.; $18.50 admission. If looking at so many fish has made you hungry to eat some, wander over to ***Bamboo Bistro*** (243–7374), where you can savor the harbor views while sampling Big Island chef Peter Merriman's culinary inventions that always feature fresh-catch specials. Open daily 11:30 A.M. to 3:00 P.M., 5:30 to 9:00 P.M. Dinner prices are investment-caliber, but lunch is moderate. Live music Thursday–Saturday nights.

If you prefer to do your whale watching from dry land, a good place to do this is the ***National Marine Sanctuary*** (879–2818; 800–831–4888) headquarters just around the bay at 1726 South Kihei Road. Scientists monitor Hawaii's whale population from here. Visitors can use the free telescopes to do a little monitoring of their own as well as peruse exhibits on marine ecology and its importance to native Hawaii culture. Open Monday–Friday 10:00 A.M. to 3:00 P.M.

On the way to the marine center, you will pass ***Kealia Pond***, a wetland bird sanctuary. Bird-watching enthusiasts should stop at the visitors office located on the inland side of the pond at mile marker six along the Mokulele Highway (Route 311). Call 875–1582.

The rest of Kihei is cluttered with condos and holds little of interest to the off-the-beaten-path traveler. Instead take advantage of the Piilani Highway to bypass them and fast-forward to the less traveled territory that begins further south at Makena. Turn seaward from Wailea Alanui Drive, onto Makena Road to swing past historic ***Keawalai Congregational Church.*** Sunday services at 9:30 A.M. are conducted half in English, half in Hawaiian. Churchgoers might also appreciate open-air services farther north in Kihei, held (weather permitting) in the ruins of a church built by David Malo, Hawaii's first native ordained minister. Look for ***Trinity-by-the-Sea Church*** off South Kihei Road.

On the horizon you can see all the islands of Maui County floating in an inland sea. From left to right, they are Kahoolawe, Lana`i, and Moloka`i. During the Ice Age, a drop in the sea level welded these lands together into a single mass. Molokini Islet, in the middle of Alalakeiki Channel, formed during this period as a tuff cone on a once-larger Haleakala. If this view sounds appealing, book a room with Ann & Bob ***Babson's Vacation Rentals*** (874–1166; 800–824–6409). They offer two B&B rooms with private baths, an apartment, and a separate cottage, all with panoramic ocean views. Prices range from $100 to $135; discounts available for longer stays. You could also try ***Makena Landing B&B*** (879–6286). The beachside studios here offer unbeatable value at $125 per night. The only catch is that they are booked solid months in advance.

Continue about a mile past the Maui Prince Hotel to the parking lot for ***Oneloa*** ("long sands") ***Beach.*** The last undeveloped beach on the coast, Oneloa glories in a half-mile of wide, white sand bordering azure waters. Rising from the northern edge of the beach, ***Puu Olai,*** a 360-foot cinder cone, resembles a pimple on the slope of Haleakala. Climb over its seaward edge to reach ***Little Beach,*** a popular unofficial nudist enclave. Dangerous conditions arise during high surf at both beaches.

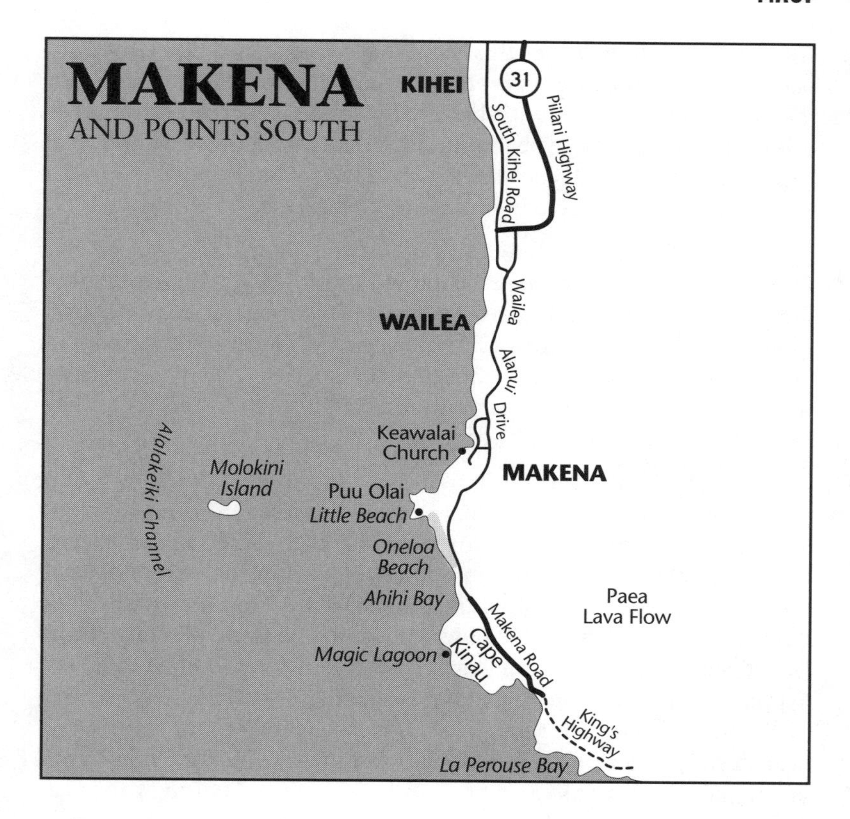

As you move south from Oneloa, you enter the ***Ahihi-Kinau Natural Area Reserve.*** A glance up the slope of Haleakala reveals a dark scar on the volcano's green flank. This black, congealed mass of lava came from the unexpected 1790 ***Paea Flow,*** the last eruption on Maui. Scientists ascribe the flow to an isolated pocket of lava trapped underground after its source had dried up. Hawaiian legend interprets it as the wrath of Pele consuming Paea, a young man who had spurned her affections. The eruption formed the massive Cape Kinau south of Ahihi Bay and has left the entire coastline rocky and barren. If you're adventurous, follow the white paint splotches on the trail that starts just before telephone pole #18; it crosses the lava for about a mile to reach ***Magic Lagoon,*** a sandy snorkeling spot.

Another mile south across the flow brings you to ***La Perouse Bay,*** named for an early French explorer who claimed it for his country, sailed off, and was never heard of again. Drivable road ends here, but remnants of the ancient ***King's Highway*** continue closer to the shore.

Oral histories testify that this stone-paved pathway once girded the island, built in the fifteenth century by the great chief Piilani. Part of the conservation zone, the waters here are a snorkeler's paradise although the center of the bay can be murky at times. Rock foundations and walls from Hawaiian houses are readily discernible, haunting the desolate lava with vestiges of a once-flourishing civilization.

Finally, to explore some more of the isthmus's north shore, head east from Kahului along the Hana Highway (Route 36). As you leave Kahului, you pass ***Kanaha Pond Waterfowl Refuge,*** once a freshwater fishpond sacred to royalty and now the nesting site for migratory waterfowl as well as native birds such as the Hawaiian heron, stilt, and coot. Birdwatchers can walk a perimeter trail accessed from the airport road. The highway continues through sugar cane and passes some of the world's most famous sailboarding beaches.

Trade winds sweeping across Maui's northern shoreline funnel into the central valley isthmus. As the sun heats the land, cooler air is sucked in from the ocean, and by afternoon the winds whip to a fury. Incoming swells generate constant surf, creating the perfect terrain for acrobatic jumps and rides. When the wind is blowing, beaches all along Maui's North Shore glisten with the butterfly wings of neon-colored sails. The latest fad here is kite surfing, a new variant that is basically windsurfing with a detachable sail. ***Kanaha Beach,*** by the airport, offers the best learning conditions for windsurfing. Most of the windsurf shops offering rentals and lessons cluster nearby on Dairy Road (straight ahead as you exit the airport). Many can also arrange beachfront accommodations. Try ***Hi-Tech/Maui Windsurfari*** (877–2111; 800–736–6284) or ***Windrigger Maui*** (800–345–6284).

Five miles east, Paia once had the largest population on Maui clustered around its still-working mill. When the new "dream city" built in Kahului lured workers around the bay, Paia dwindled to a virtual ghost town. In the sixties, the town acquired a hippie tinge that it has not entirely shed, but Paia's revival dates to the advent of windsurfing. Hordes of mostly European sailboard fanatics have descended upon the town environs, renting beach bungalows and filling the streets with rental cars laden with windsurfing gear.

Paia's ramshackle plantation buildings spread along the T formed by the Hana Highway and Baldwin Avenue. They house an incongruous mix of surf shops, old-style markets, and clothing boutiques. Near the western entrance to town, the ***Maui Crafts Guild*** (579–9697) offers a sampling of Maui artistry in media from *raku* pottery to hand-painted silks. A cooperative society of artists stock and staff the green two-story home, allowing you to meet creator and creations under the same roof. Open daily 9:00 A.M. to 6:00 P.M. Paia's shopping scene also includes a pair of antiques stores and a custom millinery shop.

Paia boasts a number of funky restaurants. The sailboarder crowds gather at ***Jacques*** (579–8844), at 120 Hana Highway, a boisterous French bistro. The menu features classic bistro standards such as duck confit, gone tropical with island fruit glazes, as well as nightly fresh-catch specials. Moderate. Open daily 10:00 A.M. to 10:00 P.M., with late night service 'till 2:00 A.M. on weekends and live music Monday and Thursday nights. Another good bet is ***Moana Bakery & Café*** (579–9999), at 71 Baldwin Avenue, which offers an eclectic menu centered on fresh island produce as well as classic French pastries. Dinners run in the expensive range. Open daily 7:00 A.M. to 9:00 P.M. ***Charly's*** (579–9453) is famous for its breakfasts. Be sure to read the story printed on the menu. Day-trippers bound for Upcountry or Hana can get gourmet box lunches from ***Picnics*** (579–8021). And vegetarians will find fine fodder at ***The Vegan*** (579–9144), a small cafe farther up Baldwin Avenue. Open daily 11:00 A.M. to 9:00 P.M.

A mile and a half east of town, in a romantic beach shack just off the highway in Kuau Cove, ***Mama's Fish House*** (579–8488) serves seafood as fresh as its oceanside views. Mama buys only from local fishers; the menu tells who caught each fish where and how. It's up to you whether the end product comes grilled, seared, sautéed, or baked. Open daily 11:00 A.M. to 3:00 P.M. and 4:45–9:15 P.M., with happy-hour *pupus* served in between. Investment-caliber prices. Reservations recommended.

Mama's also rents well-equipped, albeit pricey, cottages clustered on the same lot from $140 to $350. Call 579–9764; (800) 860–4852. For lodging with more historic character, consider the ***Kuau Cove Plantation House B&B*** (579–8988), a former plantation doctor's home nestled beneath a giant monkeypod tree. Rooms run $85, with studios for $95.

Back in Paia itself, the ***Nalu Kai Lodge*** (579–9107) is ideally situated at the corner of Baldwin Avenue and the Hana Highway. Rates start at $40 for one night. For additional lodging options, check the bulletin board outside Mana Health Foods.

As you head east of town, take a look at ***Mantokuji Buddhist Temple.*** The huge gong sounds daily at dawn and dusk. The windsurfing faithful worship 2 miles farther at ***Hookipa*** ("hospitality") ***Beach Park.*** Their mecca, a small rocky beach with less-than-hospitable currents and surf, offers experts unbeatable windsurfing terrain. When conditions are right,

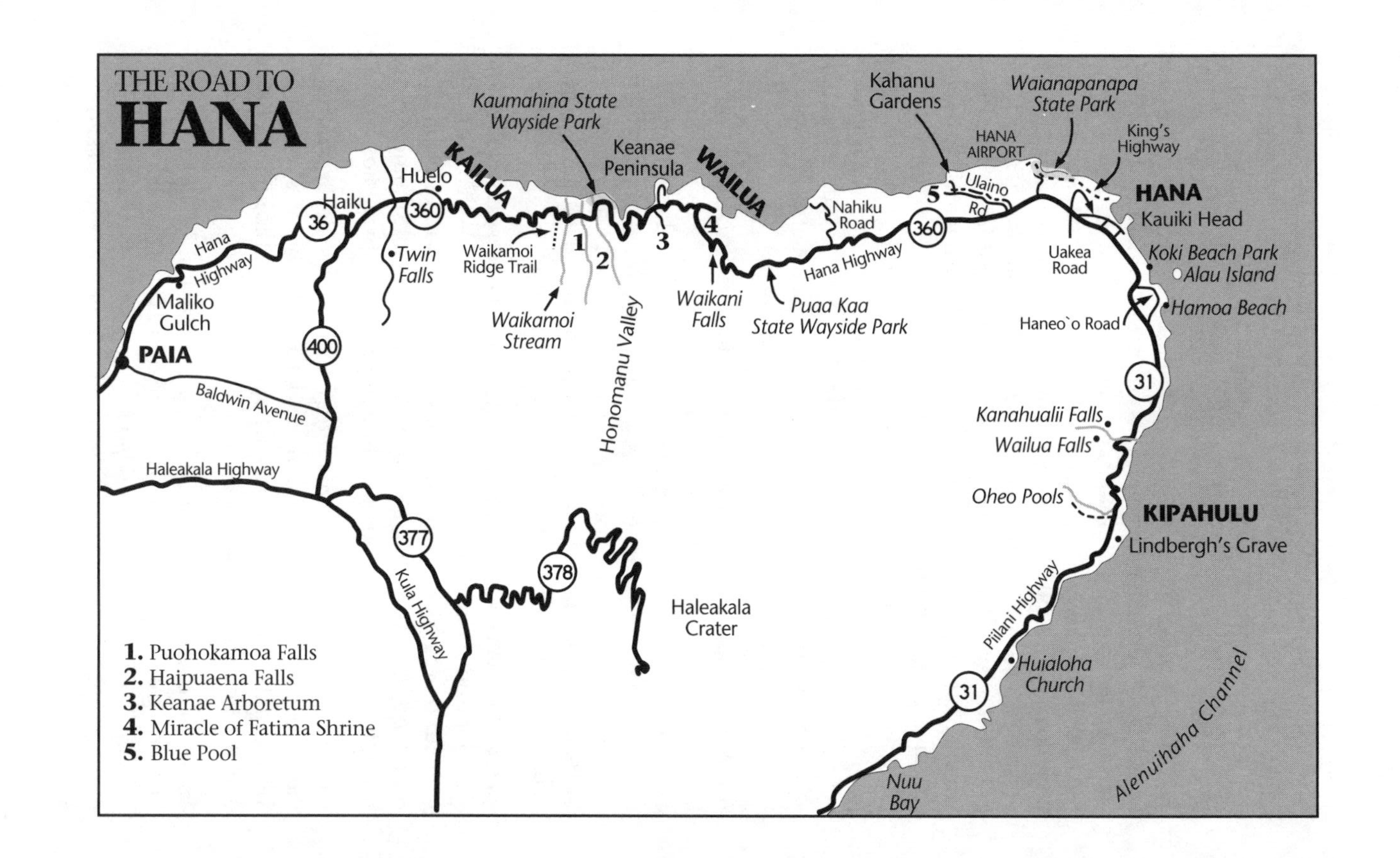
THE ROAD TO
HANA
Kaumahina State Wayside Park
Keanae Peninsula
Kahanu Gardens
Waianapanapa State Park
HANA AIRPORT
King's Highway
KAILUA
WAILUA
HANA
Huelo
Haiku
36
360
Hana Highway
Maliko Gulch
PAIA
400
Twin Falls
Waikamoi Ridge Trail
Waikamoi Stream
Honomanu Valley
Waikani Falls
Puaa Kaa State Wayside Park
Hana Highway
Nahiku Road
Ulaino Rd
Uakea Road
Kauiki Head
Koki Beach Park
Alau Island
Hamoa Beach
Haneo`o Road
31
Kanahualii Falls
Wailua Falls
Oheo Pools
KIPAHULU
Lindbergh's Grave
Piilani Highway
Huialoha Church
Nuu Bay
Alenuihaha Channel
Baldwin Avenue
Haleakala Highway
377
Kula Highway
378
Haleakala Crater
1. Puohokamoa Falls
2. Haipuaena Falls
3. Keanae Arboretum
4. Miracle of Fatima Shrine
5. Blue Pool

you can watch the world's top talents launch themselves into aerial loops off the face of mountainous waves, then jibe to surf the next breaker in.

The Road to Hana

The road to Hana is perhaps the most famous "off the beaten path" adventure in Hawaii. A constant stream of rental cars embarks on this 52-mile odyssey, negotiating fifty-six single-lane bridges and more than 600 curves. You should, too—but resist any temptation to motor compulsively for three hours nonstop just to buy your "I Survived the Hana Highway" T-shirt and return disappointed. Consider breaking up the trip by stopping overnight; it'll take the pressure off your drive. The road to Hana is like life: It's not the destination that counts, but what you do along the way.

The Hana Highway (Route 360) traverses Maui's shoulders, the rainy northeast slopes of Haleakala. You pass isolated valleys, hidden (and not-so-hidden) waterfalls, and stunning seascapes. Along the way grow tropical plants of every description. Roll down your windows and smell the flowers—there's always something in bloom. Do, however, check the weather before leaving (877–5111). Heavy rains along this windward coast can cause landslides and close the highway entirely. Beyond Hana, the southern route to Ulupalakua Ranch (Route 31) is poorly maintained and often impassable.

Stock up before you leave Paia because it's a long, empty road ahead. East of Hookipa Beach Park, Route 36 winds around ***Maliko Gulch.*** This was the last obstacle in building the Hamakua Ditch, an early irrigation channel bringing water to the isthmus sugar fields, and weary workers balked when they saw its steep walls. To rally his troops, Henry Baldwin—who had lost an arm in a mill accident only months before—grabbed a rope and lowered himself into the ravine using his one good hand. He repeated this feat every day until the gulch was spanned.

After leaving Maliko, the highway climbs inland past pineapple fields, smaller gulches, before reaching Haiku, a semirural community once anchored by a pair of pineapple canneries. The canneries closed long ago, and have been converted to commercial space. For a taste of Maui's surf culture, turn inland from the highway at arond the 12-mile point and follow Kuiaha Road to ***Pauwela Cafe*** (575–9242), at #375. The cafe shares space in the former cannery building with a surfboard manufacturer; other elite surfers who come here are drawn to Haiku by the

Trivia

The 52-mile road to Hana consists of 56 single-lane bridges and more than 550 hairpin curves.

chance to tackle "Jaws," Haiku's infamous winter surf spot that breaks on an offshore reef only during the biggest winter surf. Towering up to 50 feet high, the waves there are so big that to catch them surfers have to be towed by Jet Skis until they reach "launch speed." Grab a table when the surf is up and listen to their war stories. Open Monday–Saturday 7:00 A.M. to 3:00 P.M., Sunday 8:00 A.M. to 2:00 P.M.

Get the jump on the drive to Hana by lodging at one of these: ***Haikuleana B&B*** (575–2890; 555 Haiku Road, Haiku 96708) offers three suites in an elegantly restored 1870 plantation home; all have private baths and rent for $120–$145, full breakfast included. ***Golden Bamboo Ranch*** (572–7824; 1205 Kaupakalua Road, Haiku 96708) offers cottages and suites on a seven-acre spread, from $90–$105; breakfast fixings supplied. Just up the road at 911 Kaupakalua, the karma-conscious might appreciate the simple lodging provided by ***Bamboo Mountain Sanctuary*** (572–5106), a former Zen monastery and current spiritual retreat. Doubles with shared bath are $60 per night. For those who really want seclusion, Ann DeWeese's ***Tea House Cottage B&B*** (572–5610; P.O. Box 335, Haiku 96708) awaits a few miles

Cave Tales

Near Hana, a well-marked trail in Waianapanapa State Park leads to two caves formed from ancient lava tubes and now partially filled with water. An old Hawaiian legend tells of a beautiful princess, Popoalaea, who ran away from her cruel husband, Kakae, and hid with her handmaiden in the first of these caves on a dry inner ledge not visible from the opening. Kakae came after her, furious at Popoalaea's betrayal. Although her tracks led to the cave, Kakae could not at first tell where she had vanished and started to move away. Unfortunately, just then the torch light he carried revealed the bright colors of the princess's feather kahili *(a standard of royalty) mirrored on the clear water of the cave. Venting his anger with savage strokes of his dagger, Kakae slew the women there on the spot, their blood spilling into the pool. The tiny* opaekaa *shrimp that live in this pool annually recall this act of cruelty. In spawning every spring, they turn the water red, supposedly in deference to the slain princess. Adventurous travelers today can swim to the inner ledge where Popoalaea hid, equipped with a flashlight wrapped in a Ziploc bag. Those interested in more extended spelunking should contact Hana Cave Tours (248–7308), which leads one- and two-hour tours through the much larger Ka`eleku Caverns nearby and explains their geologic origins.*

down the highway. You have to hike about 200 yards from the driveway to reach it (a wheelbarrow does bellhop service), but the tropical jungle setting and ocean views make it worthwhile. The rustic cottage relies on solar power for electricity but is comfortably furnished with most modern conveniences, except that the bathroom is separate. It rents for $95 per night, with a three-night minimum.

The Hana Highway officially begins after the 16-mile marker at the intersection with Route 400. Route 36 changes to Route 360, for whatever reason, and the mileage markers begin at zero. As if to justify this symbolism, the road immediately launches into wild turns through lush jungle. Continue to the first bridge (Hoolawanui Stream) past mile marker 2. A trail leads from a gate on the near side of the bridge a quarter-mile inland to ***Twin Falls.*** You can swing from a rope into the swimming hole below the falls. A larger falls waits a half-mile upstream; bear left along the irrigation ditch. Daredevils leap from the top of this one as well. WARNING: As with all streams on the Hana Coast, beware of flash flooding.

A mile farther, roughly one-third of the way to Hana, ***Huelo Point*** boasts a couple of old churches and some very new, splashy vacation rentals in a tropical jungle setting. The most extravagant of these, ***A`a Pali Cliffhouse*** (573–0693; 800–861–9566) offers all the opulence and privacy of a Sultan's pleasure palace. Its perch on the edge of a 300-foot cliff affords a dramatic view of a waterfall toppling into an oceanfront gorge, with the Hana coastline and Haleakala Crater framed in the background. The sumptuous decor includes landscaped gardens, Balinese statuary, and a detached octagonal bedroom to go with the fully equipped cottage. Yours for $350 a night. On the other side of the point, the ***Cliff's Edge*** (572–4530) offers far simpler quarters but an equally stunning view of Waipio Bay. The two B&B rooms go for $125 and $135, with a separate two-bedroom rental for $250. Three nights minimum. WARNING: Whales splashing offshore at night might disturb your slumber. Other distinctive rentals are offered by ***Huelo Point Flower Farm*** (572–1850) and ***Huelo Point Lookout*** (573–0914; 800–871–8645).

Kailua Village, at 5.5 miles, is the headquarters of the East Maui Irrigation Company, Alexander & Baldwin's irrigation arm. All along the Hana Highway you will see E.M.I. CO. signs, and portions of the original nineteenth-century stone aqueducts shadow the road. Rainbow and robusta eucalyptus trees planted for lumber at the turn of the century predominate for the next few miles.

At 9.6 miles, a wide pullout space marks the start of the short ***Waikamoi Ridge Trail,*** a half-mile nature walk with scenic overlooks with picnic tables at beginning and end. Exotic plants along the trail, including mahogany, paperback, and tree ferns, are labeled. The trail also passes through a "musical" forest of bamboo; the slightest wind sets these hollow trees creaking and sighing cacophonously. A sign at the trailhead reads QUIET, TREES AT WORK.

Waikamoi Stream, at the next bridge, has a small pool for swimming, but most people stop here for the spring water that runs from a metal pipe in the rock wall just past the bridge. For splashier aquatic antics, continue to ***Puohokamoa,*** the next stream at mile marker 11. There are three waterfalls here, involving hikes of graduated difficulty. A leisurely stroll on a paved pathway leads past picnic tables to the nearest falls and swimming hole below. *Laua`e,* a multilobed, spore-studded fern that was a symbol of romantic love in Old Hawaii, grows here. For a bit more seclusion, cross the stream and hike up the steep left bank to a larger pool and falls upstream. The really adventurous hiker can rock-hop a half-mile downstream (there is no trail) and peer over the edge of a 200-foot cascade that tumbles into a narrow gorge below.

The next stream after Puohokamoa, ***Haipuaena,*** has two less well-known falls with swimming pools to enjoy. A white cross painted on a rock marks the start of the trail upstream along the left bank past coconuts, *ti* leaves, and heliconia flowers. The first pool and falls are pleasant, but they are really only a false front for the true beauty upstream. Getting there requires a short but treacherous climb.

Past the 12-mile marker, ***Kaumahina State Wayside Park*** has rest rooms and a picnic area that serves up coastal views stretching to Keanae Peninsula and beyond. African tulip trees flame with frilly orange blossoms. The heart-stopping scenery continues as the highway winds along a narrow ledge above the ocean to descend into ***Honomanu Valley,*** one of the few ancient valleys not flattened by subsequent flows from Haleakala.

Just past mile marker 15, the YMCA's ***Camp Keanae*** (248–8355; e-mail: ymcacampkeanea@aol.com) perches on an isolated headland. Run as a sanctioned American Youth Hostel, the camp offers both dorm berths and camping at $15 per person. A two-bedroom cottage being built is expected to rent for $85. Bring your own bedding. Just around the bend on the inland side, ***Keanae Arboretum*** spreads over six acres of labeled botanical specimens. Amble up Piinaau Stream past ginger and banana to enter the arboretum grounds. There are three main sections. In the first, you encounter native trees, huge sheaths of bamboo, and all manner of palms. The second showcases taro and other Hawaiian crops. A tougher trail forges through the last section, a mile of rain forest. Free.

Beyond the arboretum, a turnoff on the left provides a bumpy but scenic detour onto ***Keanae Peninsula.*** Lava from Haleakala's last crater eruption funneled through the Ko`olau Gap, filling Keanae Valley to form this flat, crusted appendage. Horses roam the grassy pastures, and an old stone church poses impassively. As you circle the perimeter road, savoring the coastal views in either direction, please respect the privacy of residents who cling to the rustic lifestyle here. The road dead-ends short of a full loop in front of extensive taro fields. Oral histories tell of the transformation of this barren peninsula into rich farmland by a thousand loads of topsoil hand-carried from the hills.

The highway, meanwhile, climbs above the peninsula and offers a lookout point near the 17-mile marker. Keanae marks the halfway point to Hana; a series of roadside food vendors lie ahead.

At 18 miles, turn left onto Wailua Village Road to enter this isolated taro-farming community. ***St. Gabriel's Catholic Church*** and the ***Miracle of Fatima Shrine*** stand on the ocean side of the road. The church features an attractive altar draped in *tapa* cloth, but the story behind the shrine is what merits a visit here. In 1860, when the Catholic community set out to construct this tiny chapel (the original St. Gabriel's church), they lacked adequate building materials. Harvesting underwater coral blocks required enormous time and effort until, answering their prayers, an ocean storm miraculously washed abundant chunks of coral onto the shore. When the grateful Catholics had taken all they needed, a second storm washed the remainder back to sea—or so the story goes.

The highway climbs on above the village. Stop a half-mile up at the ***Wailua Wayside Lookout*** on the right. Steps tunneled through a thicket of *hau* lead to a panoramic view of the patchwork taro paddies below, and inland up the broad slopes Wailua Valley rises to Haleakala Crater. A 0.5 mile farther, the spectacular ***Waikani Falls*** plunges forcefully from cliffs above the highway.

Near 22 miles you pass the smaller ***Kopiliula Falls,*** and 0.5 mile farther, you can pause for a breather at ***Puaa Kaa*** ("rolling pigs") ***State Wayside Park.*** Spread along the banks of a stream, the park has picnic tables overlooking shallow pools and small waterfalls.

The next 3 miles of highway break into stretches of open country in between overgrown streams and waterfalls. Roadside ginger grows along this section of the road; be sure to inhale the natural perfume. Rainfall in the hills above the highway here averages an inch a day. At 27 miles, the road breaks clear again into pastureland with ocean and crater views. Notice the cluster of giant travelers' palms by the upcoming ranch house on the left. These fantastic fan-shaped specimens can store up to a quart of water at the base of their leaves for thirsty travelers to access. Around 30 miles, the road shakes free from its final bends and descends to the flat expanses of the Hana Coast.

A little farther down the highway past the 31-mile point, turn left and bump your way seaward on Ulaino Road. About 1.5 miles in, a sign points to ***Kahanu Gardens*** (248–8912). You drive in past dense groves of coconut, *hala, kukui, hau,* and breadfruit trees, all of which played key roles in the ethnobotany of ancient Hawaii. Even plant haters should come here, if only to gaze in awe at ***Piilanihale Heiau,*** the largest such temple in the state. Built by the Piilani chiefs in the fifteenth century, this massive stone complex rises 40 feet above the ground and spreads over more than an acre. Unfortunately, the gardens are open only by appointment; one-and-a-half-hour tours are offered Monday–Friday at 11:00 A.M. and 1:00 P.M. Admission is $10.

If Kahanu's schedule does not match yours, you might stop at ***Kaia Ranch*** (248–7725), a half-mile back up Ulaino Road. This twenty-seven-acre fruit and flower farm owned by a native Hawaiian family offers its own self-guided "botanical walk" for $3.00 It's fairly primitive, but owner JoLoyce Kaia is a pleasant lady to chat with. (Ask her how she got her first name.) Open daily 9:00 A.M. to 5:00 P.M. The ranch also rents simply furnished studios for $100 the first night, $75 thereafter.

If it has not rained recently, and the road is passable, you can follow Ulaino Road as it curves around left until its end near the ocean; continue walking across the stream straight ahead to reach the waterfall-fed ***Blue Pool,*** right at the edge of the ocean.

Back on the highway, the next crossroad leads to Hana's tiny airport. Continue past the 32-mile point before turning seaward to ***Waianapanapa*** ("glistening water") ***State Park*** (248–8061). Notice the many breadfruit trees on the way in. The bowling ball–size fruit provided a starchy Hawaiian staple, and the sticky tree sap was used to trap birds. Pass the housekeeping cabins at the park office (book at least six months in advance for these) and drive on to the second parking lot to explore the park's caves and beach.

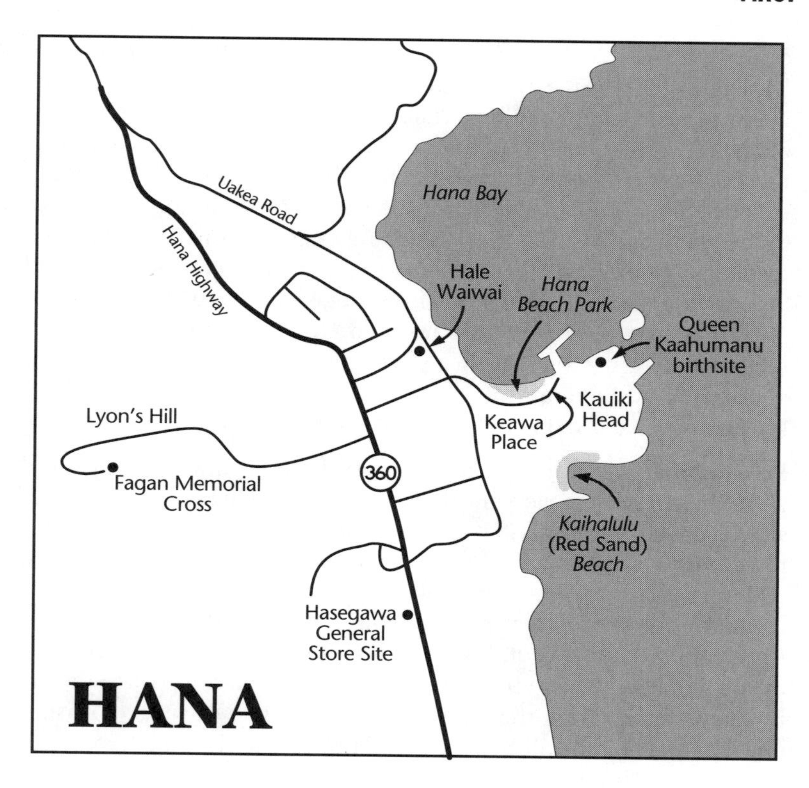

A lovely nature trail loops around the lava tube caves. Begin on the left fork and descend to the first water-filled cavern where, according to legend, a Hawaiian princess hid from a jealous husband. With a flashlight in a plastic bag, you can swim a short distance to the ledge of a dry inner chamber where she hid. The trail continues past other caves, then returns through a tunnel-like thicket of *hau* trees.

Another short trail descends to the black "sand" beach, actually composed of fine lava gravel. A rugged sea arch juts from the mouth of the bay, and seabirds nest in the rock islands offshore. Swimming becomes dangerous during periods of high surf. Coastal footpaths follow remnants of the ancient ***King's Highway*** for miles in either direction past burial mounds and *heiau.* The stark vegetation, composed predominantly of beach naupaka and *hala* trees, evokes images of a much older Hawaii.

Just ahead, a fork in the road marks the entrance to Hana proper. Forty-eight percent of the population here claims native ancestry. To explore this cultural heritage, veer left from the highway onto Uakea Road and continue 0.5 mile to the ***Hana Cultural Center*** (248–8622). Begin at the museum building, Hale Waiwai. The treasures here resemble family heirlooms, which many of them are. Coila Eade started the museum as a retirement project, and it blossomed with community support. She carved the beautiful koa doors at the entrance as well as the busts inside of prominent Hana residents. Hawaiian artifacts on display include a hundred-year-old *olona* fishnet, coconut-frond brooms, and all manner of specialized stones used by a Stone Age people. The center also includes a restored 1871 courthouse, which still sees occasional use and a replica of a traditional Hawaiian village complete with ethnobotanical gardens and authentic thatched *hale.* Museum open daily 10:00 A.M. to 4:00 P.M. Donation.

Past the museum, turn left onto Keawa Place to unwind at peaceful ***Hana Beach Park,*** a pleasant, dark-sand swimming beach on the right side of Hana Bay. ***Tutu's*** (248–8224), a concession stand in the community center across the street, serves inexpensive plate lunch, sandwiches, and fresh Hana fish when available. Open daily 8:30 A.M.–4:00 P.M. Rising above the beach, tree-covered ***Kauiki Head*** blushes with oxidized iron. Kauiki dominates its surroundings as it does Hana history. The extinct cinder cone served as a natural fortress guarding Hana during invasions to and from the Big Island. In 1773, two decades of clashes between Maui's Kahekili and Big Island invaders led by Kalaniopuu culminated in a dramatic siege in which the Maui forces surrounded the hill, and by cutting off his water supply, forced Kalaniopuu to withdraw. Polished sling stones thrown in the battle litter Kauiki's slopes.

From the wharf at the mouth of the bay, you can follow the narrow trail around Kauiki's red flank. A five-minute walk brings you to the tip of the headland where a small copper plaque marks the cave in which Queen Ka`ahumanu was born to exiled *alii* and hid during Kalaniopuu's first invasion. She was almost lost as an infant when, unbeknownst to her parents, she fell off a canoe. While Hana remained under Big Island rule, Ka`ahumanu met and married the up-and-coming Kamehameha, and her fortune began to shift. She became his favorite wife, but although he placed a *kapu* (taboo) on her body, she tormented him by sleeping with other men. Visiting British Captain Vancouver helped reconcile the couple, and upon Kamehameha's death she became queen regent. To reinforce her position, Ka`ahumanu led the way in breaking the old taboos restricting women and later became the most important convert of the missionaries.

Continue on Uakea Road until it ends at the beach cottages of Hotel

Hana-Maui. From here, another trail winds around the opposite flank of Kauiki to **Kaihalulu** or ***Red Sand Beach.*** Erosive cinders along the path make the footing treacherous, and the hotel keeps the trailhead deliberately obscure to discourage its use. The reward for the fleet of foot is a gorgeous pocket of red cinder sand enveloped in a secluded cove. A protective wall of jagged lava rock just offshore keeps swimming conditions safe, and the crystalline waters are a vision of blue on red. Clothing optional.

Backtrack a block on Uakea Road, and turn left onto Hauoli Street. At the corner of the Hana Highway is ***Wananalua Church,*** dated 1842. Hana's first missionaries deliberately built this coral block temple over the site of a pagan *heiau.* A lava stone cross on nearby ***Lyon's Hill*** honors the memory of Paul Fagan, who introduced ranching to Hana after sugar died out. Fagan built the ***Hotel Hana-Maui*** (248–8211; 800–321–4262; www.hotelhanamaui.com) in 1946 as a guest house for his millionaire friends. Rooms start at $235 at this gorgeous oceanfront property.

Nonmillionaires who wish to stay overnight in Hana have several choices. The ***Heavenly Hana Inn*** (248–8442; www.heavenlyhanainn.com; P.O. Box 146, Hana 96713), 2 miles north of town, cultivates the atmosphere of a *ryokan,* the traditional country inn of Japan; its four suites rent from $185–$250.

For those who prefer lodging with a Balinese motif, ***Hamoa Bay House & Bungalow*** (248–7884) sits on four acres of tropical splendor within walking distance of Hamoa Beach. The studio cottage rents for $165. More moderately priced lodgings can be booked through ***Hana Plantation Cottages*** (800–228–4262; www.tropical-hideaways.com/hawaii/maui/hpc/hpc.htm), which offers a range of vacation rentals for $72–$140. Some actually are renovated plantation homes.

Simpler quarters in town can be found at ***Aloha Cottages*** (248–8420; P.O. Box 205, Hana 96713) on Keawa Place. Mrs. Fusae Nakamura, the owner, offers her guests fresh fruit from her garden and will even provide laundry service during longer stays. The cottages almost all have full kitchens and rent for $65–$85. Bargain-basement rooms await at ***Joe's Place*** (248–7033; P.O. Box 577, Hana 96713), around the block at 4870 Uakea Road. Rooms with communal bathrooms and kitchens go for $45. A private bath costs $10 more.

Kitchen facilities may come in handy because dinner options are limited to the hotel and ***Hana Ranch Restaurant*** (248–8255), uphill from Hana Highway on Mill Road. The restaurant offers moderately priced breakfasts and lunches daily 8:00–10:00 A.M and 11:00 A.M. to 3:00 P.M.

with take-out food served until 7:00 P.M., plus pizza on Wednesday night and expensive sit-down dinners on Friday and Saturday 6:00–8:00 P.M. The hotel's main dining room serves decent, if pricey renditions of Hawaii Regional Cuisine, with a buffet Sunday night. Open daily 7:30 to 10:30 A.M., 11:30 A.M. to 2:30 P.M., 6:15 to 9:00 P.M. Investment-caliber prices at dinner, and reservations recommended. Otherwise, for do-it-yourself options, the Hana Ranch Store sells groceries. Hana's most famous retail establishment—celebrated in bumper stickers and in song—is nearby ***Hasegawa General Store*** (248–8231). Occupying the former Hana theater building, it stocks an amazing hodgepodge of goods crammed under one roof.

One-and-a-half miles south of town on what has now become Route 31, a county road, you reach another prominent cinder hill, ***Ka Iwi o Pele*** ("the bones of Pele"). According to the legend, "the bones" are an anatomical monument from the fire goddess' defeat by her older sister, the ocean. Turn onto Haneo`o Road to loop around the coast. ***Koki Beach Park,*** left of Ka Iwi, faces Alau Island offshore. To the right of the beach park are some ancient fishponds. On the far side of the loop, Haneo`o Road passes ***Hamoa Beach,*** a pearly strand in a semicircular cove encased by tall cliffs. Hotel Hana-Maui guests get shuttled in between 10:00 A.M. and 4:00 P.M., but the beach belongs to everyone to enjoy.

Trivia

In Ulupalakua, upcountry Maui, the Ranch Store has the distinction of maintaining the oldest Levi Strauss account in the world.

The highway continues through pastureland, and white-faced Herefords return your stares as you drive past. After another mile or so, the road narrows and begins to wind as the pavement deteriorates and lush jungle returns. About 7 miles from Hana, you will see ***Helio's Cross*** marking his grave on a hill just ahead. Helio Koa`eloa left this valley of his birth to learn the forbidden faith of Catholicism and returned to win converts by the thousands. He died in 1848.

Around the bend comes ***Kanahualii Falls,*** followed shortly by ***Wailua Falls.*** You can descend a 0.5-mile trail opposite the former to the valley floor and take a dip in the secluded pools where the river meets the rocky shoreline. Around you lie the ruins of an abandoned village. The road winds on past the ***Virgin by the Roadside*** shrine cut into the cliffside. Ocean vistas alternate with stream-fed jungle. Near the 10-mile point, you enter Haleakala National Park's ***Kipahulu District*** at Oheo. Tourist crowds come here to see the "Seven Sacred Pools" formed as Pipiwai Stream spills down a watery staircase of hollowed-out lava basins. The pools actually number more than twenty and never were sacred. You have a choice of trekking a few hundred yards down to the lower pools or hiking 0.5 mile uphill to ***Makahiku Falls*** and an optional 2 miles farther to the ***Waimoku Falls.*** The descent to the lowest pools takes you near the ocean past some archaeological remains of Hawaiian house sites. You can see the Big Island offshore on a clear day. Sharks and currents make ocean swimming a bad idea. Instead, try a dip in one or all of the pools, working your way upstream where the crowds thin out. Currents are gentle, but heed warning signs of flash flooding. Look for the reddish conical flowers of the *awapuhi* (ginger) plants that grow here. The Hawaiians crushed these bulbous hand grenades to extract a natural shampoo. Lather up and rinse in a waterfall!

If you choose the hike, you get a great overlook of Makahiku Falls cascading 200 feet below. From here, an old irrigation ditch allows you to cross to more secluded pools above the falls. The main trail continues through pastures studded with guava trees, then meanders through darkened thickets of dense bamboo that creak and rattle in the wind. The trail gets muddy at stages, but the park service has placed boardwalk planks over the worst spots. The trail ends beneath 400-foot cliffs from which the threadlike fingers of Waimoku Falls descend in shimmering rivulets. Park rangers lead regular hikes and conduct other interpretive activities. Call 248–7375 to check the current schedule. Primitive camping facilities are also available.

A mile past Oheo, aviation buffs and old-timers make the pilgrimage to ***Lindbergh's Grave*** at Ho`omau Church, on the ocean side of the road. Here the "Lone Eagle" chose to die, enveloped in the remote beauty of the land. His epitaph reads from Psalm 139: "If I take the wings of the morning and dwell in the uttermost parts of the sea."

The next 6 miles of road reach an axle-grinding low and constitute forbidden territory for rental cars. Frequently washed out after rainfalls, the rugged terrain may require four-wheel-drive even when dry. Call the Hana Public Works Office at 248–8254 to check road conditions before you chance it. Ahead, you pass the 1857 ***Huialoha Church*** on a barren windswept point. Peer uphill into the Kaupo Gap through which ancient lava flows once poured from Haleakala Crater; today, hikers travel the gap's trails.

The variably open ***Kaupo Store,*** founded in 1886 by Chinese immigrants, waits just up the highway. Three miles farther, the road edges back toward the shoreline at ***Nuu Bay,*** the best swimming beach on the coast. Then the road begins to climb slowly inland through the desolate landscape along Maui's hairless underbelly. Remains of ancient villages haunt the lava, and the endless miles of parched terrain overlook wide horizons of ocean. Above it all, the Haleakala Crater dominates the landscape, with much steeper slopes on this side. Twenty-one miles after leaving the Kaupo Store, the Tedeschi Winery signals your arrival in Upcountry.

West Maui

The West Maui Mountains are older, lusher, and more scenically eroded than Haleakala. Good highway rings the entire landmass. Departing southwest from the isthmus, the Hanoapiilani Highway climbs high bluffs overlooking the ocean. As you round Maui's chin, the island of Lana`i joins Kaho`olawe on the horizon, rising from the ocean like a giant humpback whale. People stop at the marked lookout here at ***Papawai Point*** to watch for real humpbacks in the Au`au Channel. The sight of a forty-ton leviathan breaching offshore has caused more than one traffic incident along this highway.

The highway continues to carve and burrow its way through the mountain slope and eventually descends through cane fields on the other side. A row of monkeypod trees and a drop in the speed limit signal your arrival at Olowalu. Snorkeling is good here at the 14-mile marker with beach facilities close at hand. Olowalu town consists of two establishments—one is a general store, the other's a gourmet French restaurant. Many consider ***Chez Paul*** (661–3843) the best on the island. You will want to reserve a table well in advance, as Belgian owner-chef Lucien Charbonnier's restaurant is only open 6:00 P.M.–8:30 P.M. nightly. Investment-caliber prices. ***Camp Pecusa*** (661–4303), a half-mile east of the store, offers the only tenting sites in West Maui, $5.00 per person per night.

The ***Olowalu*** region is steeped in history. In 1790 an American captain, Simon Metcalf, opened fire on native canoes he lured into range, killing more than eighty Hawaiians to avenge the theft of his longboat and the murder of a Western sailor. The Hawaiians retaliated by seizing a companion ship captained by Metcalf's son and slaughtering most of the crew. Two English survivors from this bloodshed, Isaac Davis and John Young, became prisoners of Kamehameha, then an ambitious Big Island chieftain. Combining their expertise with the firepower of the cannons also acquired in the incident, Kamehameha won his bloody victory later that year in the alluvial Iao Valley above Olowalu. An ancient trail through a now-blocked mountain pass once connected Olowalu with Iao Valley. Refugees from Kamehameha's triumph at Kepaniwai escaped over this trail, bringing events full circle.

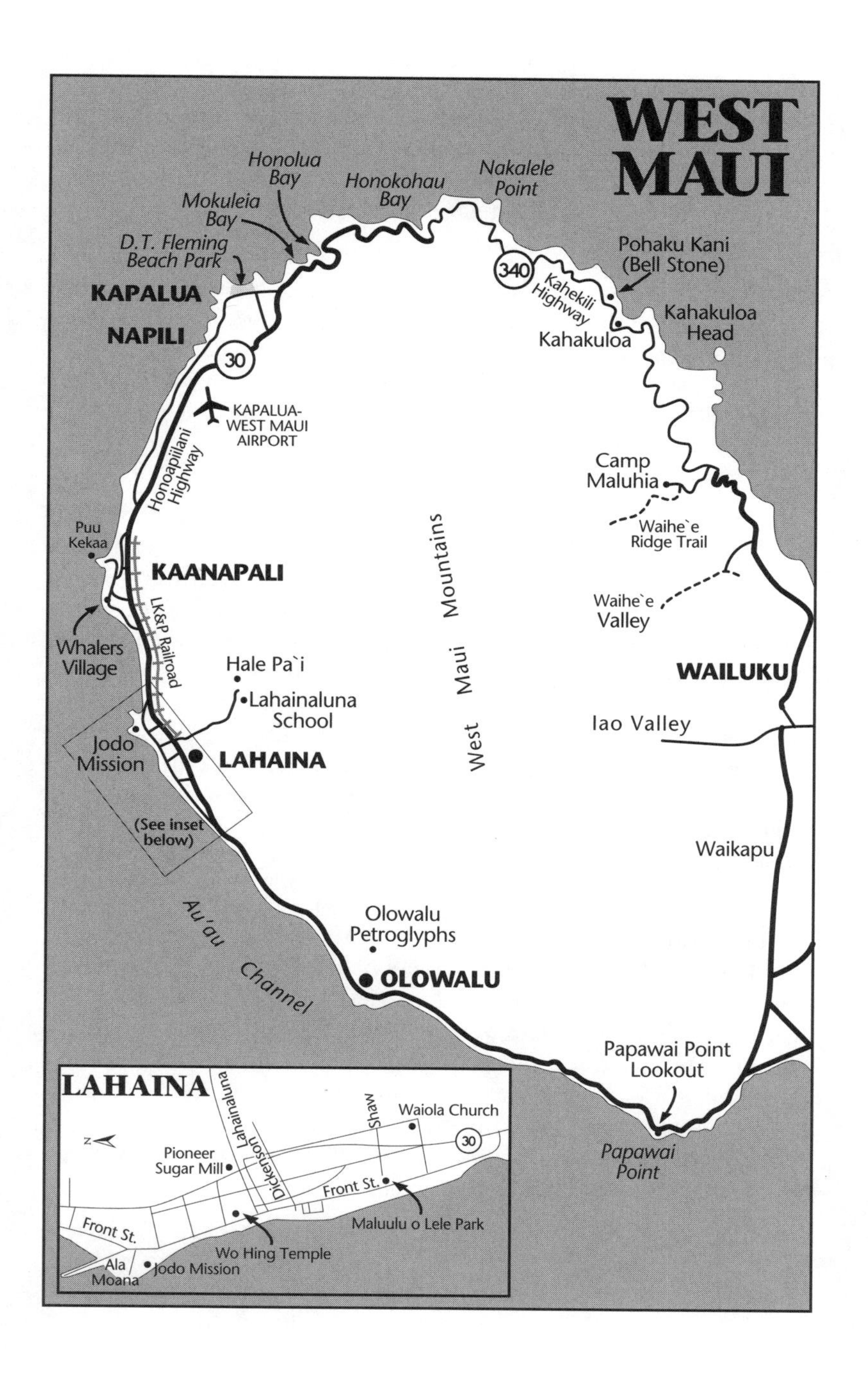

WEST MAUI
Honolua Bay
Honokohau Bay
Nakalele Point
Mokuleia Bay
D.T. Fleming Beach Park
KAPALUA
NAPILI
340
Kahekili Highway
Pohaku Kani (Bell Stone)
Kahakuloa Head
Kahakuloa
30
KAPALUA-WEST MAUI AIRPORT
Honoapiilani Highway
Camp Maluhia
Waihe`e Ridge Trail
Puu Kekaa
KAANAPALI
West Maui Mountains
Waihe`e Valley
LK&P Railroad
Whalers Village
Hale Pa`i
Lahainaluna School
WAILUKU
Iao Valley
Jodo Mission
LAHAINA
(See inset below)
Waikapu
Au'au Channel
Olowalu Petroglyphs
OLOWALU
Papawai Point Lookout
Papawai Point
LAHAINA
Lahainaluna
Shaw
Waiola Church
N
30
Pioneer Sugar Mill
Dickenson
Front St.
Front St.
Maluulu o Lele Park
Wo Hing Temple
Ala Moana
Jodo Mission

Hidden in the cane fields here is an impressive collection of ***petroglyphs.*** Because of vandalism, the site is no longer advertised to the general public. If you take the paved cane road that parallels the highway and turn right at the water tower a few hundred yards west of the Olowalu Store, an unpaved cane road leads a half-mile to these markings. The petroglyphs are carved into a cliff face just after the road forks. Look for the former viewing platform.

Trivia

Piilanihale Heiau, Maui, the largest such temple in the state, was built by the Piilani chiefs in the fifteenth century.

Those wishing to explore more of the area's history and ecology can hike the 5-mile ***Lahaina Pali Trail,*** which crosses the West Maui Mountains to reach a 1,600-foot elevation before emerging north of Ma`alaea.

Five miles northwest of Olowalu, a flotilla of yachts anchored offshore signals your arrival at the town of ***Lahaina,*** reminiscent of the whaling fleet parked in these "Lahaina Roads" more than a century ago. More than any other place in the islands, Lahaina embodies a feeling of old and new superimposed. The town has gone through many incarnations over the years: a center of royalty, then a raucous whaling port, then a sleepy sugar settlement. Although thriving today as a tourist center, Lahaina has retained its sense of romance and history. The active Lahaina Restoration Foundation moved early to preserve many of the historic sites, and building codes keep new developments in line with the old. Pick up a free copy of the *Lahaina Historical Guide* at any of the commercial centers in town to read more about the town's many landmarks. Plan on spending some time; there's lots to see.

Front Street serves as the town's main drag, with a boardwalk strip running partway along the ocean. At the corner of Front and Diickenson stands the ***Baldwin Home,*** Lahaina's oldest building, now run as a museum. In 1838, newlywed missionaries Edwin and Charlotte Baldwin moved into this home after a 161-day honeymoon trip around stormy Cape Horn. The museum displays some of their possessions, among them Charlotte's sewing kit and china brought from Connecticut. Mosquito nets over the four-poster beds reflect the arrival in 1872 of the winged parasites, carried unwittingly aboard the *Wellington,* a merchant ship docked at Lahaina.

Rev. Edwin Baldwin ran a medical clinic in an adjacent room and serviced three islands in addition to his pastoral duties. His medical instruments fill the shelves of his study. Notice the hilarious English translation of his official posted rates. Licensed native doctors in 1865 could levy charges ranging from $50 for "very great sickness" to $3.00 for "incantation to find out disease" and could even assess a $10 fee for "refusal by patient to pay." The museum is open daily 10:00 A.M. to 4:30 P.M.; token admission; 661–3262.

Lahaina's first missionaries, the Richardses, used to live in a house next door. In 1827 these stubborn crusaders had to crouch in their cellar while cannonballs whistled overhead, fired by a sea captain furious at the edicts of Christian morality that the Richardses had persuaded local chiefs to impose. Whalers had begun arriving in large numbers about the same time as the missionaries, setting the stage for epic battles between the two groups. Rallying to the motto "No God West of the Horn," the lusty sailors rioted to win back their grog and women, but as whaling gradually died as an industry, the missionaries won by default.

Walk a block seaward to the waterfront, where you'll see the stone foundations from Kamehameha I's 1802 ***Brick Palace,*** the first Western building in the islands. Kamehameha never lived here because his wife, Ka`ahumanu, refused to move in. Kamehameha III later tended a wetland taro patch nearby to demonstrate "the dignity of labor." Walk to the seawall at the edge of the lot. The ***Hauola Stone,*** just below, is shaped like a reclining chair. You're supposed to sit here with legs dangling in the surf to activate the stone's curative powers.

Docked offshore near the Brick Palace, its square-rigged sails fluttering in the breeze, is the brig ***Carthaginian*** (661–8527), a Baltic Sea schooner

Fright Night

If you frighten easily, stay away from Front Street on October 31. Monsters, witches, and an assortment of scary creatures will be on the prowl during the annual Halloween festivities. No one is really sure how the tradition started, but Halloween in Lahaina has grown into an event of mythic proportion. Last year almost a third of the island turned up, and Lahaina hotels charge special Halloween rates. No costume is too bizarre, far out, or ghoulish. In fact, the weirder, the better.

Lahaina's popular holiday involves residents and visitors. At lunch, your waitress may give you a Dracula smile if you order a "horrorburger" from the menu. Festivities begin with the children's parade at 4:00 P.M. down Front Street, followed by dancing in the streets as hundreds of weird-looking people vie for thousands of dollars worth of prizes in a costume contest.

Trivia

Early whalers didn't go after humpbacks because they sink upon death.

refitted to replicate an early nineteenth-century freighter. Because of crowding in Lahaina Harbor, the *Carthaginian* is moored outside the breakwater. The narrow gangplank sways with every surge in the surf; those prone to seasickness might best stay ashore.

Below deck, a few displays touch on Lahaina's whaling heritage, but most focus on humpback whales. The two topics are not as closely related as most people assume: Lahaina merely served as a central staging ground for the North Pacific fleet's pursuit of sperm whales off Japan and Alaska. With modern technology, humpbacks were indeed hunted to near extinction, but this happened long after the last whaleships left Hawaiian waters. Open daily 10:00 A.M. to 4:00 P.M.; nominal charge.

Inland from the *Carthaginian* stands the historic ***Pioneer Inn*** (661–3636 or 800–457–5457; 568 Wharf Street, Lahaina 96761). George Freeland, a Canadian Mountie, tracked a notorious criminal to Lahaina and stayed to open in 1901 what for many years was the only hotel in town. Now a Best Western, its raucous atmosphere has tamed considerably. To get a sense of the inn's former clientele, ask for a copy of inn's original House Rules written in comical pidgin English. Rooms start at $110.

Next to the Pioneer Inn, Lahaina's massive ***Banyan Tree*** shades almost an acre of the central courthouse square. Planted in 1873, the tree has aerial roots that have grown into twelve major trunks, giving it the appearance of a small forest. The ***Courthouse*** next to the tree, built in 1859, served as a center of Maui government. Inside, the ***Lahaina Art Society*** (661–0111) exhibits its members' works. Check out the Old Jail Gallery in the basement, where iron-barred cells now imprison painted canvas. You will find works from some of the island's top talents in mediums ranging from *sfumato* (smoke painting) to basket weaving. On weekends, member artists gather to display additional works under the Banyan Tree outside. Open daily 9:00 A.M. to 5:00 P.M. In the corner of the square, you will notice "ruins" of the original waterfront fort built in the 1830s to intimidate rowdy sailors. The fort was actually torn down completely in 1854. Rather than damage the Banyan Tree, the Restoration Society settled on this partial reconstruction.

Farther south on Front Street, take a peek inside the ***Episcopal Church*** to see the painting by DeLos Blackmar of a Hawaiian Madonna. The area around here overflowed with sites of royalty. ***Maluulu o Lele Park*** once held a pond called Mokuhinia, home of a legendary *mo`o* (lizard). Maui's royal *alii* lived on an island in this pond, protected by the *mo`o,* and

Kamehameha's heirs enjoyed its seclusion while growing up. The island even housed a royal mausoleum for a time. In 1918, the pond was filled in and the ground leveled. Today all you see is an ordinary ballfield.

Turn inland up Shaw Street to the corner of Wainee Street and ***Waiola Church.*** The church has an interesting history. Formerly named Wainee Church, the original 1832 edifice could seat 3,000 people and was the first stone church in the islands. In 1858 a whirlwind funneled out of Kaua`ula Valley and tore off the roof, and in 1894 royalists protesting Hawaii's annexation burned the church to the ground. Rebuilt, it burned down again in 1947 and was restored only to be demolished by another Kaua`ula windstorm. Reoriented with its front door facing Kaua`ula Valley and renamed Waiola, the church has remained standing . . . so far. In the old cemetery next door, elaborate tombstones designate the likes of Queens Ka`ahumanu and Keopuolani and Maui Governor Hoapili. Next to Ka`ahumanu lies Kamualii, the husband she kidnapped from Kaua`i.

Return north on Wainee Street past the Indian-style ***Hongwanji Mission.*** A block farther, ***Hale Paahao*** ("stuck in irons house") is surrounded by a high wall built from coral blocks from the old fort. The wall and wooden jailhouse inside were built by the prisoners themselves, most of whom were jailed for disorderly conduct. You can peer inside one of the cells where prisoners were locked up at night and listen to a recorded account of prison life. Notice the list of crime statistics from the period. It seems that 1857 was a big year for "giving birth to bastard children," "violating fish taboos," and "felonious branding." You enter Hale Paahao appropriately on Prison Street.

Other historical sites lie north of the Bailey House on Front Street. Don't miss ***Wo Hing Temple,*** a colorfully restored two-story building affiliated with the Chee Kung Tong fraternal society. Exhibits chronicle the history of Chinese immigrants, the first Asian group to arrive in Hawaii. Commercial sugar production on the islands was started by Chinese entrepreneurs, although most of the Chinese came later as field workers for plantations run by white owners. In the Taoist temple upstairs, incense burns alongside offerings on a richly decorated altar honoring Kuan Ti, the god of wealth. The cookhouse outside shows footage from Thomas Edison's movies of Hawaii shot in 1898 and 1903.

The ***U.S. Seamen's Hospital,*** farther north, was originally built as a bachelor pad by Kamehameha III. Here he could escape his missionary advisors' watchful eyes to drink, gamble, and even meet for clandestine trysts with his sister, Princess Nahienaena. Such incestuous unions between high-ranking *alii* had been a sacred duty in the old days to assure offspring of the purest bloodlines. The new Christian morality of the missionaries condemned incest. Distraught by the strain of these conflicting moralities, Nahienaena suffered an early death. A special path was cleared through the breadfruit trees of Lahaina for her body to be carried to Maluulu o Lele; the path today exists as Luakini Street. The word *luakini* describes temples where human sacrifices were performed. To the grieving Hawaiians, Nahienaena was similarly a sacrifice to the new morality of the missionaries. The United States later leased the building as a home for destitute and disabled American sailors. Consular officials in charge of the hospital ran a profitable racket charging the U.S. government inflated prices and even billing for "patients" interred in the nearby seamen's cemetery.

Continue north along Front Street to meditate beneath the giant Buddha of ***Lahaina Jodo Mission.*** To find it, look for the helpful JESUS IS COMING SOON sign and turn seaward onto Ala Moana Street. The majestic Buddha sits lotus-style atop an outdoor platform against a backdrop of green hills. The mission compound also includes a three-story pagoda housing cremated ashes and a large bell whose "voice of Buddha" speaks nightly at 8:00 P.M.

Lahaina means "merciless sun." If you're ready to "holler uncle," take to the cooler hills. Lahainaluna Road leads uphill past the Pioneer Sugar Mill to ***Lahainaluna*** ("above Lahaina") ***School.*** Founded by missionaries in 1831, it's the oldest school west of the Rockies. Boarding students from as far away as California once enrolled here. On the campus you will find ***Hale Pa`i*** (667–7040), the old mission printing house. The printery's hand press cranked out Hawaiian translations of the Bible as well as an early newspaper, paper money, and even drafts of the Hawaiian constitution. Hale Pa`i is open 10:00 A.M. to 4:00 P.M. weekdays.

Stargazing

For an off-the-beaten-path experience that's out of this world, try stargazing from the rooftop of the Hyatt Regency Maui. Open to guests and visitors, an in-house astronomy expert leads attendees on a tour of the evening sky with "Big Blue," a super-powered telescope programmed to find more than 1,000 objects. In an hour-long show, Big Blue will show you the locations of planets, nebulae, galaxies, and star clusters. Big Blue runs three shows nightly starting at 8:00 P.M., with a "champagne special" for couples at 11:00 P.M. on Friday and Saturday; call 661–1234. Admission is $25.

Lahaina Jodo Mission

Among Lahainaluna's first students was David Malo, a brilliant scholar whose book *Hawaiian Antiquities* forms the basis for much of our knowledge of precontact Hawaiian culture. A Christian minister himself, Malo respected the missionaries for their spiritual exertions. At the same time, he saw clearly the devastating impact of Western contact on Hawaiian society. He died a bitter man, asking to be buried "above the tide of foreign invasion." His grave rests on top of Mount Ball, near the giant L cut into the forest above the school.

To many people, Lahaina doesn't mean history but shopping. Rows of Western-style arcades lining Front Street create a carnival atmosphere. Art is a major commodity here. Notice how many galleries carry works showing dual underwater-surface landscapes in the "two worlds" style pioneered by Robert Lyn Nelson. Every Friday evening, local galleries host special "Art Night" receptions. For those who like their art aged, ***Lahaina Printsellers*** (667–7843) has amassed an amazing collection of antique maps and prints. They specialize in drawings made by early Pacific explorers, with a selection from Captain Cook's voyages second only to the British Museum. Their main store is located in the Lahaina Cannery Complex, on the highway near the north edge of town. Open daily 9:00 A.M. to 9:00 P.M.

Moving from art to crafts, ***Na Mea Hawaii*** (661–5707) sells a broad range of craftwork, clothing, and other gift items all made by island artists. It's located on Front Street in the ground floor of the 1847 Masters Reading Room. Open Monday–Friday, 9:30 A.M. to 7:00 P.M.; and weekends from 10:00 A.M. This being Lahaina, you should also stop in at ***Lahaina Scrimshaw*** at 845 Front Street. Sailors of old started this tradition of engraving ivory teeth from sperm whales to while away the hours at sea. Upon returning to their home port, they would present the completed work to their sweethearts as a testament to their undying ardor and constancy. In fact, stores like Lahaina Scrimshaw were cottage industries even in those days. Lazy sailors could purchase mass-produced art from these early precursors of the airport gift shop. The ***Crazy Shirts*** outlet (661–4775), two doors down from Lahaina Scrimshaw, has a wall devoted to whaling memorabilia.

Restaurants rival shops in Lahaina in variety, number, and mutability. Popular standbys overlooking the waterfront on the 800 block of Front Street include ***Kimo's*** for seafood and ***Longhi's*** for hip Italian, both expensive. ***Pacific O*** (667–4341), farther south at 505 Front Street, serves its trendy Pacific Rim creations right on the beach, with live jazz on weekend nights. Open daily 11:00 A.M. to 4:00 P.M., 5:30–10:00 P.M. Investment-caliber prices. For local plate lunch with a gourmet flair, walk a few blocks north to ***Aloha Mixed Plate,*** at 1285 Front Street. Their coconut prawns won an award. Open daily from 10:30 A.M. to 10:00 P.M. Moderate.

Devotees of elegant French dining will delight in ***Gerard's*** (661–8939) at 174 Lahainaluna Street. Housed in the Plantation Inn, Gerard's offers a choice of garden, lana`i, or interior dining to assure an intimate setting. Gerard Reversade's cuisine reflects his Gascogne upbringing, modified to embrace Maui's island produce. He specializes in seafood dishes, such as Hawaiian snapper in orange-ginger sauce. Open for dinner nightly, 6:00–8:30 P.M. Investment-caliber prices.

The ***Plantation Inn*** (667–9225; 800–433–6815; www.theplantationinn.com; 174 Lahainaluna Road, Lahaina 96761) deserves mention of its own as an elegant Victorian-inspired hostelry. A white balustrade surrounds the two-story building. The interior features lavish use of natural woods, stained-glass windows, and polished brass. Floral wallpaper, lace curtains, and Persian rugs add to the indulgent feel. The rooms have authentic period furniture, from pull-chain toilets to four-poster beds; a few have ceilings with faux paintings; and suites include whirlpool baths and kitchenettes. Modern conveniences are discreetly concealed. Rates range from $145 to $215 and include a full breakfast.

The success of the Plantation Inn has inspired emulation by the ***Lahaina Inn*** (661–0577; 800–669–3444; www.lahainainn.com; 127 Lahainaluna Road, Lahaina 96761) just down the road. Extensive renovation by Crazy Shirts founder Rick Ralston has outfitted each of the twelve rooms with a period look. Touches such as leaded-glass lamps and needlepoint handwork on pillowcases supply authenticity. Rooms start at $99, with harbor views from $109, including continental breakfast.

Next door is ***David Paul's Lahaina Grill*** (667–5117), whose new American kitchen creates a rotating menu with Southwestern touches such as Tequila Shrimp and Firecracker Rice served in a chic black and white tile salon with molded tin ceilings. Open daily 6:00–10:00 P.M. Investment-caliber prices.

A block north of Lahainaluna Road on the highway is the Lahaina terminal of the ***Lahaina-Kaanapali Railroad,*** also known as the Sugar Cane Train (661–0089). The islands' only remaining steam locomotives now haul tourists instead of sugar cane along the 4-mile tracks for $11 one way and $15 round-trip. Behind the station at 991C Limahana Place, ***Lahaina Bakery*** (667–9062) prepares made-to-order sandwiches and scrumptious pastries. Open Monday–Friday 5:30 A.M. to 3:00 P.M., Saturday until 2:00 P.M., and Sunday until noon.

Kaanapali, north of Lahaina, is the first planned resort in the Hawaiian islands. In the middle of 3-mile-long Kaanapali Beach, ***Puu Kekaa,*** commonly called Black Rock, is an eroded black cinder cone that rises from the ocean. Hawaiians believed that spirits of the dead leaped from this rocky bluff to enter the world beyond. Maui's powerful eighteenth-century ruler, Kahekili, inspired his men by diving into the ocean alongside the invisible spirits. Today the Sheraton-Maui sprawls over Black Rock, and during its nightly torch-lighting ceremony this leap is dramatically reenacted.

If Lahaina has piqued your interest in whaling, be sure to visit the ***Whalers Village Museum*** (661–5992) in the Kaanapali shopping complex by the same name. James Campbell, who founded Pioneer Sugar Mill, began his career as a carpenter on a whaling ship. The museum is funded in his memory by his estate and does a good job of conveying the story of whaling in Hawaii. Relive the drama of the chase as tiny whaleboats row stealthily into battle with "the enemy." Learn how the economic factors governing whaling's rise and fall included women's fashions in hoopskirts and the discovery of petroleum in Pennsylvania. You can even see a life-size model of a fo'c'sle where common sailors slept. A separate gallery focuses on the whales themselves; its extensive interactive displays include videos of humpbacks at play accompanied by recorded whalesongs. Open daily 9:30 A.M.–10:00 P.M. Free.

Newer resort developments, alternating with cane fields, have sprouted north of Kaanapali. King Cane is shutting down, and soon the scent of "West Maui incense" from burning cane (the most efficient method of harvesting) may no longer waft through the luxury hotels. After Napili, the fields switch to pineapple cultivation but this, too, is being phased out. Other islands fade from view as East Moloka`i looms across the channel. Kapalua, the last tourist enclave on this coast, ends at the 30-mile marker. The demons of development have left three beautiful beaches beyond. WARNING: These northern strands can become dangerous for swimming, especially during winter surf.

At 31 miles, a side road leads to ***D. T. Fleming Beach Park,*** in Honokahua Bay. The facilities here are the last you will find before Wailuku. A half-mile past the 32-mile marker, the road winds above ***Mokuleia Bay.*** Beachgoers descend very steep trails from either side to the secluded beach below; locals call this "Slaughterhouse" because such a facility once stood on the cliffs above. The bay belongs to a marine-life conservation zone.

Honolua Bay, the northern limit of the conservation zone, awaits a half-mile farther at the mouth of a lushly tropical valley. The beach here, accessed by several trails down from the highway, suffers seasonal depletions of its sand and can be quite rocky during winter. The right side of the bay receives the best winter surf on the island, rivaling O`ahu's North Shore. In calmer months, snorkelers take advantage of the abundance of marine life in the conservation zone. The inner bay can be murky, but excellent coral formations farther out await exploration.

The road continues through pineapple fields and open forest. Near the 36-mile point, it rounds a sharp corner and begins a dramatic descent into Honokohau Bay. The Honoapiilani Highway ends here at the last of six bays (*hono*) claimed by the fifteenth-century chief Piilani. As you curve around the bend, glimpses of the rugged coastline beyond beckon. Route 340, a narrow county road, continues up the other side of the bay with mile markers enumerated in the reverse direction, descending from 22. Don't miss this road. It wriggles through the mountains, passing remote farms and villages. The tiny town of ***Kahakuloa*** is the epitome of Small Town, Hawaii, where lazy dogs sleep in the middle of the road, the air is fragrant with sweet ginger, the cobalt blue ocean laps at the shoreline, and the neighbors are welcoming.

Route 340 begins innocuously enough, winding through sisal and ironwood forests alternating with grassy cattle range. About a mile along, a white Coast Guard beacon marks ***Nakalele Point.*** Bizarre rock formations spewed from a volcanic spatter cone close to the shoreline give this region its nickname of Hobbitland, after author J. R. R. Tolkien's fantasy world. To the right of Nakalele Point, a blowhole powered by this coast's constant surf sends ocean sprays wafting through the air.

As you continue along the highway, signs warn of falling rocks. Hidden hands have stacked many of these rocks into cairns that line the road like sentinels. Clinging to the edge of cliffs, the road winds through knobby green hills and past remote valleys with abandoned settlements. The tree cover fades as the scenery grows more and more dramatic, and almost every turn begs you to pull over. Below the highway, the blue vastness of the Pacific Ocean hisses and seethes, crashing in fury and then retreating in restless agitation. Grazing bovines seem oblivious to the savage drama around them.

Around the 17-mile mark, the narrow, winding road reaches its roughest stretch, with more potholes than pavement. Just shy of the 16-mile point, near the top of a hill, ***Pohaku Kani,*** an enormous solitary boulder, squats above the highway on the inland side. Now marred by graffiti, the rock once served as a bell stone, struck by ancient Hawaiians to produce a resonant, bell-like tone. A mile and a half farther, the road narrows to a single lane as it climbs around the twin valleys of Kahakuloa Bay. ***Kahakuloa Head*** ("the tall lord") towers above the far edge of the bay. Visible for miles along this coast, this green volcanic knoll shelters a tiny Hawaiian settlement in the valley floor below. Residents of Kahakuloa Village tend taro fields and fish in the traditional manner.

From here, the road turns uphill through mountain pastures past the Honolua Ranch headquarters. The contortions of this single-lane road reach a climax as it winds in and out of deserted valleys high above the coast. By the 10-mile point, the road begins a slow descent with views along the coast and across the isthmus to East Maui. Just beyond the 7-mile marker, a side road leads to Maluhia Boy Scout Camp. A mile up this road, just before it curves into the camp, is the start of the ***Waihe`e Ridge Trail.*** Hardy hikers can climb 3 miles to scenic Lanilili Peak. For a less-strenuous

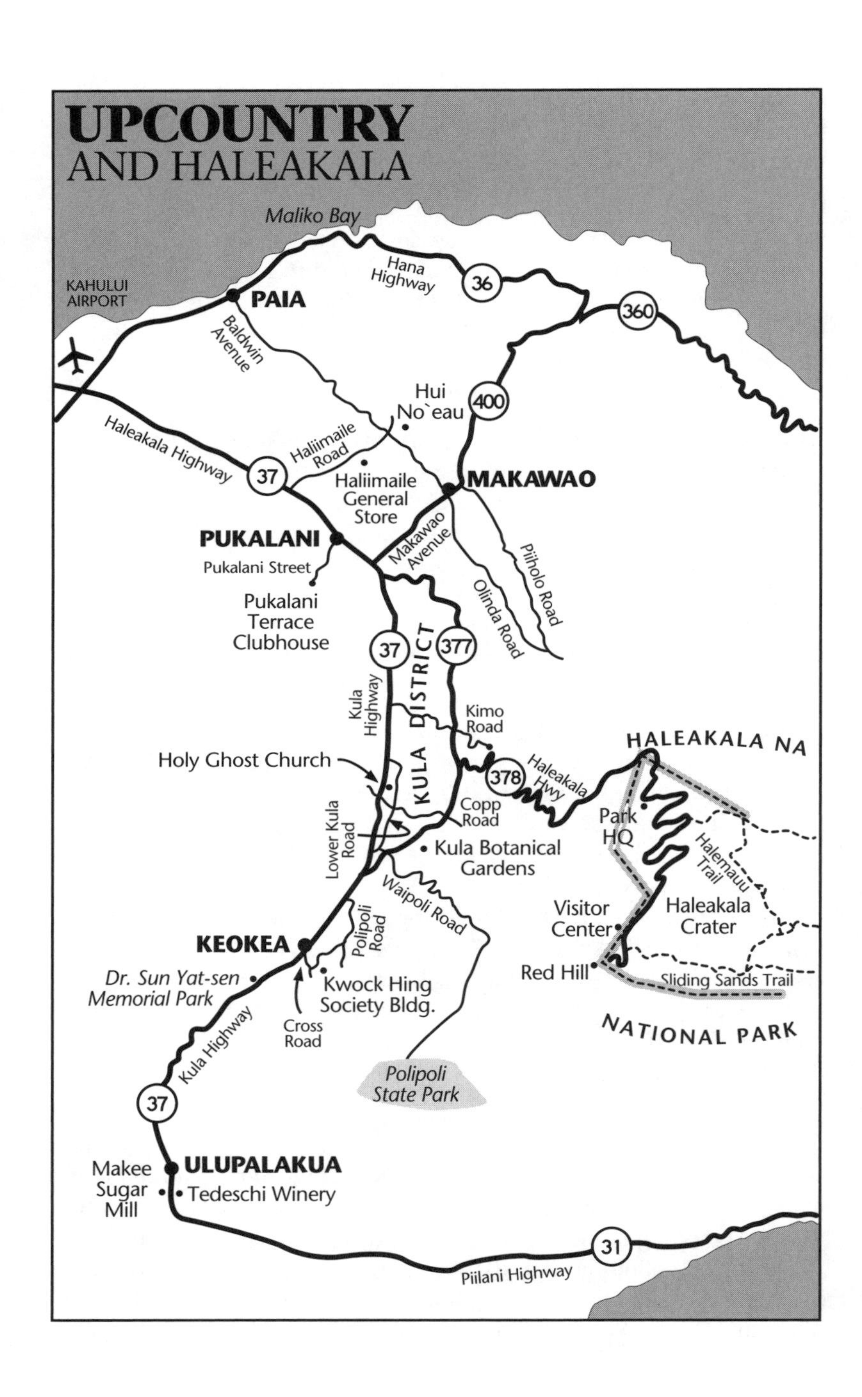
UPCOUNTRY
AND HALEAKALA
Maliko Bay
KAHULUI AIRPORT
PAIA
Hana Highway
36
360
Baldwin Avenue
Hui No`eau
400
Haleakala Highway
Haliimaile Road
37
Haliimaile General Store
MAKAWAO
PUKALANI
Makawao Avenue
Pukalani Street
Piiholo Road
Olinda Road
Pukalani Terrace Clubhouse
37
377
KULA DISTRICT
Kula Highway
Kimo Road
HALEAKALA NA
Holy Ghost Church
378
Haleakala Hwy
Copp Road
Park HQ
Lower Kula Road
Kula Botanical Gardens
Halemauu Trail
Waipoli Road
Polipoli Road
Visitor Center
Haleakala Crater
KEOKEA
Red Hill
Sliding Sands Trail
Dr. Sun Yat-sen Memorial Park
Kwock Hing Society Bldg.
Cross Road
NATIONAL PARK
Kula Highway
Polipoli State Park
37
Makee Sugar Mill
ULUPALAKUA
Tedeschi Winery
31
Piilani Highway

hiking option, continue a mile farther to Waihe`e Valley Road. Follow the road until the pavement ends at a T-junction with a former cane road. Take this road to the right for a stroll up the valley, past streamside taro patches, across a hanging footbridge, to reach a natural pool 2 miles in. Enjoy the pristine beauty while you can. The road soon improves, and before you know it you're on a two-lane highway, speeding back to civilization.

Upcountry and Haleakala

Unlike Vesuvius, St. Helens, Fuji-san, and Kilimanjaro, ***Haleakala*** ("the house of the sun") lacks the classic upsloping shape and explosive pedigree of its volcanic peers. Hawaiian volcanoes form through comparatively gentle eruptions that spread layer upon layer of viscous lava over a broad area. The flattened appearance of the "shield volcanoes" that result can be deceiving. Haleakala does not look 10,000 feet tall because it is so wide—it spreads over most of the island. In mass, its concave dome packs more solid rock than a dozen of the world's more visually impressive "tall" volcanoes put together.

Wrapped around Haleakala's gentle western slopes, a loosely defined agricultural zone known as Upcountry takes advantage of the temperate climate and fertile volcanic soil. Truck farmers grow a variety of vegetable crops; floral nurseries cover hillsides with exotic blooms; and two of Hawaii's largest ranches herd cattle along Haleakala's upper slopes. Upcountry residents are an easygoing lot. Comforted by cool breezes and chilly nights, they boast that their sunset views across West Maui can't be beat.

The many different routes to Upcountry all climb through pineapple-covered foothills planted in countered rows like the whorl of a fingerprint. The Haleakala Highway from Kahului passes through Pukalani, the largest settlement. Two "back-door" routes lead first through Makawao, an Upcountry outpost with far more character. These roads, Baldwin Avenue, which climbs from Paia, and Route 400, which starts farther along the Hana Highway and turns into Makawao Avenue, intersect each other at right angles in the center of Makawao town.

If you take Baldwin Avenue up, stop at the ***Holy Rosary Church*** on the right past the sugar mill to see Maurice Felbier's rendition of Father Damien comforting a leper. Three miles farther, look for the sign to ***Hui No`eau*** (572–6560) at 2841 Baldwin Avenue. A beautiful lawn drive lined with trees leads to a tile-roofed Mediterranean mansion, built by noted architect C. W. Dickey for Harry and Ethel Baldwin in 1917. Ethel helped to found Hui No`eau, the oldest art society on Maui, and today the *hui* maintains the home as a workshop center for the benefit of its membership and visiting artists. Although it is not set up as a commercial gallery, various artists exhibit their works here and frequent shows and art classes are held. Wander around the garden courtyard and peek into the stables where potters manipulate their wheels. Open Monday–Saturday 10:00 A.M. to 4:00 P.M.

Two miles farther, Makawao, Maui's cowboy town, keeps up its "Machowao" image through periodic rodeos. Horses may no longer be hitched at the lampposts, but four-by-four pickups crowd the main streets, and the wooden architecture simulates a transplanted Dodge City. Most cowpokes work at the surrounding ranches during the week, leaving Makawao to a more precious set. No longer selling rawhide and rope, many of Makawao's shops have gone yuppie, stimulated not only by a boost in tourism but also by a rash of Upcountry subdivisions. The main streets are choked with fashionable boutiques and art galleries. Note the store selling fireplaces and chimneys, however, as an indication of Upcountry's chilly nights.

Start your browsing amid the former Makawao Theater complex at the lower end of Baldwin Avenue. Yet another artists' collective exhibits here, and in back, ***Hot Island Glass*** (572–4527) displays its own form of artistry. Watch colored lumps of glass being shaped in the 2,000-degree furnace. Open daily 9:00 A.M. to 5:00 P.M., with glass blowing starting at 10:30 A.M. The complex also has a very pleasant courtyard cafe.

As for restaurants, Makawao has plenty. ***Kitada's*** (572–7241) across the street, serves a mean bowl of saimin (a kind of ramen in broth) to a mostly local clientele. Open Monday–Saturday 6:00 A.M. to 1:30 P.M. Old-timers also favor the cream puffs from ***Komoda Bakery*** (572–7261). Meanwhile, at the top of Baldwin Avenue, ***Casanova's Italian Deli*** (572–0220) embodies Makawao's new upscale persona. The deli was established by four Italian schoolfriends from Milan who moved to Makawao because they heard it "had horses." Casanova's has expanded into an adjacent property to operate a *ristorante* and *discoteca,* but it's cheaper to order from the deli counter. Park yourself on the front porch and watch life in Makawao pass by. Open Monday–Saturday 7:00 A.M. to 6:00 P.M., Sunday 8:30 A.M. to 5:00 P.M. The restaurant stays open until 9:00 P.M., with live music starting 10:00 P.M.

A number of alternative-lifestyle people live here, too, close to the spiritual "power source" of Haleakala Crater. Seekers or those merely curious can enter ***The Dragon's Den*** (572–2424) at the corner of Baldwin and Makawao Avenues. This oriental lair has shelves filled with jars of exotic herbs, teas, and medicines. William Malik grew up in China and acquired a formal education in Chinese healing. He opened this shop as the pharmaceutical wing of his adjacent practice. Other alternative practitioners have joined him.

Above Makawao Avenue, Baldwin Avenue becomes Olinda Road, which leads past the 1843 coral-block ***Po`okela Church*** and climbs steeply through lush hills. Eucalyptus line the narrow road, filling the air with a spicy fragrance. Designer homes alternate with rustic farmhouses. Gaps in the tree cover offer dramatic vistas of the coast far below. Higher up, you'll pass the state's Captive Rearing Project for endangered *`alala* crows and *nene* geese. To stretch your legs at the top of Olinda, follow the dirt road that continues from the gate through rolling pastures. If you take the left fork, you can follow a large irrigation pipe east through several miles of variegated forest to end up in Haleakala's moss-covered watershed.

Just before it dead-ends, Olinda connects with Piiholo Road, which winds through a pine forest to loop back to Makawao. On the way down, look for ***Aloha o Ka Aina,*** a plant nursery that specializes in ferns. Turn left at the bottom of Piiholo to return to town.

Makawao Avenue continues southwest as Route 365 to Pukalani. Here, amid this elevated wasteland of shopping malls and suburban homes, one of Maui's few authentic Hawaiian kitchens lurks in an unlikely place, the Pukalani Country Club. To reach it, go 0.5 mile downhill on Haleakala Highway from Makawao Avenue, turn left on Pukalani Street past the shopping center, and follow to its end. The ***Pukalani Terrace Clubhouse*** (572–1325) serves all your local favorites, such as squid in coconut milk. Large picture windows overlook the golf course with views of West Maui beyond. Open weekdays 7:00 A.M. to 2:00 P.M., weekends 6:30 A.M. to 2:00 P.M., and nightly 5:00–9:00 P.M. Inexpensive.

Ever since its opening in a forgotten plantation camp, a stampede of savvy locals have flocked to the ***Haliimaile General Store*** (572–2666). To follow their footprints, turn from Haleakala Highway onto Haliimaile Road, just south of Pukalani. Beverly and Joe Gannon have forsaken a background in show business to team up with two local chefs and convert this 1929-vintage plantation store into a gourmet restaurant. The partners share cooking duties and collaborate on recipe ideas to maintain an ever-changing menu of eclectically blended ingredients based around "fish, pasta, duck, lamb, and a smoked something." Delicatessen-style lunches command moderate prices, while dinners approach the investment-caliber range. Open Monday–Friday 11:00 A.M. to 2:30 P.M. and nightly 5:30–9:00 P.M.

Beyond Pukalani, the Haleakala Highway splits off to the left as Route 377, while Route 37 continues south as the Kula Highway. These parallel routes traverse the Kula District, some of Maui's most fertile farmland. Kula onions are prized throughout the state for their sweet, mild flavor. Kula potatoes, first planted to feed hungry forty-niners during the California gold rush, now appear in island markets as Maui-style potato chips. Kula's flower farms have blossomed into a multimillion-dollar business, thanks largely to the commercial success of the South African protea. Like the Greek god Proteus, for whom they are named, these striking flowers take many forms, from the regal powderpuffs of the king protea to the spiky bristles of pincushions. Dressed in metallic hues, they have a texture ranging between feathers and stiff felt, and from exotic bouquets that retain their beauty fresh or dry. Although primarily a winter crop, some varieties bloom year-round. Many of Kula's flower nurseries post signs welcoming visitors and will sell retail. You can arrange a guided tour of Kula's largest protea farm, ***Kula Vista*** (878–3251; 888–878–3251); if you call on a weekday morning, they can generally accommodate visitors that afternoon.

Most of the farms lie along side roads running between the two highways. Plot your own course on these steep country lanes, perfect for a lazy Sunday drive. As clouds descend upon and lift from the mountain slopes, the landscape alternates between a misty gray and a bouquet of color. The panorama of the isthmus and West Maui stretches below, shimmering like a mirage.

Take the high road first, not for moral reasons, but because the scenery's better. Chrysanthemum and carnation farms decorate the surrounding hillside. In spring the jacaranda trees erupt in a blaze of lavender/periwinkle blossoms. A mile farther, the Haleakala Highway turns uphill again, becoming Route 378, while Route 377 continues as Kekaulike Avenue and soon begins to descend. About 3 miles along, the ***Kula Botanical Gardens*** (878–1715) on the left might merit a visit. In case you're planning a vendetta, the "taboo garden" near the top features an assortment of some of the world's most poisonous plants. Open daily 9:00 A.M. to 4:00 P.M.; small admission fee.

The next left is Waipoli Road, which narrows to a single lane as it climbs 10 miles of switchbacks through cattle land to reach ***Polipoli State Park*** (984–8109). The last few miles are unpaved and may require four-wheel-drive. If you can make it to the top, the combination of serenity and scenery can't be beat. Tall stands of redwood mingle in an experimental forest composed of trees from around the world. A variety of hiking trails beckon, and campers can enjoy the park's unearthly views overnight by booking the state-owned cabin (587–0300) well in advance.

Immediately past Waipoli Road, Route 377 rejoins the Kula Highway. If you take this lower road to or from Pukalani, look for the silver roof of the ***Holy Ghost Church*** on the uphill side. Portuguese Azores islanders built this unusual octagonal structure in 1894. To reach it, you have to get onto Lower Kula Road, which runs parallel to the highway. Inside the church, you'll find a lovely gilded altar and bas-relief sculptures depicting the stations of the cross. Notice the statue of Saint Antone, with a pig underfoot. Volunteers bake *pao doce* (Portuguese sweetbread) every Monday and Thursday morning for sale in the adjacent hall. Church members also throw an annual free luau in a tradition stemming from the Old Country. Their ancestral village had faced a severe drought, and the villagers had vowed that if God brought forth rain, they would feed the entire island. Centuries later, on a new island, in a faraway land, this vow is still remembered.

Just past the church on lower Kula Road, ***Cafe 808*** (878–6874) has a menu as local as its clientele. At $9.95, the fresh-catch special is the most expensive thing on the menu. Grab a table inside this former plantation store or carry out to enjoy the sumptuous hilltop views from the parking lot. Open daily 6:00 A.M. to 8:00 P.M.

As you continue south along the Kula Highway, moving farther around the volcano's flank, Moloka`i disappears from the north and reappears behind the south end of West Maui. Every mile brings you farther into Haleakala's rain shadow. In contrast with the lush hills of Olinda, *panini* (prickly pear) cactus already carpets lower elevations. A couple miles south from the second junction of Route 37 and 377, you reach tiny Keokea, a one-time community of Chinese immigrants. Downtown Keokea has four stores, two of them rival gas stations. ***Keokea Gallery*** (878–3555) takes its ties to local art seriously; many of the paintings depict scenes in or around town while the owners paint new ones in the back of the room. Open daily 9:00 A.M. to 5:00 P.M. A real treat awaits you in ***Grandma's Coffee*** (878–2140), where owner Alfred Franco roasts his own homegrown beans just like Grandma taught him, using a century-old roaster. Peek through the counter window to see the original machinery he uses. Grandma's also serves breakfast and lunch, with local specials like sweet-sour spare ribs. Paintings of Upcountry rodeos by local artist Sharon Shigekawa decorate the walls. Open daily 7:00 A.M. to 5:00 P.M.

Holy Ghost Church

To tour Chinatown, backtrack to Cross Road, near the town entrance, which angles above the park. A half-mile uphill, the ***Kwock Hing Society Building*** serves as a solitary reminder of the immigrant farmers who flocked to the area. Among the village's early residents was Sun Yat-sen's brother. The future Chinese leader often visited Keokea while studying in Honolulu, and he sent his family here for safety while plotting his revolution, and was funded heavily by Hawaii Chinese through societies like Kwock Hing. A mile and a half past Keokea town on the highway, look for the newly dedicated ***Dr. Sun Yat-sen Memorial Park.*** Two enormous mock-stone lions face off in opposing corners, while a statue of the great man gazes down the hill to the site of his brother's former home.

From here, Route 37 begins a gradual, bumpy descent as it continues south across miles of cactus-studded pastureland partitioned by crumbling walls of lava stone. Most of Moloka`i swings out of view as the island of Lana`i seizes center stage on the horizon. Farther along, uninhabited Kaho`olawe appears with tiny Molokini in midchannel. Five miles out of Keokea, the highway reaches the headquarters of the vast Ulupalakua Ranch. James Makee, a whaling captain turned gentleman planter, founded the ranch in 1856 to complement his sugar ventures. Makee's lavish social life included the entertainment of royalty. The white ***King's Cottage,*** built for King Kalakaua's use during his visits, peeks through the trees behind the ranch office.

Across the street, the ***Ranch Store*** boasts the oldest Levi Strauss account in the world. Bags of swine and horse feed have yielded shelf space to tourist bric-a-brac as well as a deli. Sitting on a porch in front of the store, two life-size sculptures impersonate a pair of old-timers who actually hung out on this very porch. Ulupalakua resident Reems Mitchell immortalized the duo in his trademark caricature style. The cowpoke standing next to them is Ikua Purdy, a famous roper from the ranch's early history. Mitchell's better-known works on exhibit elsewhere include the "old salts" fronting the Pioneer Inn in Lahaina. The artist makes his home inside the ruins of the old Makee Sugar Mill, a quarter-mile up the road.

Across the street from the mill, you can visit ***Tedeschi Vineyards*** (878–1266) and reward yourself with a glass of bubbly for coming this far. Emil Tedeschi has brought family know-how from Napa Valley to open Hawaii's first vineyard and winery, in cooperation with Ulupalakua Ranch. You can take a free tour of the winery to learn the painstaking steps through which grapes and pineapples become bottled wines and champagne. Almost everything gets done by manual labor according to traditional methods. Despite its founder's credentials, the winery likes to boast that "this is not Napa Valley." After the tour, stop at the visitors center. An adjacent gallery filled with historic photos chronicles a century of ranching life, including visits from royalty. Open daily 9:00 A.M. to 5:00 P.M.; half-hour tours are offered at 10:30 A.M. and 1:30 P.M.

Beyond the winery, the highway deteriorates further. A narrow, winding road rattles its way east to Kaupo across 22 miles of old lava flows covered by scrub bushes that barely sustain the scattered cattle that graze here. Consider going at least the first couple of miles to visit the bleak solitude of the landscape. As you round the corner to Haleakala's southern slopes, the ink-black path of the Cape Kinau lava flow below draws the eye, in vivid contrast with the tree-covered cinder cones higher up.

Those who wish to devote more than a day to Upcountry or position themselves midway to Haleakala's summit for a predawn ascent have several options. The ***Gildersleeves*** (878–6623; 2112 Naalae Road, Kula 96790), in lower Kula, offers perhaps the most outstanding value. A retired couple from Alaska, Murray and Elaine, spent five years building their dream home on this small Upcountry farm. Resplendent with natural woods, the split-level home enjoys breathtaking views across the isthmus. The three guest rooms on the lower level have a private entrance and share separate cooking facilities and living space. The Gildersleeves also rent a fully equipped cottage with a cozy fireplace and berths for up to six people. Murray still tends the pineapple fields and harvests other fruits and vegetables, of which guests can partake. Rooms go for $70 double and the cottage for $125 as a quad, with a surcharge for stays of less than three nights. The hosts prefer that smoking and drinking be done elsewhere.

Farther south toward Ulupalakua, ***Silver Cloud Ranch*** (878– 6101, 800–532–1111; www.silvercloudranch.com; RR 2, Box 201, Kula 96790) occupies a nine-acre lot within the larger, still-functioning

Aviation in Miniature

One of the more improbable museums you'll find on Maui—or anywhere else—is Ray Robert's Paper Airplane Museum (877–8916), which occupies a small space in Kahului's Maui Mall (on Ka`ahumanu Avenue). The museum displays an impressive array of paper airplanes and models—mostly packaged as kits for sale. Evidently the science of paper aviation has advanced considerably since the third grade. Started as a retirement project by Roberts, the museum also has amassed an extensive collection of photographs illustrating milestones in Hawaii's aviation history. Most of these were donated by members of the community, and Roberts is more than willing to walk visitors around the display area, recounting the anecdotes that accompany each photograph. Roberts is also known as the "Tin Can Man" on Maui. He builds miniature aircraft and other models to order out of recycled juice cans. "They fly like a rock," he deadpans. The museum is open Monday–Thursday, 10:00 A.M. to 7:00 P.M., Friday until 9:00 P.M. Saturday and Sunday, 10:00 A.M. to 4:00 P.M.

Thompson Ranch. The original ranchhouse, bunkhouse, and cottage have been converted to B&B units. Six ranchhouse rooms rent from $85 to $145; bunkhouse suites with kitchenettes go for $110–$150, except the Haleakala Suite with fireplace for $150. Nicest of all is the Lana`i Cottage, which has a porch hammock and an antique wood stove and radio inside; it costs $160. All rooms have scenic views and include a hot breakfast.

Olinda Country Cottages & Inn (572–1453; 800–932–3435) offers a variety of lodging spread over a seven-acre former protea farm with hilltop views. The owner, a former antiques dealer, has decorated the property with an abundance of country charm. Two B&B rooms in the upstairs of the main Tudor mansion rent for $120, with a studio for $130. A pair of secluded, fully equipped cottages rent for $195 and $220. Two nights minimum.

Malu Manu (878–6111; 888–878–6161; www.mauisunrise.com) offers two options, a two-bedroom house and a log-cabin studio, each nestled within a wooded seven-acre lot, with views spanning three islands. The cabin, built in the 1920s as a writer's retreat, rents for $135; the house goes for $170. Both feature simple Hawaiian decor, with wood-burning stoves. An outdoor Japanese *ofuro* (wooden bathtub) and paddle-tennis court await use by guests. Other Upcountry B&B cottages with hilltop views include Bloom Cottage (878–1425), Country Garden Cottage (878–2858), Moonlight (878– 6977), and Kula Cottage (878–2043).

Located just below Makawao, the ***Banyan Tree*** (572–9021; www.banyantreehouse.com) offers historical charm and leafy tranquility in lieu of unobstructed views. Built in the 1920s as a plantation manager's home abutting the pineapple fields, the property became the residence of Ethel Baldwin, one of Maui's early patrons of the arts. Ethel painted here daily and even got her chauffeur to join her. The main, three-bedroom house has antique furnishings with an understated island decor. It rents for $275; individual rooms are occasionally rented on a last-minute basis. If not, you'll have to make do with the servants' quarters, which, refurbished as studios, rent for $85–$100. A swimming pool is on site. Another Makawao home of similar vintage, ***Hale Ho`okipa*** (572–6698), was built by a Portuguese financier who raised thirteen kids here. Remnants of the original twenty-two-acre estate (since subdivided) include a small Madeira vineyard, Portuguese bread oven, and water tower. B&B rooms rent for $85–$145. Owner Cherie Attix also offers hiking tours.

The voyage to the top of ***Haleakala Crater*** provides in every way the crowning experience of a Maui visit. After driving to the volcano's

10,023-foot summit, you peer over the rim of the 3,000-foot-deep crater inside. Measuring 7.5 miles long by 2.5 miles across, this mind-boggling space could swallow Manhattan, skyscrapers and all. Erosive stream action cut the original basin during a lull between eruptions, after which subsequent flows filled in the floor and restored the crater's volcanic appearance. Rust-streaked colors paint a lunar landscape of cinder cones and crusted lava flows. Mark Twain called it "the sublimest spectacle" he had ever seen.

To receive the quintessential Haleakala experience, purists insist you must arrive at the mountain early enough to watch the sun rise above the far rim of the summit wall. Shadows creep along the crater-pocked floor as the first rays ignite the smoldering embers of the volcano in a blaze of colorful light. Such a vision entertained the demigod Maui, who waited here in ambush and used a magic lasso to snare the sun's legs as they poked above the crater rim. Threatened with its life, the sun promised to travel across the sky more slowly, giving Maui's mother time to dry her *kapa* cloth. Almost as impressive as the show itself is the number of pilgrims willing to brave frigid early-morning temperatures to follow in Maui's footsteps.

The Art of Maui

The unsurpassed beauty of the Hawaiian islands has always attracted a steady stream of artists. Maui has perhaps more than its share, however. More to the point, it has made a cottage industry out of "art tourism" as a means of exploiting the synergy between local talent and tourist pocketbooks. The hotbed of such activity is undoubtedly Lahaina, which claims more art galleries per capita than any other American city. Local galleries promote Friday night as "Art Night," with special shows, featured artists-in-residence, and free refreshments offered from 7:00–10:00 P.M. The weekend outdoor showings of the Lahaina Arts Society beneath the central Banyan Tree provide another chance to get acquainted with local artists. The art on Maui should not be dismissed as only made-for-tourists kitsch. The many artist cooperatives scattered around the island nurture some genuine talents. Moreover, the Maui Arts and Cultural Center in Kahului showcases rotating exhibits from the world over. Call 242–2787 for details. It is also possible to visit certain artists in their studios. Sheldon and Elizabeth Wallau of Upcountry's Keokea Gallery do their painting right in the back of their gallery. Jan Kasprzycki, another Upcountry painter whose work is shown in many of the island's better restaurants, such as David Paul's and Mama's, welcomes visitors by appointment to his Olinda studio. Call 572–0585.

Those preferring to rise at a more civilized hour will be pleased to know that Haleakala's sunsets claim a following of their own, even though clouds that descend into the crater during the day sometimes linger after dark, obscuring the view. Call 877–5111 for the exact times of sunrise and sunset and general weather conditions. Allow an hour and a half for the drive up.

From the junction of Routes 377 and 378, a series of switchbacks ascends 6,800 feet over 20 miles, reaching the summit a total distance of 38 miles from Kahului. You'll pass a number of biking groups cruising "the world's steepest downhill ride." If that sounds impressive, how about the autumn "Run to the Sun," an annual footrace going up! The road quickly climbs above the tree line through open cattle land. Signs advise you to TURN ON LIGHTS IN CLOUDS. The ***Haleakala National Park*** boundary and turnoff to the ***Hosmer Grove*** campground arrive at roughly the halfway mark. A brochure available at the campground will guide you along the quarter-mile nature trail nearby. Just ahead you can pay the $10 entrance fee and proceed to the ***Park Headquarters*** building. Inquire here about the morning schedule of ranger-led talks and hikes, and collect camping permits, if desired. Call 572–9306 for live bodies 8:00 A.M. to 4:00 P.M. A small collection of displays chronicles the natural history of the park. You can learn about the campaign to restore the *nene* goose, Hawaii's state bird, to the unique habitats of Hawaii's tall volcanoes. Somewhat-tame *nene* often hang out in the parking lot.

As you continue zigzagging up the barren rubble that covers Haleakala's upper slopes, you will come to two crater overlooks that deserve a stop on the way up or down. ***Leleiwi Overlook*** at 8,800 feet offers the chance to view the elusive "Specter of the Brocken." During late afternoon on cloudy days, you may see your own rainbow-shrouded shadow reflected in the mist. ***Kalahaku Overlook*** at 9,320 feet features a patch of silversword plants, which thrive atop Hawaii's highest volcanoes. These exotic bushes resemble metallic porcupines. After growing for five to twenty years, they erupt once in a spectacular display of tiny flowers, then wither and die. Because silverswords have fragile, shallow roots adapted to the volcanic soil, take care not to walk within 6 feet of any plant.

Near the summit, the park service operates another ***visitor center,*** open from sunrise to 3:00 P.M. daily. In addition to natural history exhibits, the center houses a much-reproduced painting by Paul Rockwood depicting Maui's encounter with the sun god, La. The metallic domes of Science City, an off-limits research center, gleam nearby. From the visitors center, the road climbs 0.5 mile to ***Red Hill,*** the actual summit. Most people watch the sunrise from the small shelter here. The 360-degree windowpanes allow you to view every island except Kaua`i on a clear day.

No one with the legs to carry them should pass up the chance to explore Haleakala crater on foot. Short of space flight, it's the closest thing to walking on another planet. Those who would rather ride than walk can contact Pony Express Tours (667–2202) or Maui Crater Bound (878–1743) to ask about crater trail rides. The ***Sliding Sands Trail*** from the visitors center provides the main access to the crater floor. The trail gets its name from the loose cinders it traverses, so watch your footing. As you descend, you pass a procession of cinder cones, some of which rise as high as 1,000 feet; when clouds roll in, these poke through the mist like islands in a sea. The crater floor below is wracked by crevices and lava caves. Hawaiians threw the umbilical cords of their newborns into one such pit called ***Keanawilinau.*** This prevented rodents from making off with them, which would give the grown child "ratlike" qualities.

The Sliding Sands Trail connects midway with the ***Halemauu Trail,*** which loops back up the crater walls, emerging near the highway at the 8,000-foot level for a hardy 8-mile round trip. A third trail allows backpackers an overnight route through the ***Kaupo Gap,*** descending to Maui's remote southeastern coast. Hawaiians often made such a trek as a shortcut across the island. Except for *kahunas* in training, Hawaiians did not live in the crater itself. Camping in the crater's two campgrounds requires a permit. If you write at least three months in advance and are flexible about your dates, you can book one of the three cabins here. Address requests to the Cabins, Haleakala Park, Box 369, Makawao, Maui 96768.

If you want a hiking guide for the crater or anywhere else on Maui, a call to ***Hike Maui*** (879–5270; www.hikemaui.com) will put the encyclopedic knowledge of Ken Schmidt at your disposal. He charges about $85 for a half-day hike, lunch included. Randy Warner's ***Maui Hiking Safari*** (573–0168; 888–445–3963) charges $49, without lunch. In a hurry to get back to the beach? ***Proflyght Hawaii Paragliding*** (874–5433) launches tandem flights from atop Haleakala weather permitting, with prices varying by flight time.

WHERE TO STAY

A`a Pali Cliffhouse, 573–0693; (800) 861–9566. One-bedroom Balinese pleasure palace perched above dramatic waterfall gorge along Hana coast. $350 per night.

Gildersleeves B&B, 878–6623, at 2112 Naalae Road in Kula, is the product of a retired couple's dream. Views and accommodations are wonderful. Rates start at $70.

Haikuleana B&B, 575–2890, 555 Haiku Road, consists of four rooms in an elegantly restored plantation home. Rates start at $120.

Hana Plantation Cottages, 800–228–4262, where you can rent private homes on the beautiful Hana coast. Rates start at $72 for a studio.

Lahaina Inn, 661–0577 or (800) 669–3444, is at 127 Lahainaluna Road. It's a wonderfully restored mansion in the center of town with 12 rooms decorated with period antique furniture. Rates start at $99.

The Old Wailuku Inn at Ulupono, 244–5897; (800) 305–4899 offers gracious hospitality in a nostalgic Old Hawaii setting. Rates start at $120.

Olinda Country Cottages & Inn, 572–1453; (800) 932–3435. Hilltop protea farm offers B&B rooms and secluded cottages, decorated in country elegance. Rates start at $120.

Silver Cloud Guest Ranch, 878–6101, in upcountry Kula, has a variety of rooms in a historic ranch house, all with great views. Rates start at $85.

For links to many other Maui accommodation options (including numerous B&Bs), plus general visitors info, visit: *www.maui.net; www.visitmaui.com.*

WHERE TO EAT

David Paul's Lahaina Grill, 667–5117. Award-winning Pacific Rim cuisine with Southwestern accents. Investment-caliber.

Gerard's, 661–8939, in the Plantation Inn, at 174 Lahainaluna Road, Lahaina, French Gascogne cuisine, modified to embrace island produce. Investment-caliber prices.

Haliimaile General Store, 572–2666, is neither "general," nor a "store." It offers a wide–ranging selection of great regional dishes and wines. Expensive but worth it.

Paia Bistro, 579–6255, at 89 Hana Highway, in Paia, serves French bistro standards with island flavorings, and fresh fish nightly. Moderate.

Koho's, 877–5588, venerable local diner in Ka`ahumanu Shopping Center, Kahului. Inexpensive.

Mama's Fish House, 579-8488, just east of Paia Town, offers fresh seafood in a romantic oceanfront setting. Investment-caliber.

Pacific Café, 879–0069, in Azeka Place II, at 1279 South Kihei Road, Kihei, serves Jean-Marie Josselin's version of Hawaii Regional Cuisine. Investment-caliber prices.

Plantation House, 669–6299, 2000 Plantation Club Drive, Kapalua. Romantic, hilltop dining, with views across three islands. Expensive.

Roy's Kahana Bay & Grill, 669–6999 and Nicolina, 669–5000, in Kahana Gateway Shopping Center, 4405 Honoapiilani Highway, Kahana. Hawaii superchef Roy Yamaguchi opened these twin venues to cope with the demand for his inventive Pacific Rim cuisine. Expensive.

Saigon Cafe 243–9560, at 1792 Main Street (next to the bridge), Wailuku, serves delicious Vietnamese fare in a no-nonsense setting. Moderate.

Sansei Seafood Restaurant, 669–6286, 115 Bay Drive, Kapalua Shops, Kapalua. Top-rated seafood venue thrives on East-West culinary fusion. Expensive.

Waterfront (244–9028), at 50 Hauoli Street, in Milowai condo near Ma`alea Harbor. "The local's Mama's" serves fresh fish in an oceanfront venue on the South Shore. Investment-caliber prices.

The Big Island

Anchoring the archipelago on its southeastern end, the island of Hawai`i represents the volcano goddess Pele's latest and greatest creation. Built on the overlapping flows of five volcanoes, the island covers almost twice the area of all its northern neighbors put together. Mauna Kea ("white mountain"), at 13,796 feet, not only tops all rival peaks in the Pacific but, viewed from its base on the ocean floor, would be the tallest mountain on earth. A nudge below Mauna Kea in height, its neighbor, Mauna Loa ("long mountain"), covers half the island with its massive girth. It's the world's largest volcano, weighing more than the entire Sierra Nevada Range, and it's still growing.

Ever vigilant, Pele continues to add to her domain, sending rivers of molten rock flowing down the hillside to form new land. The goddess makes her principal abode inside Kilauea, the pygmy of the Big Island volcanoes at 4,000 feet. Kilauea ("spewing") has spewed the hot stuff almost daily since 1983, averaging 300,000 cubic yards per day, making it the world's most active volcano. The steady pattern of these "drive-in" eruptions has delighted tourists but brought woe to homeowners in lava-inundated areas. Still, each acre of expanded shoreline buys Pele added security against the encroachments of her arch rival, the ocean.

Thanks to the conquests of Kamehameha I, another famous Big Island resident, the island of Hawai`i came to bestow its name on the entire chain. Today locals distinguish the island from the state by referring to the former simply as the Big Island. It's big not just in size. The variety of terrain rivals that of a continent. Mark Twain, gazing from the desert of Ka`u to the rain forest of Hamakua, from the snowcapped peak of Mauna Kea to the beaches of Kona, boasted that he "could see all the climes of the world at a single glance of the eye." Hilo and Kona, the two population centers, spread over opposite coasts, 95 or 124 miles apart, respectively, by the northern or southern route.

For those who wish a guided hiking experience, Hugh Montgomery's ***Hawaiian Walkways*** (775–0372) and Rob Pacheco's ***Hawaii Forest & Trail*** (331–8505; 800–464–1993) both provide the service and have

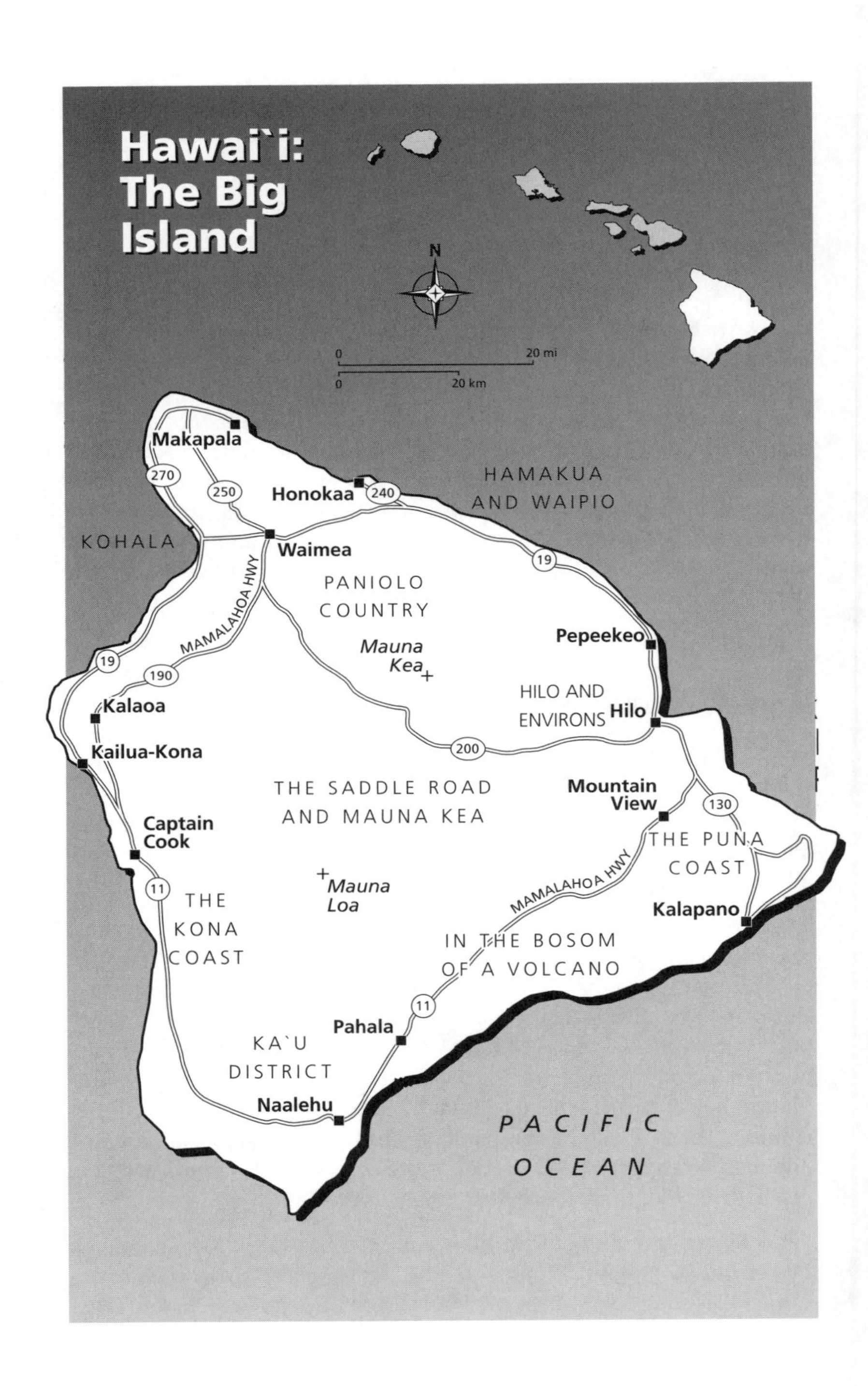
Hawai`i:
The Big
Island
N
0
20 mi
0
20 km
Makapala
270
250
Honokaa
240
HAMAKUA
AND WAIPIO
KOHALA
Waimea
MAMALAHOA HWY
19
PANIOLO
COUNTRY
Pepeekeo
Mauna
Kea
19
190
HILO AND
ENVIRONS
Hilo
Kalaoa
200
Kailua-Kona
THE SADDLE ROAD
AND MAUNA KEA
Mountain
View
130
Captain
Cook
THE PUNA
COAST
MAMALAHOA HWY
11
Mauna
Loa
THE
KONA
COAST
Kalapano
IN THE BOSOM
OF A VOLCANO
11
Pahala
KA`U
DISTRICT
Naalehu
PACIFIC
OCEAN

access to private land not otherwise available. Hawaii Forest is by far the larger of the two, and not all their trips involve hiking; these range from stargazing atop Mauna Kea to caving in a lava tube, plus two trips of special interest to birders. The vertiginous hike behind North Kohala's Kapoloa Falls will wow even jaded waterfall connoisseurs. They charge $95 for half-day outings that include a snack. Hawaii Forest is based in West Hawaii, so if you are staying on the east side, Hawaiian Walkways' meeting points are more convenient, and two of their half-day trips on the Hamakua Coast offer unique experiences such as a waterfall swim. These cost $85, including a picnic lunch. Both companies also offer longer outings as well as custom tours. Those of a scientific bent may also want to check out geologist Seth Bloom's ***Hawaiian Eyes*** (937–2530). His half-day tours of Kilauea's volcanic terrain and full-day visits to Mauna Kea's observatories are primarily by four-wheel-drive van, with short hiking stops; these cost $99 and $149, respectively. Finally, if your visit coincides with the first Saturday of the month, you can join members of the ***Kona Hiking Club*** on the trail. Call Roger Knoblauch at 325–0012; check local Sunday newspapers for hikes offered by other island groups.

Hilo and Environs

The Big Island is unique in that its principal settlement lies on the lush windward coast. More than 100,000 people make their home around north-facing Hilo Bay, making Hilo the largest town outside O`ahu. Its 130 inches of annual rainfall nourish all the greenery of

Geography of the Big Island

The youngest island in the chain, the Big Island of Hawai`i is by far the largest, and it is the only one still growing. Its 266 miles of coastline have relatively few beaches. Except for a remote northern section, most of the island is encircled by the Hawai`i Belt Highway; the name it goes by varies between segments. The Big Island has five main volcanoes, two of which top 13,000 feet. Kilauea, the pygmy of the bunch, has the distinction of being the most active volcano on the planet. Its current eruption has continued almost daily since 1983, much of the time allowing visitors to witness one of nature's most awesome and spectacular forces in action. The Big Island's terrain varies enormously from dry, barren lava fields to lush tropical jungle to snow-capped peaks. The many state-of-the-art telescopes atop 13,796-foot Mauna Kea take advantage of the world's clearest night skies.

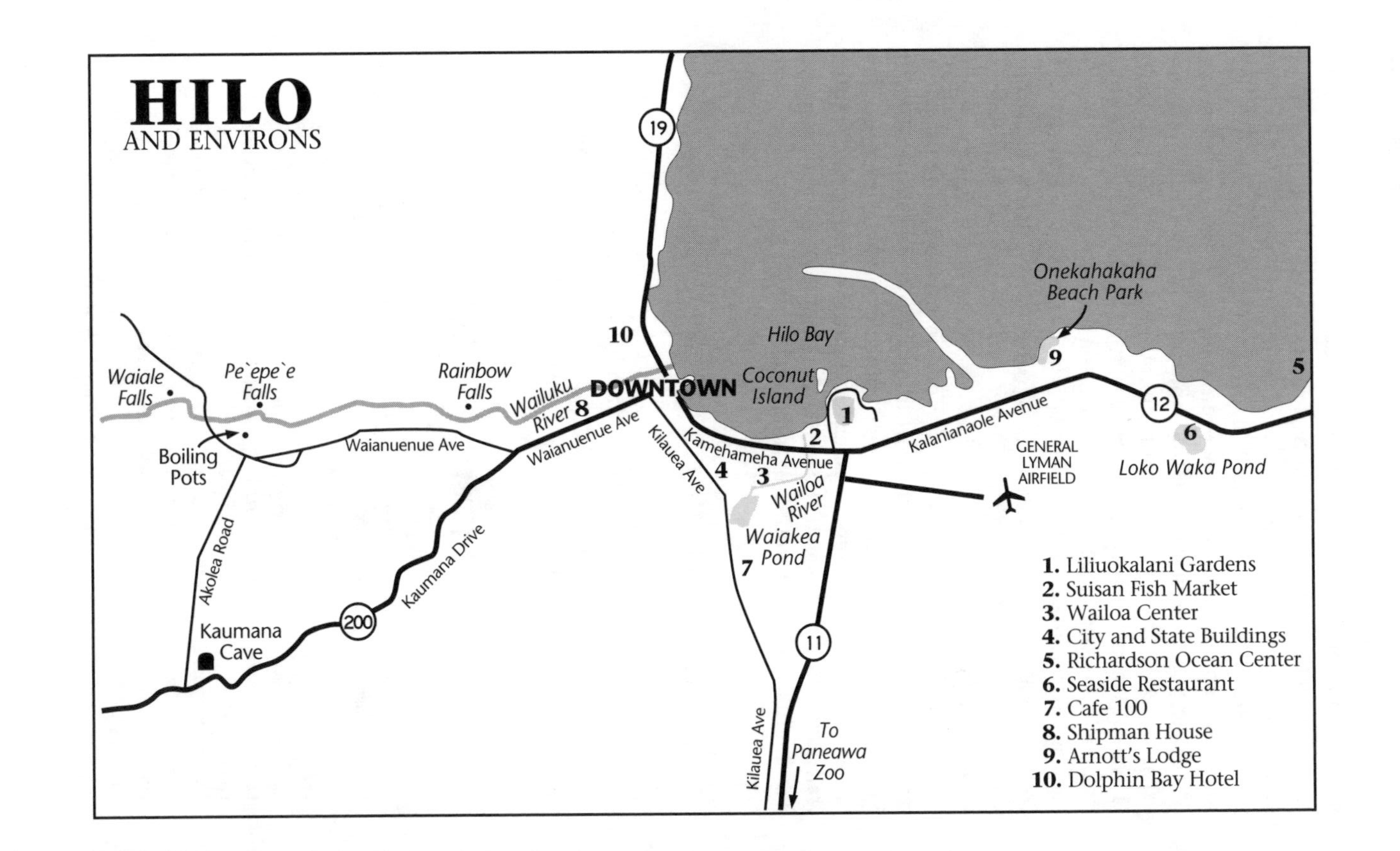
HILO
AND ENVIRONS
19
10
DOWNTOWN
Hilo Bay
Coconut Island
Onekahakaha Beach Park
Waiale Falls
Pe`epe`e Falls
Rainbow Falls
Wailuku River
Boiling Pots
Waianuenue Ave
Kilauea Ave
Kamehameha Avenue
Kalanianaole Avenue
Wailoa River
Waiakea Pond
GENERAL LYMAN AIRFIELD
Loko Waka Pond
Akolea Road
Kaumana Drive
Kaumana Cave
200
11
12
To Paneawa Zoo
1. Liliuokalani Gardens
2. Suisan Fish Market
3. Wailoa Center
4. City and State Buildings
5. Richardson Ocean Center
6. Seaside Restaurant
7. Cafe 100
8. Shipman House
9. Arnott's Lodge
10. Dolphin Bay Hotel

a rain forest. The visitors bureau may tell you that Hilo's rainfall arrives mostly at night, but expect passing showers throughout your stay. You shouldn't let these bouts of precipitation discourage you from enjoying Hilo's offerings. It keeps things cool and makes the flowers grow—to the tune of a $20-million orchid-anthurium industry. Hilo has survived two devastating tidal waves, at least four close calls from advancing lava flows, and countless earthquakes. Residents of this indomitable city by the bay are not about to let a little rain dampen their lifestyle. And neither should you.

If your visit should happen to coincide with the arrival of a foreign cruise ship (usually September through May), head to pier one of the harbor to partake in the free entertainment by Hilo's ***kupuna*** (old-timers). The *kupuna* entertain inter-island arrivals onboard, however, so those performances are restricted to passengers. Call 933–8850 for the schedule of foreign arrivals.

Route 11 passes Hilo's airport as it approaches from the south. The highway ends at the junction of Kamehameha and Kalanianaole Avenues, which reach west and east, respectively, around the bay. Instead, continue straight onto ***Banyan Drive*** to loop around Waiakea Peninsula in the center of the bay. Rows two and three thick of mammoth banyan

Brief History of the Big Island

The Big Island's pivotal role in Hawaiian history centers around the life and death of Kamehameha I, its most famous native son. Kamehameha's inheritance of the family war god, Kukailimoku ("Ku the devourer of lands") gave him a psychic edge in warfare. When an army belonging to Keoua, Kamehameha's cousin and principal rival on the Big Island, was destroyed by an erupting volcano in 1790, it was taken as a sign that the volcano goddess, Pele, favored Kamehameha. Kamehameha's victories on the battlefield owed as much, however, to the modern weapons and training that he received from his Western advisors as it did to the gods of ancient Hawaii. By conquering the other islands, Kamehameha gave the name of his home island, Hawai`i, to the unified kingdom he created. But this victory came at a price. The old gods died with him at Kailua-Kona where his heirs conspired to abolish the system of kapu *just in time for the arrival of the first missionaires in 1820. Moreover, Western ships, which continued to come in ever greater numbers, avoided the Big Island because it lacked a protected harbor. As the center of trade and commerce shifted to Lahaina and then Honolulu, the preeminence of the Big Island became steadily undermined.*

trees line the drive, planted by celebrities. Search for those planted by your favorite public figures, from Amelia Earhart to Richard Nixon.

At the end of a strip of hotels, Keliipio Place detours to the footbridge to Coconut Island. The Hawaiians called this island Mokuola ("healing island") because underwater springs supposedly gave curative properties to waters around it. In addition to affording vistas across the bay, this palm-covered plot provides an excellent vantage point from which to view the Big Island's twin peaks, Mauna Kea and Mauna Loa. Come in the early morning before the clouds roll in.

Next, take a stroll in nearby ***Liliuokalani Gardens.*** While this attractive park bears the name of Hawaii's deposed queen, it exhibits Japanese motifs in its miniature stone pagodas, pavilions, teahouse, and footbridge over reflecting ponds. On the far side of the gardens, ***Suisan Fish Market*** stages a daily morning auction. Night fishers bring in their catches beginning at 6:00 A.M., and local vendors gather to inspect the colorful platters of fish and core samples cut from giant tuna. Show up by 7:30 A.M. to listen to the bidding.

Turn right from Lihiwai Street, the extension from Banyan Drive, and follow Kamehameha Avenue across Wailoa River and the estuarine waters of ***Waiakea*** (or Wailoa) ***Pond.*** On the west bank, inland from the highway, Hilo's ***King Kamehameha Statue*** gazes out across the bay that he loved to surf. This is a replica of two statues originally cast in 1880, which stand in Kapaau and Honolulu, respectively. This modern-day

Big Island Trivia

- *Ka Lae is the southernmost point in the fifty United States.*
- *Kilauea is the world's most active volcano.*
- *Hawai`i is the worldwide leader in harvesting macadamia nuts and orchids.*
- *Parker Ranch is the largest privately held ranch in the United States.*
- *Mauna Kea is the tallest mountain in the world (measured from its base at the ocean floor).*
- *The world's largest and most powerful telescopes top Mauna Kea's summit.*
- *The world's first and only known specimen of olymanite, a mineral discovered by a Lyman descendant, is on display in the Lyman Museum and Mission House in Hilo.*
- *Pahoa, in Puna, is home to the oldest theater in the state—Akebono Theater.*

duplicate was commissioned by the Princeville Resort on Kaua`i, but community elements there opposed its display on the one island that the great conqueror had failed to subdue. Instead, the statue ended up here at Waiakea, the staging grounds for many of his war fleets. Almost 150 million gallons of fresh water empty daily into the spring-fed pond to the right of the statue. Hilo's original downtown once centered around this former Hawaiian fishpond. The area was devastated by the 1946 and 1960 tidal waves that funneled into Hilo Bay with deadly force. The area has been converted into a public park as a kind of buffer zone. Near the statue, the ***Shinmachi Tsunami Memorial*** stands in front of the ***Wailoa Information Center*** (933–0416). The center itself houses rotating exhibits as well as a photo-history of the tsunami. Closed Wednesday morning and Sunday.

Big Island Facts

Nickname: *"The Big Island" or "Orchid Isle"*

Dimensions: *93 x 76 miles*

Highest elevation: *Mauna Kea (13,796 feet)*

Population: *137,531 (1995)*

Principal city: *Hilo*

Flower: *Red lehua*

Color: *Red*

Above the center, on Aupuni Street, stand Hilo's county and state buildings. Their controversial location in this flood-ravaged tsunami zone was designed to reinspire confidence in the city's renewal. You can get the scoop on camping in the county or state parks around the island by applying to the appropriate agency. Some county parks have pavilion shelters, and many state parks have well-maintained housekeeping cabins at affordable rates. Call 961–8311 for county, or 974–6200 for state parks. Satellite county offices can also be found in Waimea, Captain Cook, and Kailua-Kona.

To get a more complete picture of awesome destruction wreaked by tsunamis, continue a mile further around the bay to the ***Pacific Tsunami Museum*** (935–0926), at 130 Kamehameha Avenue. Here you will learn how tsunamis can cross the Pacific as fast as a jet airplane and form waves as high as 100 feet tall. The tsunamis that twice struck Hilo this century moved houses and scattered boulders around town "like a giant hand shooting marbles." Hundreds drowned, but you can also read amazing accounts of survivors swept out to sea for days as well as a legendary Hawaiian said to have surfed an 1868 tsunami in to safety (not recommended). The museum occupies the space of the former First Hawaiian Bank, an 1930 edifice that itself withstood both recent tsunamis. The bank vaults serve as theaters for video screenings. Open Monday–Saturday 10:00 A.M. to 4:00 P.M. Small admission charge.

The buildings around here constitute Hilo's new downtown and its (surviving) historic center. Note the dark gray sidewalks, a consequence

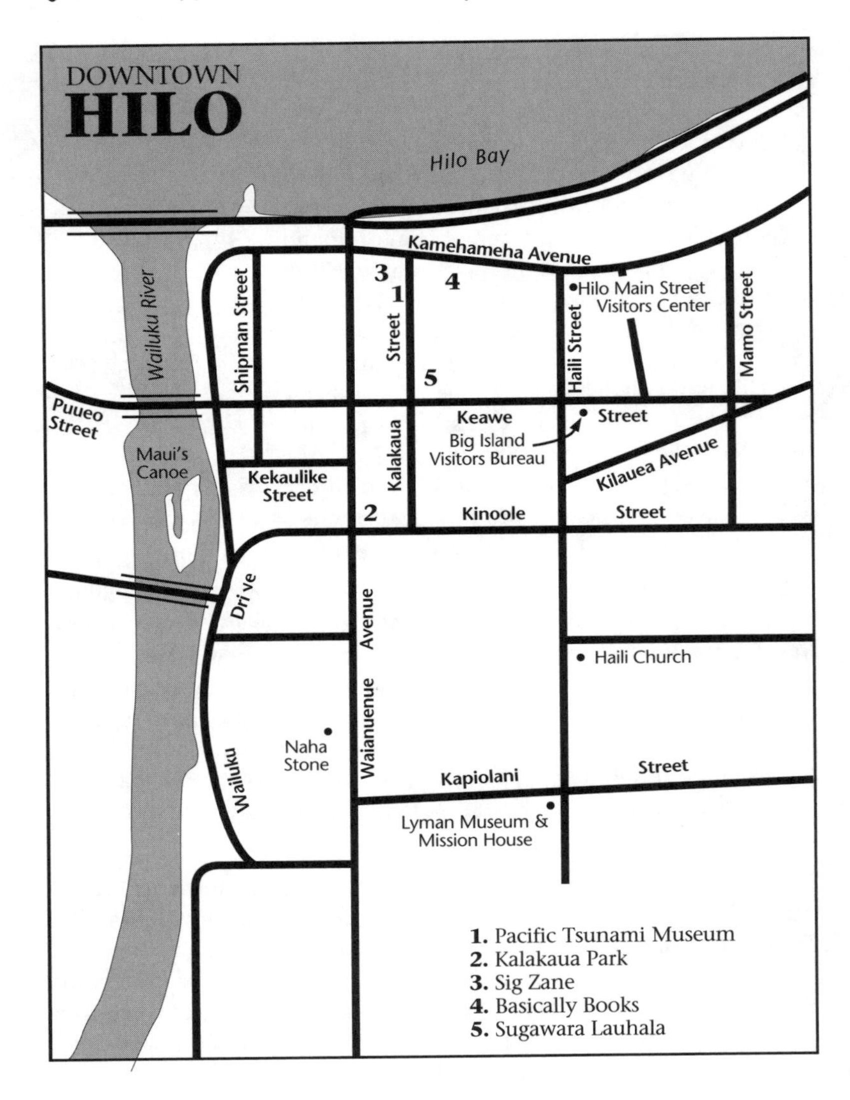

of pouring concrete mixed with black sand from Hilo's bayfront. Look for the original hitching rings embedded in some of these sidewalks. (You'll find one on Haili Street, a few yards inland from Kamehameha). To explore more of Hilo history, you can pick up a self-guided tour map from the ***Big Island Visitors Bureau*** at 250 Keawe Street (corner of Haili Street). The Lyman Museum also leads a free guided tour of downtown Hilo on the third Saturday of each month at 9:00 A.M. In fact,

Hilo's historic district is fairly compact. You may find it just as nice to wander at random.

The census bureau may call Hilo a city, but it still feels like a small town. Strangers greet each other in the street, and parking meters extort a mere quarter for two hours.

A few highlights to look for: 2 blocks up from the museum, at the corner of Kalakaua and Kinoole Street, ***Kalakaua Park*** honors Hawaii's last king, "the Merrie Monarch," who helped revive traditional Hawaiian culture. Hilo's annual Merrie Monarch Festival in April is the biggest hula competition in Hawaii. A statue of Kalakaua by Henry Bianchini in the park kneels in front of the banyan tree he planted. The king is depicted in military dress, balancing in his right hand an *ipu hula,* a gourd instrument symbolic of the culture he helped revive. The buildings around the park once served as Hilo's center of government. On the other side of Kalakaua Street stands the Old Police Station, now home to the ***East Hawaii Cultural Center.*** Rotating exhibits can be viewed Monday–Saturday 10:00 A.M. to 4:00 P.M. Continue your sightseeing on Haili Street, 1 block off Kinoole, past a trio of vintage church buildings. The oldest, Haili Church, was founded by the original missionaries.

To see the secular trappings of these soul seekers, follow Haili Street uphill to the adjacent buildings of the ***Lyman Museum and Mission House*** (935–5021). Hourly tours guide you through the mission home, built in stages by David and Sarah Lyman beginning in 1839. The four-poster beds have mattresses stuffed with wood shingles, handy chamber pots sit in the corners, and whale-oil lamps illuminate the desks. A curio shelf displays toys brought by whaling captains as well as autumn leaves that Mrs. Lyman obtained to illustrate to her children the meaning of seasons. Because of fire hazards, cooking had to be done in an outdoor oven. The house doubled as mission school, with boarders lodged upstairs.

Besides saving souls, the Lymans made at least two unwitting contributions to science. Mrs. Lyman's diary remains of interest to geologists today for its detailed record of earthquakes and eruptions. Her son Frederick collected hundreds of land snails in a drawer, all of which are now extinct. It is fitting that these items in their home should stand beside a museum of science that houses the world's first and only known specimen of olymanite, a mineral discovered by a Lyman descendant.

You can explore the museum while waiting for your tour of the mission house. The ground floor displays Hawaii's cultural heritage, while the upstairs exhibits focus on the natural history of the islands. The collection

Kalakaua, "The Merrie Monarch"

of Hawaiian artifacts includes a full-scale *hale pili* (grass hut). Representations from other ethnic groups range eclectically from the altar of a Chinese Taoist temple salvaged after a Hilo tidal wave to a formal wedding kimono shared by brides in Miyazaki, Japan, that was sold to finance a village son's education in America. Upstairs, glow-in-the-dark natural fluorescents highlight a top-notch mineralogy collection, and a new astronomy exhibit contrasts the stargazing of the ancient Hawaiians with the cutting-edge research performed at Mauna Kea observatories. The museum and mission house are open Monday–Saturday 9:00 A.M. to 4:30 P.M. Admission $7.00.

Walk back 1 block over to Waianuenue Avenue and the Hilo Public Library. Two mammoth boulders lie out front. The larger one, lying horizontally, is the ***Naha Stone,*** brought from the Pinao Temple on Kaua`i in days of yore. A kind of Hawaiian Excalibur, the Naha Stone could reveal male descendants of its royal house. By moving the three-and-a-half-ton stone, Kamehameha symbolically "overthrew a mountain" and proved his worthiness to conquer the islands. Visitors are welcome to try to duplicate this feat.

In addition to its historic attractions, downtown Hilo boasts a wealth of mom-and-pop shops perfect for browsing. Look for the following, open Monday through Saturday. ***Sig Zane's*** fashion center has a bayfront roost at 122 Kamehameha Avenue, near the corner of Kalakaua. Sig designs aloha wear in 100 percent cotton with patterns incorporating the indigenous flora of Hawaii. His knowledge of the plants that inspire his creations draws from a lifelong involvement in the art of hula. Those with a literary bent will enjoy ***Basically Books*** (961–0144) at 160 Kamehameha Avenue, one block farther. An excellent selection of Hawaiiana includes the owner's own publishing line of Hawaiian folklore anthologies. Just uphill on Kalakaua, the ***Sugawara Lauhala Gift Shop*** has a tiny showroom filled with products made through this traditional form of Hawaiian leaf weaving. Lastly, if you're in Hilo on a Wednesday or Saturday morning, don't miss the colorful ***farmers' market*** staged near the corner of Kamehameha and Mamo Street, a few blocks over.

The Wailuku River serves as the northern boundary of downtown Hilo and harbors scenic attractions of its own. Straddling the river near its mouth, between the second and third bridges, is ***Maui's Canoe,*** a low rock island. According to legend, the outrigger canoe was beached here in a flood unleashed when the demigod Maui rescued his mother, Hina, from Rainbow Falls. To this day, foam from the falls accumulates alongside the canoe.

To see the other half of the legend, head upstream on Waianuenue Avenue (one block in from the river), and bear right at the fork. Turn right again into ***Rainbow Falls State Park,*** where the Wailuku River cascades down a drop of 200 feet. After rains, the waters crash with thunderous volume and send up clouds of mist that produce the falls' trademark rainbows in the sunlight. When a rebuffed suitor trapped Hina in the hollow cavern behind the falls, sealing the entrance with dammed waters, her dutiful son smashed the dam with his canoe paddle. Walk to the upper platform above the falls for a view up and down the river. Bananas, red ginger, mango trees, and other tropicals festoon the park with exotic lushness.

Continue 1.5 miles to ***Pe`epe`e Falls State Park*** for a glimpse of this smaller falls upstream. Directly below the overlook, the river spills its way over a series of lava pools. The bubbling rapids thus produced give the pools their nickname, ***Boiling Pots.*** Some say the body of the mo`o dragon, Kuna, slain by Maui, snakes along the river bottom, churning the waters. Despite the warning signs, locals take a path down to the river and swim in these natural (cold) Jacuzzis during low-water periods. If you follow them, beware of underwater sinkholes and flash floods. It's not for nothing that *Wailuku* means "waters of destruction." A third cascade, ***Waiale Falls,*** waits just up the road at the bridge over the river.

For a different outdoor experience, return to the first fork at Waianuenue Avenue and take the other branch 3 miles up Kaumana Drive to ***Kaumana Caves County Park.*** The "caves" are actually two ends of a lava tube whose ceiling collapsed. Such tubes form as surface rocks cool around an underground river of swiftly flowing magma. When the current of molten rock dwindles, the empty tunnels often remain. Sightless insects found nowhere else in the world have evolved inside these dark chambers. The tube at Kaumana formed during Mauna Loa's 1881 eruption and stretches for miles underground. Surface lavas came within a mile of the then-smaller city limits and stopped only when Princess Ruth came overland from Kona to appease Pele with prayers and offerings—much to the missionaries' chagrin.

A steep stairway descends into a tropical pit of green, speckled with impatiens flowers. Continued collapses make the upper cave unsafe, but with a flashlight you can explore the lower tunnel as far as you dare. Tree roots hang from the 20-foot-high ceiling, the walls are smooth, and the hardened lava floor resembles rippled fudge. In this damp, mossy environment, it's hard to picture the torrent of glowing molten rock that flowed here a century ago. Kaumana Drive continues as Route 200, or the Saddle Road, running across the center of the island.

For beaches in Hilo, folks head to the east rim of the bay along Kalanianaole Avenue. The Big Island's young age means most of its shoreline is bare, but prevailing currents have hidden strands of white and black sand in between the rocky tidepools along this coast. ***Onekahakaha Beach Park*** just off Kalanianaole, 2 miles in, has the best swimming with its wide, sand-bottomed pools protected by lava rock barriers. Farther on, as you approach Kealoha Beach Park, look for the large fishponds on the inland side of the road, many of which still function.

Continue on to ***Richardson Ocean Center*** at the far end of Leleiwi Beach Park. The center has beautiful gardens surrounding it as well as a former fishpond. Ask for a trail guide pamphlet detailing the many interesting plants on the property. Open Monday–Saturday 9:00 A.M. to 3:00 P.M.

Restaurants in Hilo are mostly family-run operations serving home-grown cooking in unvarnished venues at unbeatable values. Everyone has his favorite, and it's hard to go very wrong. The following are clustered downtown. For creative island sushi, try ***Ocean Sushi Deli*** (961–6625), at 235 Keawe. The same family runs ***Tsunami Grill*** across the street. It's not unusual for folks eating at either restaurant to place orders at both. Open daily 10:30 A.M. to 2:00 P.M., 4:30 to 9:00 P.M. The local Thai favorite, ***Royal Siam*** (961–6100) waits just around the block at 70 Mamo Street. Open 11:00 A.M. to 2:00 P.M., 5:00–8:30 P.M.; closed Sunday. A few doors up, ***Elsie's Fountain*** (935-8681) at the corner of Kilauea and Mamo is the oldest soda fountain in the state. Recently refurbished to restore its original charm, this 1940 landmark still pours old-fashioned malts and floats from antique mixers Monday–Saturday; they also serve a local American menu, with Korean specials.

For something completely different, try ***Hawaiian Jungle*** (934–0700), on Kalakaua Street, across from the post office, near the park. Despite the name, the menu here is really Mexican-Peruvian; tamales are specially recommended. Open Tuesday–Sunday 11:00 A.M. to 11:00 P.M. Moderate. For upscale dining, Hilo residents split their allegiances between two Italianesque eateries, downtown, both open daily for lunch and dinner. ***Café Pesto*** (969–6640), at 308 Kamehameha Avenue, specializes in Pacific Rim designer pizzas. ***Pescatores*** (969–9090), at 235 Keawe, unsurprisingly emphasizes seafood. Neither is superb.

A more original choice is ***Seaside Restaurant*** (935–8825), at 1790 Kalanianaole Avenue, on the east side of the bay. Despite its name, the restaurant is actually across the street from the ocean, but it overlooks Loko Waka, an enormous freshwater fishpond. Your featured entree will probably come right out of the pond, netted just a few hours before you arrive. Colin Nakagawa tends the pond by day and cooks fresh fish dinners by night from its stocks of mullet, rainbow trout, golden perch, and *aholehole* (a type of bass). The menu also includes ocean-caught fish bought fresh at market (plus a handful of nonseafood choices). The rest of the Nakagawa family pitches in to help, as they have since 1926; the friendly service more than compensates for the somewhat primitive decor. As for the food, you can choose fish in a number of preparations. Drawing on traditional island recipes, the techniques, such as steaming in *ti* leaves, emphasize simple, natural flavors in lieu of gourmet high-concept creations. Considering that the entrees come as complete dinners, the prices are quite moderate. Open Tuesday–Sunday, 5:00–8:30 P.M.

For another lakeside venue, you might try ***Miyo's*** (935–2273) at the Waiakea Villas, 400 Hualani Street, for moderately priced Japanese meals served in a idyllic setting. Open Monday–Saturday 11:00 A.M. to 2:00 P.M. and 5:30–8:30 P.M.

Finally, no discussion of Hilo eateries can be complete without a mention of plate lunch. These quintessentially local meals revolve around ethnic entrees, from teriyaki chicken to *kalua* pork, accompanied by a standard two scoops of rice and macaroni salad. In a city where plate lunch is king, ***Café 100*** (935–8683), Hilo's first drive-in, presides as grand poobah. The menu includes Hawaiian and local staples, including several variations on the *loco moco.* Reputedly invented in Hilo, this dish revolves around rice, a fried egg, a hamburger patty, and ample gravy. In case you wondered, the cafe takes its name from the 100th Infantry Battalion, the all Japanese-American unit in which founder Richard Miyashiro fought during World War II. Miyashiro learned to cook in the foxholes of Italy and returned to open the restaurant after the war—just in time for the 1946 tsunami. A second newly built restaurant opened in 1960—to be demolished just as promptly by the tsunami of that year. Rebuilt safely inland, at 969 Kilauea Avenue, the cafe has thrived ever since and remains in the family. Open Monday–Saturday 6:45 A.M. to 8:30 P.M. For traditional Hawaiian plate lunch, feast yourself on ***Ka`upena's*** (993–1106) foot-long *lau lau.* You'll find them next to Ken's at the corner of Kamehameha and Route 11. Open Monday–Saturday 11:00 A.M. to 5:00 P.M. Finally, those in search of a late-night feed after an evening of lava viewing can slurp hot saimin and other local fare at ***Nori's*** (935–9133), in the Kukui Plaza at 688 Kinoole Street. On Sunday and Monday it closes at 9:30 P.M., but other nights they stay open until at least midnight.

As for lodging, Hilo has many fine choices. If it's an ocean view you want, ***Hale Kai B&B*** (935–6330; 111 Honolii Pali, Hilo 96720) is hard to beat. It sits on a bluff directly above Honolii Cove, Hilo's premier surfing spot, with sweeping views stretching across the entire bay. All five rooms face the ocean and cost $90 to $110. Owner Evonne serves a full breakfast, while husband Paul, a native Hawaiian born in Hilo, offers inside tips. If it's whale season, ask him about his "girlfriend" who's been visiting for 11 years. Book well in advance for this one.

For historic flavor, it's hard to beat the ***Shipman House*** (934–8002; 800–627–8447; bighouse@bigisland.com; www.hilo-hawaii.com), at 131 Kaiulani Street, 96720. Nicknamed "the Castle," this 1900 Queen Anne Victorian mansion crowns a hill on Reed Island, a verdant residential district separated from downtown Hilo by a wooden bridge over Waikapu Stream. Owned by a great-granddaughter of the original Shipmans, Barbara-Ann Anderson and her husband, Gary, the impeccably refurbished two-story building is furnished almost entirely with antiques, most original to the home. Almost every piece has a story to relate; the hosts have prepared a four-page leaflet for those wishing a self-guided tour. Queen Liliuokalani was a frequent guest, playing the 1912 Steinway grand piano in the living room before slipping out to the porch to smoke her cigars. Jack London stayed here for more than a month while his ship, the *Snark,* awaited repairs.

The Shipman family has an interesting history itself (to which a book—placed in each room is devoted). The first Shipmans came to Hawaii as a missionary couple destined for Micronesia. The wife's pregnancy prevented them from continuing any farther. A grandson, Herbert, made two notable contributions to Hawaii: He's credited with saving the native *nene* goose and introducing the first orchids to the Big Island, which now bears the nickname of "Orchid Isle." Indeed, the family boasted several ardent horticulturists, and the sumptuous five-acre grounds surrounding the mansion form a large part of its appeal. Royal palms line the driveway and exotic flowers abound, several of which bear the Shipman name. In addition to the streambed, the house overlooks a sunken gulch whose wild jungle foliage has yet to be explored.

There are three B&B rooms in the main house, with two in the 1910 guest cottage. Some of the rooms have four-poster beds and claw-foot tubs. All have private baths and fridges. They rent for $155–$175. A generous continental breakfast is served on the lana`i, overlooking the bay, featuring fruit from one of the twenty different kinds of fruit trees on the premises. Guests can also watch a hula troop rehearse on Tuesday evening. Staying at the Shipman House provides a rare glimpse of a bygone lifestyle. Be warned, though, that Barbara-Ann is (understandably) protective of her house and its contents. Guests should be prepared to tread lightly. Smoking is absolutely forbidden.

For a very different historic mansion-turned-B&B, consider ***Maureen's*** (935–9018, (800) 935–90918; 1896 Kalianaole Avenue, Hilo 96720; maurbnb@hilo.net). This 1932 Japanese banker's home retains a funky charm, despite its somewhat disorderly appearance and furnishings. Built from redwood and cedar, its vaulted central salon opens onto a formal oriental garden. Doubles with shared bath start at $75. Staying here puts you within easy walking distance of Hilo's east shore beaches.

Also on the east side of the bay, near Onekahakaha Beach Park, budgeteers will rejoice in ***Arnott's Lodge*** (969–7097; www.arnottslodge.com), tucked away on a side street, at 98 Apapane Road. This congenial backpacker's haven offers dorm rooms for $17. Private rooms cost $47 or $57 with private bath. The lodge also runs excellent daily ***Hiking Adventures*** using four-wheel-drive vans to tour remote regions of the island. The expeditions cater to an adventurous clientele and start at $48 ($96 for nonguests).

For those preferring hotels, the ***Dolphin Bay*** (935–1466; www.dolphinbayhilo.com) stands out for its friendly, ever-helpful staff. Located at 333 Iliahi Street in a quiet residential area north of downtown, the hotel has eighteen rooms, each with a full kitchen and private bath. Rates start at $72 for a double and include pastries and fresh-picked fruit from the garden.

Finally, for those longing for the serenity of a private waterfall, ***Kulani'iapia*** (966–6373; 888–838–6373; www.waterfall.net; waterfalls@prodigy. net) offers $99 B&B rooms that overlook a 120-foot cascade on a very remote macadamia farm above Hilo.

South of Hilo, Route 11 becomes the Mamalahoa Highway. The name means "law of splintered paddle," commemorating an event that happened not far from here. As a young chief on a raiding party, Kamehameha impetuously attacked an old fisherman but tripped and fell in the act. The fisherman promptly brained him with a canoe paddle and ran away. Later, when the man was brought to him, instead of seeking revenge for this affront to his chiefly dignity, Kamehameha admitted he was in the wrong. His "law of the splintered paddle" instructs that the elderly and infirm should not be molested.

Many people consider Hilo's nicest attractions to be its gardens, most of which lie south of the city along Route 11, on the way to Volcano. The rainfall here transforms almost any residential street into a tropical wonderland, and commercial plant nurseries have grown from cottage industries to major moneymakers. Some of these cater to the tour-bus set, while others just tolerate visitors.

For a different kind of garden with more dynamic life forms, turn west onto Mamaki Road, just past the 4-mile point. You pass the Rainbow Tropicals Nursery before reaching Stainbach Highway and ***Panaewa Rainforest Zoo*** (959–7224). This county-run facility takes full advantage of its lush setting. Enter through a wire tunnel "cage" crossing the middle of the first animal enclosure. Tiny monkeys clamber along the wire above, following you as you walk and making you wonder who's on display. Elsewhere, peacocks and guinea fowl roam the grounds amid native Hawaiian birds, pygmy hippos, and tigers penned in natural-style enclosures. Open daily 9:00 A.M. to 4:00 P.M. Free.

Much of the former sugar land south of here and throughout the island has switched to macadamia nut orchards, a mainstay of the Big Island's move toward diversified agriculture. If you want to learn more about this exotic export industry a sign guides you to the ***Mauna Loa Macadamia Nuts Visitors Center*** (966–8618) just ahead. Open daily 8:30 A.M. to 5:30 P.M.

Trivia

It takes 345 pounds of pressure to crack the macadamia's outer nutshell; no wonder the trees were long thought of as purely ornamental.

The Puna Coast

Two miles farther south, you reach Keaau, an aging sugar settlement, at the crossroads of Route 11 and Route 130. Now that the ongoing eruptions have cut the latter's coastal link with the Chain of Craters Road, few people head this way, yet the Puna Coast has attractions of its own that you shouldn't miss. The region has one of the fastest-growing populations in the United States, a substantial portion of whom live on remote homestead plots "off the grid."

Ten miles farther along is the town of ***Pahoa,*** which Route 130 bypasses but you should not. It takes only a few moments to detour through Pahoa's colorful strip of vintage false-front shops. Unlike the other towns in the Puna area, Pahoa predates the sugar industry, having begun as a logging town. The golden spike linking the Trans-Continental Railroad was driven into an *ohia* wood tie milled in Pahoa. The town's Akebono Theater claims to be the oldest in the state. Stroll down Pahoa's wooden sidewalks to absorb the multiple personalities of Puna's main town. Parked pickup trucks display bumper stickers calling for the legalization of marijuana, one of Puna's principal cash crops. ***Pahoa Natural Groceries*** serves as a social center for the many alternative-lifestyle people inhabiting the region. Dreadlocks and tie-dye predominate here. New Agers gather in ***Huna Ohana,*** where the aroma of coffee beans blends with incense and an Internet cafe shares space with a women's sexuality center. Folks at ***Malama Puna*** (965–9254), an environmental community group, fight the good fight against corporate aggression. Inside, a bewildering array of printed matter will get you up to speed on regional issues. Next to the theater, the ***Village Inn*** (965–6444) rents rooms in this former lumberjack boardinghouse. As of press time, the inn had changed management, and was temporarily closed.

In addition to its flower children, Pahoa bills itself as the anthurium capital of the world, with many nurseries operating in the area. You may

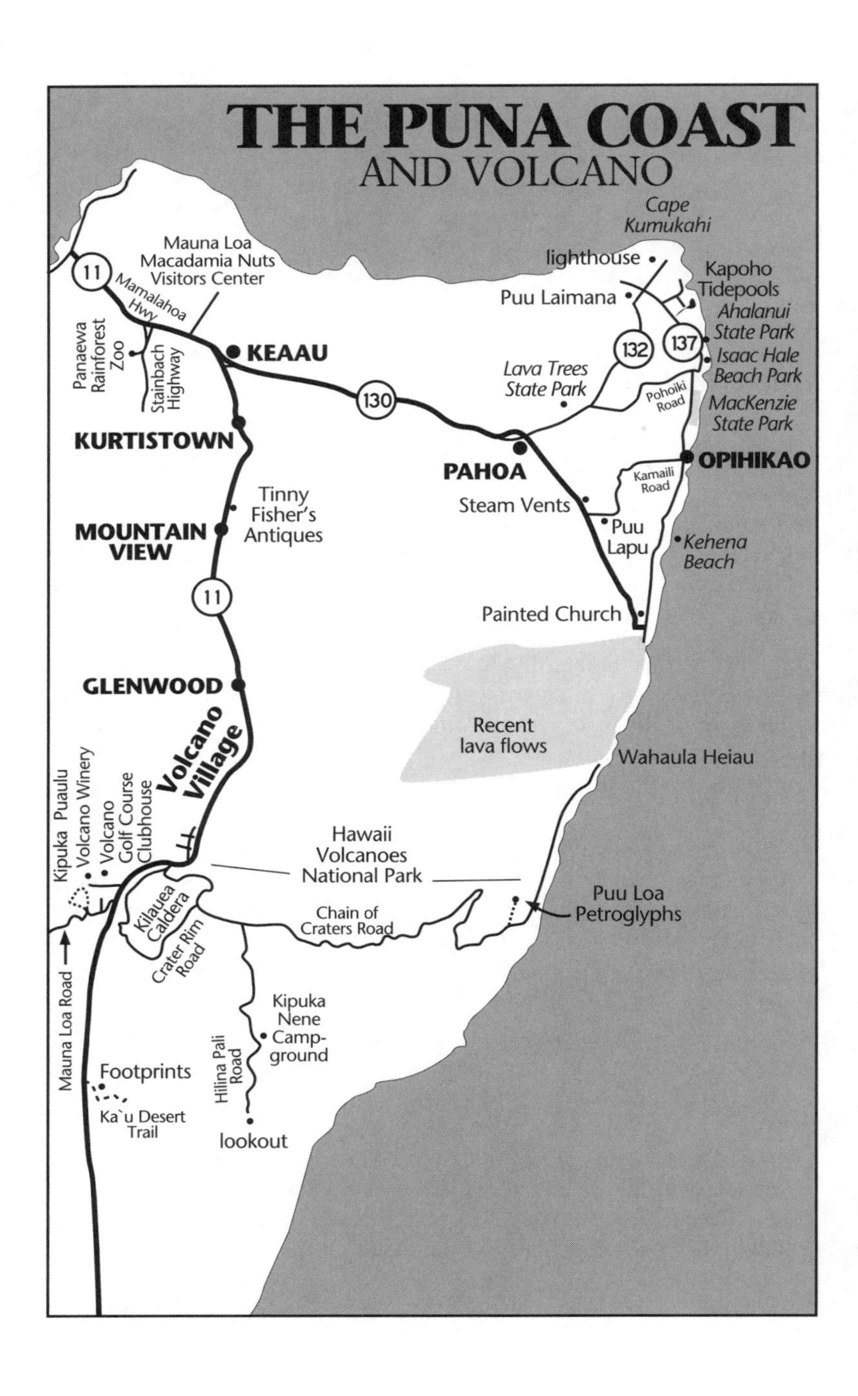
THE PUNA COAST
AND VOLCANO
Cape Kumukahi
lighthouse
Kapoho Tidepools
Ahalanui State Park
Isaac Hale Beach Park
MacKenzie State Park
Puu Laimana
132
137
Lava Trees State Park
Pohoiki Road
OPIHIKAO
Kamaili Road
PAHOA
Steam Vents
Puu Lapu
Kehena Beach
Painted Church
130
Mauna Loa Macadamia Nuts Visitors Center
11
Mamalahoa Hwy
Panaewa Rainforest Zoo
Stainbach Highway
KEAAU
KURTISTOWN
Tinny Fisher's Antiques
MOUNTAIN VIEW
11
GLENWOOD
Volcano Village
Recent lava flows
Wahaula Heiau
Kipuka Puaulu
Volcano Winery
Volcano Golf Course Clubhouse
Hawaii Volcanoes National Park
Kilauea Caldera
Crater Rim Road
Chain of Craters Road
Puu Loa Petroglyphs
Mauna Loa Road
Kipuka Nene Camp-ground
Hilina Pali Road
Footprints
Ka`u Desert Trail
lookout

also see signs around Pahoa advertising the sale of *`awa. `Awa* (also known as kava) is a medicinal plant with mildly narcotic properties and was used by ancient Hawaiians for ritual purposes. It's legal and is now being marketed as an herbal remedy. You can find products made from both *'awa* and *noni,* another traditional, island-grown medicinal, on sale at Pahoa Natural Groceries.

Pahoa also offers an impressive array of ethnic restaurants, many run by foreign expatriates. ***Sawasdee*** (965–8186) is run by a pair of Thai wives of local Americans. It's a cozy cafe with bamboo wainscoting. You order through the counter window and watch your selection being freshly prepared in the wok. Open every day but Wednesday, 5:00–8:30 P.M. Inexpensive. ***Paolo's Bistro*** (965–7033) next door features the cuisine of owner-chef Paolo Bucchioni's native Tuscany. Almost every ingredient is prepared from scratch, from mozzarella to pasta. A gazebo in back affords pleasant outdoor dining. Open Tuesday through Sunday 5:30–9:00 P.M. ***Luquin's Mexican Restaurant*** (965–9990) serves a tasty tortilla across the street. You'll find the biggest crowd in the adjacent tavern. Open daily 7:00 A.M. to 9:00 P.M. Finally, for Filipino fare and fruit smoothies, stop in at ***L&T.*** Open Sunday–Friday 8:00 A.M. to 7:00 P.M.

As you leave Pahoa's commercial section, look for ***Sacred Heart Church*** ahead on the left and you'll be seeing double. A miniature replica flanks the church building on its left. Originally built as a parade float, the model now sees its use from juvenile churchgoers. Continue on the main road out of Pahoa until it becomes Route 132, after it crosses Route 130. The road leads into a tunnel of tall albezia trees drenched in philodendron vines. Two miles along be sure to stop at ***Lava Tree State Park*** to view some unique monuments to Madame Pele's destruction. As lava from a 1790 flow engulfed the *ohia* forest in this area, moisture from the trees caused the molten rock to harden around their trunks. As the trees rotted away, a hollow shell of lava rock remained. A one-hour nature loop takes you through the park, but plenty of examples of these "lava tree" pillars stand near the entrance. The same eruption also left deep crevices in the surrounding terrain, so this is one place *not* to stray off the beaten path.

After Lava Tree State Park, the road forks again. If you take Pohoiki Road, on the right about a mile further, you will pass the wooded site of ***Puna Geothermal Venture*** (965–6233). Geothermal power in Hawaii is as hot an issue as the 358°C volcanic steam that it taps. Many Hawaiians oppose drilling as a desecration of Pele, environmentalists fear its impact on the pristine rain forest, and local residents complain about noise and sulfur pollution. The state remains committed to geothermal power, however, to alleviate the islands' almost total dependence on imported oil. Plans even envision an underwater cable to transmit electricity from Big Island wells to O`ahu. Interested parties can arrange a tour of the 25-megawatt power plant by calling in advance

Continuing on Pohoiki Road bypasses part of the Puna Coast scenery, so if you have time, backtrack and take the left fork on Route 132. As you descend to the coast, you emerge from low *ohia* forest to cross the undulating terrain of the 1955 lava flow. As the road descends to a lower basin, you pass through vast papaya fields. No one will object if you pick up a fruit or two from the ground. Route 132 intersects Route 137 just past ***Puu Laimana*** ("Lyon's Hill") on the left. A 1960 eruption from this cone destroyed the once-large settlement of Kapoho.

You can continue east along the cinder road extension of Route 132 for 1.7 miles across the crusty 1960 flow almost to the tip of Cape Kumukahi. Kindness to an old crone (one of Pele's incarnations) figures in various latter-day legends that explain why lava flows parted to spare the ***lighthouse*** at the end of this road. Cape Kumukahi ("first beginning") ends a few hundred yards farther. As the easternmost point of the island, this is where the sun's first rays greet the Aloha State.

Backtrack to Route 137 and turn left. A mile south brings you to the Kapoho Kai/Vacationland subdivision on the ocean side and the older Kapoho Cone inland. Turn left on Kapoho Kai Road, just shy of the 9-mile marker, and drive about a mile seaward; bear left at the end of the road to ***Kapoho Tidepools,*** a network of interconnecting tidepools extending 200 yards out to a protective reef and stretching along almost a mile of coastline. Snorkeling is first-rate here thanks to an unusual diversity of coral not found elsewhere in the state. Some of the pools are brackish and springfed; some are volcanically warmed. The property owners here try to discourage outside visitors, but state law guarantees shoreline access.

Continuing south, the lava fields give way to mixed forest and coastline vegetation. About 2 miles farther, when the road bends right, look for the telltale portable toilets that mark ***Ahalanui County Park*** (sometimes referred to as Pu`ala`a). Park across the road and follow the footpath to bathe in the large thermal pool near the ocean's edge. It's an idyllic spot ringed with coconut palms. The water comes from geothermal springs but gets its salinity from the ocean waves that break across the lava shelf. The mud bottom smells faintly of sulphur.

Just under a mile farther, the highway turns sharply inland at the entrance to ***Isaac Hale Beach Park*** on the eastern edge of Pohoiki

Bay. Visitors come here to bathe in another warm spring just outside the park property. To get there, take the narrow path around the edge of the bay and then inland into vine-choked jungle. A five-minute walk brings you to a small lava rock basin whose clear spring waters are warmed by volcanic heat.

Just beyond Isaac Hale, Route 137 meets the other end of Pahoiki Road. From here the coastal highway, dubbed the "red road" after its tinted asphalt mixed with volcanic ash from the 1960 Kapoho eruption, narrows as it continues south. Brushing against the coastline and rolling over gentle hills, you pass through a lush canopy of tropical vegetation that alternates with open seascapes. Two miles down the red road, ***MacKenzie State Park*** provides a peaceful picnic spot amid a grove of ironwood trees. The park borders low sea cliffs, and waves crashing below send saline mists billowing through the trees. A sign by the parking lot marks the site of the old King's Highway, a traditional Hawaiian trail improved in the 1850s by convict labor. Follow the trail a few hundred yards north (left, when facing the ocean) to enter an exposed lava tube. Halfway along, a collapsed "skylight" helps you find your footing. The tunnel exits just across the highway. Camping here is allowed by state permit, but MacKenzie has a bad reputation. Not only have thefts occurred, but the park sits athwart a notorious route of the "night marchers," a ghostly train of ancient Hawaiians who walk the earth under the new moon. If you see them, you should fall to the ground and not look up till they've passed.

Another 1.6 miles brings you to Opihikao junction, where Kamaili Road climbs 5 miles uphill to meet Route 130. Just under a mile from the top, you come to a runaway truck ramp. Locals call this stretch of road immediately preceding the ramp ***Puu Lapu*** ("haunted hill"). If you put your car in neutral, you coast in reverse and get the illusion of rolling uphill.

Continuing on Route 137, the landscape grows drier and more open as you pass ***Kalani Oceanside Eco-Resort*** (965–7828; 800–800–6886; www. kalani. com), a New Age retreat/cultural center spread over twenty acres. You can visit the craftshop to see works by local artists and participate in various workshops or cultural activities, including weekly hula lessons. Double rooms start at $135 with private bath, $110 without.

Just past the (partly obscured) 19-mile marker, turn onto the overlook above ***Kehena Beach.*** This black-sand beauty splits into two sections. The staircase leading to the section beneath the overlook collapsed in a 1975 earthquake, but a rough trail closer to the mile marker allows you to scramble down to the "clothing optional" beach on the north side.

Coconut and ironwood trees provide some shade. Dolphins often frequent the waters offshore, but heavy surf can make swimming dangerous.

Route 137 ends 3 miles past Kehena, closed by a 1990 lava flow that engulfed the town of Kalapana, destroying 103 houses as well as two of the island's most famous black-sand beaches. The black, steaming crust of lava piled across the highway provides a vivid portrait of man's powerlessness against the forces of nature. It's hard to imagine that almost all the land on the ocean side of the road was created in a few fiery months. Those feeling sure of foot can disregard the posted danger signs and walk out onto the 0.5-mile-wide flow. Charred trunks of coconut palms that once grew along Kaimu Beach lie toppled on the lava. Yet, as the molten rock poured into the Pacific, deposits of black sand formed anew at the flow's edge. Like the Hindu god Shiva, Pele must destroy in order to create. Local residents have done their part, planting hundreds of baby coconuts along the shore.

Scuba Spectacular

Readers of Rodale's Scuba Diving *voted the Big Island the world's best overall diving destination in 1998. Given the diversity of dive sites around the island, it's not hard to see why. Moreover, as a young island, Hawai`i's lava coastline has steep dropoffs that permit divers to come into contact with a variety of open ocean marine life that don't normally come in close to shore. In addition, the extensive system of lava tubes all along the island make for interesting cave diving.*

One of the more unique diving experiences on the island is the nightly manta ray dives off the Kona Coast. Divers shine lights from below which attract plankton on which the mantas feed. These enormous (up to 15-foot wingspan), yet harmless, creatures sail in graceful arcs through the column of light, spiraling from top to bottom. (Snorkelers can watch the action from the surface.) A number of companies offer manta ray dives; try Manta Ray Dives of Hawaii (325–1687). The mantas don't come every night, though; there are no guarantees.

Perhaps the most exciting dives the Big Island offers—and probably the most dangerous too—are the hot lava dives offshore from the volcano. Because water is such a great conductor of heat, it's possible for divers to get right close to a zone of active lava intrusion and watch the red molten stuff ooze and billow into unique formations known as "pillow lava." Eruption sites are unstable areas and conditions have to be right for the dive to happen, but it's a once-in-a-lifetime experience for advanced divers only. The Nautilus Dive Center in Hilo (935–6939) is one of the few that offers the trip when conditions allow.

The current eruption, which began in 1983, has shifted its active zone farther south, with hot lava flows accessible from the National Park's Chain of Craters Road at the other end of the coastal highway's broken circuit.

A native Hawaiian family whose home survived the lava has opened a snack/gift shop-cum-visitor center at the highway's end. You can view photographs of Kalapana before, during, and after the eruption, and follow a meandering foothpath through a backyard ethnobotany garden with native crafts demonstrated at stations along the way. It's all rather amateurish, but genuine.

A new junction links Routes 130 and 137. The famous ***Star of the Sea Painted Church*** from Kalapana has been "evacuated" and rests by the roadside just around the bend on Route 130. A wooden statue of Moloka`i's Father Damien stands in front. As you return on Route 130, stop at the scenic turnout a half-mile north of the top junction of Opihikao/Kamaili Road, at the 15-mile marker. If you follow the narrow trail that leads through *ohia* forest, you will pass a series of volcanic steam vents. The fifth and last crater, about 0.25 mile in, provides a natural steam bath. Be careful if you go in—it can be scalding!

In the Bosom of a Volcano

Moving southwest from Keaau, Route 11 passes a series of former sugar camps as it climbs a gentle 4,000 feet over 21 miles to the summit of Kilauea Volcano. Macadamia nut orchards are muscling their way into cropland that sugar has vacated, and flower nurseries also abound. One that accepts visitors is ***Akatsuka Orchids*** (967–8234), at the 22.5-mile point, past Glenwood. Open daily 8:30 A.M. to 5:00 P.M.

For a different sort of plant nursery, visit the ***Fuku-Bonsai Cultural Center*** (982–9880) in Kurtistown, on Olaa Road between the 9-mile and 10 mile-markers, to learn about this pan-Asian art of cultivating diminutive trees. Open Monday–Saturday 8:00 A.M. to 4:00 P.M. For yet another local art form, stop at Dan de Luz's ***Woods Inc.*** (968–6607) in Mountain View at the 12-mile marker. A bearlike Portuguese-American, Dan welcomes visitors to tour his shop room in back. You learn the different stages through which his collector's item bowls emerge. Open daily 9:00 A.M. to 5:00 P.M. On weekends you can find Dan in his Waimea shop. Also worth a gander in Mountain View is ***Tinny Fisher's Antiques*** (968–6011), in a blue plantation house on the left between the 12- and 13-mile markers. Open Tuesday–Sunday 10:00 A.M. to 5:00 P.M.

Continuing uphill on Route 11, you enter an impressive rain forest, and temperatures cool as you gain elevation (an average of 15°F cooler at the summit than the coast). As you approach the summit of Kilauea, don't expect any lofty peak. Viewed from the air, the mountain appears as but a faint swelling on the flank of the far larger Mauna Loa. Kilauea's flattened dome shape reflects the gently oozing flows from which it arose. Don't get the impression that Hawaiian volcanoes are pussycats. It's just that they lack the pent-up gases that cause their continental cousins to blow their tops. Instead, the frequent and controlled nature of their eruptions makes the Big Island one of the few places in the world where people run *to*—not *from*—a live volcano.

Hawaii Volcanoes National Park (985–6000) encompasses some of the wildest terrain on Earth. Extending from sea level to 13,667 feet, the park covers a range of habitats, from desert to rain forest to the subarctic summit of Mauna Loa. Two of the most active volcanoes in the world lie within its boundaries, which makes this one of the most volatile areas on Earth. If Pele truly lives here, she's been a busy deity of late. When Mauna Loa last erupted in 1984, visitors could see both volcanoes going off simultaneously. Scientists estimate that Mauna Loa and Kilauea will cover themselves entirely with new surface lavas before they finish.

Seismic rumbles register constantly in the park. Most go unfelt by humans, but they do build to violent earthquakes every now and then. New phases of eruptions often open with spectacular fountains of lava that drain into glowing ponds of red-hot rock. As these lavas flow down the mountain slopes and into the sea, they recontour the landscape and often create geological formations of rare beauty. A word of warning: Taking rocks as souvenirs violates federal law and risks angering Madame Pele. The park service gets packages every day from visitors who want to return things they took to rid themselves of lingering bad luck.

From the park entrance at the highway's 29-mile point, the 11-mile Crater Rim Road loops around Kilauea Caldera, doling out a crash course in volcanology. Pay your $10 per vehicle admission (valid for a week's re-entry) and proceed first to the ***Visitors Center*** to get oriented. You can take in some natural history exhibits, get information on hiking trails and camping, and watch some stellar footage of past eruptions while getting the scoop on current volcanic activity. The park staff runs various interpretive programs mostly during the summer months; check the schedule. Open daily 7:45 A.M. to 5:00 P.M.

Take a moment to browse in the ***Volcano Arts Center*** (967–7565; (800) 670–8345) next door, which occupies the original Volcano House lodge

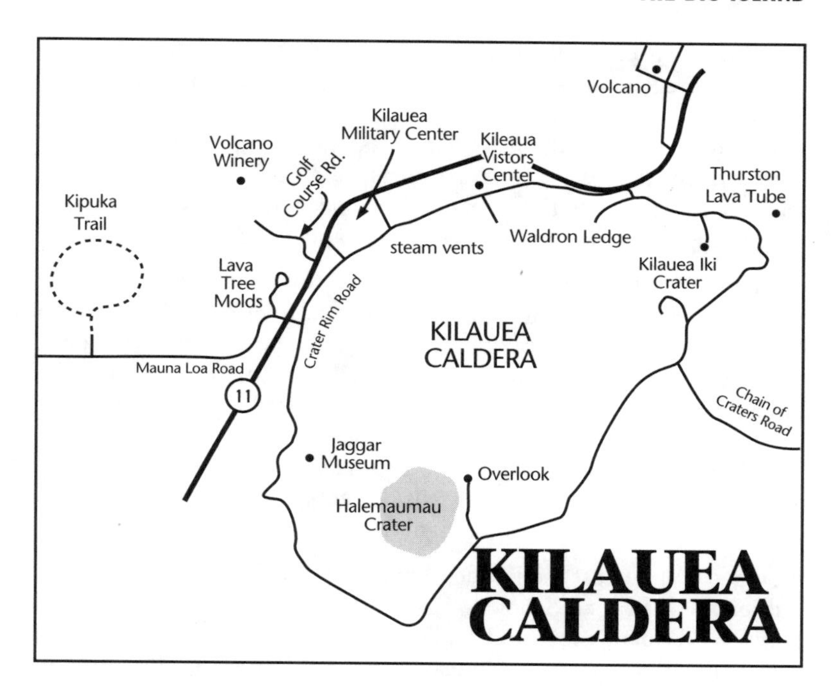

built in 1877. This nonprofit venture showcases the work of local artists, including some striking eruption photography, and sponsors workshops and occasional hula performances. You can also arrange visits to local studios. Call 967–8222 for program information. Open daily 9:00 A.M. to 5:00 P.M.

Across the street sits the new Volcano House, perched right on the rim of Kilauea Caldera. Four hundred feet below, the volcano's gaping maw measures almost 3 miles across, textured by lava flows and craters of varying ages. To appreciate the violent collapses that formed this sunken pit, walk left from the Volcano House along Waldron's Ledge. Until 1983, the Crater Rim Road ran this way. On November 16 of that year, a 6.6-magnitude earthquake shredded the road and tore away part of the ledge.

As you walk, pay attention to the rain forest around you. Reaching heights up to 30 feet, the many *hapuu* tree ferns evoke a primeval atmosphere. You half expect to see a triceratops lurking behind one. Look also for the red-tinged *amaumau* ferns, sacred to Pele. And keep your eyes peeled for the wild orchids that thrive in these misty uplands. Towering above this lush undergrowth, *ohia* trees grow here as they do throughout the park, from the coastal desert to the 9,000-foot elevation level. This versatile tree is one of the first life forms to inhabit a new lava flow and begin its revegetation, and it can be identified by its red, tassel-like *lehua* blossoms (sacred to Pele's sister, Hiiaka). In Hawaiian tradition, the ohia-lehua represents the male-female essence, a yin-yang duality that legend traces to a pair of lovers, transformed by the gods. Picking the lehua blossoms parts the lovers, and supposedly brings rain (divine tears). Judging by the weather, it seems to happen quite often here.

Start your driving tour around the Crater Rim, moving counterclockwise. Just around the bend from the visitors center a side jog leads to ***Sulfur Banks,*** where some of the park's most active fumaroles emit noxious fumes that reek of rotten eggs. Yellow sulfur streaks paint the landscape and oxidize iron in the lava to create striking colors. As Mark Twain joked, "The smell of sulfur is strong, but not unpleasant to a sinner." Nonsulfuric ***steam vents*** are also nearby. In the early morning cool, the "steaming bluff" from trailside vents along this section of the crater rim makes an impressive sight.

As you continue past the Kilauea Military Center, look for *ohelo* berry bushes along the road. Sacred to Pele, the pale-red fruits resemble cranberries and ripen year-round. (Any clue yet what's the goddess' favorite color?) To indulge, you are supposed to toss the first handful toward the caldera as an offering. Next up at Uwekahuna Bluff, the ***Hawaii Volcano Observatory*** overlooks Halemaumau Crater. Awestruck Hawaiians left offerings at a *heiau* here, cringing before the sight of their fearful deity. Today's scientists are more clinical as they monitor Pele's vital signs to try to predict eruptions.

The ***Jaggar Museum*** (985–6049) here explains the dangers and difficulties of studying an active volcano. Watch as working seismographs monitor the constant shifting in the area. You might just spot the big one! Other displays teach you to distinguish the two main types of lava: *A`a* lava travels as rough, slow-moving clinkers and hardens the same way. The hotter *pahoehoe* flows in streams or seeps out in narrow fingers; it hardens in smooth, wavy surfaces or curls into ropy formations. Other oddities strike your eye, like Pele's "hair" and "tears," as well as pumice, cinder, and "lava bombs." You can find examples of all these in the park. For those who prefer myth to science, a beautiful set of photomurals done by Herb Kawainui Kane introduces visitors to Pele and her family. Kane, a Big Island native, specializes in portrayals of Hawaiian history and legends and has been designated a "living treasure of Hawaii." The museum is open daily 8:30 A.M. to 5:00 P.M. Free.

As you continue around the crater drive, the vegetation becomes stunted, then almost barren. This is the dry side of the mountain, and below stretches the stark wasteland of the Ka`u Desert. What little rain falls here is full of sulfur from the eruptions, a naturally occurring version of "acid rain." Some of that sulfur hits you in fumes as you round the southwest corner of the caldera and heralds your approach to ***Halemaumau Crater,*** Pele's firepit. This "crater within a crater" measures 3,000 feet across and drops 280 feet to a smoothly paved lava floor. The goddess maintained a more formidable presence here before 1924, when the crater bubbled with a constant lake of molten lava. Subsequent lava flows have "ponded" the crater, with the last summit eruption in 1982. The following year a new eruption started at Pu`u`O`o, along the east rift zone, and lava has flowed from there ever since; today only wisps of steam reveal the presence of magma beneath the surface of Halemaumau. An early Christian convert, Princess Kapiolani, won followers by defying Pele here in her own home. But Hawaiians in the area still purchase "lava insurance" through offerings of gin and other commodities favored by the goddess.

Continuing from Halemaumau, you'll pass the turnoff to Chain of Craters Road, which descends to the coast. Stay on Chain of Craters Road for now to complete the last leg of the loop. The crater around which you are looping at this stage is ***Kilauea Iki*** ("little Kilauea"). This kid brother of the main caldera erupted in 1959 with fountains of lava that towered as high of 1,900 feet. Two overlooks allow you to peer into this yawning fissure, a mile long and almost 400 feet deep. As with Halemaumau, a smooth tarmac of jet-black lava covers the floor where a molten lake once churned. You can see traces of the "bathtub ring" left on the walls by the high-water mark of the ponded lava.

Near the first overlook is ***Puu Puai*** ("gushing hill"), formed on the southwest crater rim from trade winds carrying pumice, cinder ash, and lava splatter from the eruption. Running alongside the hill (beginning at the overlook) is the popular 0.5-mile "Devastation Trail," which passes through an *ohia* forest caught in the firestorm.

Between the two Kilauea Iki overlooks is another "must," the ***Thurston Lava Tube.*** A 300-yard loop descends through gorgeous rain forest into a sunken crater, where the entrance to the lava tube drips with ferns. The inside is well lighted and smoothly hollowed. (Souvenir collectors stripped all the stalactites from the ceiling—the curse of Pele be upon them.) The sound of bird songs greets you on the other side.

Those for whom the Thurston tube sounds too tame may want to sign up for the park service's free weekly hike through ***Pua Po'o Lava Tube,*** a pristine lava tube only accessible on this guided tour. The trip involves four miles of hiking and takes about four hours (with an hour spent in the tube itself). Some climbing/crouching is required, and you must bring your own flashlight. The trip size is limited, so reserve ahead. Currently offered on Wednesday afternoon, the park service starts its sign-up list on the Wednesday of the week prior. Call 985–6017.

From the southeast corner of the caldera, the Chain of Craters Road leads 24 miles downslope to the site of the recent eruptions along the coast. As its name implies, the road passes a series of impressive craters along Kilauea's east rift zone. The constant eruptions since 1983 have all flowed from points east of this road.

The seldom-traveled Hilina Pali Road, 2 miles long, detours right to ***Kipuka Nene campground,*** a *pali* overlook, and the start of several backcountry trails. The main road descends an impressive *pali* of its own with several pulloffs overlooking the blackened shelf of Hawaii's newest lands. The perennially overcast skies reflect "vog" formed by lava entering the ocean. At the bottom of the hill, about 17 miles along, look for the sign to the ***Puu Loa Petroglyphs.*** A 1-mile trail leads to one of Hawaii's largest concentration of stone carvings. Some are recognizable images, others abstract symbols. Puu Loa translates to "long hill," but the Hawaiians read this as "long life." The top of the hill is pocked with thousands of tiny holes drilled by Hawaiian parents of old in the belief that burying the *piko* (umbilical cord) in such a hole would ensure a long life for their child.

The road continues toward the sea and then travels about 5 more miles along the coast. Several turnoffs allow you to walk to the edge of rugged lava cliffs overlooking the deep blue of the open ocean. Driven by the sea goddess' fury, constant waves rip against the land, battering against Pele's island stronghold. The eroded shoreline reveals striking sea arches and rock islands. Farther north, Pele has struck back, pouring her lava into the sea to build new land. Towers of steam rise above this epic battle between two great forces of nature. Underwater, the superheated lava cools explosively, splintering into glassy fragments that ocean currents collect and deposit to form black-sand beaches. Most of these fledgling strands get covered by encroaching flows, but just as steadily new ones form downcurrent.

The road ends somewhere short of the park's eastern border at Wahaula where a visitors center, campground, and 1,000-year-old *heiau* have been consumed by recent flows. If lava is still flowing in the area, you will probably have to walk to see it. Conditions change daily. Slow-moving surface flows sometimes extend molten fingers that allow visitors to safely approach close enough to roast marshmallows in the 2,000° F heat. At other times, the flow funnels underground through lava tubes extending to the water's edge. Spectators watching from a distance catch glimpses of the red stuff as it drips over a ledge into the ocean amid clouds of steam. The radiant glow of the lava provides the best spectacle when viewed at night. (The park stays open twenty-four hours a day.) The park service regulates access as conditions warrant. Unstable surfaces, dangerous fumes, and other potentially life-threatening hazards make extreme caution imperative. Call 985–6000 for a recorded eruption update.

Return up Chain of Craters Road and turn right to return to the visitors center; if you are still game, there's more to see in the park off Route 11. (If you are headed to Kona, you can make these stops on the way.) Take the second right 2 miles from the park entrance onto Mauna Loa Road. Immediately after turning, take another right along the loop road to the ***Lava Tree Molds.*** These manhole-size oddities formed in a manner similar to the "lava trees" in Puna: Lava inundated a forest and crusted around the water-laden trunks of large trees. In this case, the flow raised the surrounding ground level. The hollow molds left after the wood burned or rotted away indicate the depth of the new lava cover. The width of the molds indicates the trees were koa, the largest of the native trees. Plenty of smaller koa grow nearby. The young saplings have fern-like leaves that change to sickle-shaped leaf stalks as the tree matures.

Two miles farther, Mauna Loa Road reaches ***Kipuka Puaulu*** ("bird park"). A *kipuka* forms when lava flows bypass a section of forest, leaving an island of vegetation surrounded by devastation. Studies of insect species cut off from the mainstream population by *kipuka* formed at a known date have shown that evolutionary changes can occur much quicker than biologists had previously thought possible. The flow that created this *kipuka* happened about 400 years ago, but a visible difference remains between the old growth and the new scrubland around it. Wildlife appreciate the difference as well. Bird-watchers can walk the 1-mile loop around the forest to see and hear many native and exotic species. The bright red *iiwi* and *apapane* have black-tipped wings and curved beaks to suck nectar from treetop blossoms. The *elepaio* has an onomatopoeic name resembling its song. It has brown feathers and a white rump. Mauna Loa Road continues 10 more miles to the mountain's 6,650-foot elevation, a launching point for the 18-mile, two-day ascent to Moku`aweoweo Caldera at the 13,679-foot summit. It's worth driving up on a clear day for the view over Kilauea.

Six miles farther on the highway, past the 37-mile point, look for the sign for the ***Ka`u Desert Trailhead*** near the western border of the national park. An easy 0.8-mile walk across lava fields brings you to some literal footprints of history from a pivotal event in Hawaii's past. The violent eruptions of 1790 spewed clouds of volcanic ash that trapped an army belonging to Keoua, Kamehameha's cousin and main rival. The victims suffocated in the noxious fumes, leaving their footprints preserved in hardened deposits of ash. Such Pompeii-like destruction is unusual for Hawaiian eruptions, and both factions interpreted the disaster as a sign that Pele favored Kamehameha. A protective shelter on the trail encases a section of these footprints.

One final attraction has nothing to do with volcanoes. Take the golf course turnoff between Mauna Loa Road and the park entrance, and continue to ***Volcano Winery*** (967–7479) at the end of the road. At present, the winery produces white wines from the Symphony grapes it grows on surrounding vineyards as well as a range of novelty wines from tropical fruits and honeys. A tasting room is open to visitors daily from 10:00 A.M. to 5:30 P.M.

Restaurant options at Volcano are limited, so you may want to pack a picnic. The Volcano House has the best views but suffers from tour-bus crowds. You're better off leaving the park to seek nourishment in nearby Volcano Village. Backtrack 1 mile on the highway toward Hilo, and turn left onto Old Volcano Road where you might eat at either ***Lava Rock Cafe*** (967–8526) for local plate lunch; or ***Surt's*** (967–8511) for Asian-European cuisine, from spicy Thai curries to seafood and pasta. Both are open daily through the afternoon. You could also try the golf course clubhouse (on the way to the winery) for local American fare; this closes at 2:00 P.M.

As for dinner, Surt's makes a fine choice, with fresh fish specials at investment prices and other options at more moderate cost; it's open until 9:30 P.M. nightly. Probably your best bet in the village, though, is ***Kilauea Lodge*** (967–7366), which serves gourmet continental dinners in the lofty central hall of a renovated 1938 YWCA retreat. Albert Jeyte, the owner-chef, won an Emmy for makeup work in the television series *Magnum P.I.* The hearty central-European flavors match the cozy warmth of the fireplace. Open nightly from 5:30–9:00 P.M. Expensive. Another solid option is ***Tai Tai*** (967–7969) for Thai food. Open nightly 5:00–9:00 P.M. For those who just want to fill the belly with decent grub at a modest price, the ***Kilauea Military Camp*** (967–8356) has a canteen that serves nightly ethnic "theme" buffets for $8.50. Although officially restricted to military personnel, the restaurant management no longer enforces this policy. It is located on the Chain of Craters Road, just past the steam vents. Open nightly from 5:30–8:00 P.M.

Given all there is to see in the park, plus the possibility of night-time lava viewing, you should consider staying overnight here. Fortunately, the Volcano has proven fertile soil for B&Bs to flourish. The oldtimer of the bunch—and first B&B on the island—is Gordon and Joann Morse's ***My Island*** (967–7216; www.myislandinnhawaii.com). Rooms with shared baths in Haleohu, the Morses' 1886 home, whose name quite appropriately means "house in the mist," cost $60. The Morses have decorated with their own works of photography and painting. Gordon has written his own travel guide to the Big Island and is a fount of information. They also offer separate studios and cottages (one has a kitchen). These start at $85. Rates include a full buffet breakfast, plus all the macadamia nuts you care to eat. Although later to enter the B&B market, Lisha and Brian Crawford have become the dominant players in town with their ***Chalet Kilauea Collection,*** which runs the gamut from budget to luxury accommodations, all managed with corporate efficiency. (They also own Surt's and the Steam Vent Café). For central reservations call (800) 937–7786; or visit www.volcano-hawaii. com. The Crawfords' upscale ***Inn at Volcano*** (967–7786) has international theme rooms decorated with objects that Lisha and Brian collected during their world travels. All have private whirlpool baths, with tariffs that run $139 to $399 and include a formal candlelit breakfast. ***Castle Suites*** offers even more elaborate digs, decorated with a kind of faux European gentility for $149–$249. ***Volcano B&B*** (967–7779) offers simple rooms with shared baths in a renovated 1912 home for $49–$69. Chalet Kilauea also offers a number of other options for B&B rooms and vacation rentals.

For a more intimate abode, consider either of the following. ***Volcano Rainforest Retreat*** (985–8596; 800–550–8696; www.volcanoretreat. com) offers three unique hideaway cabins created by owner-architect Peter Golden, who seems mildly obsessed with polygonal shapes. Nestled within a mossy, tree-fern forest, the smaller two cabins have central skylights and floor-length picture windows; their tightly efficient design includes a tiny kitchenette. The guest house is more spacious, with full kitchen and more conventional geometry; this was the Goldens' first residence on site. All units have private entrances and access to an outdoor hot tub. Prices range from $110–$170, with discounts for longer stays. Even more private is ***Volcano Teapot Cottage*** (967–7112; 800–670–8345; www.volcanoteapot.com), a two-bedroom bungalow built in the early 1900s on its own two-and-a-half-acre plot. Painted a cheery red with white trim on the outside, the interior displays such Victorian touches as a four-poster bed and original claw-footed tub. Owner Antoinette Bullough leaves daily breakfast fixings, and naturally there is plenty of tea. $115 per night, two night minimum.

Hale Ohia (967–7986, 800–455–3803; www.haleohia.com) features lodging on the sumptuous grounds of the 1931 Dillingham summer estate at similar prices. Other good choices include ***Carson's Volcano Cottages*** (967–7683; 800–845–LAVA; www.carsons cottage.com) and ***Kilauea Lodge*** (967–7366). Finally, for those on a bare-bones budget, Satoshi Yabuki's ***Holo Holo Inn*** (967–7950; www.enable.org/holoholo/) offers dorm beds for $17. Call after 4:30 P.M. Tent space at the two national park campgrounds is free with a permit from the park visitors center.

Ka`u District

Route 11 descends south from the volcano through miles of scrubland followed by cane fields and macadamia nut orchards. At about the 51-mile marker, you pass Pahala, the largest settlement in the area. The town began as a sisal plantation, switched to sugar, and is now moving into macnuts. Scattered cane camps dot the foothills above Pahala, monuments to a fading way of life.

Punaluu, 4.5 miles farther, boasts the most famous ***black-sand beach*** left on the island. Turn left down the beach road and park by the coconut trees at the bottom. The rhythmic ebb and flow of the surf create mesmerizing patterns of white foam on black beach. Punaluu means "diving springs"; Hawaiians would dive into the bay to fill stoppered containers with fresh water from the underwater springs that empty into the ocean here. You can find one such spring near the shoreline to the left of the boat ramp. Turtles gather to feed on algae that flourish in the brackish waters. The north side of the bay guards the ruins of a *heiau.* The cluster of mock Polynesian buildings bordering an old fishpond, just inland of the beach, formerly housed a restaurant and cultural center, with an excellent mural by Herb Kane depicting Punaluu of old. Unfortunately, both have closed indefinitely.

The beach road loops uphill to rejoin Route 11. The Seamountain Resort along the way takes its name from Loihi Seamount, the heir apparent in the Hawaiian island chain, located 20 miles offshore. Fueled by a very active sea volcano, Loihi has risen to within 3,000 feet of the surface. Geologists estimate the new island could appear within a mere 10,000 years. Stay tuned.

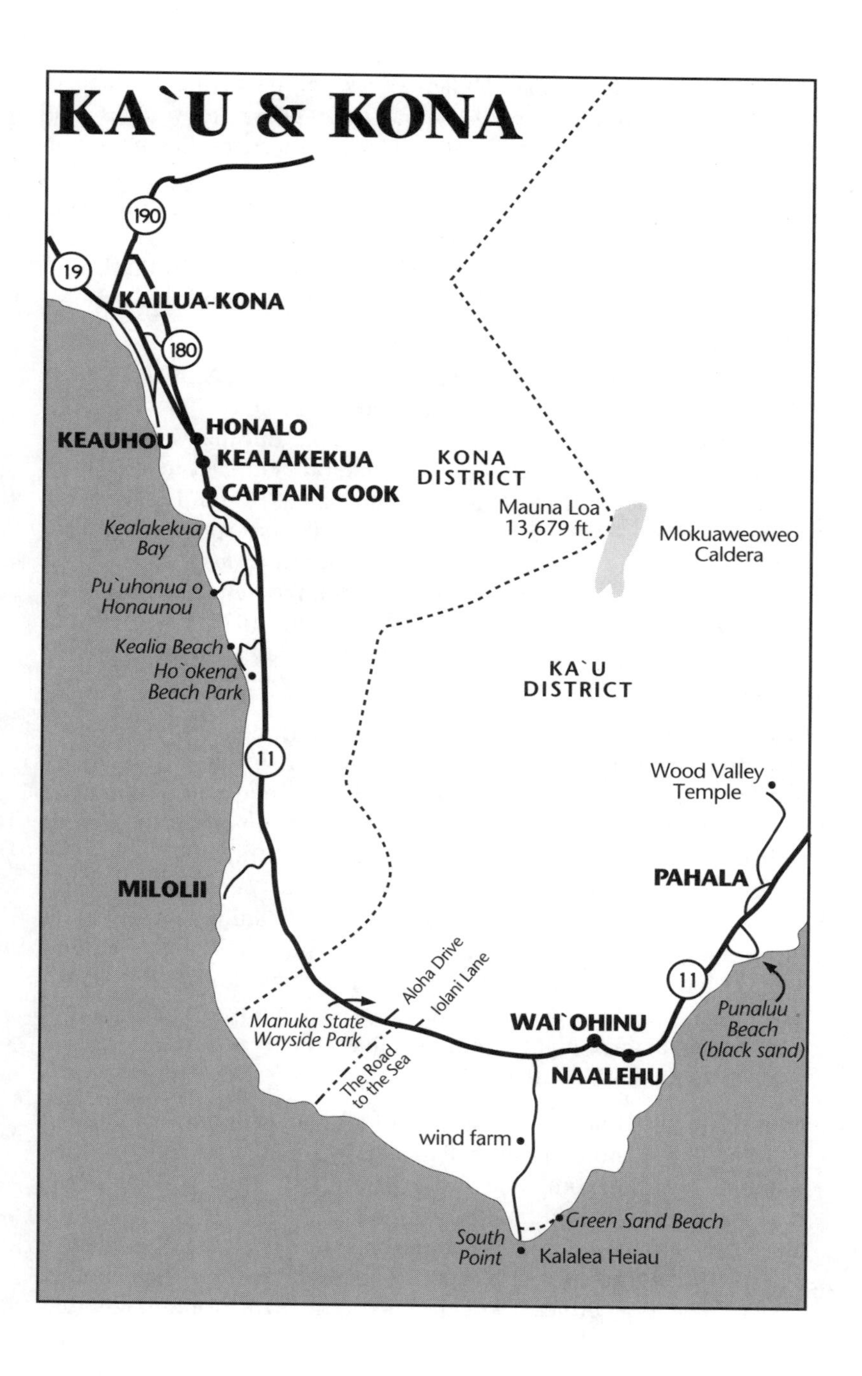
KA`U & KONA
190
19
KAILUA-KONA
180
HONALO
KEAUHOU
KEALAKEKUA
CAPTAIN COOK
KONA
DISTRICT
Mauna Loa
13,679 ft.
Mokuaweoweo
Caldera
Kealakekua
Bay
Pu`uhonua o
Honaunou
Kealia Beach
Ho`okena
Beach Park
KA`U
DISTRICT
11
Wood Valley
Temple
PAHALA
MILOLII
Aloha Drive
Iolani Lane
11
Manuka State
Wayside Park
WAI`OHINU
Punaluu
Beach
(black sand)
The Road
to the Sea
NAALEHU
wind farm
Green Sand Beach
South
Point
Kalalea Heiau

As you continue along Route 11, you can alleviate the monotony of its flat, linear course by gazing uphill at a series of interesting flat-topped craters clinging to the slopes of Mauna Loa. At 60.5 miles you pass the turnoff to ***Whittington Beach Park,*** which has a swimming pond but no beach. The crumbling pier offshore once served to load sugar for shipping. The road begins to climb inland through dairy pastures with great coastal vistas. Like everything in this area, the tree-lined town of Naalehu, at 64 miles, bills itself as "the southernmost in the USA." Notice the bumper stickers that read NO ROCKETS, reflecting local opposition to a proposed spaceport in the area.

Try a meal in the country's southernmost restaurant, ***Naalehu Coffee Shop*** (929–7238). Owned by the Toguchi family since 1941, the large dining room has Hawaiiana decor and serves full meals. Fresh fish caught daily at South Point tops the moderately priced menu. Open Monday–Saturday 8:00 A.M. to 3:00 P.M. and 5:30–7:30 P.M. The ***Naalehu Fruit Stand*** (929–9009) provides a cheaper take-out option. They bake their own bread for wholesome sandwiches as well as tasty pizzas. Try a Ka´u orange for dessert; the uglier the skin, the better it tastes. The nearby ***Punaluu Bakeshop and Visitors Center*** (929–7343) tempts visitors with samples of island-flavored sweetbread as well as a pair of eye-catching murals depicting island life.

Naalehu has a roadside B&B, but for the southernmost motel, you have to continue 2 miles to ***Shirakawa's*** (929–7462) in Waiohinu. A monkeypod tree planted by Mark Twain grows near the motel. Rooms start at $35. Not quite as southerly, but considerably more unique, is the ***Hobbit House*** (929–9755; www.hi-hottit/Hawaii.bnb.htm; P.O. Box 269, Naalehu 96772), a whimsically designed in remote Waionihu Valley, with sweeping coastal views. Bill Whaling is a former building contractor and successful inventor who got tired of building houses "straight." He and wife Darlene spent eight years constructing their abode using hand-hewn beams and handcrafted stained-glass windows. A private unit rents for $150, three night minimum. To stay here, you need to have a four-wheel-drive vehicle to negotiate the road up.

From Waiohinu, Route 11 climbs out of a broad valley onto a forested plateau. The turnoff to South Point arrives at the 70-mile marker. Although rental car companies forbid its use, the 12 miles of single-lane road are in good drivable condition. You pass an orange grove near the top of the road, then continue through open cattle pasture. A wind farm of sleek, three-armed windmills towers above the savannah, yet another alternative energy project. Near the end of the road, take the right fork and park by the fishing platforms built onto the cliffs. As you look back, the panoramic sweep of the cliffline bordering the western edge of the peninsula illustrates in relief the elevated plateau from which you have descended.

A Coast Guard beacon a quarter-mile along the coast marks ***Ka Lae*** ("the point"), as Hawaiians call the southernmost border of the fifty states. Beneath the beacon stands ***Kalalea Heiau,*** a small rock enclosure with a wooden *ahalele* (offering stand) inside. Archaeological remains litter the area, many carbon-dated to the fifth century, if not earlier. Oral traditions hold that the first Polynesian voyagers landed here. In the rocks below the *heiau,* holes drilled with Stone Age tools served as ancient canoe moorings, allowing Hawaiians to fish in the often stormy, current-swept waters below. In calmer periods, daredevils sometimes take the plunge. The left fork of South Point Road leads to the headquarters of ***Ka Ohana o Kalae,*** a curatorship project working to protect the area's archaeological sites. From the end of the pavement, a hot and dry 3-mile hike along a jeep road leads to ***Green Sand*** (or Papakolea) ***Beach.*** Olivine grains eroded from the base of a cinder cone behind the beach give the sand its distinctive green tint; swimming conditions are often unsafe. There is a $5 charge to park at the trailhead.

West of South Point, Route 11 begins to cross a series of ancient lava flows. The only other accessible beaches in Ka`u lie at the end of the ***Road to the Sea.*** This unmarked cinder road departs from the highway 0.4 mile north of the 79-mile point, between Iolani Lane and Aloha Drive but on the opposite side of the road. Two-wheel-drive vehicles can handle all but the very last section of the 7-mile descent. Park and hike down to a string of green- and black- sand beaches tucked beneath Humuhumu Point and extending west about a mile. The striking littoral cones along this coast were formed from spattering ash thrown back by blasts of steam as lava entered the ocean. Two miles farther along the highway, the road-weary can rest at ***Manuka State Wayside Park*** and bask in the tranquility of its arboretum.

The Kona Coast

The Mamalahoa Highway continues around the west slopes of Mauna Loa to enter the Kona District. As the highway climbs higher, broad vistas open up over the ocean below. Rainfall here varies by elevation from a parched dry coast to rain forest in the uplands. Coffee bushes thrive on the middle slopes of South Kona, shaded by the afternoon cloud cover. Kona Coffee, the oldest commercial beans grown in the islands, has gained worldwide recognition. North Kona reaps its own growing crop in tourism. Heeding pressure from Hawaiian activists, many of the new hotels preserve the historical sites on their properties as minimuseums.

At the 89-mile point, you pass the turnoff to ***Milolii,*** a traditional Hawaiian fishing village. Local fishermen still use traditional outrigger canoes (powered by nontraditional outboard motors) to net *opelu* (mackerel) that have been tamed and fattened by repeated feedings. It's a steep 5-mile descent to the village. From the end of the road, a fifteen-minute hike south leads to a secluded black-sand beach at Honomalino Bay.

One and a half miles past the 100-mile point, a narrow bumpy road descends 2 miles to ***Hookena Beach Park.*** Shaded by coconut palms, the gray sand beach faces cliffs across Kauhako Bay. The bay's protective arms make Hookena an excellent swimming beach. ***Kealia Beach,*** a short walk to the north, has smaller pockets of white sand and offers good snorkeling.

Continue on Route 11 for another 2.5 miles and turn seaward to Honaunau Place of Refuge. A sign halfway down directs you on a short detour right to ***St. Benedict's Painted Church.*** A Belgian priest, Father John Velghe, took four years and a healthy dose of imagination to paint the interior. Biblical scenes decorate the side panels for the benefit of illiterate churchgoers. The wall behind the altar gives the illusion of being in the Cathedral of Burgos in Spain. For a tropical touch, Father Velghe made the interior pillars sprout palm fronds curving onto the painted ceiling.

Back on the Honaunau Road, a few hundred yards past the church turnoff, you might stop at ***Wakefield Botanical Gardens and Restaurant*** (328–9930). The restaurant has a standard soup-and-sandwich menu and specializes in homemade pies for dessert. Golden coconuts mark a path through the gardens behind the restaurant. En route through the five-acre spread you will pass almost 1,000 labeled varieties of tropical plants. The restaurant is open daily 11:00 A.M. to 4:00 P.M., but you can tour the gardens free any time between dawn and dusk.

Other eating options in this stretch of South Kona cluster along the highway, ensconced in vintage plantation buildings, all on the ocean side. ***Keei Cafe*** (328–8451) serves an eclectic mix of Thai, Mexican, and New American dinners, whose gourmet flavorings and presentation belie the unassuming decor. The cafe may move north to Kainaliu but will keep its old name. It's worth looking for. Open Tuesday–Saturday 5:00–9:00 P.M.; reservations recommended. Moderate. Open for breakfast and lunch, the ***Coffee Shack*** (328–9555) offers decent grub, but the real reason to stop here is its sweeping views of the coastline below. Open

Coffee Tourism

The rich, mellow taste of Kona coffee has earned it an elite status among world coffees. But until recently, visitors to Kona never actually saw coffee growing. This $6 million crop is scattered among more than 500 small farms in South Kona. Many of these are now promoting coffee tourism much in the same way that vineyards in wine-producing regions do, by opening visitors centers and tasting rooms.

The Kona Coffee Belt spans roughly 20 miles of coastline between Honaunau and Holualoa. It begins about 2 miles inland at 800-foot elevation and extends about another mile upward to the 1700-foot level. Sheltered beneath the slopes of giant Mauna Loa, the Coffee Belt has a unique climate: It's one of the few places in Hawaii that gets more rain in summer than in winter. The typical weather pattern of morning sun followed by afternoon clouds and rain has proven ideal for coffee to thrive. From March to May, coffee bushes in Kona erupt in a cloud of fragrant, white blossoms known as "Kona snow." From the blossoms grow "cherries," which ripen to a brilliant red when ready for harvest in the fall. Harvest times vary by elevation, and the clusters of cherries on each bush ripen individually, requiring harvesting to be done by hand in several rounds. Stripped of pulp, the cherry pits become "green" (unroasted) coffee beans. Usually there are two beans per cherry, but about 5 percent of cherries yield only one bean, called a "peaberry." Many coffee farms produce a special peaberry coffee, which has a distinctive taste.

The first coffee was planted in Kona around 1828 by Samuel Ruggles, a missionary. Although commercial coffee was once grown on all the islands (a trend that is now reviving), a collapse in the world coffee market in 1898 put the large-scale plantations out of business. In Kona, small five-acre plots were instead leased as crop-shares to Japanese farmers, who carried on the coffee-growing tradition (sometimes harvesting fields at night to escape the watchful eyes of their creditors). For many years, Kona coffee remained the only commercial coffee crop grown in the United States.

To learn more about coffee growing first hand (and sample some of the house product), plan to visit at least one coffee farm while in Kona. For a complete guide to coffee tourism, look for the free brochure/map entitled "Kona Coffee Country Driving Tour" distributed at various visitors centers. Besides the Greenwell Farm and Kona Historical Society tours mentioned in the text, other places welcoming visitors include Kona Le`a Plantation (322–9937) at the 2-mile marker on the Mamalahoa Highway (Route 180) and Old Hawaii Coffee Farm (328–2277), just south of the 105-mile marker on the main highway (Route 11). Kona Le`a offers tours from tree to cup on weekdays from 3:30 A.M. to 4:00 P.M. Call ahead for Old Hawaii as owner Misha Sperka runs a one-man show. A former aquanaut and museum historian, Sperka's tours cover everything from coffee history to organic methods involving Chinese geese and avocado trees.

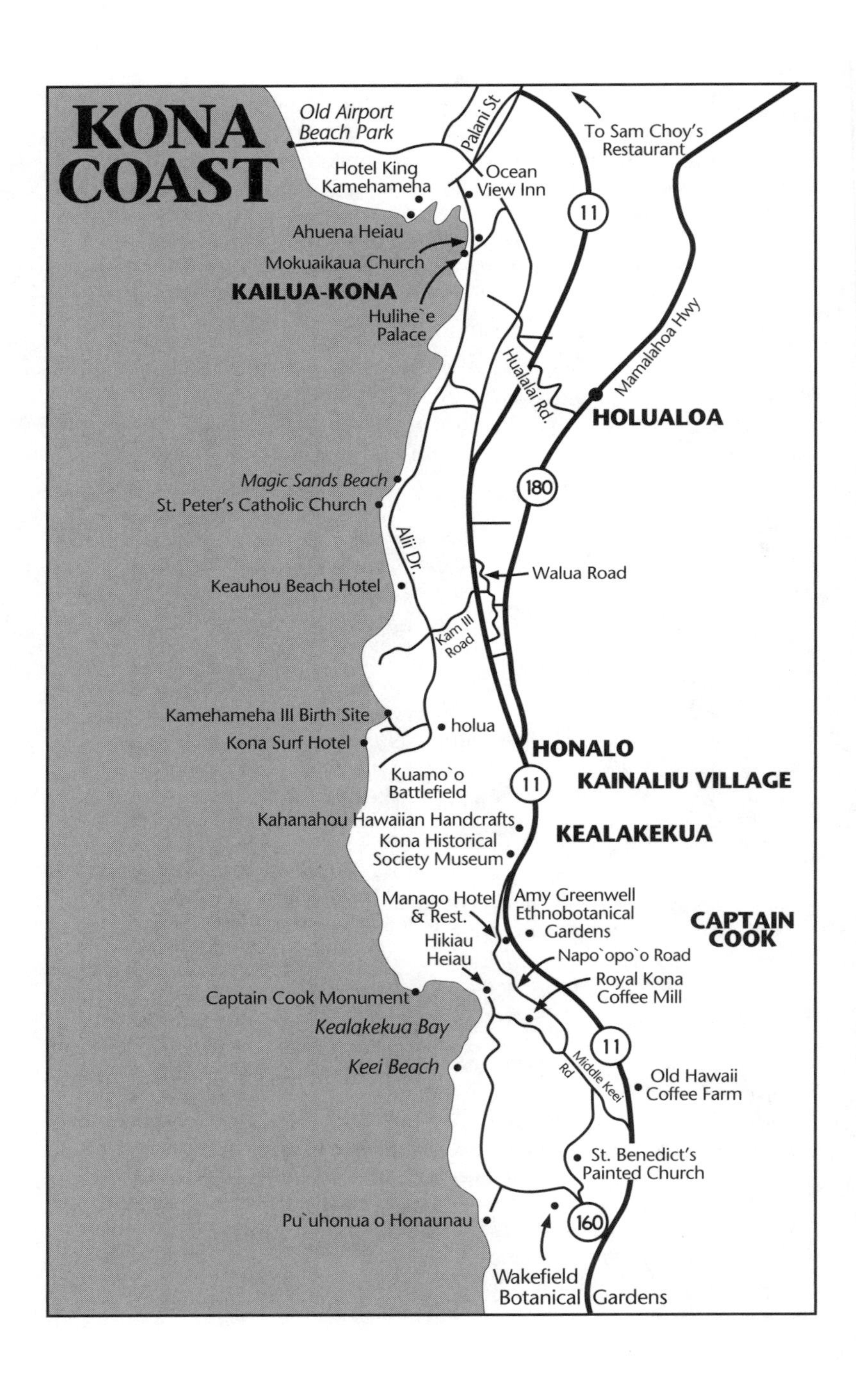
KONA COAST
Old Airport Beach Park
Palani St
To Sam Choy's Restaurant
Hotel King Kamehameha
Ocean View Inn
11
Ahuena Heiau
Mokuaikaua Church
KAILUA-KONA
Hulihe`e Palace
Mamalahoa Hwy
Hualalai Rd.
HOLUALOA
180
Magic Sands Beach
St. Peter's Catholic Church
Alii Dr.
Walua Road
Keauhou Beach Hotel
Kam III Road
Kamehameha III Birth Site
holua
Kona Surf Hotel
HONALO
Kuamo`o Battlefield
11
KAINALIU VILLAGE
Kahanahou Hawaiian Handcrafts
KEALAKEKUA
Kona Historical Society Museum
Managao Hotel & Rest.
Amy Greenwell Ethnobotanical Gardens
CAPTAIN COOK
Hikiau Heiau
Napo`opo`o Road
Royal Kona Coffee Mill
Captain Cook Monument
Kealakekua Bay
11
Keei Beach
Middle Keei Rd
Old Hawaii Coffee Farm
St. Benedict's Painted Church
Pu`uhonua o Honaunau
160
Wakefield Botanical Gardens

daily 7:00 A.M. to 5:00 P.M. ***Super J's*** (328–9566) serves authentic Hawaiian food Monday–Saturday 10:00 A.M. to 6:00 P.M. Farther on, the ***Manago Hotel Restaurant*** (323–2642) commands a loyal following with a variety of local favorites, from fried *opelu* (mackerel) to pork chops. Open daily except Monday, 7:00–9:00 A.M., 11:00 A.M. to 2:00 P.M., and 5:00–7:30 P.M.

The ***Manago Hotel*** (323–2642; www.managohotel.com) is an equally fine choice for lodging. Run by the third generation of Managos, the hotel's roadside rooms are backed up by a plush new wing overlooking the ocean. A Japanese garden and carp pond enhance the courtyard in between. Rates vary by wing and floor, from $28 to $50 for doubles. For a touch of Oriental luxury, ask for the Japanese suite, which rents for $64. Furnished in memory of Kinzo and Osame, the hotel's immigrant founders, the room features *ofuro* tubs, tatami mats, and futons.

Several B&Bs also operate in the area. ***Affordable Hawaii at Pomaika'i Farms*** (328–2112; 800–325–6427; www.luckyfarm.com) offers four rooms, with private bath, on a four-acre working coffee and macadamia nut farm. By far the most unusual is the coffee barn, a seriously rustic private shack with huge screen windows and an outdoor shower. Rooms rent for $55–$65 and include a full breakfast. Even funkier lodging can be had at the ***Dragonfly Ranch*** (328–2159, 800–487–2159; P.O. Box 675, Honaunau 96726; www.dragonflyranch.com), a New Age center of sorts. The "designer hippie" lodgings have a treehouse feel. They range from a room with shared bath for $90 to the honeymoon suite complete with outdoor waterbed for $200. The suites all have private outdoor showers and views of the coast. Breakfast fixings are supplied and snorkeling gear is available. Host Barbara can provide Hawaiian *lomilomi* massage and other homeopathic treatments upon request. For touch more luxury, consider a stay at ***McCandless Ranch*** (328–8246; www.alala.com). The guest room in the main house comes in a dainty white; it rents for $115. The much larger Kalahiki Cottage for $150 features lavish splashes of *koa* wood trim (mostly from the ranch's own woodshop) plus some antique *koa* furniture. It also has an open-air kitchen facing the pool and Jacuzzi. The ranch itself belongs to an old kamaaina family. Its 20,000 acres reach high up the slopes of Hualalai and include the only wild population of *`alala* (the Hawaiian crow) known to exist in the islands. The ranch offers expensive day-long "ecotours," catering to birders.

At the bottom of Honaunau Road you will find ***Puuhonua o Honaunau National Historic Park*** (328–2288). Life in ancient Hawaii was governed by a system of rigid *kapu* (taboos). Women couldn't eat bananas; commoners had to keep their shadows off the pathway of a chief; fish remained off-limits during spawning. Transgressions of any *kapu,* however minor, offended the gods and could provoke a natural disaster, such as a tidal wave. To protect the community, offenders had to be killed immediately—unless they could reach a *puuhonua* ("hill of sanctuary"), such as the one here at Honaunau, to receive spiritual cleansing within. Defeated warriors and noncombatants also took sanctuary here.

The National Park Service has worked to restore the area sites to the way they appeared in the late 1700s. You enter through the palace grounds of the ruling chief of the area, whose courtyard adjoined the *puuhonua.* Numbered coconuts designate points of interest as you stroll through the living compound and canoe landing. Ask at the visitor counter for a copy of the rules for *konane* (Hawaiian checkers). A stone *papamu* (playing board) with light and dark pebbles sits in a shaded spot awaiting players. The "Great Wall"—a miracle of mortarless construction 10 feet high, 17 feet thick, and 1,000 feet long—separates the palace grounds from the sanctuary itself. At the far edge of the wall, ***Hale o Keawe Heiau*** features a reconstructed thatched building, a *lele* stand for offerings, and ferocious carved tikis standing vigil around the perimeter. The buried bones of twenty-three high chiefs imbue the seventeenth-century temple with its sacred *mana.* Two older *heiau* remain unreconstructed. Look for the Ka`ahumanu Stone, under which Kamehameha's favorite wife hid until her pet dog gave her away. Ka`ahumanu swam to this sanctuary to escape her husband's jealous wrath. Only the intercession of British Captain George Vancouver persuaded the couple to make up. Coconut and *noni* trees are the only vegetation within the *puuhonua* grounds. Other native plants grow around the periphery. The park visitors center is open daily, 8:00 A.M. to 5:00 P.M., but the grounds stay open until evening. You can enjoy excellent snorkeling on the north side of the bay or follow a hiking trail 0.5 mile south along the coast through the ruins of an ancient Hawaiian fishing village to find an exposed lava tube overlooking the sea; token admission charge.

If the *puuhonua* at Honaunau Bay preserves something of the old system, the next bay to the north bears witness to the coming of the new. To get to ***Kealakekua Bay,*** where Captain Cook landed, you can either drive 4 miles along the coast on a narrow road through barren scrub-covered lava fields or backtrack uphill and take either the middle road past the Painted Church through scenic coffee country or the main highway farther up; then turn down Napo`opo`o Road.

The highway route is the longest, but it compensates by offering the following attractions en route. Just ahead, on the ocean side, look for the wind socks of ***SKEA Gallery*** (328–9392), a nonprofit cooperative of local artists, located in a former schoolhouse. You will find works exhibited in a variety of media and can visit the potters' guild studio nearby. Open Tuesday–Saturday 9:00 A.M. to 5:00 P.M.

Also on the ocean side of the highway, look for the ***Royal Kona Coffee Mill*** (328–2511). The historic mill mostly serves as a museum with exhibits on coffee growing, but the antiquated machinery inside still mills and roasts coffee beans once a week. You get a complimentary cup of the local brew just for visiting. Open daily 7:45 A.M. to 5:00 P.M.

Just shy of the 110-mile marker on the uphill side, the ***Amy Greenwell Ethnobotanical Garden*** (323–3318) spreads over twelve acres of hillside. Designed as a microcosm of Kona agriculture in ancient times, with plantings varying by elevation from ocean to mountain, the gardens have helpful labels throughout as well as a series on interpretive panels along a short nature walk. Open Monday–Friday 8:30 A.M. to 5:00 P.M., with guided tours Wednesday and Friday at 1:00 P.M. and the second Saturday of each month at 10:00 A.M. Donation.

Just past the Manago Hotel, Napo`opo`o Road descends from the highway to Kealakekua Bay with sweeping views of the coast fanning out

Wood Valley

Five miles inland from Pahala, a sleepy cane village on the sparsely populated south side of the Big Island, lies Wood Valley, a largely inconspicuous indentation in the slopes of Mauna Loa. This misty valley is one of the most remote places on the island, its one-time plantation camp now abandoned as are the sugar-cane fields that line the road leading into it. The cane gives way to tall trees once you reach the valley, and the bright gaudy colors of Wood Valley Temple (928–8539; www.nechung.org) come into view. This improbable sanctuary was built by Japanese cane workers as a Nichiren Mission, with its upper level later taken from a Japanese Shingon shrine in Pahala. The temple now belongs to Tibetan Buddhists and was inaugurated by the Dalai Lama himself in 1973 as Nechung Dorje Drayang Ling ("Immutable Island of Melodious Sound"), a spiritual retreat center affiliated with two other temples in Tibet and India. Visiting Buddhist scholars, monks, and lamas often host lectures and workshops here, and anyone is welcome to attend the daily services at 7:00 A.M. and 7:00 P.M. or stop by for quiet meditation alone during the day. You can also find lodging here for $50 for a double with shared bath and kitchen, or $25 for a dorm. To get to the temple, turn off the highway at Pahala and take Pikake Street 5 miles north into Wood Valley. Because this is a place for spiritual contemplation, casual visitors are discouraged.

below. Whichever route you chose to get here, you end up at ***Napo`opo`o Beach Park,*** one corner of which edges against the bay. A famous *heiau* dedicated to the harvest god, Lono, once stood here. Contrary to common belief, however, it was separated from ***Hikiau Heiau,*** the terraced platform you see today. When Captain Cook sailed into Kealakekua Bay, the Makahiki Festival honoring Lono was in full swing. The billowing white sails of the English vessels matched the white *tapa* (bark cloth) banners erected to herald the season; this recalled a prophecy that Lono would return atop a "floating island." Cook was taken for Lono and welcomed as a god.

When Cook returned a month later to repair storm damage, the Makahiki was ending; his ship's broken mast paralleled the lowering of Lono's sacred *tapa* banners. This time the welcome was more grudging. A skirmish erupted over a stolen lifeboat and led to Cook's death. In a bizarre overlap of cultures, this accidental conflict symbolically reenacted a ritual in which devotees of the war god, Ku, would "defeat" Lono to end the Makahiki's annual hiatus from warfare. The wars to come would be bloodier than ever, thanks to Western weapons, and would lead to Kamehameha's ultimate conquest of the islands.

Still, the murder of "Lono" could not spare the other Hawaiian gods and beliefs from falling victim to Western ways. A plaque in front of Hikiau Heiau commemorates the first Christian service in Hawaii, a burial ceremony performed by Captain Cook on temple grounds. Another plaque salutes Henry Opukahaia, a young Hawaiian apprenticed at the *heiau* who turned his back on the old gods and sailed to New England to receive a Christian education. His passionate pleas would inspire the first missionaries to come to Hawaii to lead his people away from idolatry.

Across the bay, steep bluffs descend from the hillside and slope down to a peninsula at the far mouth of the bay. At the base of this peninsula, a white marble obelisk stands near the spot where Captain Cook fell. To get there, you can hike down, starting at the jeep road turnoff on the right off Napo`opo`o Road, just below its junction with the highway. It takes about two hours. Another option is horseback riding (323–2388), which should be arranged in advance. A number of roadside shops also rent kayaks upon the highway. It's a 1-mile paddle to reach the monument. Technically, this is British soil you'll be standing on—ceded land akin to a consulate. An Australian ship still comes annually to tend to the monument's upkeep. The waters offshore are a popular snorkeling spot; a pod of spinner dolphins frequents the bay as well as others to the south.

Depending on which route you took to get to Kealakekua Bay, you passed one of two nearby attractions. Just south of the bay, a turnoff from the coastal road to Honaunau leads to the white sands of ***Keei Beach,*** which has a place in history all its own. Kamehameha fought his first battle to subdue the Big Island here, defeating his cousin, Kiwalao, the son of former ruling chief Kalaniopuu. Luckily, the losers had a *puuhonua* nearby.

Return up Napo`opo`o Road to Route 11 and the town of Captain Cook, and continue north on the highway 1 mile to the ***Kona Historical Society Museum*** (323–3222) just outside Kealakekua Village. Housed in an 1875 store built by rancher Henry Nicholas Greenwell, the museum features photographs, memorabilia, and artifacts from Kona's past. Open Monday–Friday 9:00 A.M. to 3:00 P.M. Admission by donation. An Englishman by birth, Greenwell came to Kona in 1850, one of the first haole settlers on the coast. The ruins of his family homestead lie adjacent to the store; those interested can get a self-guiding tour sheet from the museum. The Kona Historical Society also offers a number of guided walking tours to other sites well worth checking into. The "living history" tour of the ***Uchida Coffee Farm*** is especially innovative. Costumed guides lead visitors back in time to visit a working Japanese coffee farm as it stood in the 1920s and interact with volunteer "interpreters" on hand to role-play, using authentic machinery and live animals. The 2½-hour tour is offered several times per week and costs $30. Call 323–2006 for information and reservations. In addition, the Society offers a walking tour of Kailua Village most mornings for $15 and can schedule a guided visit to the historic sites of Keahou or Kealakekua Bay for groups of three or more with advance notice. Call 323–3222. Finally, the Society organizes periodic tours by land or sea to other remote spots of historic interest; these alone may be worth the price of membership.

Among H. N. Greenwell's many ventures was the export of coffee. He began selling beans harvested by native Hawaiian farmers; his wife later had many acres of their own land planted with coffee trees. Her great-grandchildren still tend some of those trees on the 35-acre ***Greenwell Farms Coffee Estate*** (323–2275; 888–592–5662). Although not connected to the historical society, a driveway down to the farm extends from the museum parking lot. You can sample a variety of house brews, including a rare peaberrry coffee at a tasting booth as well as take a brief tour of the farm. Open Monday–Friday 8:00 A.M. to 5:00 P.M.; Saturday until 4:00 P.M.

On the north end of Kealakekua, don't miss a stop at ***Kahanahou Hawaiian Handcrafts*** (322–3901). Founded by *kumu hula* Lanakila Brandt in 1968 to revive traditional Hawaiian art forms, the center has a showroom filled with authentic craftwork and hula implements for sale, from bamboo nose flutes to the gourd helmets worn by priests of Lono, all of which Brandt and his apprentices make in an adjacent workshop. Ask for a free demonstration of their use. Hula *halau* rehearse on the premises, and traditional medicinal plants grow around the perimeter. This is a rare chance to visit a place where the Hawaiian culture truly lives.

Continue on Route 11 to the tiny town of Kainaliu. The highway strip here has a number of interesting shops and galleries. ***Kimura Fabrics*** (322–3771) inhabits a 1926-vintage general store. Inside, Hawaiian *palaka* and *tapa* prints hang alongside hand-batiked silks. Open Monday–Friday 9:00 A.M. to 7:00 P.M., Saturday till 6:00 P.M., and Sunday till 5:00 P.M.

Just up the road, also in Kainaliu, you can dine at the ***Aloha Theatre Cafe*** (322–3383). Order over the counter in the theater lobby, which is decorated with posters from cinema classics; then carry your meal around to the terraced veranda overlooking a hillside meadow. The moderately priced menu centers around health food and Mexican fare, with fresh fish daily. The 1928 theater still functions as an art-house cinema and occasional concert venue. Open Thursday–Sunday 8:00 A.M. to 3:00 P.M., dinner 5:00–9:00 P.M.

Next up on Route 11 comes Honalo, where ***Teshima's*** (322–9140), a long-standing local favorite, serves Japanese meals at honest prices. The wooden paneled mock-shoji decor showcases paintings by the Teshimas' grandson, Jason. Open daily 6:30 A.M. to 1:45 P.M. and 5:00–9:00 P.M. The Teshimas also rent out two simply furnished rooms in back, facing a Japanese garden; $35 for a double.

Next door to Teshima's, take a moment to peek inside ***Daifukuji Buddhist Temple.*** (Remove your shoes before entering.) This large wooden complex, painted red with a silver corrugated roof, has several rooms and a Japanese garden in back. The main entrance opens onto a lovely altar embellished in gold and silver brocade. Giant ceremonial drums fill an adjacent side room.

Just outside town, Route 180 splits off on an uphill route to Holualoa. If you stay on the main highway, three miles farther, Kamehameha III Road crosses Route 11 and plunges down toward the coast, intersecting Alii Drive, a lower coastal road, just above Keauhou Bay. Turn left (south) on Alii Drive, and take the next right down to the bay. Kamehameha III was born here. An interpretive garden trail follows the cliffline leading to the birth site. The story goes that the royal prince was delivered stillborn but was revived miraculously in a nearby spring by an attending *kahuna.* In gratitude, his father, Kamehameha I, built a 1-mile-long *holua* (sledding) track on the hillside above the bay. An HVCB marker designates the royal birth site, and a bronze plaque on a nearby boulder notes where the resuscitation took place. Golf course development has destroyed most of the holua course, but if you look uphill from Alii Drive, you might make out the parallel walls of the ramp where wet leaves greased the original course. You can see one of the long, incredibly narrow sleds used for the sport at Hulihe`e Palace in Kailua.

Alii Drive ends a short distance farther south at the sacred burial ground of ***Kuamo`o Battlefield.*** A pivotal battle was fought here in 1819, pitting Liholiho, Kamehameha's heir, against his cousin, Kekuaokalani. The pretext for the clash was Liholiho's abolishment of the *kapu* system, which traditionalists opposed. As keeper of the war god, Kekuaokalani's challenge threatened Liholiho's authority. In similar circumstances, Kamehameha himself had overthrown Kalaniopuu's heirs using Western weapons, but this time the overwhelming weight of musketry favored Liholiho. The death of the old guard and their gods was assured, and the way was paved for the Christianization of the islands. Today, a rough trail leads across the barren lava field to the Lekeleke burial grounds where more than 300 warriors lie entombed beneath rocky cairns. The golf course across the road provides an almost surreal contrast to the stark surroundings.

Going north, Alii Drive hugs the coastline for 6 miles to Kailua, past various hotels and unusual vegetation draped in a dense curtain of vines. If you come at night, you will see some of the hotels' floodlights that shine out to sea to attract and illuminate the giant manta rays that gather offshore. By day, stop at ***Aston Keauhou Beach Resort*** (877–532–8468) near the 5-mile marker and ask for a free copy of the self-guided walking tour of the hotel's historic grounds. You'll find the remains of three *heiau,* a fishpond, a cluster of petroglyphs, and various fishing shrines as you learn the legends that accompany them. A replica of a beach house belonging to King Kalakaua stands beside a sacred pool; cultural activities are scheduled inside. The hotel offers a free guided tour daily at 8:30 A.M. Rooms here start at $185.

On the other side of Kahaluu Bay, a popular snorkeling spot north of the hotel, sits tiny ***St. Peter's Catholic Church,*** a pretty vision in blue built on the grounds of an old *heiau.* ***Magic Sands Beach,*** just up the road, gets its name from its seasonally varying deposits of white sand. Continue on Alii Drive into the town of Kailua (often called Kona and officially hyphenated as Kailua-Kona). Tourist dollars and rampant development have transformed the town into an endless strip mall, sprawling across poorly laid out streets. The heart of historic Kailua clusters around the harbor at the end of Alii Drive.

Begin your tour at ***Hulihe`e Palace*** (329–1877), a two-story stone structure built in 1838 by John Kuakini, the Big Island's first governor. His daughter-in-law, Princess Ruth, inherited the building, but at 6'10" and 410 pounds, she couldn't fit up the stairs and preferred to sleep in a grass house she built outside. Various members of the Hawaiian royalty used Hulihe`e as a vacation home until 1914, when Prince Kuhio sold the property and auctioned off all its contents. By 1924 the empty palace had fallen into disrepair, and the Daughters of Hawaii acquired an easement over the property to restore it as a museum. Fortunately, the Daughters were able to recover many of the original palace possessions. The ensemble of beautiful furniture and historical artifacts spans the entire century of the Hawaiian monarchy.

As you enter the building, a marble bust of King Kalakaua flanked by feather *kahilis,* the standards of royalty, greets you at the foot of the stairs. An adjacent room contains possessions belonging to Kamehameha I, including his *`awa* (a mild narcotic) pipe and his stone exercise ball weighing 200 pounds. Upstairs, you'll find some of the gifts received by King Kalakaua on his travels around the world, including the busts of Grecian gods that inspired him to commission his own. Pause to read an original copy of a poem written by Robert Louis Stevenson to Princess Kaiulani, then enter the bedrooms to admire the sumptuous furniture. Finally, step onto the balcony for a refreshing view across Kailua Bay.

Before you leave, take a look at ***Kiope Pond*** behind the gift shop. This spring-fed pool was the original water source for the palace. Later, when pipes supplied fresh water throughout Kailua, the well was enclosed and converted to a small fishpond, which still functions today. Hulihe`e Palace opens its doors Monday–Friday 9:00 A.M. to 4:00 P.M., Saturday and Sunday 10:00 A.M. to 4:00 P.M. Admission $5.00.

Across the street, ***Mokuaikaua Church*** has a rich history of its own. When the first twenty-three-member troop of missionaries came to Hawaii in 1820, they landed in Kailua for an audience with Kamehameha II. The king granted the missionaries a one-year probationary stay and ceded them land in Kailua. The brethren immediately broke ground for the islands' first church, leaving Asa Thurston as its minister. Governor Kuakini built the current building in 1838. It took 4,000 workers to erect the 3.5-foot-thick walls, incorporating lava stones from a fifteenth-century *heiau* built on the site by Chief Umi, and a lime mortar prepared from burned coral. Beautiful stained-glass windows grace the interior, the gift of a church member in 1970. Behind the pews, a koa wood panel separates the royal section, which is backdropped by four *kahilis* colored to represent the four major islands.

Browse among the exhibits in the rear of the church to learn more about the church and missionary history. A model of the brig *Thaddeus*, "Hawaii's *Mayflower*," which carried the first missionaries on their 164-day voyage around Cape Horn, occupies a prominent place. Also intriguing is the Micronesian navigation stick chart obtained from a sister church on Kwajalein Island. The carefully shaped latticework of crossed sticks schematically represents the currents, swell patterns, and flotsam drift lines learned for a given region through prolonged observation. Such an intimate relationship with the environment around them enabled Polynesian navigators to conquer the Pacific.

Walk along the harbor seawall. You might see coconut-frond weavers sitting on the wall above the small, white-sand pocket bordering Hulihe`e Palace grounds. As you approach the pier, note the marked finish line for Kona's annual Ironman Triathalon, held in October, the original and most famous race of its kind. Competitors must survive a 2.6-mile rough-water swim, run a marathon, and cycle a hilly 117 miles to earn the right to cross this line. Across the bay, ***Kailua Pier*** becomes a popular hangout at the end of the day when the charter fishing boats weigh in their prize catches. Kona waters are world famous for their game fish, so if someone's been lucky, you might see a 1,000-pound marlin dangling from the scales. (If not, the King Kamehameha Hotel lobby has several stuffed giants in its lobby.) The International Billfish Tournament in late July/early August brings a circuslike atmosphere to town as competitors from around the world vie to land the big ones. Other tournaments happen throughout the year.

To the right of the pier, ***Kamakahonu Beach*** cozies up inside a small cove fronting the King Kamehameha Hotel. Kamehameha I spent his last days here, enjoying the peace and prosperity of his reign. A mortuary platform marks the spot where the king was buried, but his bones were removed and secretly hidden according to ancient custom. After Kamehameha's death in 1819, his son and heir, Liholiho, overthrew the *kapu* system when he permitted his mother-in-law Queen Ka`ahumanu to dine at his table here at Kamakahonu. This left a void that the arrival of the missionaries and their new god, Jehovah, would fill in the following year. ***Ahuena Heiau,*** a relic of the gods Liholiho forsook, sits at the mouth of the cove. Restored by the Bishop Museum, the small complex

Ahuena Heiau

includes a thatched *hale mana* (main prayer house), *hale pahu* (house of drums), *anuu* (oracle tower), and several beautifully carved *kii akua* (temple idols). The adjacent ***Hale Mahina*** ("house to watch the farm land") has a thatched roof of sugar cane leaves. Kamehameha came here to relax and gaze along the fertile expanse of the Kona coast. He himself tended a taro plot on the slopes of 8,000-foot Mount Hualalai.

In addition to the *heiau* on its grounds, the lobby of ***King Kamehameha Kona Beach Hotel*** (329–2911, 800–367–2111; www.konabeachhotel.com) constitutes a quasi-museum. Display cases house artifacts from ancient Hawaii ranging from feather capes to hula instruments. Ask the concierge for an informative brochure on the collection. A prominent mural by Herb Kane portrays King Kamehameha's court at Kamakahonu with the same view toward Ahuena Heiau as the hotel's side entrance affords today. The hotel offers free tours of the grounds weekdays at 1:30 P.M. Rooms start at $130.

Kailua's less-conventional lodgings range from a youth hostel to a luxury B&B. The former, ***Patey's Place*** (326–7018; 75–195 Ala-Ona Ona), is located on an obscure side street. It offers both shared and private rooms for $20 and $46, respectively. The B&B, ***Kailua Plantation House*** (329–3727; www.kphbnb.com), has a stunning oceanfront location and an elegant interior to match. Rattan furniture, hanging plants, and Hawaiiana decor create an intimate ambience. The five individually furnished suites range in price from $160 to $235. Children must be twelve or older.

Restaurants in Kailua mostly cater to tourist tastes and wallets, but there are a few good bets. ***Oodles of Noodles*** (329–9222) will take you on an international tour de noodle, navigated by culinary whiz, Amy Ferguson Ota. Open Monday–Saturday 10:00 A.M. to 9:00 P.M., Sunday from noon. You'll find it in the Crossroads Mall on Henry Street, above Route 11, near Safeway. ***Sibu Cafe*** (329–1112) in the Banyan Court Mall specializes in Indonesian *satay* at moderate prices. To dine in Kailua away from the tourist crowds, backtrack from the pier a few hundred yards to the ***Ocean View Inn*** (329–9998). This is a family-run Kona institution, whose namesake view filters along with the harbor breezes through jalousie windows with insect screens. The extensive menu features Hawaiian, Chinese, and local American staples. A separate shaved-ice counter serves refreshing island desserts like Li Hing Mui ice cream. Open Tuesday–Sunday 6:30 A.M. to 2:45 P.M. and 5:15–8:45 P.M. Inexpensive.

For a true gastronomic treat, visit ***Sam Choy's Restaurant*** (326–1545), located in the Kaloko Industrial Center, 3 miles north on Route 19. (Turn right off the highway, then take the first right and second left.) The place may look like a truckstop diner, but that just underscores the emphasis placed on the kitchen. Chef Choy has his own cooking show on TV, and this is where he practices what he preaches. He differs from Hawaii's other leading chefs in his emphasis on down-to-earth cooking over pretentious cuisine. Lunch specials include a beef-stew omelette and go for moderate prices. Dinner always features fresh fish and runs in the expensive range. Humongous portions are the norm. Open daily 6:00 A.M. to 2:00 P.M. and Tuesday–Saturday 5:00–9:00 P.M.

When Kailua's heat and crowds begin to press, Hualalai Road offers an escape up inland to the cool coffee country of Holualoa. As you climb the 4 miles up the slopes of Mount Hualalai, the vegetation grows more lush with every foot of elevation. At the intersection with Route 180, stop for a moment at the ***Kimura Lauhala Shop*** (324–0053) to browse among handcrafted creations woven from the fibrous leaves of the *hala* tree. Open Monday–Saturday 9:00 A.M. to 4:00 P.M. The store has been run by the Kimura family since 1915.

Turn left on Route 180 and continue uphill 0.5 mile, enjoying coastal views over Keahole Peninsula as you enter the town of Holualoa ("long sled run"). This former coffee town has gone artsy, with galleries galore. Fresh paint livens up the tin-roofed clapboard buildings. The old coffee mill now houses the ***Kona Arts Center,*** an artist workshop and studio. Another gallery occupies a former gas station. Most are open Tuesday–Saturday 10:00 A.M. to 3:00 P.M.

The oldest gallery in town, and one of the nicest, is ***Studio 7*** (324–1335). This was owner Hiroki Morinoue's parents' store, when they ran it as a pool hall and laundry business. He has transformed it into a gallery that is a work of art itself, with pebble paths and wooden partitions. Hiroki and his wife, Setsuko, display their work and that of a few others, including their daughter Miho. Open Tuesday–Saturday 11:00 A.M. to 5:00 P.M.

Accommodations in Holualoa come in two forms, economy and deluxe. Deluxe is the ***Holualoa Inn*** (324–1121 or 800–392–1812; inn@aloha.net; P.O. Box 222, Holualoa 96725), built as a mountain retreat by *Honolulu Advertiser* publisher Thurston Twigg-Smith and now run as a B&B by the family. Eucalyptus wood milled on Maui covers the floors, while the walls inside and out luxuriate in natural cedar. Creature comforts include a pool, game room, library, wet bar, and hot tub. The entire property overlooks a forty-acre coffee plantation with captivating views of the Kona coast. Prices for the six rooms range from $150–$195 and include full breakfast with Kona coffee grown on the premises as well as afternoon pupus. Children must be twelve or older. The budget option in town is the venerable ***Kona Hotel*** (324–1155), which rents rooms for $20 for a single, $26 for a double. Take a peek in back at the scenic "toilet in the sky."

North to Kohala

To enjoy Kona's legendary blue waters in relative seclusion, head north from Kailua. Kuakini Highway (the middle road between Alii Drive and Route 11) runs through the town's industrial section and ends a mile farther along at the ***Old Kona Airport State Park.*** The broad swath of white sand here stretches along the coast for almost a mile. A sandy inlet on the south end offers the best shelter for swimming during periods of surf. You won't have to worry about parking—there is an entire runway left from the old airport. To reach other beaches, take Route 19, the extension of Route 11, a straight, flat road that crosses lava flows of varying vintage. The turnoff to Honokohau Harbor comes 3 miles up the coast. The marine vessels here seem to

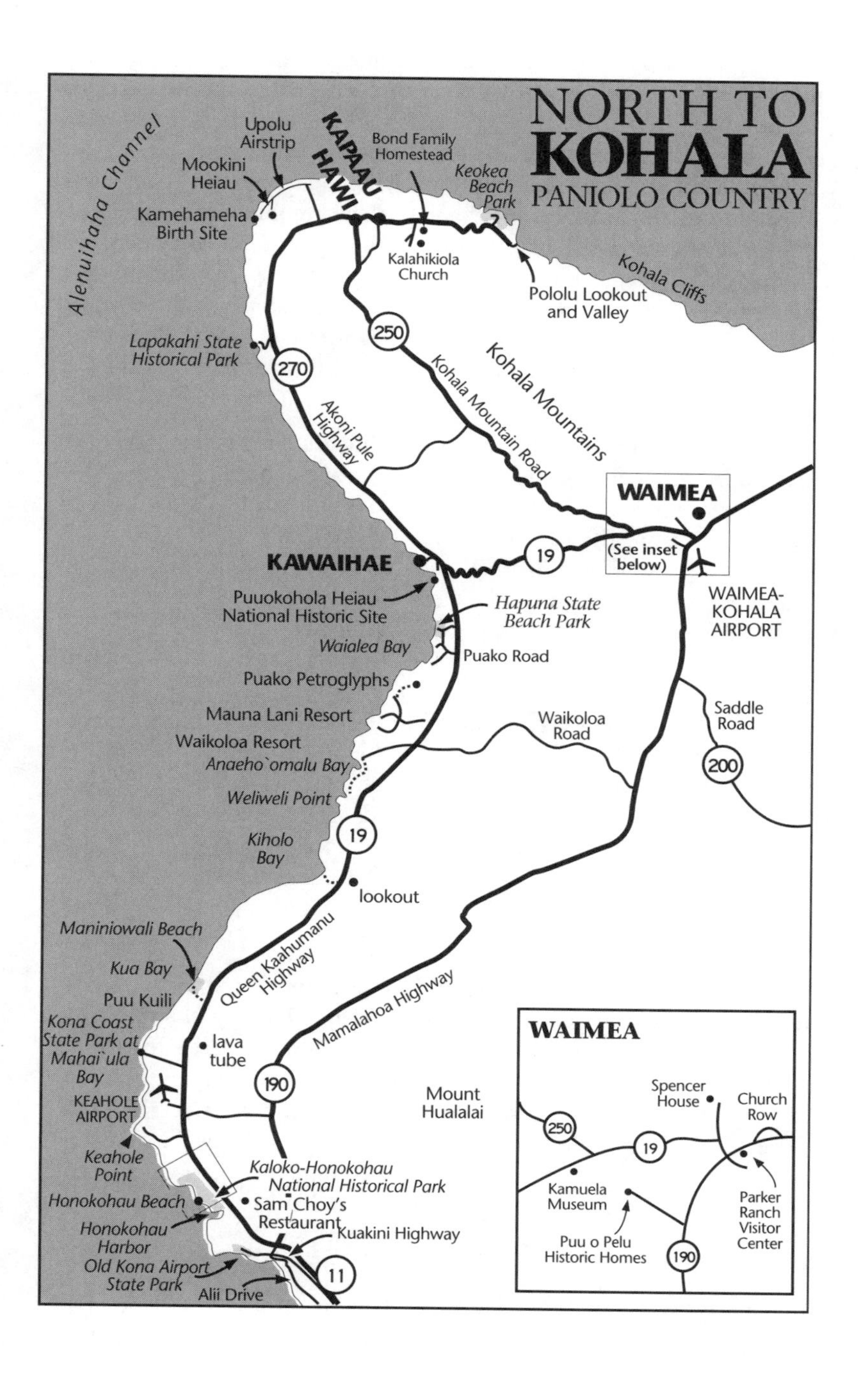
NORTH TO
KOHALA
PANIOLO COUNTRY
Alenuihaha Channel
Upolu Airstrip
Mookini Heiau
Kamehameha Birth Site
KAPAAU
HAWI
Bond Family Homestead
Keokea Beach Park
Kalahikiola Church
Kohala Cliffs
Pololu Lookout and Valley
Lapakahi State Historical Park
270
250
Kohala Mountains
Kohala Mountain Road
Akoni Pule Highway
WAIMEA
(See inset below)
19
KAWAIHAE
Puuokohola Heiau National Historic Site
Hapuna State Beach Park
WAIMEA-KOHALA AIRPORT
Waialea Bay
Puako Road
Puako Petroglyphs
Mauna Lani Resort
Saddle Road
Waikoloa Road
Waikoloa Resort
Anaeho`omalu Bay
200
Weliweli Point
19
Kiholo Bay
lookout
Maniniowali Beach
Queen Kaahumanu Highway
Kua Bay
Puu Kuili
Mamalahoa Highway
Kona Coast State Park at Mahai`ula Bay
lava tube
190
KEAHOLE AIRPORT
Mount Hualalai
Keahole Point
Kaloko-Honokohau National Historical Park
Honokohau Beach
Sam Choy's Restaurant
Honokohau Harbor
Kuakini Highway
Old Kona Airport State Park
11
Alii Drive
WAIMEA
Spencer House
Church Row
250
19
Kamuela Museum
Parker Ranch Visitor Center
Puu o Pelu Historic Homes
190

float in a sea of lava, but in fact the harbor connects to the ocean through an artificial channel. This is another great place to watch charter boats weigh in their catch. Or hoist a schooner at the harbor restaurant and hear salts young and old bemoan "the one that got away." Sandy patches line both sides of the harbor entrance. Most people take the right fork of the harbor road and park where the road becomes private property. Cross the lava barrier on the right to follow a paved trail through 0.5 mile of *kiawe* scrub to ***Honokohau Beach,*** which used to be a popular nude beach until the feds started cracking down. *Kukui* trees border the salt-and-pepper sands, and a low lava shelf dogs the waterline for much of the beach. The central portion offers the best swimming and has a good snorkeling reef offshore.

The archaeologically rich land bordering the beach has been purchased by the federal government for ***Kaloko-Honokohau National Historical Park*** (329–6881). If you follow a trail inland from the northern edge of the beach, you can rinse off after your swim in the cool, brackish waters of ***Kanini`ini`ula Pond,*** popularly known as the ***Queen's Bath,*** where Queen Ka`ahumanu supposedly dipped the royal derriere. Park archaeologists say this never happened. But the area is definitely full of sacred memories. Rock cairns surround the spring-fed pool. A *holua* (sled) track lies to the south. The nearby Aimakapa fishpond covers twenty acres inland of the beach, providing an important waterfowl habitat. Kaloko Pond to the north reputedly guards the bones of King Kamehameha I in a secret underwater cave. Other sites of interest include *heiau,* petroglyph fields, and burial mounds. To find these, enter the park through the unpaved access road opposite Kaloko Industrial Park, 0.5 mile north on Route 19. A skeleton ranger staff is on duty from 7:30 A.M. to 4:00 P.M. daily, although a permanent visitor center is planned.

A few miles up the coast, near the 94-mile marker, another turnoff leads past Wawaloli Beach Park to the ***Natural Energy Lab of Hawaii*** (329–7341) at Keahole Point. Part of the lab's research focuses on ocean thermal energy conversion (OTEC), which exploits differences in ocean temperatures at varying depths to generate electricity. This experimental technology holds the promise of a renewable, environmentally safe energy source. In the meantime, the nutrient-rich cold water that the lab pumps up from the ocean depths allows for successful aquaculture of black-pearl oysters, Japanese flounder, and Maine lobster. The lab offers a two-hour "presentation" to visitors on Thursday morning by advance reservation.

A mile farther, Keahole Airport shares space with the ***Onizuka Space***

Center (329–3441), dedicated to the memory of Holualoa-born astronaut Ellison Onizuka, who perished in the 1986 *Challenger* space shuttle disaster. Various space-themed exhibits, interactive displays, and NASA paraphernalia can be examined. Open daily 8:30 A.M. to 4:30 P.M.; token admission charged. Two miles north of the airport, look uphill to spot a gaping lava tube. All the lava here came from Hualalai's last flow in 1801. A mile farther, a sign marks the turnoff to the beachfront ***Kona Coast State Park*** at Mahai`ula Bay. For a more secluded strand, continue on the highway. As you drive, look for Puu Kuili, a grassy 341-foot cinder cone on the downhill slope. Just north of the cone, immediately after the 88-mile marker, you can rattle your way down to Kua Bay on a jeep road. Passenger cars can make the drive almost to the end; alternatively, the walk takes only about twenty-five minutes. Rock-hop across the final yards of lava field between the road and ***Maniniowali Beach,*** the bay's hidden gem. Turquoise waters and a gently sloping sandy bottom make for perfect swimming conditions, although winter surf can create hazards and deplete the sand.

Not far from Maniniowali, the ***Kona Village Resort*** (325–5555; 800–367–5290; www.konavillage.com) delivers a tame version of the great Gauguin getaway. Individual *hale* (thatched Polynesian bungalows) border a picturesque bay and fishpond, with all-inclusive meals-lodging-activities rates beginning at $480 for two.

As you continue north on the highway, note the yellow donkey-crossing signs. The donkeys, known as "Kona nightingales," run wild in the hills and come down at night to drink from coastal springs. Stop at the lookout near the 82-mile point and let your gaze travel the barren lava coast below until it strikes the bright cobalt blue of ***Kiholo Bay.*** The sparkling waters of this coconut-fringed lagoon wink an unspoken invitation. Tempted? If you pull off the highway at the wide shoulder just south of the 81-mile marker, you can hike down a jeep trail to reach this remote oasis. A half-hour's exertion brings you to the north end of the bay, where sea turtles nest by the brackish five-acre lagoon. Black-sand beach lines the shore, and to the south lies Luahinewai, a freshwater pond.

Past Kiholo, on a clear day, you can see all the island's volcanoes except Kilauea. Note the Jello-mold shape of Puu Waawaa, a pumice cone, on Hualalai's northern flank. The highway passes through more lava flows that came mostly from distant Mauna Loa. A series of artificial Edens relieves the monotony of this lava desert as luxury resorts sprout along the arid South Kohala coast. Two of the hotels here (listed below) have developed extensive "historical parks" on their grounds. Interpretive trails lead past a variety of archaeological sites.

Both employ a "court historian" to lead tours and staff minimuseums. Call for the current schedule.

The turnoff to the ***Outrigger Waikoloa Beach Hotel*** (886–6789) at Anaehoomalu Bay comes first at the 76-mile point. Petroglyphs fill a two-acre lava field by the golf course. Two large fishponds that Kamehameha I claimed for his own front a narrow coconut-fringed beach strip edging the bay. If you walk to the far south end of the beach and continue over ancient lava flows from Mauna Kea, you reach, after about a mile, a beautiful spring-fed pond at Weliweli Point. Locals call this hidden oasis "one coconut." What do you think grows here?

The ***Mauna Lani Hotel*** (885–6622), 2 miles up the highway, has even more elaborate sites to explore. You can pick up an excellent brochure from the concierge. A historical trail starts through an underground

Sailing Hawaiian Style

Five hundred years before the Vikings, when European galleys hugged the coastline of the Mediterranean, afraid to risk the open sea, Polynesian navigators had conquered the Pacific, the largest ocean on Earth, making regular crossings from one isolated group of islands to the next across thousands of miles of open ocean. By the late twentieth century, however, Polynesian sailing canoes had disappeared from island waters as western vessels built from modern materials supplanted them. The Orchid at Mauna Lani is the homeport for one of the few exceptions: The Hahalua Lele *("flying manta ray") is a replica of the double-hulled sailing canoes of old, built from native woods and incorporating traditional techniques. The sail is of the triangular "crab claw" design used by the ancients. The cross-boom lashings were done by Hawaiian Studies students at a local high school. There is not a single nail or screw in the entire 35-foot vessel. Its owner, Capt. Casey Cho, offers visitors a unique opportunity to experience firsthand the thrill of authentic Polynesian sailing. The two-hour voyages begin with a traditional Hawaiian prayer and the blowing of a conch shell. Cho issues commands to his crew in the Hawaiian language. Once underway, the vessel sails along the magnificent Kohala coastline with views of four Big Island volcanos, plus Maui just across the channel. This is not just a glorified pleasure cruise, it's a cultural journey. Cho shares with passengers some of the secrets of ancient sailing and navigation. Weather permitting, he may anchor the canoe for swimming or demonstrate traditional fishing techniques. Hawaiian refreshments are served, including a fresh coconut, husked at sea and a cocktail made from* `awa. *Sailing trips depart several times weekly and cost $95. Call the Orchid Beach Club at 885–2000, ext. 7320, for reservations.*

"city" of interconnecting lava tubes in an old *pahoehoe* lava flow. The trail then meanders around the two picturesque fishponds that the resort maintains in working condition. Watch as the large captive fish inside wiggle and splash on the surface to shake off parasites. On the ocean side, *makaha* (sluice gates) help circulate the water and let small fish enter while keeping big fish from getting out. You can walk south along the coast to find more interesting sites. Most of the area remains undeveloped and separate from the resort.

At Holoholokai Beach Park, north of the Orchid Hotel end of the Mauni Lani resort, a public access leads to the ***Puako Petroglyphs,*** one of the finest petroglyph fields in all Polynesia, with more than 3,000 rock carvings in all. You can take rubbings from fake petroglyphs placed here to spare the originals. Scattered in an old cracking *pahoehoe* flow overgrown with *kiawe,* stick-figure images of warriors and canoes float in the frozen lava sea. Part of the fun is trying to make out the different images and symbols. Were they ritual markings or prehistoric doodles? Their mystery reaches across time.

A mile to the north, ***Hapuna State Beach Park*** wins the Big Island popularity poll hands down. This nicely landscaped park has it all. Inviting waters accommodate a variety of recreational activities. The wide expanse of white sand is backdropped by grassy hills equipped with picnic table pavilions. And with less than 10 inches of rain annually, you can count on the sunniest skies on the island. Hapuna does get dangerous surf in winter, although a shallow cove on the north side offers some protection. Farther up the hill you can rent A-frame cabins that sleep four for $20. Bring your own bedding. Call 974–6200 for reservations.

For a more hidden beach, turn south onto an unmarked side road just below the cabins on the Hapuna access road. Look for the dirt-road access to the beach at Waialea Bay, 0.5 mile along. Locals call this "Beach 69" because the turnoff comes just before the utility pole with that number.

Back on Route 19, the vegetation picks up near the Kawaihae junction. Most people stay on Route 19 as it climbs inland along the south slopes of the Kohala Mountains to Waimea; instead, turn left to continue along the Kohala coast on Route 270. The North Kohala peninsula is the oldest part of the Big Island geologically and harbors many of the island's most beautiful and historic spots. Just below the junction, turn left again into ***Puuokohola Heiau National Historical Site*** (882–7218). Kamehameha I built this last great monument to the gods of Old Hawaii atop Puu o Kohola ("the hill of the whale") in response to a prophecy. A famous Kaua`i *kahuna* had predicted that if Kamehameha built this temple to honor his family war god, Kukailimoku, he would conquer the islands, a feat never before achieved.

Kamehameha's rivals joined forces in 1790 to try to stop the temple's completion, but their attacks failed. That same year, Pele's violent eruption destroyed an army belonging to Keoua, Kamehameha's main opposition on the Big Island, showing which side the gods favored. By 1791, the temple had been completed, and Kamehameha invited Keoua to the dedication ceremony as guest of honor. Apparently, Keoua knew his fate but came anyway. As he stepped ashore, he and his companions were struck with spears and carried to the temple as the first sacrifices. The prophecy began to be fulfilled. With the death of his rival, Kamehameha reigned supreme on his home island and proceeded to conquer the others. By 1810, Kamehameha had become the first ruler of a unified Hawaiian kingdom.

Stop first at the visitors center to receive an orientation to the park grounds and view Herb Kane's depiction of Keoua's fateful arrival. In addition to Kamehameha's temple, two older *heiau* occupy the park grounds. ***Mailekini Heiau*** sits in ruins midway down the slope. This temple was converted into a fort and mounted with cannons by John Young, a British sailor who became Kamehameha's confidant. ***Haleoka-puni Heiau,*** dedicated to the shark gods, once rested on a reef below the hill. The park is open daily 7:30 A.M. to 4:00 P.M.

Nearby Kawaihae Harbor has heavy industrial overtones complete with cattle loading docks, an oil refinery, and a chemical plant. Across the highway from the harbor, the ***Blue Dolphin Restaurant*** (882– 7771) serves a tasty menu of local favorites, including Hawaiian plates for moderate prices. Crowds turn up for the live music on Thursday, Friday, and Saturday nights. Another good bet for lunch or dinner in South Kohala is ***Roussels*** (883–9644) in Waikoloa Village (off Waikoloa Road, 8 miles south on Highway 19 from Kawaihae). This New Orleans trans-plant serves all your Creole and Cajun favorites daily from 11:00 A.M. to 2:30 P.M. and Tuesday–Saturday 5:00–8:30 P.M. Expensive.

Route 270, the Akoni Pule Highway, turns uphill immediately after the restaurant and heads north above the coast.

At the 14-mile marker, explore the shadows of the past that haunt ***Lapakahi State Historical Park*** (882–6207). The rocky remains of an ancient fishing village spread over several acres along the sea. Scattered among this dry, seemingly inhospitable scrubland are all the essentials needed to sustain life. Pick up a pamphlet at the entrance if no ranger is available to guide you. Marked stations along the way point out the architectural plan of the village as well as the native trees and plants used by its inhabitants. A now-brackish well used to provide drinking water. Selected rocks could serve as salt pans, lamps, or even fishing shrines. Lapakahi, like every community, had its recreation area. Here you are invited to try your hand at Hawaiian games like *o`o ihe* (spear throwing) or *ulu maika,* a version of bowling that requires you to roll stone disks between wooden stakes.

Although a few upland fields were tended, the ocean was the focus of village life. Koai`e Cove provided a safe landing for canoes. Fishers congregated on the low bluffs overlooking the sea, mending nets or playing *konane,* but always keeping a watchful eye for signs of fish. Displays show some of the common fishing tools and techniques, like the lift nets used to lure the timid *opelu.* Lapakahi's rich marine life is now protected by conservation statutes. During the calm summer months, the waters offshore offer first-rate snorkeling. Look for whales during winter. Open daily between 8:00 A.M. and 4:00 P.M.

As you continue north and begin to round the point to the island's windward side, the landscape rapidly becomes greener and more shapely. To visit a pair of sites pivotal in Hawaiian history, turn seaward at the 20-mile point, proceed 2 miles to Upolu Airstrip, and follow a dirt road back along the coast for 1.6 miles and then a few hundred yards uphill to ***Mookini Heiau.*** Oral histories date this massive temple to as early as the fifth century, making it one of the oldest and most important in the islands. A human chain is said to have carried the stones from Pololu Valley overnight to build the temple's 30-foot-high walls in an irregular parallelogram covering a quarter-acre. If a stone was dropped, it was left where it lay; a trail of scattered stones taken from Pololu can still be found en route. With the arrival of the high priest Paao from Tahiti in the twelfth century, the site became one of the first *luakini heiau,* where human sacrifices were offered to the new, bloodthirsty god that Paao brought with him, Ku Waha Ilo ("Ku of the maggot mouth").

Walk around to the western entrance, where green lichen tints these leeward walls. Outside the temple, an authentic grass *hale* rests on a stone foundation. Imagine similar structures standing amid the patchwork of stone walls and platforms of the temple interior. *Kahuna nui* Leimomi Mookini Lum, a direct descendant of the Mookini line of high priests, lifted the *kapu* against commoners a decade ago, so feel free to go inside. The main scalloped altar stood at the rear left, flanked by prayer houses.

Continue along the coast another half-mile to the ***birthplace of Kamehameha the Great*** at Kokoiki. On a stormy night, sheltered within these concentric walls on a remote windswept plain, the high chieftess Kekuiapoiwa gave birth to the child who would be named "the Lonely One." As Kamehameha's political fortunes rose, the legends surrounding his childhood multiplied. Under missionary influence, two have assumed Christlike parallels. Accounts of a strange light in the heavens on the night of his birth have tempted astronomers to fix the date at 1758, when Halley's Comet returned to view. Another story relates a prophecy that the newborn child would grow to become "a slayer of chiefs." Hearing this, Alapai, the ruling chief, supposedly played Herod, ordering the infant to be put to death. Kamehameha spent a lonely childhood in hiding. Initiated into the worship of Ku at Mookini, the young warrior became the war god's most dedicated follower. Maui, whose southern face looms directly offshore, would be the first island Kamehameha conquered.

A mile farther east on Route 270 brings you to Hawi, the largest town in North Kohala, and the junction with Route 250, the mountain road. By now you have rounded the point, and the landscape has become lushly tropical.

Hawi itself has an interesting collection of Western storefronts, some gentrified by tourist dollars, others left unvarnished. The ***Bamboo Inn*** (889–5555) occupies a cavernous plantation-era building in the center of town that began life as a hotel, was converted to a grocery store, and has ended up somewhere between the two as a restaurant-cum-gallery. Definitely the culinary hotspot of North Kohala, the inn serves fresh island cuisine with Pacific Rim accents as well as a famous passion-fruit margarita. The Hawaiian nostalgia decor combines colorful artwork with old Hawaii kitsch, such as Matson menu covers from the 1950s (on the walls). The oversized wicker chairs come from the old Moana, Waikiki's first hotel. (Yes, there is bamboo here as well). On weekends, live music plays in the evening and the wait staff has been known to dance an impromptu hula when the spirit moves them. Open Tuesday–Sunday 11:30 A.M. to 2:30 P.M., Tuesday–Saturday 6:00–8:30 P.M. Prices verge on investment-caliber; however, half-portions are available.

For lodging in town, the ***Kohala Village Inn*** (889–0419) offers basic rooms with bath in a venerable motel from $55 and up. Even better value can be had up the road at ***Kohala's Guest House*** (889–5606; home1.gte.net/svendsen). These modern, comfortably equipped rental units are within walking distance of Keokea Beach Park. Prices range from $49 for a master bedroom to a mere $125 for a three-bedroom apartment.

Hawi is also headquarters for the ***Kohala Mountain Kayak Cruise*** (889–6922; 877–449–6922), one of the island's most unique adventures. Like most sugar-growing areas, the North Kohala plantations needed a constant flow of water to irrigate their thirsty crops. In 1906 one of them built the Kohala Ditch, a 23-mile miracle of engineering, whose fifty-seven tunnels bored through 16 miles of solid rock to reach the rainy valleys of Kohala's windward slopes. For children in the plantation camps of North Kohala, "fluming the ditch" proved an irresistible lure. Despite the penalties for trespassing, the bravest kids would head for the hills, clutching improvised flotation devices for an exuberant ride down the waterway. When the sugar plantations closed in Kohala, the ditch fell into disrepair. However, Mountain Kayak has restored a section of the ditch and now offers guided flume rides using inflatable five-person kayaks. The 3-mile descent through upland rain forest offers adventurous travelers a fascinating and authentic journey into plantation nostalgia. Although the water flow varies with rainfall, it's a fairly gentle trip, but you do pass through a number of long dark tunnels. As you travel, the guides (all of them local) point out various natural features along the way and relate plantation stories from their childhood. They also describe the almost inhuman conditions in which original (mostly Japanese) ditch workers toiled; at $1.00 a day their labor was cheaper than using machines. Counting transport to and from the ditch, the tour takes about three hours. It's offered twice daily, costs $85, and requires advance reservation. The company also offers rain forest "safari" tours in a hummer Tuesday–Saturday that include a swim in a waterfall pool; $95.

Two miles past Hawi comes Kapaau, with another row of plantation storefronts and galleries. Every tourist who wanders into town stops for the obligatory snapshot of the ***King Kamehameha Statue.*** This is the original casting of the statue that stands in Honolulu and Hilo. A plaque on a rock near the statue commemorates Hawaii's version of *Saving Private Ryan,* the World War II rescue of the "Lost Battalion" trapped behind German lines in Italy. Japanese-American soldiers, recruited primarily from Hawaii (at a time when their kinsmen were imprisoned in concentration camps on the West Coast), fought heroically in the 100/442nd Battalion to liberate the trapped Texan unit. Eight hundred Japanese-Americans perished to save 221 Texans.

While here, be sure to peruse the bulletin boards outside the old courthouse building behind the statue (now converted into a senior citizen center). The billboards contain fascinating snippets and photographs revealing area history with further displays inside. Seniors operate an information table weekdays from 9:00 A.M. to 3:00 P.M. to dispense travel tips and "talk story" about bygone days.

A 0.5 mile east from Kapaau, just before the 24-mile marker, turn uphill at the sign for Bond Historic District. The palm-lined drive passes through macadamia orchards. On the right look for the buildings of the ***Bond Family Homestead*** (889–0615). Arriving in 1841 to take over North Kohala's mission, the Reverend Elias Bond dominated the area's history in his time. Besides building churches and schools and practicing medicine for the mission, he founded a sugar company and served in a variety of government roles. The Bond family home is currently being restored, but visitors are welcome to wander the compound and view the buildings from the outside so long as they first check in at the office. In addition to the original 1841 home, built from stone and wood with whitewashed stucco walls and corrugated tin roof, Father Bond built separate quarters for his son, Dr. Bond, where the latter ran a clinic. As the only doctor for miles, Dr. Bond's services were often in demand. A horse was kept at the ready in a special stall for emergencies that a sign labels as "Kohala's first ambulance." When Dr. Bond eventually tried to retire, his patients did not stop coming. One day, the good doctor simply walked away from it all, boarding a ship in Hilo, never to return. The Bond home has remained uninhabited since, with the original furnishings intact, just as he left them. A nonprofit foundation backed by a private philanthropist is overseeing its restoration as well as managing the surrounding property. Be sure to walk behind the buildings, to enjoy the extensive gardens that include a lily pond and citrus orchard, as well as all manner of tropical fruit.

Continue up the road to ***Kalahikiola*** ("the day salvation comes") ***Church***, a somewhat squat stone structure with a square wooden steeple. Father Bond rallied his flock to build the first meetinghouse here. It took three years of toil, hauling timber sawed by hand across the mountains. The church lasted only four years until a storm blew it down. (The carpenter's helper had forgotten to put pins in the tie beams.) Father Bond was not fazed. He decided to build its replacement in stone. Men carried boulders from neighboring gulches on their backs, lime came from coral harvested underwater, and sand was brought in calabashes from Kawaihae. Two years later, the community had built its spiritual home. The church is still used for Sunday services, which are the only opportunity to view the interior. Past the church, the (often muddy) road continues to the ***Kohala Girls' School,*** the final cluster of buildings within the district. Operating from 1874 until 1955 as a boarding facility, the school primarily taught Christianity and homemaking.

About a mile farther along the highway, the road winds around a gulch.

On the far side of the bridge, look for a small boulder on the side of road. Kamehameha supposedly carried this rock up from the coast to prove his strength. It has remained here ever since. Just around the bend is the ***Tong Wo Society*** building above the road, fronted by a tiny cemetery plot. The building served as a community center/dining hall for Chinese immigrants from 1886 to 1948. At its peak, it fed 2,000 Chinese men daily. A temple altar remains intact; however, the gambling/opium den in back has entirely rotted away. Draw your own moral conclusions. The building is usually open on Sunday. The ***Wo On*** general store next door now houses a gallery.

Two highway turns farther you reach the turnoff to ***Keokea Beach Park.*** The road descends past another Buddhist cemetery, then curves into the gulch of Niuli Stream. The beach park at the bottom enjoys a picturesque setting amid rugged coastal bluffs. A boulder breakwater guards a small, sandy swimming hole.

The final 1.5 miles of Route 270 treat you to spectacular countryside as it winds around lush hillsides overlooking the sea. Trees and meadows alternate in harmonious proportion until all of a sudden your scenery gauge blows off the chart as the sheer cliffs of the east Kohala Coast confront you straight ahead. Dotted with islands and silhouetted ridge upon ridge, this unpopulated and almost inaccessible terrain stretches for more than 11 miles. The end of the road overlooks ***Pololu Valley,*** the first in a chain of remote valleys that corrugate this coastline. Pololu's taro fields used to yield productive harvests until the Kohala Ditch diverted most of the valley's water supply to leeward sugar fields. Today the valley lies deserted, its taro terraces overgrown by vegetation. A steep 20-minute hike from the lookout takes you to the wide, flat valley floor. The black-sand beach here is *not* recommended for swimming. For nonhikers Hawaii Forest & Trail (331–8505; 800–464–1993) offers three-hour tours on muleback; $95.

Make your return along Route 250, the mountain road, for a scenic counterpoint to the coastal route's historic interest. Climbing swiftly above Hawi, the road curves along the spine of the Kohala Mountains to descend upon Waimea 20 miles south. You wind around knobby hillocks whose timeworn form and lush coating belie their dimpled volcanic tops. Along the way, herds of multicolored cattle and sheep fatten themselves on the rolling green hillsides. Lines of evergreens planted as windbreaks provide a darker contrast to the lime green pastures. It's hard to imagine these hills were covered with sandalwood forest until two centuries ago, when wholesale logging of this fragrant wood left the hills barren. As you climb to nearly 4,000 feet, the views over the South

Kohala coastline and central tableland grow ever more impressive. The road then begins a swift descent from its aerielike perch, dropping 1,000 feet to the already elevated town of Waimea.

Paniolo Country

Surrounded by cattle range in the elevated foothills of Kohala and Mauna Kea, Waimea remains Hawaii's premier *paniolo* town (see map on page 275). *Paniolo* was the Hawaiian pronunciation of "español," the language spoken by early Mexican *vaqueros* brought to help drive the cattle. By extension, the word became the name for island cowboys whose heritage predates their mainland counterparts of the American West by almost four decades. Ranching at Waimea began with John Parker, a young American who jumped ship in 1809 at age nineteen and went to work for King Kamehameha, rounding up wild cattle descended from stock brought by Captain Vancouver two decades earlier. Parker befriended the king and married a royal granddaughter. Combining the land she inherited and the choice cattle stock culled during his prior employment, he started his namesake ranch in 1847—just in time to market beef to the 49ers of the California Gold Rush.

The ranch now covers 225,000 acres and is the largest independently owned ranch in the United States. It produces 10 million pounds of beef annually, one-third of the amount raised in Hawaii and a tenth of the state's consumption. At an elevation of 2,500 feet, Waimea's cool mountain breezes keep things fresh, so bring a sweater.

Coming down from Route 250, you intersect Route 19 just west of Waimea. Backtrack a few hundred yards on the latter from the junction to see the unique and truly eclectic exhibits of ***Kamuela Museum*** (885–4724). The contents of the museum represent a lifetime of collecting by Albert Solomon and his wife, Harriet, a great-great-granddaughter of John Parker. The Solomons built this display house beside Waikoloa Stream just to exhibit their collection.

Many of the intentionally jumbled contents carry labels like "very rare" or "unique in the world." The items come from all over the world, though most relate to Hawaii. They range from old to new: from ancient *kahuna* "love stones," used by witch doctors to create instant romance, to a piece of rope used by astronauts. They include both the exotic and the mundane: Stone "money" used on Yap Atoll rests beside an 1897 hand-cranked sausage-stuffing machine from St. Louis. Much of the contents "acquired" from Iolani Palace by the 1893 revolutionaries has ended up in this museum. Also here you will spot *ti*-leaf slippers worn by Franklin Delano Roosevelt, a captured Nazi flag, a set of hand-painted ruby crystal goblets from Italy's famous Murano glass works, an ostrich-feather fan belonging to Queen Emma, and two stuffed bears. Detailed explanations accompanying the exhibits convey an encyclopedic wealth of knowledge. Stay long and grow wise. Open daily 8:00 A.M. to 5:00 P.M. Admission $5.00.

Inside town itself, Route 19 makes another junction with Route 190, the inland road from which it split in Kailua. Those with an interest in military history should head south on 190 to view the ***Camp Tarawa Monument*** on the outskirts of town. Twenty-thousand marines were stationed here during World War II at what became the largest marine training facilty in the Pacific. The green knolls of Parker Ranch served as stand-ins for Pacific atolls to practice a new kind of amphibious warfare that would lead these troops on their tortuous path to Iwo Jima.

To learn more about Parker Ranch, visit the ranch ***visitors center*** (885–7655) at the rear of the Parker Ranch Shopping Center just across the main intersection. Exhibits here portray the intimate links between the history of the ranch and the history of Hawaii over 144 years. The center is open daily 9:00 A.M. to 5:00 P.M. Admission is $5.00. You can also sign up for a covered wagon ride through the ranch, offered hourly Tuesday–Saturday from 10:00 A.M. to 2:00 P.M. Cost $15.

Even if you skip the visitors center and wagon ride, don't miss the historic homes at ***Puu o Pelu*** ("folding hills") (885–5433). Head 0.5 mile south on Route 190 and turn up the tree-lined drive to the main estate. "Colonel" Samuel Parker built his "Hawaiian Victorian" residence here away from the family homestead so he could entertain in accustomed luxury such guests as King Kalakaua. (Kamuela, the Hawaiian translation of Samuel, is Waimea's alternate name.) Richard Smart, the ranch's sixth-generation owner who died in 1992, renovated the ranch house with European flourishes. French doors open onto a formal rose garden overlooking a lake. Smart also amassed an impressive art collection. Works by Degas, Renoir, and Pissarro, among others, crowd the walls of the house. To complete the illusion of a grand chateau, a tape of European songs sung in three Romance languages by Richard Smart himself (a Broadway wannabe) plays constantly.

Next door stands a replica of the original Parker residence, ***Mana Hale.*** The interior and contents come from the actual family homestead, Mana Hale, in the Kohala uplands and are fashioned almost entirely from native

Trivia

Mauna Loa mountain is the largest volcano in the world. Its surface area covers almost half the island, and its massive weight—more than the entire Sierra Nevada range—creates a depression in the ocean floor more than five miles deep. What's more, it's still growing!

koa wood. The wooden saltbox design evokes memories of John Parker's childhood in Massachusetts. Photos and other memorabilia recount Parker family history for those who missed the visitors center. You can visit both historic homes Tuesday–Saturday between 10:00 A.M. and 5:00 P.M. for a combined admission of $8.50.

If historic homes and wagon rides sound too tame for your cowboy soul, a number of Waimea ranches will put you back in the saddle for some unique horseback riding. Native Hawaiian owned and operated, ***Dahana Ranch*** (885–0057) lets guests ride across open range on the slopes of Mauna Kea. Unlike the usual nose-to-tail trail-rides offered elsewhere, experienced riders can trot, canter, and even take part in a cattle drive on this working ranch; novices are also welcome. Prices range from $55 for a one-and-a-half hour ride to $100 for the two-hour cattle drive. ***Paniolo Riding Adventures*** (889–5354) also offers adventurous "off-trail" riding in the panoramic Kohala Mountains at similar prices.

As one might imagine, Waimea has no shortage of steakhouses. The ***Koa House*** (885–2088), in the Waimea Shopping Center, makes a fine choice for cowpokes wielding a fork instead of lasso with plenty of Hawaii's native Koa wood splashed around the interior. Open daily 11:30 A.M. to 2:30 P.M., 5:00–9:00 P.M. Expensive. But Waimea doesn't cater to just cowboys anymore. Many of the observatories atop Mauna Kea have their ground headquarters here. Perhaps due to this international clientele, the town's dining options improve every year. A steady exodus of accomplished chefs have departed the luxury hotels of South Kohala to open their own establishments here in Waimea. Most of them congregate west of the town center on Highway 19 (Kawaihae Road) and serve moderately priced lunches, with dinners in the expensive range.

First to arrive was ***Edelweiss*** (885–6800). Owner-chef Hans Peter Hage went from being a butcher in the Black Forest to a chef at the ultraluxurious Mauna Kea Resort; he now conjures up the hearty *hofsbrau* fare of his native Bavaria. Uncut *ohia* posts, silver oak paneling, and a koa bar create a sylvan atmosphere. Open Tuesday–Saturday 11:30 A.M. to 1:30 P.M. and 5:00–8:30 P.M. Across the street from Edelweiss in the Opelu Plaza, ***Merriman's*** (885–6822) boasts the culinary wizardry of an ex–Mauna Lani chef. Peter Merriman bases his Pacific Rim concoctions around novel produce grown on the Big Island. Some grumble that the kitchen quality has slipped now that Merriman's has expanded to Maui. However, it remains top dog in town, and some would say on the island. Potted palms and parasols seem to sprout from the floral carpet interior in an exuberance of tropical colors. Moderately-priced lunches served Monday–Friday 11:30 A.M.–1:30 P.M.; dinners nightly 5:30–9:00 P.M. are investment caliber.

Also at Opelu Plaza, ***Aioli Cafe*** (885–6325) belies its bare-bones decor (guests are encouraged to decorate the walls with their own doodles) by producing surprisingly sophisticated meals, often featuring unusual meats from ostrich to venison. Moderate prices. Open Tuesday 11:00 A.M. to 4:00 P.M., Wednesday–Thursday until 8:00 P.M., Friday, Saturday until 9:00 P.M. and Sunday 8:00 A.M. to 2:00 P.M. Even more down-home is local favorite ***Hawaiian Style Cafe*** (885–4295), on the other side of Merriman's. The naugahyde-backed booths and formica counters recall diners of yore. Open for breakfast/lunch Monday–Friday 6:00 A.M. to 1:00 P.M., Sunday 7:30 A.M. to noon, and for dinner Wednesday–Saturday 4:00–8:00 P.M. Come on Friday to try authentic Hawaiian food. Just up the road from Opelu in the historic Chock In ranch store, newcomer ***Daniel Thiebault*** (887–2200) has won fans by offering a French-accented Pacific Rim menu at prices slightly lower than Merriman's. Note the safe at the entrance; no one knows what's in it, as the original Chock family forgot the combination. Open nightly 4:30–9:30 P.M.

Another recommended breakfast and lunch spot back in the town center is ***Maha's Cafe*** (885–6822), located in the 1852 Spencer House, a one-time courthouse and hotel, in the Waimea Shopping Center. The owner/chef, Harriet-Ann "Maha" Schutte, is another Mauna Lani refugee. From a closet-size kitchen, she turns out an impressive menu relying on fresh, local produce and fish served with a gourmet touch. The Koa cabinet inside is original to the house. Open daily, except Tuesday, 8:00 A.M. to 4:00 P.M. Moderate.

Waimea also has an equally fine array of shops and galleries to browse. Anyone with an interest in Hawaiiana collectibles should pay a visit to ***Mauna Kea Gallery*** (877–2244; 969–HULA). Owner Mark Blackburn literally wrote the book on the subject (it's on sale there). Everything in the store predates 1960. The offerings range from 1950s kitsch such as dancing hula dolls to vintage aloha shirts, Matson menu covers, and rare books, photos, and prints. Display cases also house museum-quality artifacts such as *lei palaao,* made from human hair. Open daily 10:00 A.M. to 5:00 P.M. Also worth checking out is the ***Gallery of Great Things*** (885–7706), in nearby Parker Square. You will find works by local artists, such as Marian Berger's portraits of rare native birds as well as authentic replicas and genuine artifacts from Hawaii and other Pacific Rim cultures. Open Monday–Saturday 9:00 A.M.–5:30 P.M., Sunday 10:00 A.M.–4:00 P.M. ***Cook's Discoveries*** (885–3633), located at the third traffic light as you approach the Hilo end of town, is a treasure house of contemporary Hawaiian arts and craftwork, from museum-caliber replicas of Hawaiian shark-tooth weapons to novelty items such as Hawaiian quilt potholders as well as Hawaiian clothing and food items. Open Monday–Saturday 10:00 A.M. to 6:00 P.M., Sunday 10:00 A.M. to 4:00 P.M. Near the Shell station at the first traffic light is ***Upcountry Connection*** (885–0623), one of the few places where artist-historian Herb Kane exhibits his paintings.

With all Waimea has to offer, you may want to stay overnight. The newly opened ***Jacaranda Inn*** (885–8813; www.thejacarandainn.com) offers eight semi-private suites on an 1897 ranch estate built by a Parker Ranch manager and later used by Nelson Rockefeller to entertain dignitaries from Henry Kissinger to Jackie Kennedy. Exquisitely decorated in styles varying from whimsical South American to Victorian elegance, many have oriental rugs, old-fashioned bedposts, Tiffany lamps, and palatial bathrooms. Each suite has its own character, but all exude an intimate luxury that bespeaks wealth and good taste. The rooms are spread among several wings, separated by garden courtyards. The eleven-acre grounds feature everything from begonias to birds of paradise—and, of course, jacaranda. From the gazebo in back, a trail leads to a swimming hole and waterfall. The inn offers two different rate plans, depending on the kind of breakfast and frequency of maid service you choose. Prices start at $149, with a three-day minimum.

For those who prefer to stay outside of town, Charlie and Barbara Campbell built their original ***Waimea Garden Cottage*** (885–4550, 800–262– 9912; P.O. Box 563, Kamuela 96743) as a honeymoon retreat for their daughter. The cottage is built around a washroom from an old Hawaiian homestead. Vintage farming tools and other antiques add a rustic note to the elegant eucalyptus floors, wainscoting, and French doors; a newer addition also boasts a fireplace. Guests are encouraged to feed the poultry and collect fresh eggs for breakfast, which they can prepare in a fully equipped kitchen. A stream, which you can follow to a natural waterfall pool, flows outside the cottage. The Campbells rent the cottage's two separate units, each with private bath, for $135 and $150. They require a three-day minimum stay. If this doesn't work for you, Barbara Campbell also operates an upscale booking agency, Hawaii's Best B&Bs. Although she lists statewide, many of her best finds are scattered around the Waimea area.

Before leaving Waimea, pause at "Church Row" on the east side of town. ***Imiola*** ("seeking life") ***Church,*** the oldest house of worship on the strip, dates to 1838 (rebuilt in 1857). The church has a beautiful koa interior. Lorenzo Lyons, one of the first Waimea missionaries, worked here until 1886, translating hymns into Hawaiian. Music was arguably the most beloved gift brought by the missionaries, as Hawaiian *mele* (chants) previously had consisted of monotonic rhythms.

Hamakua and Waipio

From Church Row, Route 19 continues east toward the lush Hamakua Coast. Waimea stands at something of a climactic fault line. Notice how much greener things are here than on the other side of town. About 2 miles out from the town center, just past the 54-mile marker, a left turn onto White Road leads to the trailhead for a forty-minute hike overlooking the spectacular rear wall of Waipio Valley. The trail can be treacherous when wet. A little bit farther along the highway, near the 52-mile point, the old Mamalahoa Highway offers a pleasant detour along a deserted mountain road. Paralleling the highway route east, the road rolls across misty hills and then descends through tall forest that segues into more recent commercial plantings of eucalyptus for paper mulch. The two roads meet up at ***Tex's,*** famous for its *malasadas* (Portuguese donuts). A half mile below you lies Honokaa, the main town of the Hamakua Coast.

Route 240 passes through the center of town as Mamane Street before heading north up the coast to Waipio Valley. At the entrance to town, next to the library, the three-legged ***Katsu Goto Monument*** recalls the grisly hanging of a Japanese labor activist in 1889. As you reach the main commercial strip just ahead, all sorts of interesting shops clamor for your attention. ***Seconds to Go*** (775–9212) and ***Honokaa Trading Company*** (775–0808) are two "used goods" stores crammed full of antiques. ***Honokaa Market Place*** (775–8255) also has a nice mix of new and old handicrafts. You can check out Manila's latest at the ***Filipino Store*** opposite the vintage People's Theater. Farther down, the Rice family runs a bizarre menagerie of shops full of "museum replicas," which range from tourist tacky to authentic Hawaiiana. The town even has a shirtmaker whose services you can hire and a barbershop whose 80-year-old proprietor is still apologizing for having to raise her haircut price to $5.00. Most of these stores operate on irregular hours, so take a stroll and stop wherever you fancy.

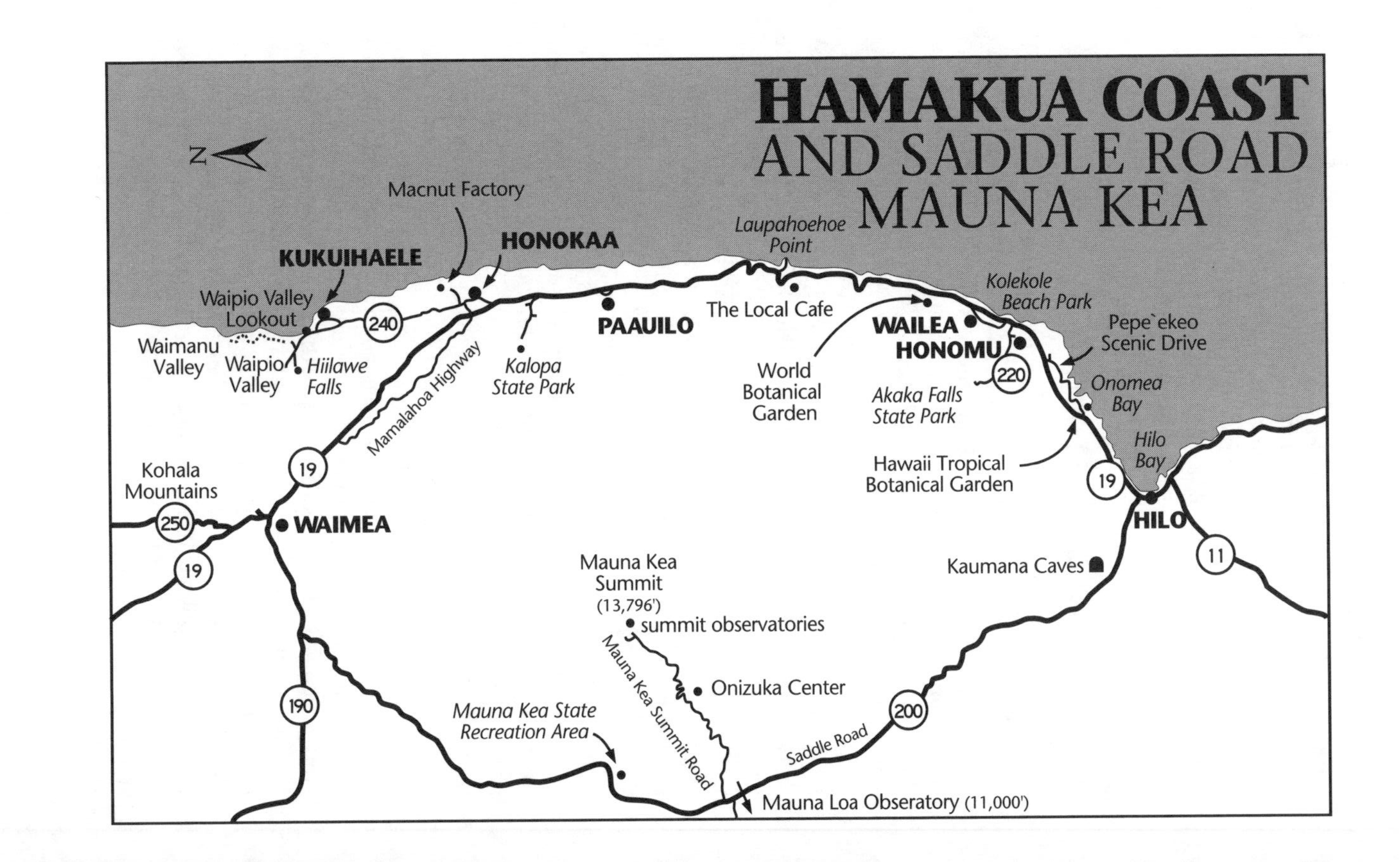
HAMAKUA COAST
AND SADDLE ROAD
MAUNA KEA
N
Macnut Factory
HONOKAA
KUKUIHAELE
Waipio Valley Lookout
240
Waimanu Valley
Waipio Valley
Hiilawe Falls
Mamalahoa Highway
Kalopa State Park
PAAUILO
Laupahoehoe Point
The Local Cafe
Kolekole Beach Park
WAILEA
HONOMU
World Botanical Garden
Pepe`ekeo Scenic Drive
220
Akaka Falls State Park
Onomea Bay
Hilo Bay
Hawaii Tropical Botanical Garden
19
HILO
11
Kohala Mountains
250
19
WAIMEA
Kaumana Caves
Mauna Kea Summit
(13,796')
summit observatories
Mauna Kea Summit Road
Onizuka Center
190
Mauna Kea State Recreation Area
200
Saddle Road
Mauna Loa Obseratory (11,000')

Social activity in town seems to converge on ***Hotel Honokaa Club*** (775–0678, 800–808–0678; home1.gte.net/honokaac), which occupies a rambling plantation building between the antiques shops. The hotel offers two classes of rooms. Beds in the "hostel" section rent from $15–$35, with a $5 rental fee for linen. Standard rooms with private bath go for $45–$65. These include a continental breakfast. Dining options in Hono Kaa are limited; you may want to drive to Waimea. ***Cafe Il Mondo*** (775–7711), near the hotel, bakes a decent *calzone*. Open daily Monday–Saturday 10:30 A.M. to 8:30 P.M. The best meal in town is probably ***Tex's*** (775–0598) fresh Ahi sandwich, back up on the highway. They also serve a range of local ethnic fare. Open daily 6:00 A.M. to 8:30 P.M.

Near the north edge of town, a sign points downhill from the main highway to what was once a macadamia nut factory. Now it is just a big giftshop where glass blowing is demonstrated, although plans call for tours of the factory innards down the road.

On the road to the factory lies ***Kamaaina Woods*** (775–7722). Bill Keb and his nephews make beautiful wooden bowls from native woods on a lathe in the back of this former Hamakua Soda Works factory. Like vintner Paul Masson, these crafters boast they will sell no bowl before its time; they wait a year or more after the first turning to allow the wood to dry out before they apply the final touches to guard against warping or defects. A large showroom exhibits the bowls as well as other items that are part of Bill Keb's private collection. Open Monday–Saturday 9:00 A.M. to 5:00 P.M.

Back on the main raod, just past the factory turnoff, stop for a moment at the "heritage center." It consists of little more than a brochure rack and a handful of photos occupying the bay of a former gas station, but the real draw is a gorgeous mural depicting a Hawaiian family in Waipio of old.

Continue north on Route 240 toward Waipio. Two miles out of Honokaa, ***Waipio Wayside B&B Inn*** (775–0275, 800–833–8849, www.waipiowayside.com; wayside@ilhawaii.net) hides behind a white picket fence. Jackie Horne rents five rooms in this 1936 sugar plantation manager's home, each individually decorated, many with antique furnishings. A frustrated would-be restaurateur, Jackie works off her culinary energies in the lavish full breakfasts she serves along with helpful travel tips. She also keeps a large selection of teas perfect for sipping in the garden gazebo out back. Double rooms start at $95 and come with extra amenities more common to a luxury hotel.

Six miles farther, take the turnoff to loop past the aging houses and shops of Kukuihaele, the last settlement topside of Waipio Valley. Kukuihaele means "traveling light," a reference to the ghostly procession of night marchers who supposedly pass by on their way into Waipio Valley.

Continue on to the ***Waipio Valley Lookout*** at the end of the highway and perched directly above the valley rim. Your eyes struggle to digest the scope of the vision before you. Almost a mile wide, the valley floor appears virtually flat, flanked on all sides by cliffs rising vertically from 1,000 to 3,000 feet. The characteristic square finish of Waipio's far wall is broken by a low, jutting peninsula near the base of which a constant waterfall tumbles. Bands of vibrant color flare as your gaze wanders. The blue Pacific presses inward on the bay, separated by a white ribbon of surf from the black-sand beach at the valley mouth. Dark stands of ironwood trees followed by lighter green fields of grass provide the next swaths of color. Taro fields form a patchwork inland, and a meandering river in the center of the valley drains these wetlands into the mouth of the bay. Beyond the taro plots, a tangled mass of jungle defies human cultivation.

A number of vacation rentals perched on the valley rim offer lodging with a similar view to the lookout. Roger Lasko's ***Waipio Ridge Vacation Rental*** (775–0603; vacationspot.com) has the best view of the valley. His simply furnished one-bedroom cottage is not for those with a fear of heights; it practically levitates above the valley edge and rents for $75. Lasko also offers lodging in a 24-foot airstream trailer with futon parked below the cottage. He's added an outdoor deck and shower. Yours for $65. ($10 surcharge on both for single night.) Jim Hunt's ***Hamakua Hideaway*** (775–7425) sits farther out on the rim, along a streambank, with views of the Kohala cliffline as well as part of the valley. It rents for $95. Richard Mastronado's ***Cliff House*** (775–0005, 800–492–4746; www.cliffhousehawaii.com), a snazzy modern two-bedroom duplex surrounded by pastureland overlooking the ocean, goes for $150.

Another way to see more of the valley from "topside" is to take a rim tour, along privately owned former sugar land. You have a choice of tours on foot (775–0372); on horseback (775–1007); by four-wheel (775–1122); or by ATV (775–1701) and, if it's been raining, you will enjoy staggering views of waterfalls along the way—you can even arrange to swim in one of them. Prices range from $75–$150.

But you should not be content only to view Waipio from on high. The valley floor holds many secrets for those with time to explore below. Known as the Valley of Kings, Waipio is the largest and most important valley in Hawaiian history. As many as 30,000 people once farmed this fertile haven, perhaps a quarter of the island's population. Young Umi came here to claim his inheritance from the High Chief Liloa. Gaining custody of the war god, Kukailimoku ("Ku-the-divider-of-lands"), Umi went on to unify the Big Island, which he ruled from this valley. Also in Waipio, Umi's descendant, Kamehameha, inherited control of the fearsome deity from his uncle, the ruling chief Kalaniopuu. With the aid of the war god, Kamehameha became ruler of all the islands. In 1791 a great naval clash between Kamehameha and Maui's Kahekili took place offshore. Known as Kepuwahaulaula ("the battle of the red-mouthed guns"), this bloody but inconclusive conflict saw the first widespread use of Western cannons, mounted on canoes.

Arriving as a cruel April Fools' joke, the 1946 tidal wave wiped out many of the farmers who remained in the valley in the modern age. In the 1960s, the Peace Corps used Waipio as a training ground to expose recruits to jungle life. Now only a handful of residents remain, far outnumbered by the wild horses that roam the valley floor. Others come from topside to tend their taro plots and reminisce about old times. If you want to join them, you have several options. A paved road does descend from the lookout to the valley floor, but its 26-percent grade requires four-wheel–drive. To hoof it takes about half an hour and strong knees. Otherwise, the following outfits will take you down and give you a valley tour for a combined price. They have courtesy phones at the lookout, but you'll do better to call in advance. None operate on Sunday.

Waipio Valley Shuttle (775–7121) in Kukuihaele offers four-wheel-drive tours for $35 that last one-and-a-half hours. ***Waipio Wagon Tours*** (775–9518) relies on mule power for its tours that cost $40. Sheri Hannum's ***Waipio Naalapa*** (775–0419) gives trail rides that last two-and-a-half hours for $75. These latter two shuttle you down to the valley where their Waipio-based operations begin.

For those hiking in on their own, there's plenty to see; but be aware that much of the valley remains private property. Begin by heading toward the beach, the largest black-sand strand on the island. Swimming is not recommended, but you can sometimes watch surfers offshore. Camping here is unofficially tolerated. If you do camp, pick your spot with care. Not only do night marchers patrol the valley, but a *lua milu* (a portal to the next world) reputedly opens at a secret spot along the beach. Other legendary denizens of the valley you might meet include Nenewe, a shark-man, and Pupualenalena, a yellow dog *kupua* (spirit).

From the mouth of the stream, facing back toward the lookout, you'll see Kaluahine Falls dropping 620 feet from the mouth of the valley. Zigzagging above the beach on the other side, a switchback trail climbs the cliffs on Waipio's western wall. Continuing along the uninhabited tableland above and crossing a series of gulches, the 9-mile trail eventually reaches Waimanu Valley, a smaller but wilder version of Waipio. The often muddy hike takes at least six hours and passes a rain shelter midway.

Trivia

Hawaii's longest unbroken waterfall is at Waipio Valley, where the water plunges more than 1,200 feet.

From the beach Waipio Valley stretches almost 5 miles inland. The interlocking Vs of its rear canyons make a stirring sight. To explore Waipio's interior, reverse course and take the main dirt road upstream. On the way, besides taro fields, you pass a commercial lily pond from which lotus flowers and roots are harvested. Farther inland you will find all kinds of tropical fruits and flowers blooming. Wild horses graze along the streambank, coming and going as they please.

Sticking to the left side of the valley leads you to a closed canyon from whose rear wall topples ***Hiilawe Falls.*** Dropping more than 1,200 feet in free fall, the waters of Hiilawe make Hawaii's longest unbroken descent. Sugar irrigation ditches divert some of the water, so usually only one of the twin falls is flowing. The harvest god, Lono, descended a rainbow to find his bride-to-be bathing at the bottom. Travelers attempting a more conventional trek overland should beware of falling rocks. You need to cross two streams to reach the right side of the valley, where the trails extend farther into the interior. After a rain, any number of waterfalls spill from the cliffs.

When and if you manage to tear yourself away from Waipio, backtrack through Honokaa and strike out south on Route 11 down the Hamakua Coast. This was one of the last areas on the island still growing sugar cane into the 1990s. The imprints of King Sugar's rule remain visible in sideroads leading through abandoned cane fields to isolated plantation camps above and below the highway. A series of gulches cuts through the landscape, draining the runoff from Hamakua's moist climate. The gulches contain spectacular rain forest, often bejeweled with sparkling waterfalls. The early plantations used to send cut cane flowing downslope in elaborate flumes.

For a taste of sylvan splendor, turn inland 3 miles south of Honokaa to visit ***Kalopa State Park.*** Follow signs that guide you uphill through 3 miles of pastureland and cane field. The road ends in the tall *ohia* forest of the park where native flora have been making a strong comeback. An easy 0.7-mile nature walk will take you through some excellent examples of endemic foliage. Other more demanding trails beckon adventurous hikers. Four well-maintained cabins each accommodate up to eight people with hot showers and linen, and a communal hall has a fully equipped kitchen and fireplace. You may appreciate the latter at this cool 2,000-foot elevation. This is your chance to enjoy the great outdoors without really roughing it. The cabins rent for $55 each regardless of how many are in your party. To make reservations, call the Hilo office at 974–6200.

About 12 miles farther, near the 28-mile marker, the road winds around a deep gulch. Turn seaward 0.5 mile farther to explore ***Laupahoehoe*** ("leaf of lava") ***Peninsula.*** The road winds 1 mile downhill past an old Jodo Mission temple to the county park on the peninsula. From the point, you can enjoy breathtaking views in both directions along the coast. A small monument in the park commemorates the deaths of nineteen children carried away from the former school grounds here by the 1946 tsunami. Past the peninsula, the highway swoops around another deep gulch to reach the current town of Laupahoehoe. At the junction with the highway, the ***Laupahoehoe Train Museum*** (962–6300) recalls the heritage of the railways that hauled island cane from field to market and linked the isolated plantation camps along this coast long before the first highway was built. The museum displays occupy a former rail employee's home and a few old stock cars gather rust in back. Open daily 9:00 A.M. to 4:30 P.M. Donation. Bread lovers should check out the ***Big Island Bakery*** (962–6955) down the road. It bakes forty-five different kinds of loaves and stone-grinds its own wheat on the premises; open Monday, Tuesday, Thursday, and Friday 10:00 A.M. to 4:00 P.M.

The highway continues to make its way south across several more deep gulches. Hakalau Gulch, at the border of South Hilo District, is still spanned by the original trestle rail bridge. Just before Hakalau Gulch, at the 16-mile marker, a turnoff leads to the royal palm-lined entrance to ***World Botanical Gardens*** (963–5427) at Umauma. The 300-acre grounds remain a work-in-progress, but already there is much to see here from the colorful "rainbow walk" and orchid wall to the children's hedge maze. The scientifically organized phylogenetic garden caters to serious botanists, but nature-lovers of any stripe will savor triple-tiered

Umauma Falls. Open Monday–Saturday 9:00 A.M. to 5:30 P.M. About a mile south of Umauma, turn uphill past the decrepit buildings of Wailea and descend into a wildly tropical gulch where ***Kolekole Beach Park*** abuts an icy-but-swimmable river. A waterfall is right at the base of the elevated highway bridge overhead. Wailea is the somewhat improbable home to ***Akiko's Buddhist B&B*** (963–6422; www.alternative-hawaii.com/akiko). Akiko Masuda was the first person to buy property here in almost forty years when this self-described former hippie/dance teacher purchased the ultimate fixer-upper that she is now gradually transforming into a place of grace and beauty. A former auto garage serves as the zendo, where Sunday yoga classes are held. The wooden floor in the retreat center comes from an Oregon high school's basketball gym. Guests can choose between lodging "Japanese monastery style," in rooms with futons adjacent to the meditation room, or quarters in rooms with conventional beds next door. Early morning meditation sessions are held daily, as well as most evenings, and various alternative retreats are staged throughout the year. The decor everywhere is sparse, and plenty of rough edges remain, but a genuine sense of aloha permeates the walls, and Akiko herself has a delightfully irreverent sense of humor. Rooms with shared bath cost $55. Continue on the same road up on the other side of the gulch to rejoin Route 19.

To see the same stream farther up, turn up Route 220 shortly after Kolekole to get to ***Akaka Falls State Park.*** On the way you will pass through the town of Honomu, worth a casual stroll. Store hours are mostly a lazy "whenevah." The ***Akaka Noodle Factory*** (963–6701) no longer makes its own noodles but still dispenses a tasty bowl of saimin. Browse the display cabinets inside to view an eclectic assortment of plantation-era relics from Manila rope slippers to a hand-cranked soybean mill. The "driftwood" you see above you is actually tree roots that were plowed under the cane fields. You can also enjoy gourmet pizza at the ***Akaka Falls Inn. Glass from the Past*** (963–6422) sells antique bottles and jars that owner David Ackerman digs up from old landfills in the area. The store also has vintage clothing, unique collectibles, and ephemera (just in case you wanted a turn-of-the-century laundry receipt written in Tagalog). At the top of the hill, a string of Buddhist temples and Christian churches congregate in ecumenical harmony.

Turn right to follow Route 220 three miles farther uphill through cane fields to the state park. A 0.75-mile trail loops down around the gulch of upper Kolekole Stream. You first overlook Kahuna Falls, whose beauty gets shown up by the 420-foot unbroken plummet of Akaka Falls farther on. It's mesmerizing to focus on an individual droplet as it descends, seemingly in slow motion. As lovely as these waterfalls are, don't ignore the rest of the park's charm. You pass by prolific growths of bamboo, ferns, orchids, hibiscus, azaleas, gingers, and heliconia. Eden never had greenery so lush.

For those who haven't yet overdosed on scenery, a blue sign 3 miles farther south at Pepeeko designates the scenic detour along the old belt road closer to the ocean. The twisting road leaves the cane fields and macadamia orchards to burrow through 4 miles of tropical jungle with breathtaking views of the coastline. Fruits and flowers litter the road as you cross a series of streams spanned by one-lane bridges.

About 3 miles along, the road overlooks the steep-faced walls of Onomea Bay. The valley bordering the bay belongs to the ***Hawaii Tropical Botanical Garden*** (964–5233). For a closer look, continue around the next bend to the headquarters. A shuttle bus takes passengers down to the valley floor, where you can wander gravel paths through labeled plantings of exotic flowers and towering palms. Flamingos preen themselves and macaws shriek. A lovely waterfall awaits at the back of the narrow gulch, while along the coast, sea stacks (pillarlike rock islands) roil a restless sea. The $15 admission is pricey, but the beauty of the spot is unquestioned. From the end of the scenic drive, it's about 7 miles to Hilo. You will pass some plots of dryland taro, a new, old crop that has taken over former sugar land.

The Saddle Road and Mauna Kea

Crossing the elevated plateau between Mauna Kea and Mauna Loa, the Saddle Road represents the Big Island's last frontier (see map on page 290). Some locals use this mountain "shortcut" to travel between Hilo and Kona, but rental car companies ban the use of the road (more because of its remoteness than its occasional rough edges). The narrow shoulders can be dangerous, however, and the road is often misted-in. Besides desolate moonscapes, the main attraction of the saddle is the Mauna Kea summit road halfway along.

If you just want to see Mauna Kea and return the same way, the more scenic approach is from the Kona/Kohala side. Start early before the clouds roll in. Mamalahoa Highway (Route 190) runs inland between Kailua and Waimea. Six miles south of the latter, take the turnoff to the Saddle Road. The terrain resembles the Kohala Mountain Road as you climb through rolling green pastures and tree-covered knolls. Behind you, Maui's Haleakala becomes the fifth volcano in a panorama of island castles floating in the sky. About six miles along, you will pass Waikii Ranch, where polo is played in the fall. Watch a demolition derby of ponies tear red-soiled streaks in the grass field for a chukker or two of action. Call 322–3880 for schedule. Small admission charge.

The road eventually climbs above the foothills and enters the wide valley of the saddle. Cinder cones dot the open savannah as the road straightens out and the tree cover fades. Looking up at the twin towers on either side of the road, you can see how much larger the smooth, flattened dome of Mauna Loa is than the more vertical, jagged-peaked Mauna Kea. Most of the cinder cones come from the older Mauna Kea, while ribbons of fresh lava run down the slopes of Mauna Loa. The highway begins to cross these flows, changing the landscape to a more barren plain. The live ammo tested at Pahakuloa Military Camp here make this one place to avoid. About 20 miles in, near the 35-mile marker, a turnoff leads to the ***Mauna Kea State Recreation Area.*** Unfortunately, as of press time, the housekeeping cabins here had been closed indefinitely for repairs. Call 974–6200 to see if that's changed.

Seven miles farther, next to the 28-mile marker, the ***Mauna Kea Summit*** Road begins its ascent through open cattle range. Switchbacks become steep as you climb 6 miles to Hale Pohaku at the 9,200-foot level. Astronomers working at the summit observatories inhabit the base camp on this flat plateau, nestled behind a wall of cinder cones. The ***Onizuka Visitor Center*** (961–2180) provides an overview of the summit observatories as well as some general information about Mauna Kea's unique environment. If continuing to the summit, you should spend at least one hour here to acclimatize to the altitude. The center is open daily 9:00 A.M. to 10:00 P.M. It also leads summit tours on weekends starting at 1:00 P.M. (You must provide your own four-wheel-drive transport. Children under sixteen not allowed.) You can also do your own astronomical observations nightly at the center using its 11- and 14-inch telescopes. Note the rare silversword plants growing outside. Found only on the top of Hawaii's three tallest volcanos, the plants here on Mauna Kea have to be hand-pollinated by biologists with a paintbrush because the insect that used to serve that function is now extinct.

The remaining 8 miles to the summit require four-wheel drive. Harper's (969–1478) rents these in both Hilo and Kona for $100 to $110. If you'd rather someone else do the driving, several companies offer summit tours; most include evening stargazing. See the hiking companies in the chapter intro for a partial list. The first part of the road traverses unpaved cinders, and the grade is very steep. Be prepared for summit weather conditions that can change rapidly, with summer blizzards not unheard of. Call 974–4203 for an updated forecast. You can also expect your car's engine to labor somewhat in the thin air. (Be sure to loosen your gas cap to prevent vapor lock.) WARNING: Children, pregnant women, and those with respiratory ailments may suffer harm from the lack of oxygen on the summit. On the way up, you pass from the space age to the Stone Age in less than a mile. An important adze quarry used by the ancient Hawaiians lies above "Moon Valley," where the *Apollo* astronauts test-drove their lunar lander. One of the cinder cones near the quarry conceals Lake Waiau, an alpine pool fed by melted runoff from the layer of permafrost that lies hidden beneath cinder topsoil. A 0.5-mile trail to get to the lake begins at the last switchback before the summit.

The actual summit consists of a cluster of red cinder hills topped with the white-and-silver domes of the world's most powerful "eyes to the sky." Mauna Kea's elevation and isolation combine to create unbeatable viewing conditions at night. While scientists on neighboring Kilauea and Mauna Loa probe the inner secrets of the earth, these lonely outposts peer across time and space, scanning the heavens for clues to the mysteries of the universe. Take the right fork to the University of Hawaii's 88-inch telescope on top of the highest peak. This and Keck I are the only observatories that permit visitors inside to watch from a viewing gallery on weekdays. Mauna Kea's most powerful telescopes, the Keck I and II, stand on nearby hills. Their unique honeycomb patterns of hexagonal mirrors function as a single unit, providing unprecedented light-gathering power.

Trivia

If viewed from its base on the ocean floor, 13,796-foot Mauna Kea mountain is Earth's tallest mountain.

Besides the observatories, Mauna Kea's summit has other attractions. In winter months, at least, you can count on snow here. Poliahu, the resident snow goddess of Hawaiian legend, had a hot-blooded sister, Pele. As with all Pele's sisters, the two got caught up in epic battles over men. Pele's eruptions on Mauna Kea would be cooled by Poliahu's frosts, only to be melted by new flows of lava, and so on. These Hawaiian legends fit geological evidence of eruptions during the ice ages when Mauna Kea had a dense glacial ice cap. Nowadays, the two goddesses maintain a truce. Poliahu's snows stick mostly to Mauna Kea, and Mauna Loa remains Pele's domain of fire. Puu Poliahu, the cinder cone on the summit most closely associated with the snow goddess, has been declared off-limits to observatory development.

After a snowfall, which can happen any time of year, families leave the beaches and flock to the mountain summit to toboggan, build snowmen,

Keck I telescope

and generally frolic in the fresh white stuff. When enough snow falls, skiing takes place. ***Ski Guides of Hawaii*** (885–4188) will provide clothing, equipment, and jeep-lift service for adventurous souls who want to earn their "Ski Hawaii" T-shirts the hard way.

Mauna Kea's sunsets, bedded across a sea of clouds, number among the world's most beautiful. All vehicles must be off the upper summit road by nightfall, however, as headlights can impair observing conditions. On your way down the mountain, scan the heavens for the circling *io,* the Hawaiian hawk. Found only on the Big Island, this high-flying hunter was a symbol of royalty. Just past the turnoff to the Mauna Kea Summit Road comes its Mauna Loa counterpart (heading in the opposite direction, naturally). This one doesn't quite make it to the summit. Scientists use it to access a meteorological observatory at the 11,000-foot level. At this elevation, the remaining 2,679-foot climb to the summit is far tougher than it seems. There is a wilderness cabin on the east rim of Moku`aweoweo Caldera. Call Volcano National Park for information at 985–6000.

Continuing along the saddle road leads you on a roller-coaster ride across undulating lava fields. As you approach Hilo, *ohia* trees crop up as dry scrub cover and grow denser and taller as you move east. The final 12 miles of curving road descend through lush *ohia* rain forest, which continues to the outskirts of the city itself.

Where to Stay

Shipman House, 934–8002, (800) 627–8447, historic Victorian mansion and five-acre grounds restored to original splendor by fourth-generation owners. Rooms from $130.

Hale Kai B&B, 935–6330, oceanfront rooms in modern home from $90.

Dolphin Bay, 935–1466, has 18 rooms in a quiet section of Hilo town. Rates start at $66.

Chalet Kilauea, 967–7786, (800) 937–7786, offers a wide selection of B&Bs and rentals from budget to luxury. Rates range from $45 to $395.

Carson's Volcano Cottages, 967–7683, (800) 845–LAVA, tropical hideaways surrounded by lush vegetation. Rates from $95 to $165.

For more B&B options and other useful visitor information, visit the following Web sites: *www.bigisland.org; www.stayhawaii.com; www.hawaii-bnb.com.*

Manago Hotel, 323–2642, is an institution in Kona, run by the third generation of Managos. A great place to soak up local graciousness, customs, and culture. Rates start at $28.

Holualoa Inn, 324–1121, (800) 392–1812, luxury B&B rooms in a hillside retreat starting at $150.

Waimea Garden Cottage, 885–4550, (800) 262–9912, rustic country charm in upcountry setting. Rates $135 to $150.

Waipio Wayside, 775–0275, (800) 833–8849, gracious hospitality in former plantation manager's home.

WHERE TO EAT

Seaside Restaurant, 935–8825, at 1790 Kalanianaole Avenue, Hilo, is a family-owned fish house serving fresh-catch from the aquaculture fishpond right outside.

Honu's Nest, 935–9321, at 270 Kamehameha, Hilo, is a tiny hole-in-the-wall that serves tasty Japanese specialties.

Kilauea Lodge, 967–7366, in Volcano town. Old World cuisine served in a former YMCA lodge. Expensive.

Keei Cafe, 328–8451, on Route 11, in South Kona. This tiny roadside outpost delivers impressive renditions of its eclectic menu offerings at moderate prices.

Teshima's, 322–9140, on Route 11 in Honalo, Kona. Family-owned local favorite for Japanese food.

Sam Choy's, 326–1545, in the Kaloko Industrial Center, north of Kailua-Kona. Hawaii superchef Sam Choy made his start serving gourmet versions of local comfort food in this bare-bones diner. Expensive.

Canoe House, 885–6622, at the Mauna Lani Hotel, South Kohala, romantic beach-front venue for Pacific Rim cuisine. Investment-caliber prices.

Roy's Waikoloa Bar & Grill, 886–4321, Waikoloa Beach Resort, South Kohala. Inventive Hawaii Regional Cuisine concoctions seared, blackened, and sauced with improbable combinations of local ingredients. Investment-caliber prices.

Bamboo Inn, 889–5555, in Hawi, North Kohala, fresh island cuisine served in a vintage building with colorful Hawaiian ambience. Expensive.

Merriman's, 885–6822, in the Opelu Plaza, Waimea. Peter Merriman's culinary wizardry revolves around innovative use of fresh local ingredients. Expensive.

Glossary

Hawaiian words are used for most place names in Hawaii and are sprinkled throughout the everyday speech of islanders. With a little practice, you too can speak like a *kama`aina.* The Hawaiian language has only twelve letters: seven consonants—*h, k, l, m, n, p, w*—and five vowels—*a, e, i, o, u.* Pronounce the consonants as you would in English, except for *w,* which is pronounced as a soft *v* after *e, i,* or *a.* (Yes, some people say Havaii.) Vowel sounds are more like Spanish: *a* as in *father,* e as in *acorn,* i as in *macaroni,* o as in *solo, u* as in *union.* Always pronounce each letter separately. Special cases are *ao* or *au,* which are usually pronounced "ow"; *ae* and *ai,* which sound like "eye"; and *ei,* which becomes "ay." A ` symbol before or between vowels indicates a slight pause or separation in the sounds. Give each syllable an even stress. When you see an eye-popper such as *humuhumunukunukuapuaa* (a tiny fish), don't panic. Just take it one group at a time: humu–humu–nuku–nuku–a–pu–a–a. It's easy!

Here is a selected list of Hawaiian terms used in this guide.

alii *(ah-lee-eee):* Hawaiian chief or royalty

aloha *(ah-loh-ha):* greetings, love

hala *(hah-lah):* pandanus, screwpine, or tourist pineapple; a Polynesian introduction, this tree has stilt-like aerial roots, pineapple-like fruit, and long fibrous leaves used for weaving. (see lauhala)

hale *(hah-leh):* house

haole *(how-leh):* Caucasian; originally the word for foreigner

heiau *(hay-ow):* ancient Hawaiian temple

hula *(hoo-lah):* Hawaiian dance

kahili *(kah-hee-lee):* a feathered standard held on a pole as the symbol of royalty

kahuna *(kah-hoo-nah):* "one who knows the secrets"; Hawaiian priest, healer, or other skilled "professional"

kalua *(kah-loo-ah):* steam-cooked in leaves in an underground oven

kama`aina *(kah-mah-eye-nah):* longtime island resident

kane *(kah-neh):* man; also the name of one of the principal Hawaiian gods

kapu *(kah-poo):* taboo, forbidden

kokua *(koh-koo-ah):* help, cooperation

konane *(koh-nah-neh):* Hawaiian game similar to checkers

kukui *(kookoo-ee):* candlenut tree; a Polynesian introduction with light green leaves whose oil-rich nuts were strung together and burnt as candles.

lanai *(la-nye):* large open-air veranda (Lana`i is the island)

lauhala *(laow-hah-lah):* "leaf of *hala*"; woven to make mats, sails, etc.

lau-lau *(laow-laow):* Hawaiian specialty featuring pork, fish, and taro leaves wrapped and steamed in a *ti* leaf bundle

lei *(lay):* garland or necklace, most often made of flowers

loco moco *(lohcoh mohcoh):* a local dish based on rice, a fried egg, a hamburger patty, and plenty of gravy

luakini *(loo-ah-kee-nee):* sacrifice; describes large state temples where human sacrifices were offered

luau *(loo-ow):* traditional Hawaiian feast

mahalo *(mah-hah-loh):* thank you

makai *(mah-kye):* toward the sea, coastal

mana *(mah-nah):* spiritual power, prestige

mauka *(maow-kah):* toward the mountains, inland

Menehune *(men-eh-hoo-nay):* legendary race of "little people"

ono *(oh-noh):* delicious

pali *(pah-lee):* cliff

paniolo *(pah-nee-olo):* cowboy

poi *(poy):* mashed vegetable paste, usually made from taro tubers

tapa *(tah-pah):* Polynesian bark cloth; called *kapa* in old Hawaiian

taro *(tah-roh):* traditional food staple, source of poi

tiki *(tee-kee):* carved idol

wahine *(wah-hee-nay):* woman

As noted in the introduction, much of the foreign-sounding speech you'll hear in the islands isn't Hawaiian but pidgin, a unique vernacular that grew out of the mongrelized vocabularies of multiethnic plantation workers. It continues to thrive today as a "locals only" slang. A glossary to pidgin is impractical, as word usages are nonstandard; you just have to get a feel for it. Peppo's *Pidgin to da Max,* available in local bookstores, takes a comic-book approach to pidgin, but it's not a Berlitz guide. Just remember to say "Howzit"—it's the way locals say hello.

Index

H

I

J

K

L

Q

R

S

T

U

V

About the Author

Sean Pager first came to Hawaii at the age of six months. It didn't make much of an impression at the time, but he enjoyed growing up in the islands and appreciated them even more when he continued to travel and live elsewhere. He currently lives in San Francisco with his wife, Sheryl. Sean did his first paid travel writing for the *Let's Go* series as a summer job while in college and liked it enough to stick with it after graduation. *Hawaii: Off the Beaten Path* is his first book-length publication. In his free time, Sean likes to go off the beaten path in the islands by hiking the hills or sailboarding the coast.